SERIOUSLY GOOD FREEZER MEALS

SERIOUSLY GOOD FREEZER MEALS

150 EASY RECIPES TO SAVE YOUR TIME, MONEY & SANITY

KARRIE TRUMAN

Robert ROSE

Seriously Good Freezer Meals
Text copyright © 2018 Karrie Truman
Photographs copyright © 2018 Charity Burggraaf
Cover and text design copyright © 2018 Robert Rose Inc.

Library and Archives Canada Cataloguing in Publication

Truman, Karrie, 1976-, author
     Seriously good freezer meals : 150 easy recipes to save your time, money & sanity / Karrie Truman of happymoneysaver.com.

Includes index.
ISBN 978-0-7788-0591-5 (softcover)

     1. Cooking (Frozen foods). 2. Frozen foods. 3. Make-ahead cooking. 4. Cookbooks.
I. Title.

TX828.T78 2018   641.6'153   C2017-907752-X

Disclaimer
The recipes in this book have been carefully tested by our kitchen and our tasters. To the best of our knowledge, they are safe and nutritious for ordinary use and users. For those people with food or other allergies, or who have special food requirements or health issues, please read the suggested contents of each recipe carefully and determine whether or not they may create a problem for you. All recipes are used at the risk of the consumer. Consumers should always consult their freezer manufacturer's manual for recommended procedures and cooking times.
     We cannot be responsible for any hazards, loss or damage that may occur as a result of any recipe use.
     For those with special needs, allergies, requirements or health problems, in the event of any doubt, please contact your medical adviser prior to the use of any recipe.

Editor: Meredith Dees
Recipe Editor: Jennifer MacKenzie
Copyeditor, Proofreader and Indexer: Gillian Watts
Cover Design: Laura Palese
Interior Design and Production: PageWave Graphics Inc.
Photography: Charity Burggraaf
Food Styling: Nathan Carrabba

Published by Robert Rose Inc.
120 Eglinton Avenue East, Suite 800, Toronto, Ontario, Canada M4P 1E2
Tel: (416) 322-6552 Fax: (416) 322-6936
www.robertrose.ca

Printed and bound in Canada

2 3 4 5 6 7 8 9 TCP 26 25 24 23 22 21 20 19 18

I dedicate this book to my freezer.
Thanks for always being so chill, even on my craziest days.
Without you I could have never finished this book.
Some may call you cold and half empty, but to me,
you'll always be my deep frigid friend.

TABLE OF CONTENTS

Introduction 9

GETTING STARTED 11

Freezer Cooking Basics 12

Freezer-Cooking Kitchen Essentials 15

Your BFF: The Freezer 16

Be A Freezer-Meal Genius 21

Thawing & Cooking Freezer Meals 23

Making Many Freezer Meals in a Day 24

For the Advanced Freezer Cook 27

How To Use This Book 28

7 Seriously Easy Freezer Meals in a Day: Beginner (2 to 3 Hours) 30

30 Seriously Easy Freezer Meals in a Day: Intermediate (8 to 10 Hours) 32

50 Seriously Good Freezer Meals in a Day: Advanced (12 to 15 Hours) 35

BREAKFAST 41

APPETIZERS & SNACKS 67

SOUPS, STEWS & CHILIS 95

POULTRY 127

PORK 173

BEEF 205

SEAFOOD 237

MEATLESS MAINS 253

SIDE DISHES 283

DESSERTS 303

BASES & SAUCES 329

Acknowledgments 356

Index 359

INTRODUCTION

When I first married my husband, I couldn't wait until dinnertime. It was a chance for me to connect with him, show off my mad cooking skills and promote a healthy lifestyle for my new family. I would flip through the pages of my favorite cookbooks or scour the Internet to find a new and intriguing recipe for the evening. Afterwards, I would head to the grocery store to pick up fresh ingredients and then spend the next hour preparing a (hopefully) tasty meal that my husband and I would swoon over. I enjoyed making my dinners more than just a meal — they were an experience.

A few short years later I became a busy mom of twins. I was in a constant chaotic whirlwind of changing diapers, feedings, chasing them around and still trying to cook an amazing dinner. The leisurely days of connecting with my husband over dinner were just blissful distant memories. Once my other two children arrived on the scene, I was so worn out at the end of the day that I would find myself picking up fast food or making something really quick, like hot dogs, cold cereal or processed mac and cheese. I knew this wasn't the food I wanted myself or my family to be eating on a regular basis, but because of the exhaustion, I could not make myself enter the kitchen to spend an hour preparing something healthy.

Thankfully, during this time I heard about freezer meals and decided I would give it a try. I cooked for a whole day, making 30 healthy freezer-meal dinners. I knew immediately that this would be my new weapon against wasted time and unhealthy eating. I left the kitchen feeling accomplished, especially knowing that I didn't have to dread dinnertime for the rest of the month. It was great to once again cook delicious meals for my family and to see my kids clearing their plates every night. This was the beginning of my love of freezer cooking.

Now I want to share with you my belief that it is possible — even if you have the world's busiest schedule — to have a seriously good-tasting, healthy meal every day. As I get older I have realized that nothing can replace lost time with my family. My core reason for freezer-meal cooking was to get some of that precious time back and to enable other families to spend more time together each day. So, if you are like I was and feel that you don't have one more ounce of energy left to cook, there is a solution. Freezer-meal cooking has changed my life, and it can change yours. So here's to eating seriously delicious, healthier food while saving time, money and possibly even your sanity!

— *Karrie Truman*

GETTING STARTED

FREEZER COOKING
BASICS

So you've decided to take the plunge and try out this whole freezer thing. You might be asking yourself, how hard can it be? All you have to do is whip up a few meals and throw them in the freezer. Instant meal, instant hero! Well, I'm sorry to say it's not *quite* that easy. Don't get me wrong — you can still be the dinner champion, but just as Superman has kryptonite, freezer meals can also have some weaknesses. Have no fear! I am here to help you navigate some of the dos and don'ts of freezer meals and give you strategies to maintain flavor, tips on how to avoid the dreaded freezer burn, and pretty much everything else freezer-related to turn you into a freezer-meal genius.

WHO ARE FREEZER MEALS FOR?

I think freezer meals are for everyone. You may not need to have meals ready for an entire month, but stockpiling a few can save you time and money. They're particularly handy if you are a working parent and want to have prepared meals in the freezer that will give you the extra hour you need to help your kids with their homework (or just want some "me" time).

It is a common misconception that you have to have a large family to benefit from freezing meals. Even one- or two-person households can benefit from freezing single-portion (or two-portion) meals. Since the freezer life of most food is between four and six months, you'll have plenty of time to finish up your meals before they're past their prime. You don't have to find recipes that are "just for two" — make your favorites from this book, divide them into portions that fit your needs, and freeze!

Besides feeding yourself and your family, freezer meals are also ideal for sharing, particularly when you want to lend a helping hand to others. Do you know an elderly person who could use a home-cooked meal and some conversation? Stop by their home with dinner, then leave an extra meal for the next day. Is someone in your family sick, or do you have a friend who is having a baby? Send over enough meals for a week. This helps to alleviate their stress and shows them that they are important to you.

Stocking your freezer full of meals is great for so many reasons. Think of all the time you'll save, and how many happy faces you'll see!

10 FREEZER-MEAL MYTHS

For those of you who haven't made freezer meals before, it's time to squash all your worries and fears. I've compiled a list of the biggest concerns people tell me about when I get excited about how freezer meals will change their life.

1 *Freezer food doesn't taste fresh.* FALSE! I used to think all freezer food tasted terrible because I was used to the heavily processed frozen meals from the supermarket. But once I started making my own recipes, I discovered the secrets to making seriously good freezer meals at home. (You'll be happy to know that all the recipes in this book have been tried, tested and approved to make sure they taste as fresh as the day they were made.)

2 *Freezer meals make too much food for my family of two.* The majority of recipes in this book make six servings. You could freeze all those servings or could get creative and downsize the recipes. If, for example, you want to make my Momma's Lasagna (page 225), make it in two 8-inch (20 cm) baking dishes, each of which will serve three people, instead of making it in one 13- by-9-inch (33 by 23 cm) baking dish.

3 *It takes a whole day to do the cooking.* You are in control of how much time you want to spend in the kitchen, whether it's making one meal or 50. If you don't want to do a ton of freezer meals in a day, consider simply making double or triple batches of the meals you make every day and freeze the others for another time. This is a great way to save some meals for later but not have to spend a whole day cooking.

4 *My family has special dietary needs, so freezer meals won't work for us.* Not a problem! There are recipes in this book for people who eat vegetarian, vegan or gluten-free diets. (See "How to Use This Book" on page 28 to get more information about the icons.)

5 *I don't know how to make freezer meals.* I get it — making freezer meals for the first time can be a bit scary. However, anyone who can read a recipe can make more than one freezer meal in a day. It's so much easier than you think! Just make one recipe at a time, freezing as you go. Using my techniques and the instructions in this book will help you to quickly become a confident freezer-meal at-home cook.

6 *You must have more than one freezer.* While it is nice to have more than one freezer, it is certainly not necessary. In fact, for the first five years that I made freezer meals, I used a standard refrigerator top freezer. It held a month's worth of meals as long as I had everything else cleaned out. I used stacks of plastic freezer bags that were frozen flat to save space.

7 *Freezer containers are bad for the environment.* There are numerous options to choose from for your freezer containers. Glass, metal and ceramic containers, as well as mason jars, can be washed and reused several times. If you use glass, make sure you get a heavy-duty glass such as Pyrex, so it will withstand the freezing process and not crack. Reusable bag options are also available.

8 *Stocking up on freezer containers costs more than I will save.* Let's be honest, not everyone can afford to go out and buy 10 environmentally safe, reusable glass baking dishes just to get started. While it is nice to use these reusable containers, the good news is that most of my recipes can be placed in freezer-safe bags or in wrapped casserole dishes that you already own. If you have these options available you can begin making freezer meals. Eventually you can add some reusable containers to your freezer-meal process as your budget allows. Just remember, by making these freezer meals, you are avoiding last-minute food outings, saving both time and money!

9 *My family won't eat casseroles.* The days of freezer meals being only cream-based casseroles are long gone. In this cookbook you will find all sorts of recipes from different cuisines, using fresh ingredients, like fajitas, lettuce wraps, fried rice, muffins and more.

10 *My family will get tired of eating the same meals over and over again.* Don't you find that your family often eats a lot of the same meals over the course of a month? My family loves pizza and we have it at least once a week. Every now and then I decide to try a new recipe for a little taste of something different, but I can't shake that weekly pizza! The same principle applies to your freezer cooking. You can rotate certain recipes every month; by the time a recipe comes back around, your family will be ready to eat it again.

10 TIPS TO GET STARTED

1. Make meals your family already enjoys. If they love mac and cheese, why not start by freezing some of my Amazing Macaroni and Cheese (page 254) so that you have it on hand. Start slowly, testing recipes first before making a large batch, then go big by doing a bunch of meals in a day once you know your family will like them.

2. Make sure to label everything. Otherwise you won't remember what you wrapped in that foil or poured into that freezable bag, not to mention how long it's been there. When I am labeling, I always write the name of the dish as well as the date. It's also helpful to include instructions, such as if it needs to be thawed first or the plastic removed, plus the oven cook time and temperature.

3. Be prepared before you begin. Clean your kitchen, make room in your freezer, and get out your dishes, pots, measuring spoons and cups.

4. Buy the freshest ingredients and look for the longest expiration or best-before dates when grocery shopping, for the best-tasting freezer meals.

5. Get yourself a slow cooker. Some of my favorite freezer meals are ones I can thaw in the fridge overnight, pour into my slow cooker in the morning and enjoy when it's dinnertime. This makes for a double whammy of time saving.

6. To save money and the environment, consider getting some reusable containers and freezer bags if you plan on doing freezer meals often.

7. When defrosting, thaw frozen meals for 24 hours or more in your fridge for the best results (if you can remember).

8. Avoid freezer burn. It's no fun and can make your food taste, well, not so great. The best way to avoid freezer burn is by removing as much air as possible when sealing your meals for freezing.

9. Make sure to use your freezer meals within 4 to 6 months for best flavor (see page 19 for more information).

10. Consider a freezer-meal swap. If you have five friends who are getting together, ask each person to bring five of the same meal, so everyone gets to take home five different freezer meals. This is a fun way to enjoy freezer cooking.

FREEZER-COOKING
KITCHEN ESSENTIALS

When you start your freezer-meal process, you want to have the right tools to make it a success. These are my absolute, must-have freezer-meal supplies that will help you move along more quickly, giving you some extra time to kick up your feet at the end of the day.

- Can opener
- Cookie scoops for fast meatballs, cookie dough, muffins
- Cutting boards (at least two, for separating meats and produce)
- Food processor
- Gallon-size (4 L) and quart-size (1 L) freezer bags
- Heavy-duty aluminum foil
- High-powered blender
- Kitchen scissors or shears
- Large skillet
- Plastic wrap
- Parchment paper
- Permanent marker for labeling
- Several baking containers (foil, glass or metal dishes)
- Measuring cups (dry and liquid) and spoons (at least two sets each or more)
- Slow cooker
- Several large rimmed baking sheets
- Several kitchen timers (cellphones count!)
- Several large and small mixing bowls
- Sharp knives
- Tongs

Optional kitchen helpers
- Bag holders
- Large 20-quart (20 L) stockpot
- Vacuum sealing machine

FREEZER BAGS, CONTAINERS AND MORE: DON'T CHOOSE JUST ONE!

There are many, many, many different types of packages and containers you can use to freeze your meals. Some work best for soups while others are more suitable for casseroles or to store individual servings of a dish. Feel free to use any and all of these various methods when packaging up your freezer meals.

- *Freezer-Safe Bags:* These come in many different sizes, including sandwich, quart (1 L; Medium; 17.7 by 18.8 cm), one gallon (4 L; Large; 26.8 by 27.3 cm) and even two gallons (8 L; Extra-large; 33 by 39.6 cm). Freezer bags are excellent for individual portions, for stacking to save space in your freezer, and to use with baking dishes wrapped in foil, for extra protection against freezer burn. NEVER reuse your freezer bags, or you risk your food being contaminated.

  Freezer-safe bags can be used to freeze a variety of items, but you will want to watch out when freezing things with sharp edges, such as bone-in meats or kabobs, because they can puncture the bag. I suggest double-bagging these items or storing them in a stronger container such as glass, plastic, metal or ceramic. These bags are not meant for hot food either, so please cool your food before adding it to bags.

- *Mason Jars:* To prevent cracking, use wide-mouth jars and leave at least ½ inch (1 cm) headspace between the top of the contents and the rim. Your food will expand as it freezes, so it will need the extra space. I often freeze chicken stock and soups in mason jars. Always check carefully for cracks, chips or deep scratches in the glass before using mason jars, since cold temperatures can cause breakage from even the smallest fracture.

- *Vacuum-Sealing Machines:* These machines are a little more expensive way to go, but they get almost all the air out of freezer bags, which keeps your meals tasting fresher, reduces the risk of freezer burn and saves space too.

- *Baking Pans or Dishes:* Metal or foil pans are best for freezing, but you can also use ceramic or glass. Just be sure never to place a frozen glass or ceramic baking container directly into a hot oven — it could shatter.

YOUR BFF:
THE FREEZER

What do you look for in a best friend? Reliable, helpful and always there when you need her or him. You probably never thought you would use those words to describe your freezer, but on days with busy schedules, it is truly your BFF. Here are some things you should know about your freezer before you get started.

WHAT KIND OF FREEZER DO I NEED?

Relax, you do not have to break the bank to buy a new deep freezer. Your meals can be stored in a standard above-the-fridge freezer. You *will* have to clean out any excess items to make room and limit your trips down the ice-cream aisle, but I can usually fit 30 meals in a standard-size freezer.

If you want to go the deep-freezer route, you will be choosing between upright and chest types. There are advantages and disadvantages to both. An upright freezer will hold a lot more food, you will easily be able to organize it and, most importantly, you will be able to find things quickly. A chest-style freezer, on the other hand, will keep your food colder, which means less freezer burn, but it can be harder to get to your meals and organize them.

POWER FAILURES AND FREEZER MEALS

Are you wondering what to do if you have just made a freezer full of meals and the power goes out? Here are some safety tips and rules if this happens to you:

- Don't open your freezer! The more you open it, the more life-sustaining cold air will be let out.
- A full freezer without power, unopened, should last safely for two days, whereas a half-full freezer will last only one day, since there is more air moving around. Cover the unit with blankets, if possible, for extra insulation to keep it cold for as long as possible.
- When organizing your food and meals in the freezer, separate meat and poultry items from everything else as much as possible. If you experience a power outage and everything begins to thaw, you'll reduce the risk of meat juices leaking onto your other items and contaminating them.

- You can add bagged blocks of ice to help keep your food cold.
- As a general rule, if the power comes back on and your food is still partially frozen or fridge-cold (40°F/4°C), you can refreeze it safely. However, your food may lose a little bit of quality because of the refreezing.

TO FREEZE OR NOT TO FREEZE, THAT IS THE QUESTION

Now that you know a bit of background about freezing meals, it's time to learn about what works and what doesn't. First, the good news: many foods will freeze well.

Here's a list of some not-so-typical items that you can freeze:

- Avocados (without skins) and guacamole
- Chicken broth
- Chocolate
- Garlic cloves
- Fresh herbs (ideal for cooking after thawing, but not as garnish)
- Hummus
- Pasta sauce
- Pesto
- Raw eggs (without shells)
- Tomato paste
- Tortillas

HELPFUL TIP: Try freezing pesto, tomato paste and other flavor-intense foods in ice-cube trays (I like to use silicone trays). Store the trays or place frozen cubes in a freezer bag so you can take out only what you need for cooking.

This is the part where I have to tell you the bad news. Not all foods are freezer friendly, which is soooo sad. Every recipe in this book has been tried and tested and is 100 percent freezer safe, but here are some foods you will want to avoid, unless you're following my techniques, if you're thinking about freezing other recipes:

- Some dairy (see box, page 18)
- Fried food. If you want your fried food to stay crispy when reheated, pass on the freezing. Anyone for a soggy chicken strip? Yeah, I didn't think so.
- Mayonnaise. It will separate after freezing.
- Raw potatoes. Uncooked potatoes will generally turn brown and get mushy when thawed. Nobody wants mushy brown potatoes in their freezer meal. The best way to use potatoes in freezer meals is to cook the potatoes first, then cool, peel, dice or chop.
- Raw vegetables. Never freeze raw vegetables unless they have been blanched (this applies to almost all vegetables). Blanching is a quick-cooking/flash-cooling method that seals in color, vitamins, texture and flavor. I have included a handy chart on page 18 that gives you a bit more detail, so please use it as a guide for best results. Instead of blanching and freezing my own veg, I often purchase already frozen vegetables to save myself a *ton* of time, since they are often very inexpensive. I usually have prefrozen carrots, potatoes, broccoli, corn, stir-fry veggies and peas on hand. You don't have to blanch diced onions, celery, bell peppers, mushrooms, tomatoes, green onions or grated zucchini (diced zucchini is a different story, though).
- Some fruits and vegetables with a high water content don't do well when thawed if you plan on eating them in their raw state. They turn limp, get waterlogged and often change color. These include cabbage, celery, lettuce, cantaloupe, watermelon, cucumber, endive and radishes. If you want to freeze cabbage or celery in marinated or fermented recipes, such as freezer pickles or slaws, they do freeze well, but they won't have the same texture as freshly made pickles or slaws.
- Pasta. Generally this will turn mushy when frozen separately or in casseroles or sauces, unless you follow my technique. In this cookbook you will notice that if a recipe uses pasta, I tell you to cook it only until it's just starting to soften. This allows it to continue cooking later, when baking the casserole or dish, so you get perfect pasta that's not mushy or overcooked.
- Beans. Cook just until cooked through, as overcooked beans will turn mushy later. Then freeze in bags, removing as much air as possible.
- Rice. For make-ahead-and-freeze rice, it's best to reduce the water content when cooking. My technique is to cook 1 cup (250 mL) long-grain rice in

1⅓ cups (325 mL) water instead of the typical 2 cups (500 mL). That way your rice will not turn mushy when reheating. You do need to be careful about adding rice to casseroles heavy with sauces, because it can absorb liquid and become mushy even while frozen. I recommend freezing the rice separately from the casserole, then thawing both overnight and mixing them together right before reheating.

I know you might be a little unsure now if your homemade recipes are going to freeze well or flop, so I will give you some advice: If you are not sure if your recipe will freeze well, search online for it. I am sure there is someone, somewhere, who has tried it and posted their results. Learn from my and their mistakes. You can feel safe knowing that all the recipes in this cookbook will freeze well.

REFREEZING MEATS

The United States Department of Agriculture says it is safe to refreeze uncooked meat that's been thawed in the refrigerator. But in my opinion, meat that has been thawed and then refrozen never tastes quite the same as meat that has been frozen only once before cooking.

My personal rule of thumb is NEVER FREEZE ANYTHING TWICE. That being said, I know many people buy ground beef when it's on sale and freeze it when they get home. On a big freezer-cooking day, they thaw and brown the ground beef and then refreeze it in a cooked recipe. They tell me it tastes just fine. I prefer to buy all my meats for freezer-cooking day fresh, never frozen. Ultimately it's all about preference, so if you are using already frozen beef in your freezer meals, don't sweat it. However, always follow food safety guidelines and never refreeze foods that have been left unrefrigerated for more than two hours (or one hour at temperatures above 90°F/32°C).

HOW TO MAINTAIN QUALITY

Now that you know what foods should or shouldn't be frozen, let's talk quality. We want our freezer meals to be as delicious as when prepared fresh. That means when choosing items, especially fruits and vegetables, it is extremely important to choose foods at their peak of freshness, so they maintain their taste and quality when thawed. It is also important to freeze your food as soon as possible after purchasing so you maintain vitamin content, color, flavor and texture.

In many of my recipes you will notice a technique I use a lot, called flash freezing, which allows you to preserve fresh produce so that you always have the freshest ingredients on hand. You'll see it a lot for

(continued on page 19)

THE DAIRY DILEMMA

Dairy can be confusing to freeze. Some dairy products freeze well when mixed into casseroles but those same products frozen alone will have serious texture changes. I find that butter and shredded hard cheeses freeze the best, while heavy or whipping (35%) cream, yogurt and sour cream change a lot once frozen. I've outlined the freezability of different dairy products below to help reduce confusion.

HARD CHEESES, such as Cheddar, Gouda, Swiss, Monterey Jack and pepper Jack freeze well. However, keep in mind that these cheeses freeze best when shredded as opposed to in blocks. Hard cheeses frozen in a solid block will take longer to thaw and will have a crumbly texture once thawed.

CRUMBLED CHEESES such as feta, blue cheese and Gorgonzola also freeze well.

SOFT CHEESES such as Brie, queso fresco and paneer do not freeze well and become grainy when thawed. These are best used fresh.

BUTTER is another dairy item that's easy to freeze. Margarine can also be frozen on its own. Your butter will lose flavor the longer it's kept in the freezer.

CREAM CHEESE, sour cream, cottage cheese and ricotta cheese, when frozen alone, will change consistency, become slightly grainy and separate when thawed. If you really want to freeze them, they work well in casseroles and baked dishes where they aren't the star of the show.

MILK can be frozen if you use a container with enough room for expansion while it freezes. (Alternatively, you can just keep the lid off the container for the first 3 to 4 hours while it begins to freeze so the container doesn't burst.) Milk can separate after freezing, but shaking it up once it's thawed helps return it to a normal consistency.

HEAVY OR WHIPPING (35%) CREAM and half-and-half (10%) cannot be frozen alone, because the consistency will change and it will separate when thawed. It will no longer be good for whipping or for any recipe requiring the fluffiness of heavy cream. However, it will still work fine in soups or chowders if you whisk it after thawing.

YOGURT will get that grainy texture after being frozen, but it still works really well for smoothies, baked goods and ice pops.

BLANCHING CHART

Bring a large pot of water to a rolling boil. Plunge vegetables into boiling water and blanch according to the time listed below. Remove vegetables with a slotted spoon and plunge into an ice-water bath to stop the cooking process. Drain, cool and freeze in bags or add to recipe.

VEGETABLE	BOILING TIME	VEGETABLE	BOILING TIME
Asparagus	2 minutes	Green beans	2 to 4 minutes
Broccoli	3 to 4 minutes	Peas	4 minutes
Brussels sprouts	4 to 5 minutes	Potatoes, quartered or diced	10 minutes
Carrots	2 minutes	Spinach, collard greens and beet greens	2 minutes
Cauliflower	3 minutes		
Celery	3 minutes	Zucchini, diced	2 minutes
Corn	4 minutes		

berries, cookie-dough balls and more. Take a rimmed baking sheet lined with freezer or parchment paper and place the food you want to freeze on it in a single layer. Transfer the baking sheet to the freezer and freeze until the food is frozen (usually 2 to 3 hours, depending on your freezer). Remove the food from the baking sheet and transfer to a freezer-safe bag or container, then seal, removing as much air as possible, and freeze for later use. One of the major benefits of flash freezing is that the pieces are frozen individually, so you can take out and use just the amount of ingredient you need instead of having to thaw a whole bag.

HOW TO MAINTAIN FLAVOR

To keep your dish tasting flavorful, you also have to consider how freezing affects the seasoning you use in your meals. Some seasonings can intensify or can lose flavor when frozen longer than the suggested length of time. Seasonings that will intensify the longer they are frozen include black pepper, sage, bay leaves, onions and imitation vanilla. However, some foods and seasonings can lose flavor, such as salt, green peppers, celery and bacon. They will still be safe to eat, but for optimal quality it's best to use up those foods in the recommended time (see below).

HOW LONG WILL MY FREEZER MEALS LAST?

When food is kept at or below 32°F (0°C), bacteria cannot grow. Therefore, food stored consistently at 32°F (0°C) or lower will never spoil and will be safe to eat indefinitely. However, after a time (usually 4 to 6 months) the quality of your food may start to diminish and this will affect the taste and texture. To use up freezer meals before the quality fades, make sure to label each container or freezer bag, listing the dish, the date you are freezing it and an expiration date. Here is my recommended freezing-time chart:

BAKED GOODS

Muffins

raw batter	1 month
baked	3 to 6 months

Rolls and Breads

unbaked	1 month
par-baked	12 months
baked	12 months

Pancakes and Waffles

raw batter	1 month
cooked	3 to 6 months

Cookies

raw dough	4 to 6 months
baked	6 months

DAIRY

butter, salted or unsalted	6 to 9 months
cheese, block, shredded or sliced	3 to 4 months
cream cheese	3 to 4 months
milk	2 to 4 months
sour cream	3 to 4 months
raw eggs (cracked)	6 months
yogurt	3 to 4 months

FRUIT AND VEGETABLES

blanched vegetables (asparagus, beets, green beans, mushrooms, corn, broccoli, cauliflower, carrots, zucchini)	8 to 12 months
bell peppers, grated winter squash, onions	12 months
puréed vegetables	6 to 9 months
strawberries, raspberries, blueberries, blackberries, boysenberries	12 months
apples, peaches, pears	6 to 9 months

BEEF

raw ground beef	3 to 4 months
cooked ground beef	6 months
raw beef steaks/roasts	6 to 8 months

PORK

raw ground pork	3 to 4 months
raw pork sausage	1 to 2 months
raw pork chops	4 to 6 months
raw bacon	2 to 3 months
raw pork sausage patties or links	2 to 3 months
ham, fully cooked	2 to 3 months

CHICKEN AND TURKEY

raw ground chicken/turkey	3 to 4 months
raw chicken breasts	9 to 12 months
cooked chicken/turkey	6 to 9 months
raw whole chicken/turkey	12 months

SEAFOOD

raw fish fillets	9 to 12 months
cooked fish	3 to 4 months
raw shrimp	4 months
crabmeat	2 months
clams, shucked	3 to 4 months

OTHER

cooked pasta	3 to 4 months
cooked rice	4 to 6 months
broth or stocks	4 to 6 months
tortillas	9 months
nuts	12 months

BE A FREEZER-MEAL GENIUS

One of the first times I made a freezer meal, I invited my sister over to show off my new and improved method of getting home-cooked meals on the table each night. I had frozen a lasagna and was sure my sister would be blown away, knowing that this meal had come from the freezer. As I removed the wrapping from the dish, I noticed that pesky little ice crystals had formed around the edges, but I didn't think twice about it, still sure that my dish would be a success. We sat down at the table and I giddily served her a heaping portion of lasagna. I watched anxiously as she took her first bite, while I did the same. I wish I could tell you that it ended well, but unfortunately it was terrible. The noodles were soggy and the lasagna had a funny taste. To be honest, it was inedible. She was polite, but I was mortified.

So where did I go wrong? Freezer burn. Not to mention that I'd overcooked my noodles. After many years of making freezer meals that ranged from embarrassing failures to wonderful breakthroughs, I have accumulated some great tips that have helped me perfect my freezing technique, and I want to share them with you!

AVOIDING FREEZER BURN

Freezer burn occurs when your frozen food comes in contact with air, creating dry, grayish-looking spots. Freezer-burned food is still safe to eat, but the texture can be dry, rubbery and chewy and the taste not as good. If possible, cut off the freezer-burned sections before or after cooking.

Air is the enemy of freezer meals. Avoiding freezer burn is all about removing air from your bags and containers. Many freezer-meal recipes are placed in freezer-safe plastic bags with the air pressed out. Other times you can use baking dishes or foil containers, wrapping them in several layers of plastic wrap while pressing out as much air as possible, then covering them with heavy-duty aluminum foil or putting them in freezer bags to keep the air out.

GETTING THE AIR OUT OF YOUR BAGS

Here are some handy tricks that will help you get all of that pesky air out of your freezer bags.

Vacuum Sealer: While vacuum sealers with bags can be more expensive than just using plastic freezer bags or containers, they do the best job of preventing freezer

burn. The machine sucks out air and seals your bag to lock out air and moisture. Using a vacuum sealer allows you to keep your food top quality while preventing freezer burn.

Straw Method: Another great way to remove air from your freezer bag is to use a straw. After putting your food in a bag, seal it, leaving an opening large enough for a straw. Place the straw in the opening and suck the air out of the bag. Finish sealing the bag and you are finished. No magic required! When you have to stop for breath, just pinch closed the straw and the opening in the bag so that air doesn't get back into the bag.

Squeeze It Out: The method I use the most is to squeeze the air out. Add the food to the bag, fold the top over, and press on the food until it comes up to the top of the bag. Then seal. For the displacement method, another effective technique, fill a bowl (or your sink) with water. Submerge the bag slowly in the bowl, letting the water pressure force out the excess air. Before the water reaches the top, quickly seal the bag so it doesn't get into the food.

FREEZE MEALS QUICKLY

Make sure everything is at room temperature or colder before adding it to your freezer bag, in order to freeze as quickly as possible. Quick freezing helps to prevent ice crystals from forming throughout your food. To speed up this process, put the food in a wide, shallow container and stick it in the refrigerator, uncovered, until cooled. If you're in a rush, you can cool recipes faster by using an ice bath, a technique in which you place your food in a metal bowl and set it in a larger bowl full of ice water, refreshing the water and ice as necessary to keep it cold.

The faster you can get your food to freeze, the better your meal will taste when it is thawed. Ideally it would be best to have the food frozen within 2 to 3 hours. On big freezer-meal cooking days, at first place the bagged food you will be freezing in a single layer in your freezer, which allows air to circulate, freezing the food faster. Once your meals are frozen completely solid, you can stack them one on top of each other to save freezer space.

Review the temperature that your freezer is set to, keeping it at 40°F (4°C) or below (use a freezer thermometer to check this). On the morning of a big freezer-cooking day, make sure to turn your freezer to its coldest setting. If you're having a hard time getting all your meals to freeze quickly on big cooking days, consider adding half of them to the freezer and leaving the other half in the refrigerator for two to three hours, until the first group of meals is completely frozen. Then stack up the frozen meals to create more room and add the refrigerated meals to the freezer.

ORGANIZE YOUR FREEZER

This is a given. Label everything with the name of the dish, the date you made it and the expiration date. I cannot stress this enough (I know I've already said it)! I use a permanent marker on freezer-safe bags and aluminum foil. I find it best to write the name of the dish and cooking instructions, to save you time later.

HELPFUL TIP: You must label your containers and freezer bags BEFORE you add the food to them. Some markers and labels won't write or stick to hot or cold surfaces. I have learned this one the hard way!

Flatten out the bag before freezing soups and stews. This gets out all the excess air, making it easier to stack, and saves space.

Use plastic bins or baskets to group similar foods together. You could make a bin for breakfast foods, slow cooker meals, soups, main dishes and more, or stack all your frozen vegetables in a basket. I prefer clear plastic bins so I can see what's in each group.

Use the "first in, first out" method. When you add new foods to the freezer, make sure you are putting them behind or below the food already in there. This ensures that food gets eaten before it expires.

Post a list. Tack a dry-erase board to your freezer door or hang a clipboard near the freezer so you can keep track of what is inside. Date your meals when you put them in the freezer so you don't forget to use them in time.

THAWING & COOKING
FREEZER
MEALS

After you've hung up your apron, taken a few brag snapshots for Instagram and strutted your stuff, the time will come to finally start eating your freezer meals. This section is dedicated to thawing and cooking your freezer meals properly so you will be able to enjoy the fruits of your efforts.

THE THAWING PROCESS

I will never forget the first time I made a Thanksgiving meal by myself. I placed the frozen turkey in the refrigerator the night before, thinking it would be ready to stick in the oven first thing in the morning. WRONG — that little birdie was still rock solid! The same principle goes for freezer meals. They need time to thaw. There are three safe ways to defrost your food: in the refrigerator, using cold water or in the microwave (not recommended but doable). Thawing in cold water or the microwave works best if you are short on time. NEVER leave your food to thaw on the counter, because that method can cause bacteria to multiply, resulting in food-borne illness.

Refrigerator: The best way to thaw your freezer meal is in the refrigerator. The food will remain good quality and can be used within a week. Here is a quick rundown of thawing times when you use the refrigerator:

- Single-serve portions: 6 to 8 hours or overnight
- Casseroles, soups and stews in freezer bags: 24 to 48 hours
- 8-inch (20 cm) square to 13- by 9-inch (33 by 23 cm) baking dish: 12 to 48 hours
- Meat (including roasts): approximately 5 hours per pound (1 lb/500 g)
- Cooked breads: 5 to 6 hours
- Uncooked breads: 6 to 8 hours or overnight

Cold Water: A quick-thawing method is to submerge your freezer meals in a sink full of cold water for about 1 to 2 hours. Make sure to change the water every 30 minutes or so to keep it cold, and double-bag or wrap your items so water doesn't get inside. You cannot refreeze your meals if you thaw them using this method, because there is a greater chance for possible bacteria growth.

Microwave: I don't really recommend this way of thawing, but if you are desperate, go ahead and nuke it. Microwaving will not work on foil pans and you must cook the thawed food IMMEDIATELY. Sometimes microwaving can cause your food to overcook in spots and change the texture of uncooked dishes. Make sure to microwave on the Defrost setting.

OOPS, I FORGOT TO THAW AND I NEED IT NOW!

There have been many times when I was so busy all day that I forget to think ahead, and dinner was only a few hours away. Has this happened to you? After working so hard making those freezer meals, we want to use them! Well, it is possible. You can put your frozen meals in foil or metal pans right into the oven, adding a little extra time and keeping them covered longer than the recipe specifies. (Do not place cold glass or ceramic pans in a hot oven — they could break.) Keep a close eye on your food, because cooking times will vary depending on your oven. Also note that the texture of the meal might be affected (the topping can sometimes get overdone), but for last-minute "oops, I forgot" moments, you can still have a great dinner.

MAKING MANY FREEZER MEALS IN A DAY

Now that you have read all the basics about freezer-meal cooking, it's time to take full advantage of your time and money by making multiple freezer meals in one day. In this section, you will learn all the best sanity-saving strategies to give you the confidence and excitement you need to fill your freezer full of seriously good freezer meals.

THE FIRST MOUNTAIN TO CONQUER: PRE-PREP

How do you "pre-prep"? Basically you are going to figure out which method of freezer cooking you want to use. Then you will list the meals you want to make and, last, get your kitchen cleaned, stocked and ready for cooking.

I am going to tell you a little secret about freezer cooking: there is no right or wrong way. It is simply choosing what will work best for you and your family. Here are some questions to ask yourself to narrow down which method will work best for you:

THE "HOW MUCH MONEY DO I WANT TO SPEND?" QUESTION

Truly one of the biggest reasons that freezer meals are so appealing (besides saving time) is the fact that you are saving lots of money! A great way to do that? Frugal shopping. One main ingredient you want to catch on sale is your meats. If I want to make a lot of one thing, I scour the sale ads from various stores to see who has the best deal on chicken, ground beef, steak, pork and any other meat I would like for my main dish. Then I take a quick inventory of my pantry to see what I already have. My recipes for the week (or month) will be based on the combination of those ingredients and the proteins I will be purchasing on sale. You can also look for sales on other ingredients that are not in your pantry.

If you are only cooking a week's worth of meals or doubling your recipe, you may want to choose your recipes based on what you already have in your pantry or your fridge. Do you have an abundance of produce lying around from your summer garden and a dozen boxes of lasagna noodles? Now would be a great time to freeze up some vegetarian lasagna. Using what we already have in stock is the best way to cut down costs!

THE "HOW MUCH TIME DO I WANT TO SPEND?" QUESTION

Double meals daily: This is one of the simplest ways to make freezer meals. For every meal you make, just double the batch and freeze the excess. You will be surprised at how quickly your freezer fills up! You can start skipping nights of cooking and eat your freezer meals and relax instead.

Mini freezer-meal session: A mini session is the next step up. It is perfect if you have a little extra time on your hands and want to knock out a week's worth of food at once. Choose three to five easy meals that don't take up too much time, and voilà! — you are ready to conquer the rest of your week.

30 to 50 freezer meals in a day: This is the biggie! This is *one whole day* of cooking (two if you include prep work and shopping). You are going to dig deep and complete a month's worth, maybe even slightly more, of freezer meals. Once you have accomplished this feat, it is smooth sailing for you — you will have an abundance of time to spend on yourself and your family!

HELPFUL TIP: I always suggest doing the big day without kids (if possible), but if you can't, don't be discouraged — you can do this! Just take some time to prepare for them to be around by keeping them busy and happy. You can try new activity books or movies to keep them entertained. Older kids can help with measuring, mixing, wrapping, labeling and even doing the dishes too!

THE POWER OF GROUP SWAPS

Group swaps are a fun way to get the freezer meals you need without having to do all the work yourself. The idea behind a group swap is that each person in the group will make a dish for everyone else. For example, if you make an awesome chili, you would prepare enough for each person, package it up so it is ready for the freezer and then swap it with the other members for what they have prepared. You get a variety of meals while only having to prepare one yourself.

So how do you get started with a group swap? First you will need to find a few friends or family members who are interested in the benefits of freezer cooking. Then schedule a time when you can get together to discuss menus, how often you want to swap (weekly or monthly), who will be preparing each dish, and what day of the week you will commence your swap.

WHAT DO I HAVE IN STOCK?

My first order of business is to go through my fridge, freezer and pantry to see what's where. I take note of items I have that I would like to use up or incorporate into the freezer meals.

I also take this time to organize my fridge and freezer by removing anything old or expired so I have space for my purchases after I return from the store. It's important as well to make sure I have room in the freezer for all my freezer meals when completed. Then I tackle the kitchen, making sure that I have a large, clean area that is clear of debris. Now I am ready to plan my meals.

MASTER LIST MAKING AND PLANNING

After you have answered the questions above, it is time to make a plan and get started! What should your plan consist of? Here is your checklist of to-dos:

1. Recipes: Create your "menu" by writing down all the meals you plan to make.

2. Shopping list: Write down all the ingredients and supplies that you need.

3. Plan and schedule: Take a look at your calendar and see if you have any holidays, birthdays or organized dinners coming up. Schedule your meals on the calendar so you don't end the month with five days of the same dish.

4. Assembly plan: Figure out the order in which you will make your multiple freezer meals.

ON THE BIG COOKING DAY

Bring out your inner OCD. Now is the time for order!

Set out all your equipment such as mixing bowls and measuring spoons before you start. Have foil and parchment ready to line baking sheets in between flash-freezing recipes and set out your timers so you can keep track of all the different items cooking at once. Label your freezer containers and bags with permanent marker or stick-on labels.

MAKING YOUR ASSEMBLY PLAN

You will need to figure out in what order you plan to make your multiple freezer meals on the big day. This may seem like a no-brainer, but being prepared with that plan is key to saving time and stress.

Look closely at your recipes and the instructions. Look for things that have similar prep instructions, such as chopped, minced, diced, puréed or shredded vegetables, meats and cheeses. Look for items you can precook all together at once, like ground beef or chopped chicken. Make a list of these.

After your calculations are complete, decide on the order in which you will assemble/cook your meals. Keep in mind that it is more time-consuming doing one recipe at a time than doing all your prep first. It's much better to combine prepping items together.

A lot of your chopping and grating can be done the night before if you have the time and energy. Some of these include:

- Chopping vegetables
- Soaking and cooking beans
- Shredding cheese
- Making stocks and sauces
- Cooking and cooling pasta or rice
- Browning and draining ground beef
- Chopping, shredding or dicing meat
- Making a meal overnight in a slow cooker, so it's ready to cool and freeze in the morning.

Just remember to package the prepped ingredients well and cool them in the fridge overnight so they will be chilled and ready to add to recipes as needed.

I like to start by preparing all the vegetables together, before moving on to the meats that need to be cooked, such as shredded chicken or ground beef. Last, I'll chop or dice any raw meats. Then I pick my recipe order: I always start with the most difficult and end with the easiest. That way, when I have the energy, I can get the hardest recipes out of the way. But it's totally up to you in which order you want to do your recipes.

I know making a list for assembly seems like a lot of work, but a well-written plan will make your big day of freezer-meal cooking so much easier.

MANAGE YOUR DAY WISELY

I think this is one of the most crucial elements to freezer cooking. If you cannot find the things you need, your kitchen turns into a disaster zone and your feet and back hurt at the end of the day, you are *not* going to want to make freezer meals again. You may even ban the words "freezer meals" from your vocabulary! Follow these tips to help your day flow smoothly.

I have created a few meal plans that include shopping lists (pages 30 to 39) to help to make a big cooking day a little easier!

- Consider your portions. Have the right containers ready and labeled.

- Try to wash bowls and pans as you go, if possible. You'll have to wash your hands frequently anyway, so washing a few bowls at the same time will make cleanup at the end of the day easier.
- Keep perishables in the fridge until you need them, to retain freshness. Don't take them all out when you get started, since they need to stay as cold as possible.
- Wear clothes you don't mind getting a little messy, comfortable shoes and an apron.
- Make sure to take a few breaks throughout the day. Eat nutritious snacks to keep your energy up.

JUST FOR FUN

While you're on a break, share pictures of your process on social media. You can use the hashtag #SeriouslyGoodFreezerMeals. I would love to see your cooking!

FOR THE ADVANCED
FREEZER
COOK

Have you made a week's worth of freezer meals at once? Have you pushed yourself to make 20 or 30 freezer meals in a day? Do you love freezer cooking to the extreme or want to push yourself harder? This section is for crazy folks like me who want to or have made 50 freezer meals in a day or more — serious freezer-meal addicts. Yes, that is what I will call us. People who do freezer meals because we seriously love it and know how truly awesome it is to have all that time saved, and do it to the extreme. These tips are for you.

BIGGER, BETTER TOOLS AND SUPPLIES

When I mention to people that I have made 50 freezer meals in one day, I first get a look of shock, followed by a look of disbelief. How is that even possible? they ask. And I always tell them that if they have a great bunch of recipes, an amazing plan and enough energy to work a full 12- to 15-hour day, they too can have a freezer full of dinners at the ready. But what I don't mention is all the extra tools and supplies I have collected and created to make this happen. Here are some fantastic secret weapons, time-saving tools and equipment I use.

Multiple Slow Cookers: I love to shop estate sales or thrift stores to find inexpensive slow cookers, and typically I use three or four all at once on a huge freezer-cooking marathon. I use them for recipes that can take hours to get to a nice pull-apart state. Sometimes I place these items in the slow cooker right before I go to bed the night before a big cooking day, so in the morning I can cool them for a few hours before placing in freezer bags.

Multiple Kitchen Scissors or Shears: I speed up meal-prep time by using kitchen scissors to cut herbs, green onions and peppers. I use a separate pair of scissors for cutting raw meat into cubes or strips and another pair for cutting up cooked meats. To keep them separate and avoid cross-contamination, you can buy several different-colored kitchen scissors or tape labels to the handles.

Homemade Super-Sized Fat Separator: I love saving money by making all the chicken stock I need for the meals at once, usually a day or two before the big cooking day. I make the recipe (page 349), simmer it on the stovetop for 10 to 12 hours and then separate the bones and vegetables from the stock. I used to just place the whole pot in my fridge for another 8 or so hours, until it cooled and the fat rose to the top and hardened so I could spoon it all off. But one day I figured out a faster method. I created my own super-sized fat separator! To make one yourself, find a large steam juicer (look online or at estate sales or thrift stores) and seal the inner center hole with duct tape. Pour the broth right into the canner. Let it sit for 30 minutes to separate, then drain the broth, using a juicing tube, into desired containers or jars. Works like a charm — and no waiting for 8 hours!

A Lot of Freezer Space: Before you begin, don't underestimate how much freezer space your meals will need. Nothing is worse than not having enough room for all your hard work!

Soapy-Water Container and Quick Rinsing: I keep a little bowl of soapy water and a drying towel by the sink to quickly wash my measuring cups and spoons throughout the day. Even though I have six or seven sets of both, I still find this helpful to keep me on track. If any of them have come in contact with raw meat, however, they must be fully washed and sanitized.

Prechopped or Frozen Veggies: Purchase minced garlic or ginger in jars to save time. Some stores also prechop onions or preshred carrots. I also buy frozen vegetables so I don't have to blanch and freeze them from fresh. In my opinion these purchases can save a lot of time and are totally worth the extra money. However, for the best results in my recipes, I do not recommend buying preshredded cheeses. They often include cornstarch or other fillers, which can create issues with texture and the melting process.

HOW TO USE THIS BOOK

As you get cooking, you'll notice a few symbols below many of the recipe titles. Hopefully you will find them very useful as you begin planning your meals.

 VEGETARIAN — meat-free; suitable for vegetarians

 VEGAN — free of meat, dairy and other animal products; suitable for vegans

 GLUTEN-FREE — made without wheat or other gluten-containing ingredients

 THRIFTY — a recipe that won't break the budget

 QUICK — prep and cook in 45 minutes or less

 TO SHARE — recipes that are great for sharing with others (for example, a new mother, a bereaved relative or a sick neighbor)

To avoid any surprises, I suggest reading through each recipe before you make it, looking for any special equipment you might need, such as a blender, stand mixer or electric hand mixer, specific freezer bags and additional kitchen tools. Another thing you will notice is that every recipe includes a large-batch calculation guide, as shown in the example below.

The bulk batch guide is super helpful when you want to make multiple freezer meals, because it does all the math for you! Each recipe begins with a single batch, which typically serves around 6 people. The bulk batch guide multiplies all the ingredients so that you don't have to bust out your calculator and can quickly make a shopping list for all your groceries.

Don't panic when you see those large amounts of ingredients! If, for example, you see 140 oz (4.5 L) coconut milk in the 5-batch column, remember that this amount will give you 30 servings of a meal. These calculations have been done to help save you money at the grocery store: it's usually more cost-effective to

buy one or two larger cans or packages than several smaller ones. (You can also save time on big cooking days because you have to open fewer cans.) Buying larger containers at bulk stores can be a great way to save money.

HELPFUL CONVERSIONS

Here are a few conversions to help you out when you are shopping, because packages may be labeled in ounces or pounds or a combination:

16 OZ = 1 LB (500 G)

24 OZ = 1½ LBS (750 G)

32 OZ = 2 LBS (1 KG)

My ultimate goal with this bulk batch guide is to make it easier for you to make multiple freezer meals at once, saving you both money and precious time.

BULK BATCH GUIDE	Servings	6 (1 batch)	12 (2 batches)	18 (3 batches)	24 (4 batches)	30 (5 batches)
	water	2 cups (500 mL)	4 cups (1 L)	6 cups (1.5 L)	8 cups (2 L)	10 cups (2.5 L)
	brown sugar	1½ cups (375 mL)	3 cups (750 mL)	4½ cups (1.125 L)	6 cups (1.5 L)	7½ cups (1.875 L)
	cornstarch	2 tbsp (30 mL)	¼ cup (60 mL)	6 tbsp (90 mL)	½ cup (125 mL)	⅔ cup (150 mL)
	tamari sauce	½ cup (125 mL)	1 cup (250 mL)	1½ cups (375 mL)	2 cups (500 mL)	2½ cups (625 mL)
	garlic	2 tbsp (30 mL)	¼ cup (60 mL)	6 tbsp (90 mL)	½ cup (125 mL)	⅔ cup (150 mL)
	sesame seeds	2 tsp (10 mL)	4 tsp (20 mL)	2 tbsp (30 mL)	8 tsp (40 mL)	10 tsp (50 mL)
	cooked chicken	6 cups (1.5 L)	12 cups (3 L)	18 cups (4.5 L)	24 cups (6 L)	30 cups (7.5 L)
	gallon bags	1	2	3	4	5

BULK CHICKEN CONVERSION AND COOKING CHART

Although the recipes in this book use a wonderful variety of different meats, I find cooking with chicken so easy, versatile, tasty and affordable, especially when using these bulk batch cooking techniques. I've included the conversions here to help you make more freezer meals with ease! Typically I buy large amounts of chicken breast or whole chickens and cook them up all at once, then use them in freezer meals. Make sure to plan ahead to decide how you will be using the cooked meat: If you need shredded chicken, it's best to use the oven, pressure cooker or slow cooker. If you need diced cooked chicken, I think grilling or cooking on the stovetop is best. While boiling and broiling chicken are also options, I recommend the methods I have just listed for the best flavor and texture in freezer-meal cooking.

CHICKEN CONVERSIONS

BONELESS, SKINLESS CHICKEN BREASTS

1 lb (500 g) raw chicken breasts	2¼ cups (560 mL) cooked diced or shredded
2 lbs (1 kg) raw chicken breasts	4½ cups (1.06 L) cooked diced or shredded
3 lbs (1.5 kg) raw chicken breasts	6¾ cups (1.675 L) cooked diced or shredded
4 lbs (2 kg) raw chicken breasts	9 cups (2.25 L) cooked diced or shredded
5 lbs (2.5 kg) raw chicken breasts	11¼ cups (2.81 L) cooked diced or shredded
10 lbs (5 kg) raw chicken breasts	22½ cups (5.625 L) cooked diced or shredded
20 lbs (10 kg) raw chicken breasts	45 cups (11.25 L) cooked diced or shredded

PRE-COOKED ROTISSERIE CHICKENS

2 lbs (1 kg) rotisserie chicken	3 cups (750 mL) diced or shredded meat
2½ to 2¾ lb (1.25 to 1.375 kg) rotisserie chicken	3½ cups (875 mL) diced or shredded meat

RAW, WHOLE CHICKEN, COOKED

3 lbs (1.5 kg) raw whole chicken	3 cups (750 mL) diced or shredded meat
4 lbs (2 kg) raw whole chicken	4 cups (1 L) diced or shredded meat

SLOW COOKER METHOD

For boneless or bone-in, skin-on chicken breasts, thighs and legs or a whole chicken (up to 5 pounds/2.5 kg): Place chicken in a large (approx. 5 quart) slow cooker and sprinkle with salt and pepper. Cover and cook on High for 4 to 6 hours or on Low for 8 to 9 hours, until so tender that it's almost falling off the bone.

OVEN METHOD

For boneless or bone-in, skin-on chicken breasts, thighs and/or legs: Preheat oven to 400°F (200°C).

Brush chicken with a little olive oil or spray with cooking spray; sprinkle with salt and pepper. Place in a baking dish (you may need to use multiple dishes, depending on how much chicken you're cooking) with 1/4 cup (60 mL) water. Cover with foil. Bake in preheated oven for 45 to 50 minutes or until breasts are no longer pink inside, leg and thigh juices run clear when pierced with a fork, and a meat thermometer inserted in the thickest part registers 165°F (74°C).

For 2 whole chickens (each about 3 to 4 lbs/1.5 to 2 kg): Preheat oven to 425°F (220°C). Brush chicken with a little olive oil or spray with cooking spray; sprinkle with salt and pepper. Bake uncovered in preheated oven for 60 to 90 minutes or until a meat thermometer inserted in the thickest part registers 165°F (74°C).

PRESSURE COOKER METHOD

For boneless or bone-in, skin-on chicken breasts, thighs and legs (about 3 to 4 lbs/1.5 to 2 kg): Place a cooking rack in the bottom of a standard (6 to 8 quart) pressure cooker. Add 1 cup (250 mL) water or chicken stock. Put chicken in pressure cooker and place lid on top, sealing tightly. Cook for 12 to 14 minutes at high pressure or until breasts are no longer pink inside, leg and thigh juices run clear when pierced with a fork, and a meat thermometer inserted in the thickest part registers 165°F (74°C). Quick release the pressure.

For a whole chicken (about 3 to 4 lbs/1.5 to 2 kg): Place a cooking rack in the bottom of pressure cooker. Add 1 cup (250 mL) water or chicken stock. Put chicken in pressure cooker and place lid on top, sealing tightly. Cook at high pressure for 25 to 30 minutes or until a meat thermometer inserted in the thickest part registers 165°F (74°C). Quick release the pressure.

7 SERIOUSLY EASY FREEZER MEALS IN A DAY: BEGINNER (2 TO 3 HOURS)

Here are 7 different freezer meals, each serving 6 to 8 people. This plan is perfect for beginners. It takes me 2 to 3 hours to make and freeze these meals, but those who are really new to freezing might take a bit longer. Note: Some of the quantities below have been rounded slightly for ease of shopping. On serving day, check the specific recipes for fresh ingredients and garnishes.

White Bean Chicken Chili (page 122)
Herbes de Provence Chicken (page 140)
Lemon Tarragon Chicken (page 144)
Teriyaki Chicken (page 170)
Boneless BBQ Pork Ribs (see Tip, page 189)
Venezuelan Steak (page 221)
French Dip Sandwiches (page 235)

GROCERY LIST

DRY GOODS/PANTRY

- 2 cups (500 mL) smoky barbecue sauce
- 2 tbsp (30 mL) yellow mustard
- 2 tsp (10 mL) Dijon mustard
- 7 tbsp (105 mL) Worcestershire sauce
- hot pepper sauce (optional, for White Bean Chicken Chili)
- 1 cup (250 mL) tamari sauce
- 1 tbsp (15 mL) red wine vinegar
- ¼ cup (60 mL) olive oil
- 3 tbsp (45 mL) cornstarch
- 2 cups (500 mL) brown sugar
- 1 tbsp (15 mL) honey
- 8 oz (227 mL) can tomato sauce
- ⅓ cup (75 mL) tomato paste
- Three 15 oz (425 mL) cans Great Northern beans (45 oz/1.275 L)
- 1 cup (250 mL) mild salsa verde (about 9 oz/250 g)
- 4 cups (1 L) chicken broth
- 6 cups (1.5 L) beef broth

SEASONINGS

- 3½ tsp (17 mL) salt
- 1¾ tsp (8 mL) freshly ground black pepper
- ½ tsp (2 mL) garlic salt
- 1 tbsp (15 mL) ground cumin
- 2 tsp (10 mL) ground coriander
- 5 bay leaves
- 1½ tsp (7 mL) herbes de Provence
- 1 tbsp (15 mL) dried oregano
- 2 tsp (10 mL) dried tarragon
- 2 tsp (10 mL) sesame seeds

PRODUCE

- 4 lemons (+ 1 optional for Lemon Tarragon Chicken)
- 1 red bell pepper
- 3 onions
- 1 large white onion
- 1 jar (about ¼ cup/60 mL) minced garlic or 12 garlic cloves

DAIRY

- 1 tbsp (15 mL) butter

MEAT

- 2 cooked rotisserie chickens, meat removed and chopped (6 cups/1.5 L)
- 3 lbs (1.5 kg) boneless, skinless chicken breasts
- 6 bone-in, skin-on chicken thighs (about 2¼ lbs/1.125 kg total)
- 3 lbs (1.5 kg) boneless pork country-style ribs
- 2 lbs (1 kg) beef flank steak, sliced if available
- 3 lbs (1.5 kg) boneless beef shoulder roast

BAGS AND CONTAINERS

- 6 gallon-size (4 L) freezer bags
- 2 quart-size (1 L) freezer bags
- 13- by 9-inch (33 by 23 cm) baking dish

PRE-PREP

Follow the order below for fastest results. If you like, some or all of the ingredients can be prepped, packaged and kept in the refrigerator for up to 24 hours before assembling your freezer meals, or you can prep and assemble them all in one go. Any perishables, such as meat, poultry, cheese, fish and dairy, should be refrigerated or frozen (as directed) immediately after prepping/cooking, until you're ready to assemble and freeze your meals.

1. Label 6 gallon-size (4 L) freezer bags with the name of the recipe, the date and any instructions you need to remember. Make sure to read each recipe to become familiar with the thawing and cooking instructions, especially when making a recipe for the first time. Here are labels to write for your freezer bags, including simplified cooking instructions:

- Teriyaki Chicken, [date]. Thaw. Pour into baking dish. Bake at 400°F (200°C) for 45 minutes.
- Boneless BBQ Pork Ribs, [date]. Thaw. Slow-cook on Low 8 to 10 hours/High 5 to 6 hours. Discard grease, add BBQ sauce and heat. [Instructions follow recipe Tip.]
- Lemon Tarragon Chicken, [date]. Thaw. Sear. Pour into baking dish with sauce and lemons. Bake, covered, at 350°F (180°C) for 20 to 25 minutes.
- Venezuelan Steak, [date]. Thaw. Slow-cook on Low 8 to 9 hours/High 5 to 6 hours.
- White Bean Chicken Chili, [date]. Thaw. Slow-cook on Low 6 to 8 hours/High 3 to 4 hours. Add sour cream and toppings; serve.
- French Dip Sandwiches, [date]. Thaw. Slow-cook on Low 7 hours. Shred; serve on toasted buns with jus.

2. Thinly slice bell pepper and mince garlic (if not using jarred minced garlic).

3. Peel and dice 1 white onion.

4. Peel 3 onions. Place 1½ onions in a high-powered blender or food processor and purée. Thinly slice 1½ onions.

5. Thinly slice 1 lemon and seal in a quart-size freezer bag. Squeeze juice from remaining lemons.

6. Drain and rinse beans in a colander under running water.

7. Using a clean cutting board, cut flank steak into 1-inch (2.5 cm) slices (if not pre-sliced).

8. Using a clean cutting board, trim any fat from raw chicken breasts. Prepare 2 lbs (1 kg) chicken according to Lemon Tarragon Chicken instructions and sprinkle with garlic salt (page 144). Chop remaining 1 lb (500 g) chicken and reserve for White Bean Chicken Chili.

MAKING THE FREEZER MEALS

Once the major recipe components are all prepped, do the final cooking, mixing and packaging to assemble the meals, putting them in the freezer as they are assembled.

1. Prepare Teriyaki Chicken freezer meal (page 170).

2. Prepare Boneless BBQ Pork Ribs freezer meal, according to Tip (page 189).

3. Prepare Lemon Tarragon Chicken freezer meal (page 144).

4. Prepare Herbes de Provence Chicken freezer meal (page 140). Label instructions: "Herbes de Provence Chicken, [date]. Thaw. Bake, uncovered, at 375°F (190°C) for about 50 minutes."

5. Prepare Venezuelan Steak freezer meal (page 221).

6. Prepare White Bean Chicken Chili freezer meal (page 122).

7. Prepare French Dip Sandwiches freezer meal (page 235).

8. Clean up and you're finished!

30 SERIOUSLY EASY FREEZER MEALS IN A DAY: INTERMEDIATE (8 TO 10 HOURS)

Here are 14 different recipes for making 30 freezer meals, each serving 6 to 8 people. This plan is perfect for those of you who have made freezer meals before and want to do a bunch of them in one day. It takes me 8 to 10 hours to make and freeze these meals, but those who are really new to freezing might take a bit longer.

Note: Some of the quantities below have been rounded slightly for ease of shopping. On serving day, check the specific recipes for fresh ingredients and garnishes.

2 batches Coconut Cashew Basil Curry Soup (page 99)

2 batches Chicken Tortellini Soup (page 107)

2 batches Beef Barley Stew (page 125)

2 batches Maple Dijon Chicken (page 147)

2 batches Cilantro Lime Chicken Tacos (page 156)

3 batches Teriyaki Chicken (page 170)

2 batches Bacon Love Pork Tenderloin (page 174)

2 batches Honey Pork Chops (page 178)

2 batches Boneless BBQ Pork Ribs (see Tip, page 189)

4 batches Perfect Pizza Any Way You Top It (page 194)

2 batches Rosemary Pot Roast (page 205)

2 batches Brown Sugar Meatloaf (page 210)

2 batches French Dip Sandwiches (page 235)

1 batch Lemon Dill Tilapia Tacos (page 245)

GROCERY LIST

DRY GOODS/PANTRY

- 6½ cups (1.625 L) smoky barbecue sauce
- 1 cup (250 mL) ketchup
- 2 cups + 2 tbsp (530 mL) Dijon mustard
- ¼ cup (60 mL) yellow mustard
- 1 cup (250 mL) Worcestershire sauce
- 2¾ cups (675 mL) tamari sauce
- ½ cup (125 mL) balsamic vinegar
- ¼ cup (60 mL) unseasoned rice vinegar
- 1½ cups (375 mL) olive oil
- ¼ cup (60 mL) vegetable oil
- 20 cups (5 L) all-purpose flour
- 6 tbsp (90 mL) cornstarch
- ¼ cup (60 mL) quick-rising (instant) yeast
- 6⅓ cups (1.575 L) packed brown sugar
- 2 tsp (10 mL) granulated sugar
- 1⅔ cups (400 mL) honey
- ½ cup (125 mL) pure maple syrup
- 2 cups (500 mL) store-bought pizza sauce
- Two 15 oz (425 mL) cans tomato sauce (30 oz/850 mL total)

- Four 14 oz (398 mL) cans coconut milk (56 oz/1.592 L total)
- 17 cups (4.25 L) chicken broth
- 8 cups (2 L) beef broth
- 1 cup (250 mL) salted roasted cashews
- ¼ cup (60 mL) sliced almonds (optional, for Cilantro Lime Chicken Tacos)
- 1 cup (250 mL) panko bread crumbs
- 1 cup (250 mL) pearl barley

SEASONINGS

- ⅔ cup (150 mL) salt
- 2½ tbsp (37 mL) freshly ground black pepper
- 3 tbsp (45 mL) onion powder
- 5 tsp (25 mL) garlic powder
- 1 tsp (5 mL) celery salt
- ¼ cup (60 mL) beef bouillon powder
- 3 tbsp (45 mL) dried parsley
- 1 tsp (5 mL) garlic salt
- 2 tbsp (30 mL) paprika
- ½ tsp (2 mL) cayenne pepper

- ¼ cup (60 mL) curry powder
- 1 tbsp (15 mL) dried basil
- 8 bay leaves
- 3½ tsp (17 mL) dried rosemary
- 1½ tsp (7 mL) dried dill
- 2 tbsp (30 mL) sesame seeds

PRODUCE

- ⅔ cup (150 mL) minced garlic or 33 garlic cloves
- 1 tbsp (15 mL) minced or grated ginger
- 1 lime
- 6 lemons
- 5 celery stalks
- 2 shallots
- 8 onions
- 1 jalapeño pepper
- 2 cups (500 mL) fresh cilantro leaves

DAIRY

- ¼ cup (60 mL) butter
- 1 cup (250 mL) freshly grated Parmesan cheese (about 3½ oz/100 g)
- 8 cups (2 L) shredded mozzarella cheese (about 1½ lbs/750 g)

FROZEN FOODS

- 3 cups (750 mL) frozen diced carrots
- 2½ cups (625 mL) frozen sliced carrots

MEAT

- 22 cups (5.5 L) chopped cooked chicken (about 10 lbs/5 kg raw; see page 29)
- 6 cups (1.5 L) shredded cooked chicken breast (about 2⅔ lbs/1.33 kg raw; see page 29)
- 4 lbs (2 kg) boneless, skinless chicken tenders
- 4 lbs (2 kg) boneless, skinless chicken breasts
- 6 lbs (3 kg) boneless pork country-style ribs
- Two 3 lb (1.5 kg) boneless beef shoulder roasts (6 lbs/3 kg total)
- Two 3 lb (1.5 kg) boneless beef chuck roasts (6 lbs/3 kg total)
- 2 lbs (1 kg) stewing beef
- 3 lbs (1.5 kg) ground beef
- 2 lbs (1 kg) skinless tilapia fillets
- 4 large pork tenderloins (about 6 lbs/3 kg total)
- 12 medium boneless pork loin chops (about 2¼ lbs/1.125 kg total)
- 2 lbs (1 kg) sliced bacon
- 120 pepperoni slices (about 12 oz/360 g)

OTHER

- 4 cups (1 L) fresh or frozen cheese tortellini (about 15 oz/430 g)

BAGS AND CONTAINERS

- 34 gallon-size (4 L) freezer bags
- 6 quart-size (1 L) freezer bags
- 12 sandwich bags
- Two 9- by 5-inch (23 by 12.5 cm) loaf pans

PRE-PREP

Follow the order below for fastest results. If you like, some or all of the ingredients can be prepped, packaged and kept in the refrigerator for up to 24 hours before assembling your freezer meals, or you can prep and assemble them all in one go. Any perishables, such as meat, poultry, cheese, fish and dairy, should be refrigerated or frozen (as directed) immediately after prepping/cooking, until you're ready to assemble and freeze your meals.

1. Label 34 gallon-sized (4 L) freezer bags with the name of the recipe, the date and any instructions you need to remember. Make sure to read each recipe to become familiar with the thawing and cooking instructions, especially when making a recipe for the first time. Here are labels to write for your freezer bags, including simplified cooking instructions:

- 4 batches Perfect Pizza, [date]. Thaw toppings in fridge. Thaw dough 3 to 4 hours on counter. Bake on a pizza stone at 500°F (260°C) for 8 to 10 minutes.
- 2 batches Cilantro Lime Chicken Tacos, [date]. Thaw. Heat in skillet to warm.
- 3 batches Teriyaki Chicken, [date]. Thaw. Pour into baking dish. Bake at 400°F (200°C) for 45 minutes.
- 2 batches Chicken Tortellini Soup, [date]. Thaw. Pour soup into large pot; boil for 5 minutes. Add chicken and tortellini; cook 3 to 4 minutes.
- 1 batch Lemon Dill Tilapia Tacos, [date]. Thaw. Pour onto baking sheet. Bake at 400°F (200°C) for 10 to 12 minutes. Chop and serve.
- 2 batches Rosemary Pot Roast, [date]. Thaw. Sear roast. Slow-cook with potatoes, carrots and marinade on Low 8 to 10 hours/High 4 to 5 hours.
- 2 batches Beef Barley Stew, [date]. Thaw. Add water and slow-cook on Low 8 to 10 hours/High 4 to 5 hours.
- 2 batches French Dip Sandwiches, [date]. Thaw. Slow-cook on Low 7 to 8 hours. Shred; serve on toasted buns with jus.
- 2 batches Honey Pork Chops, [date]. Thaw. Place in baking dish. Bake at 350°F (180°C) for 25 to 30 minutes.
- 2 batches Boneless BBQ Pork Ribs, [date]. Thaw. Slow-cook on Low 8 to 10 hours/High 5 to 6 hours. Discard grease, add BBQ sauce and heat. [Instructions follow recipe Tip.]

- 2 batches Bacon Love Pork Tenderloin, [date]. Thaw. Place in baking dish. Bake uncovered at 300°F (150°C) for 1½ hours. Broil for 2 to 3 minutes to crisp bacon.
- 2 batches Maple Dijon Chicken, [date]. Thaw. Slow-cook on Low 4 to 6 hours/High 3 to 4 hours.
- 2 batches Coconut Cashew Basil Curry Soup, [date]. Thaw. Heat in large saucepan.

2. Bulk cook 12⅔ lbs (6.33 kg) boneless, skinless chicken breasts (page 29). Chop cooked chicken to make 22 cups (5.5 L); separate 18 cups (4.5 L) for Teriyaki Chicken and 4 cups (1 L) for Chicken Tortellini Soup. Shred 6 cups (1.5 L) cooked chicken for Cilantro Lime Chicken Tacos; refrigerate.

3. Mince garlic and mince or grate ginger (if not using jarred products).

4. Peel onions. Quarter 3 onions and place in a high-powered blender or food processor; purée for Beef Barley Stew. Quarter 2 onions and reserve for soup. Dice 2½ cups (625 mL) for stew. Peel and quarter shallots.

5. Dice 2 stalks celery for soup and chop 1½ cups (375 mL) for stew.

6. Seed and devein jalapeño pepper.

7. Grate zest of 2 lemons. Squeeze juice from all lemons. Store each separately in a small container in the refrigerator. Squeeze juice from 1 lime.

8. Grate Parmesan cheese. Shred mozzarella cheese.

9. Using a clean cutting board, cut stewing beef into 1½-inch (3.5 cm) chunks, if necessary.

10. Using a clean cutting board, trim any fat from raw chicken breast. Dice 4 lbs (2 kg) raw chicken, sprinkle with garlic salt and reserve for Coconut Cashew Basil Curry Soup.

11. Using a clean cutting board, cut each pork tenderloin crosswise into 3 pieces.

MAKING THE FREEZER MEALS

Once the major recipe components are all prepped, do the final cooking, mixing and packaging to assemble the meals, putting them in the freezer as they are assembled.

1. Prepare 4 Perfect Pizza Any Way You Top It freezer meal kits (page 194). You will have 8 separate pizza kit bags.

2. Prepare 2 Cilantro Lime Chicken Tacos freezer meals (page 156).

3. Prepare 3 Teriyaki Chicken freezer meals (page 170). Using an extra-large bowl, make a triple batch of marinade, then proceed with recipe.

4. Prepare 2 Chicken Tortellini Soup freezer meals (page 107).

5. Prepare Lemon Dill Tilapia Tacos freezer meal (page 245).

6. Prepare 2 Rosemary Pot Roast freezer meals (page 205).

7. Prepare 2 Beef Barley Stew freezer meals (page 125). Make sure to rinse barley.

8. Prepare 2 French Dip Sandwiches freezer meals (page 235).

9. Prepare 2 Brown Sugar Meatloaf freezer meals (page 210). Label for baking dish: "Brown Sugar Meatloaf, [date]. Thaw. Pour sauce over top. Bake at 350°F (180°C) for about 50 minutes."

10. Prepare 2 Honey Pork Chops freezer meals (page 178).

11. Prepare 2 Boneless BBQ Pork Ribs freezer meals, according to Tip (page 189).

12. Prepare 2 Bacon Love Pork Tenderloin freezer meals (page 174).

13. Prepare 2 Maple Dijon Chicken freezer meals (page 147).

14. Prepare 2 Coconut Cashew Basil Curry Soup freezer meals (page 99).

15. Clean up and you're finished!

50 SERIOUSLY GOOD FREEZER MEALS IN A DAY: ADVANCED (12 TO 15 HOURS)

Here are 21 different recipes for making 50 freezer meals, each serving 6 to 8 people. This plan is for the cray-cray folks (like me) who love a huge challenge and want to work super hard for a day, then take a month and a half off from making dinners every night. It takes me 12 to 15 hours to make and freeze these meals, but those who are really new to freezing might take a bit longer. Note: Some of the quantities below have been rounded slightly for ease of shopping. On serving day, check the specific recipes for fresh ingredients and garnishes.

3 batches Coconut Cashew Basil Curry Soup (page 99)

2 batches Smoky Ham and White Bean Soup (page 103)

2 batches Seriously Good Chili (page 119)

3 batches Lemon Tarragon Chicken (page 144)

3 batches Maple Dijon Chicken (page 147)

2 batches Broccoli Chicken Alfredo Bake (page 151)

2 batches Old-Fashioned Chicken Pot Pie (page 155)

3 batches Cilantro Lime Chicken Tacos (page 156)

3 batches Teriyaki Chicken (page 170)

2 batches Island Pork (page 180)

4 batches Perfect Pizza Any Way You Like It (page 194)

2 batches Hash-Brown Casserole (page 199)

2 batches Smoky Pulled Pork Sandwiches (page 200)

2 batches Rosemary Pot Roast (page 205)

3 batches Mongolian Beef and Green Beans (page 217)

2 batches Thai Beef Stir-Fry (page 218)

2 batches Venezuelan Steak (page 221)

2 batches Baked Ziti (page 222)

2 batches French Dip Sandwiches (page 235)

1 batch Savory Salmon in Foil (page 238)

3 batches Cashew Mushroom Fried Rice (page 265)

GROCERY LIST

DRY GOODS/PANTRY

- 4 cups (1 L) smoky barbecue sauce
- 3 cups (750 mL) Dijon mustard
- ¼ cup (60 mL) yellow mustard
- 1⅓ cups (325 mL) Worcestershire sauce
- 4½ cups (1.125 L) tamari sauce
- ½ cup (125 mL) balsamic vinegar
- ⅔ cup (150 mL) unseasoned rice vinegar
- 2 tbsp (30 mL) fish sauce
- 2¼ cups (560 mL) olive oil
- 2 cups + 1 tbsp (515 mL) vegetable oil
- 20 cups (5 L) all-purpose flour
- ¼ cup (60 mL) quick-rising (instant) yeast
- 3⅓ cups (825 mL) cornstarch
- 4½ cups (1.125 L) packed brown sugar

- 1½ cups (375 mL) packed dark brown sugar
- 1 tsp (5 mL) unsweetened cocoa powder
- ½ tsp (2 mL) xanthan gum
- 1¼ cups (310 mL) honey
- ¾ cup (175 mL) pure maple syrup
- Four 8 oz (227 mL) cans tomato sauce (32 oz/908 mL total)
- Three 14 oz (398 mL) cans tomato sauce (42 oz/1.194 mL total)
- 12 oz (312 mL) tomato paste
- Two 28 oz (796 mL) cans diced tomatoes (56 oz/1.592 L total)
- 2 cups (500 mL) store-bought pizza sauce
- 2 lbs (1 kg) fusilli pasta
- 2 lbs (1 kg) ziti or penne pasta

- 6 cups (1.5 L) long-grain brown rice
- Four 15 oz (425 mL) cans black beans (60 oz/1.7 L total)
- Two 15 oz (425 mL) cans red kidney beans (30 oz/850 mL total)
- Four 15 oz (425 mL) cans Great Northern (white kidney) beans (60 oz/1.7 L total)
- Six 14 oz (398 mL) cans coconut milk (84 oz/2.388 L total)
- 12 cups (3 L) beef broth
- 18 cups (4.5 L) chicken broth
- 16 cups (4 L) low-sodium chicken broth
- Two 12 oz (355 mL) cans root beer (24 oz/710 mL total)
- 3 cups (750 mL) halved raw cashews
- 1½ cups (375 mL) salted roasted cashews
- ¼ cup (60 mL) sliced almonds (optional, for Cilantro Lime Chicken Tacos)

SEASONINGS

- ¾ cup + 1 tbsp (190 mL) salt
- 1 tsp (5 mL) sea salt
- 2 tbsp (30 mL) freshly ground black pepper
- 12 to 15 whole pink peppercorns (optional, for Savory Salmon in Foil)
- 3 tbsp (45 mL) onion powder
- 2½ tbsp (37 mL) garlic powder
- 1 tbsp (15 mL) garlic salt
- 4 tsp (20 mL) celery salt
- 1 tbsp (15 mL) beef bouillon powder
- 6 tbsp (90 mL) curry powder
- 2 tbsp (30 mL) ground cumin
- 2 tsp (10 mL) whole cumin seeds
- 2 tbsp (30 mL) chili powder
- ½ tsp (2 mL) cinnamon
- 2 tsp (10 mL) cayenne pepper (optional, for Seriously Good Chili)
- 2 tsp (10 mL) ground ginger
- ½ tsp (2 mL) ground cloves
- 2 tsp (10 mL) garam masala
- ½ tsp (2 mL) poultry seasoning
- 17 bay leaves
- 3 tbsp (45 mL) dried parsley
- 2 tbsp (30 mL) dried oregano
- 2 tbsp (30 mL) dried tarragon
- 1½ tbsp (22 mL) dried basil
- 1½ tbsp (22 mL) dried rosemary
- 1½ tsp (7 mL) dried thyme
- 1 tsp (5 mL) dried dill
- ½ tsp (2 mL) hot pepper flakes
- 2 tbsp (30 mL) sesame seeds

PRODUCE

- 2 cups (500 mL) minced garlic or 88 garlic cloves
- 2 tbsp (30 mL) minced or grated ginger
- 12 red bell peppers
- 19 onions

- 8 celery stalks
- 18 white mushrooms
- 1½ cups (375 mL) shredded carrots (about 3)
- 1½ lbs (750 g) asparagus, (4½ cups/1.125 L thinly sliced, trimmed asparagus)
- 9 lemons (+ 3 optional, for Lemon Tarragon Chicken)
- 1 lime
- 3 cups (750 mL) chopped fresh cilantro (about 1 bunch fresh)
- 1½ jalapeño peppers

DAIRY

- 7½ cups (1.875 L) grated Parmesan cheese (about 1 lb 10 oz/800 g)
- 3½ lbs (1.75 kg) mozzarella cheese
- 6 cups (1.5 L) shredded Cheddar cheese (about 1½ lbs/750 g)
- 30 oz (900 g) ricotta cheese
- 2¾ cups (675 mL) butter
- 4 cups (1 L) half-and-half (10%) cream
- 4 cups (1 L) milk
- 1 cup (250 mL) heavy or whipping (35%) cream
- 2 large eggs
- 4 cups (1 L) sour cream

FROZEN FOODS

- 5½ lbs (2.75 kg) frozen diced hash browns
- 2 lbs (1 kg) frozen broccoli florets
- 4 cups (1 L) frozen peas and carrots (about 24 oz/750 g)
- 3 lbs (1.5 kg) frozen whole green beans

MEAT/FISH

- 26 cups (6.5 L) chopped cooked chicken (about 12 lbs/6 kg raw; see page 29)
- 13 cups (3.25 L) shredded cooked chicken breast (about 8 lbs/4 kg raw; see page 29)
- 12 lbs (6 kg) boneless, skinless chicken breasts (about 24 breasts)
- 6 lbs (3 kg) boneless, skinless chicken tenders
- 4 lbs (2 kg) beef flank steak, cut across the grain into 1-inch (2.5 cm) slices (if possible, get your butcher to slice it for you ahead of time)
- 10 lbs (5 kg) beef flank steak, sliced across the grain into ¼-inch (0.5 cm) strips (if possible, get your butcher to slice it for you ahead of time)
- Two 3 lb (1.5 kg) boneless beef shoulder roasts (6 lbs/3 kg total)
- Two 3 lb (1.5 kg) boneless beef chuck roasts (6 lbs/3 kg total)
- 4 lbs (2 kg) boneless beef chuck (to be cut into 1-inch/2.5 cm cubes)
- 3 lbs (1.5 kg) lean ground beef
- Two 3 lb (1.5 kg) boneless pork shoulder roasts (6 lbs/3 kg total)

- 7 lbs (3.5 kg) boneless pork shoulder roast (to be cut into 4-inch/10 cm chunks)
- 120 pepperoni slices (about 3 oz/90 g)
- 1¼ lbs (600 g) cooked ham (to make 4 cups/1 L diced)
- 2 lbs (1 kg) ham steak
- 2 medium smoked ham hocks
- 2 lbs (1 kg) salmon fillet, cut into 6 equal pieces

OTHER
- 4 store-bought pie crusts

BAGS AND CONTAINERS
- 48 gallon-size (4 L) freezer bags
- 15 quart-size (1 L) freezer bags (+ 3 optional, for Lemon Tarragon Chicken)
- 12 sandwich bags
- Four 13- by 9-inch (33 by 23 cm) baking dishes
- Two 13- by 9-inch (33 by 23 cm) metal or foil pans
- Four 10-inch (25 cm) metal or foil deep-dish pie plates

PRE-PREP

Follow the order below for fastest results. If you like, some or all of the ingredients can be prepped, packaged and kept in the refrigerator for up to 24 hours before assembling your freezer meals, or you can prep and assemble them all in one go. Any perishables, such as meat, poultry, cheese, fish and dairy, should be refrigerated or frozen (as directed) immediately after prepping/cooking, until you're ready to assemble and freeze your meals.

1. Label 48 gallon-size (4 L) freezer bags with the name of the recipe, the date and any instructions you need to remember. Make sure to read each recipe to become familiar with the thawing and cooking instructions, especially when making a recipe for the first time. Here are labels to write for your freezer bags, including simplified cooking instructions:

- 3 batches Maple Dijon Chicken, [date]. Thaw. Slow-cook on Low 4 to 6 hours/High 3 to 4 hours.
- 3 batches Lemon Tarragon Chicken, [date]. Thaw. Sear chicken. Pour into baking dish with sauce and lemons. Bake, covered, at 350°F (180°C) for 20 to 25 minutes.
- 2 batches French Dip Sandwiches, [date]. Thaw. Slow-cook on Low 7 hours. Shred; serve on toasted buns with jus.
- 2 batches Venezuelan Steak, [date]. Thaw. Slow-cook on Low 8 to 9 hours/High 5 to 6 hours.
- 2 batches Thai Beef Stir-Fry, [date]. Thaw meat bag only; leave vegs frozen. Stir-fry.

- 2 batches Rosemary Pot Roast, [date]. Thaw. Sear meat. Slow-cook with potatoes, carrots and marinade on Low for 8 to 10 hours/High 4 to 5 hours.
- 2 batches Island Pork, [date]. Thaw. Slice fresh pineapple. Slow-cook with pineapple skins on Low 10 to 12 hours.
- 2 batches Smoky Pulled Pork Sandwiches [date]. Thaw. Slow-cook on Low 8 to 10 hours. Shred and add barbecue sauce. Serve in buns.
- 1 batch Savory Salmon in Foil, [date]. Thaw. Bake at 400°F (200°C) for 15 minutes.
- 2 batches Smoky Ham and White Bean Soup, [date]. Thaw. Slow-cook on Low 3 to 4 hours. Remove ham hock and bay leaves. Add ham and cook for 10 minutes.
- 2 batches Seriously Good Chili, [date]. Thaw. Slow-cook on Low 8 to 10 hours/High 4 to 6 hours. Stir in lime juice; serve.
- 3 batches Mongolian Beef and Green Beans, [date]. Thaw sauce bag. Stir-fry.
- 3 batches Cashew Mushroom Fried Rice, [date]. Thaw. Microwave 5 to 6 minutes, stirring every minute.
- 4 batches Perfect Pizza, [date]. Thaw toppings in fridge. Thaw dough 3 to 4 hours on counter. Bake on a pizza stone at 500°F (260°C) for 8 to 10 minutes.
- 3 batches Teriyaki Chicken, [date]. Thaw. Pour into baking dish. Bake at 400°F (200°C) for 45 minutes.
- 3 batches Cilantro Lime Chicken Tacos, [date]. Thaw. Heat in skillet to warm.
- 3 batches Coconut Cashew Basil Curry Soup, [date]. Thaw. Heat in large saucepan.

2. Cook a triple batch of brown rice for Cashew Mushroom Fried Rice. Fluff with a fork. Transfer to a shallow dish. Let cool for 10 minutes, then cover and place in refrigerator for 4 to 5 hours, until completely cooled.

3. Mince garlic and mince or grate ginger (if not using jarred products).

4. Peel all the onions. Quarter and place 3 onions in a high-powered blender or food processor and purée; divide equally into 3 labeled gallon-size (4 L) freezer bags for French Dip Sandwiches. Quarter and purée 2 onions; place in a medium bowl for Red Sauce. Quarter 3 onions and reserve for Coconut Cashew Basil Curry Soup. Dice 5½ onions; place in a large bowl. Thinly slice 5 onions; place half of 1 sliced onion in each of 2 labeled gallon-size (4 L) freezer bags for Venezuelan Steak. Label 2 quart-size (1 L) bags for Island Pork and place 1 sliced onion in each bag. Place all bags and containers in refrigerator. Arrange 2 sliced onions on a baking sheet lined with parchment paper for Thai Beef Stir-Fry.

5. Thinly slice 5 bell peppers. Add 2 to bag with onions for Venezuelan Steak. Add 3 to baking sheet with onions for Thai Beef Stir-Fry; freeze for about 30 to 45 minutes. Dice remaining 7 peppers, 4 for Seriously Good Chili and 3 for Cashew Mushroom Fried Rice; place in separate bags or containers and refrigerate.

6. Chop 2 celery stalks and place in slow cooker for Red Sauce. Chop remaining celery and place in a bowl.

7. Thinly slice mushrooms.

8. Trim and thinly slice asparagus.

9. Shred 1½ cups (375 mL) carrots (if not using pre-shredded).

10. Seed and devein jalapeño peppers.

11. Squeeze juice from about 7 lemons. Thinly slice 3 lemons, if using, for Lemon Tarragon Chicken; divide equally into 3 quart-size (1 L) freezer bags. For Savory Salmon in Foil, cut six ¼-inch (1 cm) slices crosswise from centers of 2 lemons, reserving end pieces for assembling foil packets. Squeeze juice from 1 lime. Store everything separately in refrigerator.

12. Shred mozzarella cheese. Shred Cheddar cheese. Grate Parmesan cheese. Store separately in bowls or containers in refrigerator.

13. Dice ham for Hash-Brown Casserole. Refrigerate.

14. Cook 1 batch Red Sauce (page 334) in slow cooker on High for 4 to 5 hours. Quick-cool (see page 21) so it is ready in time to assemble Baked Ziti. (Sometimes I start my Red Sauce the evening before my big cooking day, letting it cook overnight on Low for 10 to 12 hours, and start cooling it in the morning.) You will have 1 cup (250 mL) sauce left over.

15. Make 4 batches White Sauce (page 336). Let cool.

16. Make 2 batches Alfredo sauce (page 333). Let cool.

17. Make 3 batches sauce for Mongolian Beef and Green Beans (page 217). Let cool.

18. Using a clean cutting board, slice 10 lbs (5 kg) beef flank steak across the grain into ¼-inch (0.5 cm) strips. Place 6 lbs (3 kg) in a large bowl for Mongolian Beef and Green Beans. Divide 4 lbs (2 kg) equally into 2 labeled gallon-size (4 L) freezer bags for Thai Beef Stir-Fry. Cut 4 lbs (2 kg) flank steak across the grain into 1-inch (2.5 cm) slices. Divide equally and add to onion/pepper bags for Venezuelan Steak. (Simply portion out the flank steak if purchased pre-sliced.) Refrigerate.

19. Cut 4 lbs (2 kg) boneless beef chuck into 1-inch (2.5 cm) cubes (if not purchased precut). Cook for the chili (step 1, page 119). Refrigerate.

20. Cook ground beef, red peppers and onion for the chili (step 2, page 119). Refrigerate.

21. Fry flank steak strips for Mongolian Beef and Green Beans. Flash-freeze.

22. Using a clean cutting board, cut 7 lbs (3.5 kg) pork shoulder roast into 4-inch (10 cm) slices. Divide equally into 2 labeled freezer bags for Island Pork. Refrigerate.

23. Using a clean cutting board, trim any fat from raw chicken breasts. Cut 6 lbs (3 kg) chicken breasts (about 12) into cutlets for Lemon Tarragon Chicken (step 1, page 144). Sprinkle with garlic salt and place in 3 labeled gallon-size (4 L) freezer bags; refrigerate. Dice 6 lbs (4 kg) raw chicken, sprinkle with garlic salt and set aside for Coconut Cashew Basil Curry Soup.

24. Bulk cook 20 lbs (10 kg) chicken (page 29). Chop 26 cups (6.5 L) cooked chicken. Shred 13 cups (3.25 L) cooked chicken. Refrigerate in separate large bowls.

25. Cook diced chicken for Coconut Cashew Basil Curry Soup. Refrigerate.

MAKING THE FREEZER MEALS

Once the major recipe components are all prepped, do the final cooking, mixing and packaging to assemble the meals, putting them in the freezer as they are assembled.

1. Prepare 3 Maple Dijon Chicken freezer meals (page 147).

2. Prepare 3 Lemon Tarragon Chicken freezer meals (page 144).

3. Prepare 2 French Dip Sandwiches freezer meals (page 235).

4. Prepare 2 Venezuelan Steak freezer meals (page 221).

5. Prepare 2 Thai Beef Stir-Fry freezer meals (page 218).

6. Prepare 2 Rosemary Pot Roast freezer meals (page 205).

7. Prepare 2 Island Pork freezer meals (page 180).

8. Prepare 2 Smoky Pulled Pork Sandwiches freezer meals (page 200).

9. Prepare Savory Salmon in Foil (page 238).

10. Prepare 2 Smoky Ham and White Bean Soup freezer meals (page 103).

11. Prepare 2 Seriously Good Chili freezer meals (page 119). Use a super-large bowl to combine ingredients for the double batch. Divide equally between freezer bags.

12. Prepare 3 Mongolian Beef and Green Beans freezer meals (page 217).

13. Prepare 3 Cashew Mushroom Fried Rice freezer meals (page 265).

14. Begin quick-cooling Red Sauce if you didn't cook it overnight.

15. Prepare 2 Hash-Brown Casserole freezer meals (page 199). Label for each baking dish: "Hash-Brown Casserole, [date]. Thaw. Bake uncovered at 350°F (180°C) for 55 to 60 minutes."

16. Make 4 batches Pizza Dough (page 332). Prepare 4 Perfect Pizza Any Way You Top It freezer meal kits (page 194).

17. Prepare 3 Teriyaki Chicken freezer meals (page 170). Use a super-large bowl to combine ingredients for the triple batch, then divide equally among labeled freezer bags.

18. Prepare 3 Cilantro Lime Chicken Tacos freezer meals (page 156).

19. Prepare 2 Coconut Cashew Basil Curry Soup freezer meals (page 99).

20. Prepare 2 Old-Fashioned Chicken Pot Pie freezer meals (page 155). Use a super-large bowl to make a double recipe of filling. Divide evenly between pie plates and proceed with recipe. Label for each pie: "Chicken Pot Pie, [date]. Poke holes. Bake on rimmed baking sheet at 375°F (190°C) for 1 hour 30 minutes."

21. Prepare 2 Broccoli Chicken Alfredo Bake freezer meals (page 151). Use a super-large bowl to make a double batch of pasta mixture. Divide equally between 2 baking dishes and proceed with the recipe. Label for each baking dish: "Broccoli Chicken Alfredo Bake, [date]. Thaw. Bake, uncovered, at 350°F (180°C) for 40 to 50 minutes."

22. Prepare 2 Baked Ziti freezer meals (page 222). Use a super-large bowl to prepare a double batch of pasta mixture. Proceed with recipe, dividing pasta and red sauce evenly between baking dishes. Label for each baking dish: "Baked Ziti, [date]. Thaw. Bake, uncovered, at 375°F (190°C) for 35 to 45 minutes."

23. Clean up and you're finished!

BREAKFAST

Blueberry Orange Smoothie Kits   43

Breakfast Burritos   44

Hearty Breakfast Bowls   47

California Breakfast Casserole   48

Maple Breakfast Sausage Patties   51

Savory Sausage Hash   52

Perfect Freezer Pancakes   55

Buttery Cinnamon French Toast Bake   56

Frosted Cinnamon Roll Granola   59

Morning Energy Bars   60

Cinnamon Mini Donut Muffins   63

Almond Lemon Poppyseed Muffins   64

Blueberry Orange Smoothie Kits

Let's just get this out of the way: I'm not a morning person. I may have to rise but I don't exactly shine. However, there is one morning item that provides me some bliss: this smoothie! It seriously tastes like an orange Creamsicle kissed with a touch of fresh blueberries. *Makes 2 servings.*

¼ cup (60 mL) plain Greek yogurt

¼ tsp (1 mL) vanilla extract

¼ cup (60 mL) frozen orange juice concentrate, partially thawed

½ banana

1 cup (250 mL) frozen blueberries

½ cup (125 mL) water

1. In a small bowl, whisk together Greek yogurt, vanilla and orange juice. Pour 1 tbsp (15 mL) each into 8 cups of an ice-cube tray. Freeze for about 2 hours, until solid.

2. Meanwhile, slice banana into ¼-inch (0.5 cm) slices and place on a baking sheet lined with parchment paper. Freeze for about 2 hours, until solid.

MAKE IT NOW Place the 8 orange juice cubes, frozen blueberries and frozen banana pieces into a blender. Add water. Blend on High until smooth. Add more water if necessary to get desired consistency. Pour into 2 glasses and serve cold.

MAKE IT A FREEZER MEAL Place the 8 orange juice cubes, frozen blueberries and frozen banana pieces in a labeled quart-size (1 L) freezer bag. Seal, removing as much air as possible, and freeze.

MAKE THE SMOOTHIES Add contents of freezer bag and water to blender. Blend on High until smooth. Add more water if necessary to get desired consistency. Pour into 2 glasses and serve cold.

VARIATIONS
Green Smoothie: Substitute 1 cup (250 mL) frozen pineapple chunks for the blueberries and add 2 cups (500 mL) packed fresh spinach leaves to freezer bag or directly to blender.

Orange Dream: Omit banana and blueberries. Add ½ cup (125 mL) frozen orange sherbet to freezer bag or directly to blender.

BULK BATCH GUIDE	Servings	2 (1 batch)	4 (2 batches)	6 (3 batches)	8 (4 batches)	10 (5 batches)
	Greek yogurt	¼ cup (60 mL)	½ cup (125 mL)	¾ cup (175 mL)	1 cup (250 mL)	1¼ cups (310 mL)
	vanilla	¼ tsp (1 mL)	½ tsp (2 mL)	¾ tsp (3 mL)	1 tsp (5 mL)	1¼ tsp (6 mL)
	orange juice concentrate	¼ cup (60 mL)	½ cup (125 mL)	¾ cup (175 mL)	1 cup (250 mL)	1¼ cups (310 mL)
	bananas	½	1	1½	2	2½
	blueberries	1 cup (250 mL)	2 cups (500 mL)	3 cups (750 mL)	4 cups (1 L)	5 cups (1.25 L)
	water	½ cup (125 mL)	1 cup (250 mL)	1½ cups (375 mL)	2 cups (500 mL)	2½ cups (625 mL)
	quart bags	1	2	3	4	5

Breakfast Burritos

HANGRY = Hungry + Angry, a condition whereby the people around you risk getting hurt if you don't get food soon. These burritos filled with crispy potato tots, savory crumbled sausage, creamy eggs and cheese, all wrapped in a soft tortilla, are the best way to cure a case of the morning hangries. Makes 12 burritos.

3 cups (750 mL) frozen potato tots (about 12 oz/375 g)

12 large eggs

¼ cup (60 mL) whole milk

1 tsp (5 mL) salt

1 tbsp (15 mL) olive oil

1 lb (500 g) breakfast sausage (bulk or casings removed)

2 cups (500 mL) shredded Cheddar cheese (about 8 oz/250 g)

12 8-inch (20 cm) flour tortillas

Salt and freshly ground black pepper

1. On a baking sheet lined with parchment paper, bake potato tots according to package instructions until extra crispy and golden brown.

2. Meanwhile, in a large bowl, combine eggs, milk and salt. Whisk like a crazy person for about 1 to 1½ minutes, until bubbles cover the entire surface when you stop. Let stand for 15 minutes at room temperature, until the mixture turns a slightly darker color.

3. In a large skillet, heat olive oil over medium-high heat. Cook sausage for 4 to 5 minutes, stirring constantly and breaking up larger pieces, or until no longer pink. (I like to turn the heat to high during the last minute to get a few crispy pieces of sausage, adding more flavor to the burritos, but that's optional.) Remove from heat and strain through a fine-mesh sieve into a small bowl. Return 2 tbsp (30 mL) drained fat to skillet; discard the rest. Set aside sausage in another large bowl.

4. Whisk egg mixture again for 15 to 20 seconds. With skillet back on medium-high heat, add eggs to sausage fat. Cook for about 4 to 5 minutes, gently scraping bottom and sides of pan continuously with a spatula, until no liquid remains. Add eggs to bowl with cooked sausage.

5. Add Cheddar cheese and potato tots to egg-and-sausage mixture and gently combine. Season to taste with salt and pepper.

6. Cut out 12 pieces of aluminum foil, each 8 inches (20 cm) square. Place a tortilla on each foil square. Spread a heaping ½ cup (125 mL) filling mixture down the center of each tortilla. Fold in opposite sides of tortilla, then roll up, burrito style. Place burrito, seam side down, on foil and wrap each individually.

MAKE IT NOW Preheat oven to 400°F (200°C). Place burritos on a baking sheet. Bake for 10 to 12 minutes or until heated through.

MAKE IT A FREEZER MEAL Place burritos in a labeled gallon-size (4 L) freezer bag. Seal, removing as much air as possible, and freeze.

REHEAT To heat up individual burritos in the microwave, remove foil, place on a plate, cover with plastic wrap and heat on High for 2 minutes or until warmed through. To reheat using your oven, preheat oven to 400°F (200°C). Place foil-wrapped burritos directly on center rack and bake for 25 to 30 minutes or until heated through.

Hearty Breakfast Bowls

Who loves a classic hot breakfast of hash browns, eggs and your favorite breakfast meat? Me too! Now, who loves slaving away over a hot stove to make it every morning? Me neither! This is why these hearty breakfast bowls are the perfect solution. Folks, we have been doing breakfast all wrong. Makes 6 bowls.

1 bag (1 lb/500 g) frozen diced hash browns

2 tbsp (30 mL) vegetable oil

6 large eggs

2 tbsp (30 mL) whole milk

½ tsp (2 mL) salt

1 tbsp (15 mL) olive oil

8 oz (250 g) breakfast sausage (bulk or casings removed)

¾ cup (175 mL) shredded Cheddar cheese (about 3 oz/90 g)

Garnish
Fresh parsley leaves (optional)

1. Preheat oven to 450°F (230°C).

2. Place hash browns in a large bowl, add vegetable oil and stir to combine. Spread potatoes evenly in a single layer on a lightly greased baking sheet. Bake in preheated oven for 25 minutes, flipping halfway through, until golden brown and crispy.

3. Meanwhile, in another large bowl, combine eggs, milk and salt. Whisk like a crazy person for about 1 to 1½ minutes, until bubbles cover the entire surface when you stop. Let stand for 15 minutes at room temperature, until the mixture turns a slightly darker color.

4. In a large skillet, heat olive oil over medium-high heat. Cook sausage, stirring constantly and breaking up larger pieces, for 4 to 5 minutes or until no longer pink. (I like to turn the heat to high during the last minute to get a few crispy pieces of sausage, adding more flavor to the dish, but that's optional.) Remove sausage from heat and strain through a fine-mesh sieve into a small bowl. Return 1 tbsp (15 mL) drained fat to skillet; discard the rest. Set aside drained sausage in another large bowl.

5. Whisk egg mixture again for 15 to 20 seconds. With skillet back on medium-high heat, add eggs to sausage fat. Cook for about 3 to 4 minutes, gently scraping bottom and sides of pan continuously with a spatula, until no liquid remains. Remove from heat and set aside.

6. Divide hash browns equally among six 2-cup (500 mL) microwave-safe containers or bowls. Evenly divide sausage between bowls, followed by eggs. Lightly mix ingredients together. Top each bowl with 1 to 2 tbsp (15 to 30 mL) Cheddar cheese.

MAKE IT NOW Place individual bowls in microwave and heat on High for 1 minute. Stir. Heat in 30-second intervals until warmed through. Sprinkle with fresh parsley, if desired.

MAKE IT A FREEZER MEAL Let container or bowl cool completely. Wrap tightly with plastic wrap, pressing down gently to remove air. Cover with foil. Label and place in freezer.

COOK FROM FROZEN Remove foil and plastic wrap. Place individual bowls in microwave and heat on High for 1½ minutes. Stir. Heat in 30-second intervals until warmed through. Sprinkle with fresh parsley, if desired.

BULK BATCH GUIDE	Bowls	6 (1 batch)	12 (2 batches)	18 (3 batches)	24 (4 batches)	30 (5 batches)
	hash browns	1 lb (500 g)	2 lbs (1 kg)	3 lbs (1.5 kg)	4 lbs (2 kg)	5 lbs (2.5 kg)
	vegetable oil	2 tbsp (30 mL)	¼ cup (60 mL)	6 tbsp (90 mL)	½ cup (125 mL)	⅔ cup (150 mL)
	eggs	6	12	18	24	30
	whole milk	2 tbsp (30 mL)	¼ cup (60 mL)	6 tbsp (90 mL)	½ cup (125 mL)	⅔ cup (150 mL)
	salt	½ tsp (2 mL)	1 tsp (5 mL)	1½ tsp (7 mL)	2 tsp (10 mL)	2½ tsp (12 mL)
	olive oil	1 tbsp (15 mL)	2 tbsp (30 mL)	3 tbsp (45 mL)	¼ cup (60 mL)	⅓ cup (75 mL)
	breakfast sausage	8 oz (250 g)	1 lb (500 g)	1½ lbs (750 g)	2 lbs (1 kg)	2½ lbs (1.25 kg)
	Cheddar cheese	¾ cup (175 mL)	1½ cups (375 mL)	2¼ cups (560 mL)	3 cups (750 mL)	3¾ cups (925 mL)
	bowls	6	12	18	24	30

California Breakfast Casserole

Want to invite all your favorite friends to breakfast? And by "friends" I mean potatoes, sour cream, salsa, cheese and everyone's best friend — bacon. This cheery morning casserole is loaded with so much taste it's almost impossible for anyone in your family not to want more. *Makes 6 servings.*

3 cups (750 mL) frozen shredded hash browns, thawed (about 12 oz/375 g)

1½ cups (375 mL) cooked diced bacon (about 1 lb/500 g uncooked)

½ cup (125 mL) sour cream

1 cup (250 mL) salsa

4 large eggs

½ cup (125 mL) shredded Monterey Jack cheese (about 2 oz/60 g)

½ cup (125 mL) shredded Cheddar cheese (about 2 oz/60 g)

Garnishes

Chopped fresh cilantro (optional)

Avocado slices (optional)

Additional salsa (optional)

1. In a large bowl, combine hash browns, bacon and sour cream. Spread mixture in a lightly greased 9-inch (23 cm) square baking dish. Spoon salsa evenly overtop.

2. In a medium bowl, beat eggs. Pour evenly over salsa layer. Top with Monterey Jack cheese and Cheddar cheese.

MAKE IT NOW Preheat oven to 350°F (180°C). Cover casserole with foil. Bake in preheated oven for 30 minutes. Remove foil and bake for an additional 20 minutes, or until golden and bubbly on top. Remove from oven and let cool for 5 minutes. Top with cilantro, avocado and additional salsa, if using.

MAKE IT A FREEZER MEAL Wrap assembled casserole tightly with plastic wrap, pressing down gently to remove air. Cover with foil. Label and place in freezer.

THAW AND COOK Place in the refrigerator for at least 12 hours or up to 24 hours to thaw. Preheat oven to 350°F (180°C). Remove plastic wrap and foil; cover with new foil. Bake in preheated oven for 30 minutes. Remove foil and bake for an additional 20 minutes, or until golden and bubbly on top. Remove from oven and let cool for 5 minutes. Top with cilantro, avocado and additional salsa, if using.

Servings	6 (1 batch)	12 (2 batches)	18 (3 batches)	24 (4 batches)	30 (5 batches)
hash browns	3 cups (750 mL)	6 cups (1.5 L)	9 cups (2.25 L)	12 cups (3 L)	15 cups (3.75 L)
bacon	1½ cups (375 mL)	3 cups (750 mL)	4½ cups (1.125 L)	6 cups (1.5 L)	7½ cups (1.875 L)
sour cream	½ cup (125 mL)	1 cup (250 mL)	1½ cups (375 mL)	2 cups (500 mL)	2½ cups (625 mL)
salsa	1 cup (250 mL)	2 cups (500 mL)	3 cups (750 mL)	4 cups (1 L)	5 cups (1.25 L)
eggs	4	8	12	16	20
Monterey Jack cheese	½ cup (125 mL)	1 cup (250 mL)	1½ cups (375 mL)	2 cups (500 mL)	2½ cups (625 mL)
Cheddar cheese	½ cup (125 mL)	1 cup (250 mL)	1½ cups (375 mL)	2 cups (500 mL)	2½ cups (625 mL)
9x9 dishes	1	2	3	4	5

BULK BATCH GUIDE

Maple Breakfast Sausage Patties

Have you ever made your own sausage patties? There is just no comparison how much better they taste than store-bought. Packed full of just the right spices and flavors, this recipe is perfection.

Makes 12 patties.

2 tsp (10 mL) dried parsley

2 tsp (10 mL) salt

1 tsp (5 mL) dried sage

1 tsp (5 mL) freshly ground black pepper

1 tsp (5 mL) dried basil

1 tsp (5 mL) dried oregano

½ tsp (2 mL) dried thyme

3 lbs (1.5 kg) ground pork

⅓ cup (75 mL) puréed or minced onion

2 tsp (10 mL) pure maple syrup

To Serve

Cooking spray or olive oil

1. In a large bowl, combine parsley, salt, sage, pepper, basil, oregano and thyme. Add pork, onion and maple syrup. Using your hands, combine to ensure it's all incorporated.

2. Place meat between 2 pieces of plastic wrap, 24 inches (60 cm) long. With a rolling pin, roll out meat to ¼-inch (0.5 cm) thickness. Remove top layer of plastic wrap. Using a 3- to 4-inch (8 to 10 cm) round cookie cutter or top of a glass, press down to cut out round patty shapes.

MAKE IT NOW Lightly spray a large skillet with cooking spray (or grease with olive oil) and heat over medium-high heat. Working in batches of 4 to 6, place patties in skillet and cook for about 4 minutes per side, until completely golden brown on the outside and no longer pink inside. Transfer to a plate lined with paper towels. Serve.

MAKE IT A FREEZER MEAL Transfer uncooked patties to a baking sheet lined with parchment paper. Freeze for about 1 to 2 hours, until solid. Transfer patties to a labeled gallon-size (4 L) freezer bag. Seal bag, removing as much air as possible, and freeze.

COOK FROM FROZEN Remove patties from freezer. Lightly spray a large skillet with cooking spray (or grease with olive oil) and heat over medium-high heat. Working in batches of 4 to 6, place frozen patties in skillet and cook for about 5 minutes per side, until completely cooked and golden brown. Transfer to a plate lined with paper towels. Serve.

	Patties	12 (1 batch)	24 (2 batches)	36 (3 batches)	48 (4 batches)	60 (5 batches)
BULK BATCH GUIDE	dried parsley	2 tsp (10 mL)	4 tsp (20 mL)	2 tbsp (30 mL)	8 tsp (40 mL)	10 tsp (50 mL)
	salt	2 tsp (10 mL)	4 tsp (20 mL)	2 tbsp (30 mL)	8 tsp (40 mL)	10 tsp (50 mL)
	dried sage	1 tsp (5 mL)	2 tsp (10 mL)	1 tbsp (15 mL)	4 tsp (20 mL)	5 tsp (25 mL)
	pepper	1 tsp (5 mL)	2 tsp (10 mL)	1 tbsp (15 mL)	4 tsp (20 mL)	5 tsp (25 mL)
	dried basil	1 tsp (5 mL)	2 tsp (10 mL)	1 tbsp (15 mL)	4 tsp (20 mL)	5 tsp (25 mL)
	dried oregano	1 tsp (5 mL)	2 tsp (10 mL)	1 tbsp (15 mL)	4 tsp (20 mL)	5 tsp (25 mL)
	dried thyme	½ tsp (2 mL)	1 tsp (5 mL)	1½ tsp (7 mL)	2 tsp (10 mL)	2½ tsp (12 mL)
	ground pork	3 lbs (1.5 kg)	6 lbs (3 kg)	9 lbs (4.5 kg)	12 lbs (6 kg)	15 lbs (7.5 kg)
	onion	⅓ cup (75 mL)	⅔ cup (150 mL)	1 cup (250 mL)	1⅓ cups (325 mL)	1⅔ cups (400 mL)
	maple syrup	2 tsp (10 mL)	4 tsp (20 mL)	2 tbsp (30 mL)	8 tsp (40 mL)	10 tbsp (50 mL)
	gallon bags	1	2	3	4	5

Savory Sausage Hash

This thrifty mama created a breakfast hash using smoked sausage for half the price of canned corned-beef hash. I love serving this with a fried egg and a sunny glass of orange juice. It's the little things in life, like this breakfast, that help me start the day with a smile. Makes 6 servings or about 8 cups (2 L) hash.

12 oz (375 g) smoked beef sausage (fully cooked), cut in half

2 tbsp (30 mL) heavy or whipping (35%) cream

1 tsp (5 mL) Worcestershire sauce

1 tsp (5 mL) onion powder

½ tsp (2 mL) garlic salt

¼ tsp (1 mL) dried thyme

⅛ tsp (0.5 mL) freshly ground black pepper

1½ lbs (750 g) frozen diced hash browns

To Serve
2 tbsp (30 mL) butter

1. In a high-powered blender or food processor, combine sausage, cream, Worcestershire sauce, onion powder, garlic salt, thyme and pepper. Pulse about 7 or 8 times, until puréed and smooth.

2. In a large bowl, combine hash browns and meat mixture. Stir until thoroughly combined.

MAKE IT NOW In a large skillet, heat 2 tbsp (30 mL) butter over medium-high heat. Add hash and cook for about 4 minutes, until crispy on one side. Flip and cook for about 4 minutes more, until crispy.

MAKE IT A FREEZER MEAL Place uncooked hash mixture in a labeled gallon-size (4 L) freezer bag. Seal, removing as much air as possible, and freeze.

THAW AND COOK Place in the refrigerator for at least 12 or up to 24 hours to thaw. In a large skillet, heat 2 tbsp (30 mL) butter over medium-high heat. Add hash and cook for 4 minutes, until crispy on one side. Flip and cook for about 4 minutes more, until crispy.

BULK BATCH GUIDE

Servings	6 (1 batch)	12 (2 batches)	18 (3 batches)	24 (4 batches)	30 (5 batches)
sausage	12 oz (375 g)	1½ lbs (750 g)	2¼ lbs (1.125 kg)	3 lbs (1.5 kg)	3¾ lbs (1.875 kg)
cream	2 tbsp (30 mL)	¼ cup (60 mL)	6 tbsp (90 mL)	½ cup (125 mL)	⅔ cup (150 mL)
Worcestershire sauce	1 tsp (5 mL)	2 tsp (10 mL)	1 tbsp (15 mL)	4 tsp (20 mL)	5 tsp (25 mL)
onion powder	1 tsp (5 mL)	2 tsp (10 mL)	1 tbsp (15 mL)	4 tsp (20 mL)	5 tsp (25 mL)
garlic salt	½ tsp (2 mL)	1 tsp (5 mL)	1½ tsp (7 mL)	2 tsp (10 mL)	2½ tsp (12 mL)
dried thyme	¼ tsp (1 mL)	½ tsp (2 mL)	¾ tsp (3 mL)	1 tsp (5 mL)	1¼ tsp (6 mL)
pepper	⅛ tsp (0.5 mL)	¼ tsp (1 mL)	⅓ tsp (1.5 mL)	½ tsp (2 mL)	¾ tsp (3 mL)
hash browns	1½ lbs (750 g)	3 lbs (1.5 kg)	4½ lbs (2.25 kg)	6 lbs (3 kg)	7½ lbs (3.75 kg)
butter	2 tbsp (30 mL)	¼ cup (60 mL)	6 tbsp (90 mL)	½ cup (125 mL)	⅔ cup (150 mL)
gallon bags	1	2	3	4	5

Perfect Freezer Pancakes

Here it is – my favorite pancake recipe of all time. These are big, beautiful, fluffy pancakes that taste as good as they look. The secret is Greek yogurt, which keeps them soft and moist even after freezing and reheating. Makes about 10 pancakes.

2 cups (500 mL) all-purpose flour

2 tsp (10 mL) baking powder

½ tsp (2 mL) baking soda

½ tsp (2 mL) salt

2 large eggs

1½ cups (375 mL) plain Greek yogurt

1½ cups (375 mL) milk

3 tbsp (45 mL) butter, melted

Cooking spray or 2 tbsp (30 mL) butter

Garnish
Pure maple syrup (optional)

1. In a medium bowl, combine flour, baking powder, baking soda and salt.

2. In another medium bowl, whisk together eggs. Add Greek yogurt, milk and melted butter; whisk until combined. Pour over dry ingredients and gently stir just until moistened and still a bit lumpy.

3. Heat a griddle to 325°F (160°C) or a medium skillet over medium-low heat. Spray with cooking spray or grease with about 1 tbsp (15 mL) butter. Working in batches, use about ½ cup (125 mL) batter per pancake. Cook for about 2 minutes, until bubbles surface and pop on top. Flip pancake and cook until golden brown. Remove from heat. Repeat with remaining batter, spraying or buttering pan and adjusting heat between batches as necessary.

MAKE IT NOW Serve warm with maple syrup, if desired.

MAKE IT A FREEZER MEAL Let cooked pancakes cool completely. Layer pancakes on a baking sheet with squares of parchment in between layers. Freeze for about 1 to 2 hours, until hard. Transfer to a labeled gallon-size (4 L) freezer bag. Seal, removing as much air as possible, and freeze.

REHEAT Heat a griddle to around 325°F (160°C) and warm frozen pancakes until heated through, or place on a plate and microwave on High for 45 seconds, until heated through. Serve warm with maple syrup, if desired.

BULK BATCH GUIDE	Pancakes	10 (1 batch)	20 (2 batches)	30 (3 batches)	40 (4 batches)	50 (5 batches)
	all-purpose flour	2 cups (500 mL)	4 cups (1 L)	6 cups (1.5 L)	8 cups (2 L)	10 cups (2.5 L)
	baking powder	2 tsp (10 mL)	4 tsp (20 mL)	2 tbsp (30 mL)	8 tsp (40 mL)	10 tsp (50 mL)
	baking soda	½ tsp (2 mL)	1 tsp (5 mL)	1½ tsp (7 mL)	2 tsp (10 mL)	2½ tsp (12 mL)
	salt	½ tsp (2 mL)	1 tsp (5 mL)	1½ tsp (7 mL)	2 tsp (10 mL)	2½ tsp (12 mL)
	eggs	2	4	6	8	10
	Greek yogurt	1½ cups (375 mL)	3 cups (750 mL)	4½ cups (1.125 L)	6 cups (1.5 L)	7½ cups (1.875 L)
	milk	1½ cups (375 mL)	3 cups (750 mL)	4½ cups (1.125 L)	6 cups (1.5 L)	7½ cups (1.875 L)
	butter	3 tbsp (45 mL)	6 tbsp (90 mL)	9 tbsp (135 mL)	¾ cup (175 mL)	¾ cup + 3 tbsp (220 mL)
	gallon bags	1	2	3	4	5

Buttery Cinnamon French Toast Bake

One truth every parent knows is that getting teenagers out of bed in the morning is like waking the dead. The only thing stronger than their need for sleep is their constant need to eat. The solution for all you parents is the sweet smell of Buttery Cinnamon French Toast Bake wafting through your house in the early morning. Makes 6 servings.

Caramel Base

½ cup (125 mL) unsalted butter

¾ cup (175 mL) packed brown sugar

Filling

1 loaf bread, any type

6 large eggs

1½ cups (375 mL) whole milk

2 tbsp (30 mL) vanilla extract

1 tbsp (15 mL) ground cinnamon

2 tbsp (30 mL) unsalted butter, melted

Topping

½ cup (125 mL) all-purpose flour

½ cup (125 mL) packed brown sugar

¼ tsp (1 mL) salt

½ cup (125 mL) unsalted butter, chilled

Garnishes

Confectioners' (icing) sugar, sifted (optional)

Heavy or whipping (35%) cream (optional)

Pure maple syrup (optional)

1. *Caramel Base:* In a small, microwave-safe bowl, combine butter and sugar. Microwave on High for about 30 seconds, until bubbly. Stir; pour into a lightly greased 13- by 9-inch (33 by 23 cm), or a similar-sized, metal or foil pan, spreading evenly.

2. *Filling:* Tear bread into 1-inch (2.5 cm) pieces and place on top of caramel base.

3. In a medium bowl, whisk together eggs, milk, vanilla, cinnamon and butter. Pour evenly over bread. Cover with plastic wrap.

4. *Topping:* In another medium bowl, combine flour, brown sugar and salt. Using two knives or a pastry cutter, cut in chilled butter until you have pea-sized pieces. Place crumble in a labeled quart-sized (1 L) freezer bag and seal.

MAKE IT NOW Place pan and topping in refrigerator for at least 6 hours or overnight. Preheat oven to 350°F (180°C). Remove plastic wrap and sprinkle topping mixture over bread. Bake for 40 to 45 minutes, until a tester inserted in the center comes out clean and topping is golden brown. Remove from oven and let cool for 5 minutes. Sprinkle with confectioners' sugar and drizzle with cream or maple syrup, if using.

MAKE IT A FREEZER MEAL Wrap the assembled pan tightly with plastic wrap, pressing down gently to remove air. Place topping bag on top of pan and cover both with foil. Label and place in freezer.

COOK FROM FROZEN Preheat oven to 350°F (180°C). Remove foil, topping packet and plastic wrap. Sprinkle topping mixture over bread. Place frozen pan directly into oven and bake for 55 to 60 minutes, until a tester inserted in the center comes out clean and topping is golden brown. Remove from oven and let cool for 5 minutes. Sprinkle with confectioners' sugar and drizzle with cream or maple syrup, if using.

BULK BATCH GUIDE	Servings	6 (1 batch)	12 (2 batches)	18 (3 batches)	24 (4 batches)	30 (5 batches)
	butter	½ cup (125 mL)	1 cup (250 mL)	1½ cups (375 mL)	2 cups (500 mL)	2½ cups (625 mL)
	brown sugar	¾ cup (175 mL)	1½ cups (375 mL)	2¼ cups (560 mL)	3 cups (750 mL)	3¾ cups (925 mL)
	bread loaves	1	2	3	4	5
	eggs	6	12	18	24	30
	whole milk	1½ cups (375 mL)	3 cups (750 mL)	4½ cups (1.125 L)	6 cups (1.5 L)	7½ cups (1.875 L)
	vanilla	2 tbsp (30 mL)	¼ cup (60 mL)	6 tbsp (90 mL)	½ cup (125 mL)	⅔ cup (150 mL)
	cinnamon	1 tbsp (15 mL)	2 tbsp (30 mL)	3 tbsp (45 mL)	¼ cup (60 mL)	⅓ cup (75 mL)
	unsalted butter	2 tbsp (30 mL)	¼ cup (60 mL)	6 tbsp (90 mL)	½ cup (125 mL)	⅔ cup (150 mL)
	all-purpose flour	½ cup (125 mL)	1 cup (250 mL)	1½ cups (375 mL)	2 cups (500 mL)	2½ cups (625 mL)
	brown sugar	½ cup (125 mL)	1 cup (250 mL)	1½ cups (375 mL)	2 cups (500 mL)	2½ cups (625 mL)
	salt	¼ tsp (1 mL)	½ tsp (2 mL)	¾ tsp (3 mL)	1 tsp (5 mL)	1¼ tsp (6 mL)
	unsalted butter for topping	½ cup (125 mL)	1 cup (250 mL)	1½ cups (375 mL)	2 cups (500 mL)	2½ cups (625 mL)
	13x9 pans	1	2	3	4	5

Frosted Cinnamon Roll Granola

I give you crispy, crunchy granola that has all the flavor of cinnamon rolls with none of the guilt. The best part about this granola? The teeny little bits of white frosting. Yes, I did go there, and it kind of rocks — a lot. Makes about 5 cups (1.25 L) granola.

Granola

⅔ cup (150 mL) packed light brown sugar

⅓ cup (75 mL) water

2 egg whites

4 cups (1 L) large-flake (old-fashioned) rolled oats

½ cup (125 mL) sliced almonds

2 tsp (10 mL) ground cinnamon

Icing

2 tbsp (30 mL) cold water

1 tbsp (15 mL) meringue powder

1½ cups (375 mL) confectioners' (icing) sugar

¼ tsp (1 mL) vanilla extract

1½ tsp (7 mL) corn syrup

1. Preheat oven to 250°F (120°C).

2. In a small, microwave-safe bowl, combine brown sugar and water. Microwave on High for 1 minute, until bubbly and sugar has dissolved. Stir and set aside.

3. Place egg whites in another small bowl. Using an electric hand mixer, whip eggs on High for about 2 minutes, until frothy and soft peaks form. Set aside.

4. In a large bowl, combine oats, almonds and cinnamon. Add brown sugar mixture and egg whites; combine until every oat is thoroughly coated. Spread evenly on a lightly greased rimmed baking sheet.

5. Bake in preheated oven for 40 to 45 minutes, stirring once after 20 minutes. Remove granola and stir well. Let cool slightly.

6. *Icing:* In a medium bowl, combine cold water and meringue powder. Using an electric hand mixer with clean beaters, mix on Low for 30 seconds, until blended. Increase speed to High and whip for about 3 to 4 minutes, until stiff peaks form. Add confectioners' sugar, vanilla and corn syrup; mix on Low for about 30 seconds, until combined.

7. Spoon icing into a piping bag or small plastic bag with a small corner cut off. Pipe icing over granola in a crisscross pattern. Without stirring, place pan back in oven and bake for 5 minutes or until icing is firm. Remove from heat and let stand for 30 minutes or until completely cool.

MAKE IT NOW Serve with yogurt and fresh fruit, if desired.

MAKE IT A FREEZER MEAL Place cooled granola in a labeled gallon-size (4 L) freezer bag. Seal, removing as much air as possible, and freeze.

THAW AND SERVE Use as desired by taking the amount you need from the freezer bag and returning the rest to the freezer. Let thaw at room temperature for 15 minutes. Serve with yogurt and fresh fruit, if desired.

BULK BATCH GUIDE — Granola	5 cups/1.25 L (1 batch)	10 cups/2.5 L (2 batches)	15 cups/3.75 L (3 batches)	20 cups/5 L (4 batches)	25 cups/6.25 L (5 batches)
brown sugar	⅔ cup (150 mL)	1⅓ cups (325 mL)	2 cups (500 mL)	2⅔ cups (650 mL)	3⅓ cups (825 mL)
water	⅓ cup (75 mL)	⅔ cup (150 mL)	1 cup (250 mL)	1⅓ cups (325 mL)	1⅔ cups (400 mL)
egg whites	2	4	6	8	10
rolled oats	4 cups (1 L)	8 cups (2 L)	12 cups (3 L)	16 cups (4 L)	20 cups (5 L)
sliced almonds	½ cup (125 mL)	1 cup (250 mL)	1½ cups (375 mL)	2 cups (500 mL)	2½ cups (625 mL)
cinnamon	2 tsp (10 mL)	4 tsp (20 mL)	2 tbsp (30 mL)	8 tsp (40 mL)	10 tsp (50 mL)
water	2 tbsp (30 mL)	¼ cup (60 mL)	6 tbsp (90 mL)	½ cup (125 mL)	⅔ cup (150 mL)
meringue powder	1 tbsp (15 mL)	2 tbsp (30 mL)	3 tbsp (45 mL)	¼ cup (60 mL)	⅓ cup (75 mL)
confectioners' sugar	1½ cups (375 mL)	3 cups (750 mL)	4½ cups (1.125 L)	6 cups (1.5 L)	7½ cups (1.875 L)
vanilla	¼ tsp (1 mL)	½ tsp (2 mL)	¾ tsp (3 mL)	1 tsp (5 mL)	1¼ tsp (6 mL)
corn syrup	1½ tsp (7 mL)	1 tbsp (15 mL)	1½ tbsp (22 mL)	2 tbsp (30 mL)	2½ tbsp (37 mL)
gallon bags	1	2	3	4	5

Morning Energy Bars

My daughter has way too much energy in the morning. To keep up with her I will eat one of these chocolatey bars filled with honey, coconut and protein powder to pump me up. Energy never tasted so good. *Makes 8 bars.*

1¼ cups (310 mL) almond flour

¾ cup (175 mL) chocolate protein powder

¼ cup (60 mL) unsweetened shredded coconut

⅓ cup (75 mL) ground flax seeds

¾ cup (175 mL) peanut butter

3 tbsp (45 mL) honey

½ cup (125 mL) unsweetened plain almond milk

1 tsp (5 mL) vanilla extract

½ cup (125 mL) mini chocolate chips

1. In a medium bowl, combine almond flour, protein powder, coconut and ground flax seeds.

2. In a separate medium, microwave-safe bowl, combine peanut butter and honey. Microwave on High for 30 seconds or until melted; stir until smooth. Add almond milk and vanilla; stir until milk is well incorporated. Pour peanut butter mixture over almond flour mixture and stir until well combined and crumbly.

3. Sprinkle half the chocolate chips in the bottom of a 9-inch (23 cm) square baking dish. Crumble dough evenly into pan and sprinkle remaining chips on top. Press mixture firmly into pan. Transfer to refrigerator to chill for 30 minutes.

MAKE IT NOW Remove from refrigerator and cut into 8 bars. Serve immediately.

MAKE IT A FREEZER MEAL Remove from refrigerator and cut into 8 bars. Wrap each bar individually in plastic wrap. Place bars in a labeled gallon-size (4 L) freezer bag. Seal, removing as much air as possible, and freeze.

THAW AND SERVE Remove desired number of bars from freezer bag, returning bag to the freezer. Let thaw on the counter to room temperature, about 20 minutes. Remove plastic wrap and enjoy.

BULK BATCH GUIDE	Bars	8 (1 batch)	16 (2 batches)	24 (3 batches)	32 (4 batches)	40 (5 batches)
	almond flour	1¼ cups (310 mL)	2½ cups (625 mL)	3¾ cups (925 mL)	5 cups (1.25 L)	6¼ cups (1.56 L)
	protein powder	¾ cup (175 mL)	1½ cups (375 mL)	2¼ cups (560 mL)	3 cups (750 mL)	3¾ cups (925 mL)
	coconut	¼ cup (60 mL)	½ cup (125 mL)	¾ cup (175 mL)	1 cup (250 mL)	1¼ cups (310 mL)
	ground flax seeds	⅓ cup (75 mL)	⅔ cup (150 mL)	1 cup (250 mL)	1⅓ cups (325 mL)	1⅔ cups (400 mL)
	peanut butter	¾ cup (175 mL)	1½ cups (375 mL)	2¼ cups (560 mL)	3 cups (750 mL)	3¾ cups (925 mL)
	honey	3 tbsp (45 mL)	6 tbsp (90 mL)	9 tbsp (135 mL)	¾ cup (175 mL)	¾ cup + 3 tbsp (220 mL)
	almond milk	½ cup (125 mL)	1 cup (250 mL)	1½ cups (375 mL)	2 cups (500 mL)	2½ cups (625 mL)
	vanilla	1 tsp (5 mL)	2 tsp (10 mL)	1 tbsp (15 mL)	4 tsp (20 mL)	5 tsp (25 mL)
	chocolate chips	½ cup (125 mL)	1 cup (250 mL)	1½ cups (375 mL)	2 cups (500 mL)	2½ cups (625 mL)
	gallon bags	1	2	3	4	5

Cinnamon Mini Donut Muffins

This recipe was discovered in my great-grandmother's recipe box. With just a few small tweaks it became something so amazing that it just had to be in this cookbook. My kids gobble up these light, bouncy and flavorful muffins like they haven't eaten in weeks. Warning, though — you'll find they never last long. Makes 24 mini muffins.

Muffins

2 cups (500 mL) all-purpose flour

4 tsp (20 mL) baking powder

1 tbsp (15 mL) granulated sugar

1 tbsp (15 mL) ground cinnamon

½ tsp (2 mL) salt

½ tsp (2 mL) ground nutmeg

1¼ cups (310 mL) milk

1 large egg

2 tbsp (30 mL) melted butter

Topping

¼ cup (60 mL) melted butter

¼ cup (60 mL) granulated sugar

3 tbsp (45 mL) ground cinnamon

1. *Muffins:* Preheat oven to 375°F (190°C).

2. In a large bowl, using a fine-mesh sieve, sift together flour, baking powder, sugar, cinnamon, salt and nutmeg. Using a large spoon, combine until thoroughly mixed.

3. In a medium bowl, whisk together milk and egg. Add egg-and-milk mixture and melted butter to flour mixture all at once. Stir until just combined and not smooth.

4. Using a small (1 tbsp/15 mL) cookie scoop or spoon, fill the cups of a greased 24-cup mini muffin pan. Bake in preheated oven for 7 to 8 minutes, or until a tester inserted in the center comes out clean. Let cool for 5 minutes before removing from pan.

5. *Topping:* Meanwhile, place melted butter in a small bowl. In a separate small bowl, combine sugar and cinnamon.

6. While muffins are still warm, dip their tops in butter, then immediately in cinnamon-sugar mixture. Let cool completely on a wire rack.

MAKE IT NOW Pop one in your mouth, because you know you want to!

MAKE IT A FREEZER MEAL Let baked muffins cool to room temperature. Place in 2 labeled gallon-size (4 L) freezer bags. Seal, removing as much air as possible, and freeze.

THAW AND SERVE Place frozen muffins on counter for 30 minutes to thaw to room temperature, or warm in the microwave on High for 15 seconds or until heated through.

BULK BATCH GUIDE Mini muffins	24 (1 batch)	48 (2 batches)	72 (3 batches)	96 (4 batches)	120 (5 batches)
all-purpose flour	2 cups (500 mL)	4 cups (1 L)	6 cups (1.5 L)	8 cups (2 L)	10 cups (2.5 L)
baking powder	4 tsp (20 mL)	8 tsp (40 mL)	¼ cup (60 mL)	⅓ cup (75 mL)	7 tbsp (105 mL)
sugar	1 tbsp (15 mL)	2 tbsp (30 mL)	3 tbsp (45 mL)	¼ cup (60 mL)	⅓ cup (75 mL)
cinnamon	1 tbsp (15 mL)	2 tbsp (30 mL)	3 tbsp (45 mL)	¼ cup (60 mL)	⅓ cup (75 mL)
salt	½ tsp (2 mL)	1 tsp (5 mL)	1½ tsp (7 mL)	2 tsp (10 mL)	2½ tsp (12 mL)
nutmeg	½ tsp (2 mL)	1 tsp (5 mL)	1½ tsp (7 mL)	2 tsp (10 mL)	2½ tsp (12 mL)
milk	1¼ cups (310 mL)	2½ cups (625 mL)	3¾ cups (925 mL)	5 cups (1.25 L)	6¼ cups (1.56 L)
eggs	1	2	3	4	5
butter	2 tbsp (30 mL)	¼ cup (60 mL)	6 tbsp (90 mL)	½ cup (125 mL)	⅔ cup (150 mL)
butter for topping	¼ cup (60 mL)	½ cup (125 mL)	¾ cup (175 mL)	1 cup (250 mL)	1¼ cups (310 mL)
sugar for topping	¼ cup (60 mL)	½ cup (125 mL)	¾ cup (175 mL)	1 cup (250 mL)	1¼ cups (310 mL)
cinnamon for topping	3 tbsp (45 mL)	6 tbsp (90 mL)	½ cup (125 mL)	¾ cup (175 mL)	¾ cup + 3 tbsp (220 mL)
gallon bags	2	4	6	8	10

Almond Lemon Poppyseed Muffins

Even though this sugar-crusted lemon-and-almond muffin was, without a doubt, the hardest recipe in the book to develop, I knew I needed to include it. I tested it nine times, until it was just as good as if it came from my favorite local bakery. Makes 12 muffins.

Muffins

2 cups (500 mL) all-purpose flour

1½ tsp (7 mL) baking powder

¼ tsp (1 mL) baking soda

¼ tsp (1 mL) salt

2 tbsp (30 mL) poppy seeds

¾ cup (175 mL) plain Greek yogurt

¼ cup (60 mL) whole milk

1 large egg

1 egg yolk

Grated zest of 1 lemon

2 tbsp (30 mL) freshly squeezed lemon juice

½ tsp (2 mL) almond extract

⅔ cup (150 mL) unsalted butter, softened

1 cup (250 mL) granulated sugar

Topping

¼ cup (60 mL) granulated sugar

¼ cup (60 mL) sliced almonds (optional)

1. *Muffins:* In a medium bowl, whisk together flour, baking powder, baking soda, salt and poppy seeds.

2. In another medium bowl, whisk together Greek yogurt, milk, egg, egg yolk, lemon zest, lemon juice and almond extract, until smooth.

3. Using a stand mixer fitted with the paddle attachment or an electric hand mixer in a large bowl, cream butter and sugar at medium speed for about 3 to 4 minutes, until creamy, fluffy and pale, stopping the motor to scrape down the bowl as necessary.

4. Add ⅓ of the yogurt mixture to the butter mixture. Mix on Low until just combined. Add ⅓ of the flour mixture. Mix on Low until combined. Repeat two more times with remaining yogurt and flour mixtures, mixing just until incorporated. Do not overmix.

MAKE IT NOW Preheat oven to 400°F (200°C). In a 12-cup muffin pan, fill greased or lined cups almost to the top. Sprinkle each muffin with 1 tsp (5 mL) granulated sugar and 1 tsp (5 mL) almonds, if using. Bake in preheated oven for 15 to 20 minutes, until golden and a tester inserted in the center comes out clean. Let cool in pan on a rack for 5 minutes.

MAKE IT A FREEZER MEAL In a 12-cup muffin pan, fill lined cups almost to the top. Sprinkle each muffin with ½ tsp (2 mL) granulated sugar and 1 tsp (5 mL) almonds, if using. Wrap muffin pan tightly with plastic wrap sprayed or brushed with oil. Place in freezer for about 6 hours or until completely frozen. Remove muffins from pan and transfer to a labeled gallon-size (4 L) freezer bag. Seal, removing as much air as possible, and return to freezer.

COOK FROM FROZEN Preheat oven to 400°F (200°C). Transfer frozen muffins to a greased muffin pan (if they were frozen with paper liners there is no need to oil the pan). Bake in preheated oven for 22 to 35 minutes, until golden and a tester inserted in the center comes out clean. Let cool in pan on a rack for 5 minutes.

BULK BATCH GUIDE

Muffins	12 (1 batch)	24 (2 batches)	36 (3 batches)	48 (4 batches)	60 (5 batches)
all-purpose flour	2 cups (500 mL)	4 cups (1 L)	6 cups (1.5 L)	8 cups (2 L)	10 cups (2.5 L)
baking powder	1½ tsp (7 mL)	1 tbsp (15 mL)	1½ tbsp (22 mL)	2 tbsp (30 mL)	2½ tbsp (37 mL)
baking soda	¼ tsp (1 mL)	½ tsp (2 mL)	¾ tsp (3 mL)	1 tsp (5 mL)	1¼ tsp (6 mL)
salt	¼ tsp (1 mL)	½ tsp (2 mL)	¾ tsp (3 mL)	1 tsp (5 mL)	1¼ tsp (6 mL)
poppy seeds	2 tbsp (30 mL)	¼ cup (60 mL)	6 tbsp (90 mL)	½ cup (125 mL)	⅔ cup (150 mL)
yogurt	¾ cup (175 mL)	1½ cups (375 mL)	2¼ cups (560 mL)	3 cups (750 mL)	3¾ cups (925 mL)
whole milk	¼ cup (60 mL)	½ cup (125 mL)	¾ cup (175 mL)	1 cup (250 mL)	1¼ cups (310 mL)
eggs	2	4	6	8	10
lemons	1	2	3	4	5
lemon juice	2 tbsp (30 mL)	¼ cup (60 mL)	6 tbsp (90 mL)	½ cup (125 mL)	⅔ cup (150 mL)
almond extract	½ tsp (2 mL)	1 tsp (5 mL)	1½ tsp (7 mL)	2 tsp (10 mL)	2½ tsp (12 mL)
butter	⅔ cup (150 mL)	1⅓ cups (325 mL)	2 cups (500 mL)	2⅔ cups (650 mL)	3⅓ cups (825 mL)
sugar	1 cup (250 mL)	2 cups (500 mL)	3 cups (750 mL)	4 cups (1 L)	5 cups (1.25 L)
sugar for topping	¼ cup (60 mL)	½ cup (125 mL)	¾ cup (175 mL)	1 cup (250 mL)	1¼ cups (310 mL)
sliced almonds	¼ cup (60 mL)	½ cup (125 mL)	¾ cup (175 mL)	1 cup (250 mL)	1¼ cups (310 mL)
gallon bags	1	2	3	4	5

APPETIZERS & SNACKS

Artichoke Dip   68

Spicy Buffalo Chicken Hot Dip   71

Fried Dill Pickles   72

Mascarpone Lemon Wontons   75

Pepperoni Blossoms   76

Sweet-and-Sour Meatballs   79

Stuffed Mini Sweet Peppers   80

Bacon-Wrapped Chicken Bites   83

Creamy Cilantro Chicken Taquitos   86

Homemade Chicken Strips   89

Empanada Hand Pies   90

Twice-Baked Potatoes   93

Artichoke Dip

"Whoa, this is SO good!" — the words of my husband when I gave him a sample of this dip for the first time. The cream cheese and Alfredo sauce lend a creamy bite that balances the savory flavors of the artichokes perfectly, while the water chestnuts add an exciting soft crunch in your mouth. *Makes 6 servings.*

1 package (12 oz/375 g) frozen artichokes

2 tbsp (30 mL) olive oil

¼ tsp (1 mL) salt

4 oz (125 g) cream cheese, softened

1 large egg yolk

1 batch Alfredo Sauce (page 333), cooled

1 cup (250 mL) shredded mozzarella cheese, divided

½ cup (125 mL) freshly grated Parmesan cheese, divided

1 can (4 oz/125 g) water chestnuts, drained and chopped

½ cup (125 mL) panko bread crumbs

Garnishes

Freshly ground black pepper (optional)

Chopped fresh parsley (optional)

Tip

Step 2 is optional. The dip is still delicious without roasting the artichokes, but that adds a delicious extra depth of flavor.

1. Preheat oven to 450°F (230°C).

2. In a large bowl, toss frozen artichoke hearts with olive oil and salt. Spread out evenly on a baking sheet lined with aluminum foil. Bake in preheated oven for 20 minutes or until starting to brown in places. Remove from oven and let cool for 5 minutes. Coarsely chop artichokes; set aside.

3. In a medium bowl, whisk together cream cheese and egg yolk until smooth. Add Alfredo sauce and whisk until smooth. Gently fold in ½ cup (125 mL) mozzarella cheese, ¼ cup (60 mL) Parmesan cheese, artichoke hearts and water chestnuts, until well combined. Spread mixture evenly in an 8-inch (20 cm) metal or foil pan.

4. In a small bowl, combine remaining mozzarella cheese, Parmesan cheese and panko crumbs.

MAKE IT NOW Preheat oven to 375°F (190°C). Sprinkle panko mixture evenly over pan. Bake in preheated oven for 35 minutes, until bubbly and golden on top. Remove from oven and let cool for 5 minutes. Top with pepper and parsley, if using.

MAKE IT A FREEZER MEAL Place panko topping mix in a labeled quart-size (1 L) freezer bag and seal. Wrap pan tightly with plastic wrap, pressing down gently to remove air. Place topping bag on top of pan. Cover both with foil. Label and place in freezer.

COOK FROM FROZEN Preheat oven to 375°F (190°C). Remove foil, topping packet and plastic wrap. Sprinkle topping mixture over dip, then cover again with foil. Bake in preheated oven for 30 minutes. Remove foil and continue baking for an additional 15 to 20 minutes, until bubbling all over and golden on top. Remove from oven and let cool for 5 minutes. Top with pepper and parsley, if using.

BULK BATCH GUIDE	Servings	6 (1 batch)	12 (2 batches)	18 (3 batches)	24 (4 batches)	30 (5 batches)
	artichokes	12 oz (375 g)	1½ lbs (750 g)	2¼ lbs (1.125 kg)	3 lbs (1.5 kg)	3¾ lbs (1.875 kg)
	olive oil	2 tbsp (30 mL)	¼ cup (60 mL)	6 tbsp (90 mL)	½ cup (125 mL)	⅔ cup (150 mL)
	salt	¼ tsp (1 mL)	½ tsp (2 mL)	¾ tsp (3 mL)	1 tsp (5 mL)	1¼ tsp (6 mL)
	cream cheese	4 oz (125 g)	8 oz (250 g)	12 oz (375 g)	1 lb (500 g)	1¼ lbs (625 g)
	eggs	1	2	3	4	5
	Alfredo Sauce	1 batch	2 batches	3 batches	4 batches	5 batches
	mozzarella cheese	1 cup (250 mL)	2 cups (500 mL)	3 cups (750 mL)	4 cups (1 L)	5 cups (1.25 L)
	Parmesan cheese	½ cup (125 mL)	1 cup (250 mL)	1½ cups (375 mL)	2 cups (500 mL)	2½ cups (625 mL)
	water chestnuts	4 oz (125 g)	8 oz (250 g)	12 oz (375 g)	16 oz (500 g)	20 oz (625 g)
	panko	½ cup (125 mL)	1 cup (250 mL)	1½ cups (375 mL)	2 cups (500 mL)	2½ cups (625 mL)
	quart bags	1	2	3	4	5
	8x8 pans	1	2	3	4	5

Spicy Buffalo Chicken Hot Dip

No game day is complete without a spicy Buffalo chicken hot dip. Whether your team wins or loses (Go, Cougs!), this creamy, mouthwatering snack will definitely score points with everyone around. Best served with corn tortilla chips, crackers, pita chips or celery sticks. Makes 6 servings.

1 lb (500 g) boneless, skinless chicken breasts

½ tsp (2 mL) salt

¼ tsp (1 mL) freshly ground pepper

1 tbsp (15 mL) butter

½ cup (125 mL) hot pepper sauce (I like Frank's RedHot)

8 oz (250 g) cream cheese

2 tbsp (30 mL) sour cream

½ cup (125 mL) shredded Cheddar cheese (about 2 oz/60 g)

¼ cup (60 mL) blue cheese dressing

½ tsp (2 mL) crumbled blue cheese (optional)

Tip

If you're baking this recipe right away, you can use a glass or ceramic baking dish.

1. Dice chicken into ½-inch (1 cm) pieces. Transfer to a large bowl and sprinkle with salt and pepper; toss to coat.

2. Heat a large skillet over medium-high heat. Add butter and heat until melted. Add chicken and cook for 4 to 5 minutes, stirring and flipping often, until chicken is golden brown with a few crispy edges and no longer pink inside. Remove from heat. Add hot pepper sauce and stir to combine. Set aside.

3. In a small bowl, whisk together cream cheese and sour cream until smooth.

4. Spread cream cheese mixture over bottom of an 8-inch (20 cm) square metal or foil pan. Spread chicken mixture on top, followed by Cheddar cheese. Spoon blue cheese dressing in lines across the top and sprinkle with blue cheese, if using.

MAKE IT NOW Preheat oven to 375°F (190°C). Bake in preheated oven for about 25 to 30 minutes, until hot and bubbling all over. Remove from oven and let cool for 10 minutes. Serve warm.

MAKE IT A FREEZER MEAL Wrap assembled pan tightly with plastic wrap, pressing down gently to remove air. Cover with foil. Label and place in freezer.

COOK FROM FROZEN Preheat oven to 375°F (190°C). Remove foil and plastic wrap. Place frozen dip directly in oven and bake for 45 to 50 minutes, until hot and bubbling all over. Remove from oven and let cool for 10 minutes. Serve warm.

BULK BATCH GUIDE	Servings	6 (1 batch)	12 (2 batches)	18 (3 batches)	24 (4 batches)	30 (5 batches)
	chicken breasts	1 lb (500 g)	2 lbs (1 kg)	3 lbs (1.5 kg)	4 lbs (2 kg)	5 lbs (2.5 kg)
	salt	½ tsp (2 mL)	1 tsp (5 mL)	1½ tsp (7 mL)	2 tsp (10 mL)	2½ tsp (12 mL)
	pepper	¼ tsp (1 mL)	½ tsp (2 mL)	¾ tsp (3 mL)	1 tsp (5 mL)	1¼ tsp (6 mL)
	butter	1 tbsp (15 mL)	2 tbsp (30 mL)	3 tbsp (45 mL)	¼ cup (60 mL)	⅓ cup (75 mL)
	hot pepper sauce	½ cup (125 mL)	1 cup (250 mL)	1½ cups (375 mL)	2 cups (500 mL)	2½ cups (625 mL)
	cream cheese	8 oz (250 g)	1 lb (500 g)	1½ lbs (750 g)	2 lbs (1 kg)	2½ lbs (1.25 kg)
	sour cream	2 tbsp (30 mL)	¼ cup (60 mL)	6 tbsp (90 mL)	½ cup (125 mL)	⅔ cup (150 mL)
	Cheddar cheese	½ cup (125 mL)	1 cup (250 mL)	1½ cups (375 mL)	2 cups (500 mL)	2½ cups (625 mL)
	blue cheese dressing	¼ cup (60 mL)	½ cup (125 mL)	¾ cups (175 mL)	1 cup (250 mL)	1¼ cups (310 mL)
	blue cheese	½ tsp (2 mL)	1 tsp (5 mL)	1½ tsp (7 mL)	2 tsp (10 mL)	2½ tsp (12 mL)
	8x8 pans	1	2	3	4	5

Fried Dill Pickles

For reals, if you haven't tried fried pickles, you are missing out! They are sooooo good — light and crunchy, with the perfect pop of tangy dill. This super-easy recipe keeps your fried pickles crisp on the inside and crunchy on the outside, perfect for dipping into some creamy ranch.

Makes 12 fried pickle slices.

12 dill pickle slices

½ cup (125 mL) all-purpose flour

Pinch freshly ground pepper (optional)

½ tsp (2 mL) dried dill, divided

½ tsp (2 mL) salt, divided

1 large egg

3 tbsp (45 mL) water

¾ cup (175 mL) panko bread crumbs

2 tbsp (30 mL) cornstarch

To Fry

2 cups (500 mL) vegetable oil (approx.)

Garnish

Ranch dressing or dip (optional)

1. Place pickle slices on a tea towel or paper towel and gently pat dry.

2. In a small bowl, combine flour, pepper, if using, ¼ tsp (1 mL) dill and ¼ tsp (1 mL) salt; set aside.

3. In another small bowl, whisk together egg and water; set aside.

4. In a medium bowl, combine panko crumbs, cornstarch and remaining dill and salt.

5. First coat pickle slices in the flour mixture, then dip in the egg mixture and then the panko mixture, pressing to coat. Place on a baking sheet lined with parchment paper.

6. Once all the pickle slices are coated, transfer to the freezer for at least 20 minutes or up to 4 hours. Discard leftover flour, egg and panko mixtures.

MAKE IT NOW In a medium, heavy-bottomed saucepan, heat vegetable oil until a candy/deep-fry thermometer registers 350°F (180°C). You'll need at least 1 inch (2.5 cm) oil; if using a deep-fryer, follow the manufacturer's directions. Fry 6 frozen pickles for 1 to 2 minutes, until lightly golden brown (do not overcook or they will disintegrate). Drain on a plate lined with paper towels. Repeat with remaining pickles. Serve hot with ranch dressing or dip, if desired.

MAKE IT A FREEZER MEAL Once uncooked pickles are frozen solid, transfer to a labeled quart-size (1 L) freezer bag. Seal, removing as much air as possible, and freeze.

COOK FROM FROZEN In a medium, heavy-bottomed saucepan, heat vegetable oil until a candy/deep-fry thermometer registers 350°F (180°C). You'll need at least 1 inch (2.5 cm) oil; if using a deep-fryer, follow the manufacturer's directions. Fry 6 frozen pickles for 1 to 2 minutes, until lightly golden brown (do not overcook or they will disintegrate). Drain on a plate lined with paper towels. Repeat with remaining pickles. Serve hot with ranch dressing or dip, if desired.

BULK BATCH GUIDE	Pickle slices	12 (1 batch)	24 (2 batches)	36 (3 batches)	48 (4 batches)	60 (5 batches)
	pickle slices	12	24	36	48	60
	all-purpose flour	½ cup (125 mL)	1 cup (250 mL)	1½ cups (375 mL)	2 cups (500 mL)	2½ cups (625 mL)
	dried dill	½ tsp (2 mL)	1 tsp (5 mL)	1½ tsp (7 mL)	2 tsp (10 mL)	2½ tsp (12 mL)
	salt	½ tsp (2 mL)	1 tsp (5 mL)	1½ tsp (7 mL)	2 tsp (10 mL)	2½ tsp (12 mL)
	eggs	1	2	3	4	5
	water	3 tbsp (45 mL)	6 tbsp (90 mL)	9 tbsp (135 mL)	¾ cup (175 mL)	¾ cup + 3 tbsp (220 mL)
	panko	¾ cup (175 mL)	1½ cups (375 mL)	2¼ cups (560 mL)	3 cups (750 mL)	3¾ cups (925 mL)
	cornstarch	2 tbsp (30 mL)	¼ cup (60 mL)	6 tbsp (90 mL)	½ cup (125 mL)	⅔ cup (150 mL)
	vegetable oil	2 cups (500 mL)	2 cups (500 mL)	2 cups (500 mL)	2 cups (500 mL)	2 cups (500 mL)
	quart bags	1	2	3	4	5

Mascarpone Lemon Wontons

Poppy seeds, creamy mascarpone and lemon curd fried in a sugar-dusted wonton — ooh la la! It takes me back to my days in France (just kidding, never been there). But I imagine this is what something from France would taste like! These delicate appetizers are very simple to make and have a sophisticated light and sweet taste. Makes 24 wontons.

4 oz (125 g) mascarpone cheese, softened

½ cup (125 mL) lemon curd

¼ tsp (1 mL) vanilla extract

½ tsp (2 mL) poppy seeds

Pinch salt

¼ cup (60 mL) cold water

24 3½-inch (8.5 cm) square wonton wrappers

2 cups (500 mL) vegetable oil (approx.)

Garnish

1 tbsp (15 mL) confectioners' (icing) sugar

1. In a small bowl, combine mascarpone cheese, lemon curd, vanilla, poppy seeds and salt; stir until smooth.

2. Place water in another small bowl; set aside.

3. Place 1 heaping tsp (5 mL) cheese mixture in center of one wonton wrapper.

4. Dip your finger in the cold water and run it along two edges of wrapper. Fold wrapper in half into a triangle to enclose filling; seal, making sure to push out any air. Moisten the two opposite corners and gently press together, so wonton resembles a large fortune cookie.

5. Wet a lint-free kitchen towel and wring out well, until barely damp. Place over filled wonton so it won't dry out. Repeat step 4 with remaining cheese mixture and wontons.

6. In a large, heavy-bottomed saucepan, heat vegetable oil until a candy/deep-fry thermometer registers 350°F (180°C). You'll need at least 3 inches (7.5 cm oil); if using a deep-fryer, follow the manufacturer's directions. Working in batches of 4 to 6, fry wontons for 1 to 2 minutes, until golden brown. Drain on a plate lined with paper towels. Repeat with remaining wontons.

MAKE IT NOW Let wontons cool for 10 minutes. Serve warm, with confectioners' sugar sprinkled evenly overtop.

MAKE IT A FREEZER MEAL Let wontons cool. Transfer to a baking sheet lined with parchment paper. Freeze for 1 to 2 hours, until solid. Transfer frozen wontons to a rigid airtight container and freeze.

REHEAT Preheat oven to 350°F (180°C). Place frozen wontons on a baking sheet lined with parchment paper. Bake in preheated oven for 10 to 12 minutes or until crunchy and warmed through (do not over-bake, or edges will burn). Serve warm, with confectioners' sugar sprinkled evenly overtop.

BULK BATCH GUIDE	Wontons	24 (1 batch)	48 (2 batches)	72 (3 batches)	96 (4 batches)	120 (5 batches)
	mascarpone cheese	4 oz (125 g)	8 oz (250 g)	12 oz (375 g)	1 lb (500 g)	1¼ lbs (625 g)
	lemon curd	½ cup (125 mL)	1 cup (250 mL)	1½ cups (375 mL)	2 cups (500 mL)	2½ cups (625 mL)
	vanilla	¼ tsp (1 mL)	½ tsp (2 mL)	¾ tsp (3 mL)	1 tsp (5 mL)	1¼ tsp (6 mL)
	poppy seeds	½ tsp (2 mL)	1 tsp (5 mL)	1½ tsp (7 mL)	2 tsp (10 mL)	2½ tsp (12 mL)
	water	¼ cup (60 mL)	½ cup (125 mL)	¾ cup (175 mL)	1 cup (250 mL)	1¼ cups (310 mL)
	wonton wrappers	24	48	72	96	120
	vegetable oil	2 cups (500 mL)	2 cups (500 mL)	2 cups (500 mL)	2 cups (500 mL)	2 cups (500 mL)
	containers	1	2	3	4	5

Pepperoni Blossoms

Maybe I love these so much because of the cute blossom shape. Or maybe it's the fact that they taste like mini pepperoni pizzas. Oh, who am I kidding? It's both! Your kids will go nuts when you cook up a batch of these right after school. Makes 16 blossoms.

1 sheet (8½ oz/250 g) puff pastry, 10 by 15 inches (25 by 38 cm)

2 tbsp (30 mL) Thirty-Minute Pizza Sauce (page 340)

½ cup (125 mL) shredded mozzarella cheese

32 slices pepperoni, halved

1 large egg

1 tbsp (15 mL) water

½ tsp (2 mL) dried parsley

¼ tsp (1 mL) garlic powder

1. Cut puff pastry sheet lengthwise into 8 strips. Then cut strips in half crosswise, so you have 16 equal thin strips.

2. Using a pastry brush, spread each strip with about ½ tsp (2 mL) pizza sauce. Sprinkle each with about 2 tsp (10 mL) mozzarella. Lay 4 pepperoni halves on each strip, with the bottom of each touching the bottom edge of the dough strip and the top sticking out slightly past the top edge. Starting at one end, roll up each strip firmly so that the pepperoni looks like flower petals.

3. Grease 16 cups of two 12-cup nonstick mini muffin pans. Place each roll in one of the greased muffin cups.

4. In a small bowl, whisk together egg, water, parsley and garlic powder. Using the pastry brush, brush egg wash all over exposed dough of each pepperoni blossom.

MAKE IT NOW Preheat oven to 400°F (200°C). Bake pepperoni blossoms in preheated oven for 10 to 12 minutes or until golden. Remove from oven and let cool for 5 minutes.

MAKE IT A FREEZER MEAL Place muffin pans with uncooked pepperoni blossoms in freezer. Freeze for 1 to 2 hours, until solid. Transfer frozen blossoms to a labeled gallon-size (4 L) freezer bag. Seal bag, removing as much air as possible, and freeze.

COOK FROM FROZEN Preheat oven to 400°F (200°C). Place frozen pepperoni blossoms in cups of 2 greased mini muffin pans. Bake in preheated oven for 14 to 15 minutes, until golden. Remove from oven and let cool for 5 minutes.

BULK BATCH GUIDE	Pepperoni blossoms	16 (1 batch)	32 (2 batches)	48 (3 batches)	64 (4 batches)	80 (5 batches)
	puff pastry sheets	1	2	3	4	5
	Pizza Sauce	2 tbsp (30 mL)	¼ cup (60 mL)	6 tbsp (90 mL)	½ cup (125 mL)	⅔ cup (150 mL)
	mozzarella cheese	½ cup (125 mL)	1 cup (250 mL)	1½ cups (375 mL)	2 cups (500 mL)	2½ cups (625 mL)
	pepperoni slices	32	64	96	128	160
	eggs	1	2	3	4	5
	water	1 tbsp (15 mL)	2 tbsp (30 mL)	3 tbsp (45 mL)	¼ cup (60 mL)	⅓ cup (75 mL)
	dried parsley	½ tsp (2 mL)	1 tsp (5 mL)	1½ tsp (7 mL)	2 tsp (10 mL)	2½ tsp (12 mL)
	garlic powder	¼ tsp (1 mL)	½ tsp (2 mL)	¾ tsp (3 mL)	1 tsp (5 mL)	1¼ tsp (6 mL)
	gallon bags	1	2	3	4	5

Sweet-and-Sour Meatballs

Growing up, I can remember stretching tall on my tiptoes to watch my mom make meatballs from scratch, which smelled so wonderful as they sizzled on the stovetop. Once they were finally cooked and coated in tangy sweet-and-sour sauce, they tasted even better than I could have imagined. This easy meatball recipe is still my all-time favorite. Makes 32 meatballs.

Meatballs

1 lb (500 g) pork sausage (bulk or casings removed)

1 lb (500 g) ground beef

¼ cup (60 mL) milk

2 slices white or whole wheat bread, torn into small pieces

1 large egg, lightly beaten

2 tsp (10 mL) dried minced onion

Sweet-and-Sour Sauce

⅔ cup (150 mL) water

¼ cup (60 mL) cornstarch

1½ cups (375 mL) packed brown sugar

¼ cup (60 mL) unseasoned rice vinegar

¼ cup (60 mL) soy sauce

1 can (20 oz/600 mL) pineapple chunks, with juice

1 bell pepper, cut into 1½-inch (4 cm) chunks

1. *Meatballs:* Preheat oven to 400°F (200°C).

2. In a large bowl, combine sausage, ground beef, milk, bread, egg and dried onion.

3. Using a medium (#40) cookie scoop or spoon, scoop up about 1½ tbsp (22 mL) meat mixture and roll into balls. Place on a rimmed baking sheet, spacing at least ¼ inch (0.5 cm) apart. Bake in preheated oven for 20 minutes or until no longer pink inside.

4. *Sweet-and-Sour Sauce:* Meanwhile, in a medium saucepan over medium heat, whisk together water, cornstarch, brown sugar, rice vinegar, soy sauce and juice from pineapple can. Cook, stirring occasionally, until it comes to a boil, about 4 to 5 minutes. Boil, stirring, for 3 minutes, until slightly thickened and smooth. Remove from heat and set aside.

5. Remove meatballs from oven. Using a spatula, transfer to a lightly greased 13- by 9-inch (33 by 23 cm) metal or foil pan.

MAKE IT NOW Add bell pepper, pineapple chunks and cooked sauce to pan. Stir gently to combine. Return to oven and bake for 10 to 12 minutes, until sauce is bubbling and pepper chunks are tender.

MAKE IT A FREEZER MEAL Let both meatballs and sauce cool completely before mixing. Add bell pepper, pineapple and cooked sauce to pan. Stir gently to combine. Wrap pan tightly with plastic wrap, pressing down gently to remove air. Cover with foil. Label and place in freezer.

COOK FROM FROZEN Preheat oven to 400°F (200°C). Remove foil and plastic wrap. Cover pan with foil and bake for 25 to 30 minutes in preheated oven, until meatballs are heated through, sauce is bubbling and pepper chunks are tender.

BULK BATCH GUIDE	Meatballs	32 (1 batch)	64 (2 batches)	96 (3 batches)	128 (4 batches)	160 (5 batches)
	pork sausage	1 lb (500 g)	2 lbs (1 kg)	3 lbs (1.5 kg)	4 lbs (2 kg)	5 lbs (2.5 kg)
	ground beef	1 lb (500 g)	2 lbs (1 kg)	3 lbs (1.5 kg)	4 lbs (2 kg)	5 lbs (2.5 kg)
	milk	¼ cup (60 mL)	½ cup (125 mL)	¾ cup (175 mL)	1 cup (250 mL)	1¼ cups (310 mL)
	bread slices	2	4	6	8	10
	eggs	1	2	3	4	5
	dried onion	2 tsp (10 mL)	4 tsp (20 mL)	2 tbsp (30 mL)	8 tsp (40 mL)	10 tsp (50 mL)
	water	⅔ cup (150 mL)	1⅓ cups (325 mL)	2 cups (500 mL)	2⅔ cups (650 mL)	3⅓ cups (825 mL)
	cornstarch	¼ cup (60 mL)	½ cup (125 mL)	¾ cup (175 mL)	1 cup (250 mL)	1¼ cups (310 mL)
	brown sugar	1½ cups (375 mL)	3 cups (750 mL)	4½ cups (1.125 L)	6 cups (1.5 L)	7½ cups (1.875 L)
	rice vinegar	¼ cup (60 mL)	½ cup (125 mL)	¾ cup (175 mL)	1 cup (250 mL)	1¼ cups (310 mL)
	soy sauce	¼ cup (60 mL)	½ cup (125 mL)	¾ cup (175 mL)	1 cup (250 mL)	1¼ cups (310 mL)
	pineapple chunks	20 oz (600 mL)	40 oz (1.2 L)	60 oz (1.8 L)	80 oz (2.4 L)	100 oz (3 L)
	bell peppers	1	2	3	4	5
	13x9 pans	1	2	3	4	5

Stuffed Mini Sweet Peppers

These mini stuffed peppers filled with a satisfying blend of garlic, cheese and tomato will surely have you wishing for more. And the spicy peach drizzle adds just the right pop of heat and sweetness to make a perfect bite. Makes 12 mini pepper halves.

Mini Peppers

6 mini sweet peppers

¼ cup (60 mL) shredded carrot

2 tbsp (30 mL) minced seeded tomato

¼ cup (60 mL) Italian blend shredded cheese (see Tip, below)

½ tsp (2 mL) minced garlic

½ tsp (2 mL) Worcestershire sauce

1 large egg, beaten

¼ cup (60 mL) Italian-seasoned bread crumbs

1 tsp (5 mL) olive oil

1 tbsp (15 mL) grated Parmesan cheese

Topping

1 mini sweet pepper, seeded and minced

¼ tsp (1 mL) celery salt

½ tsp (2 mL) dried dill

¼ tsp (1 mL) cayenne pepper

Spicy Peach Drizzle

¼ cup (60 mL) peach jam

1 tbsp (15 mL) Dijon mustard

¼ tsp (1 mL) hot pepper flakes

Tip

If you can't find Italian cheese blend, combine equal parts shredded mozzarella, Asiago, Parmesan, provolone and Romano cheeses, or a combination of two or three.

1. *Mini Peppers:* Cut mini peppers in half lengthwise, leaving the stem intact. Remove seeds and veins.

2. In a medium bowl, combine carrot, tomato, shredded cheese, garlic, Worcestershire sauce, egg, bread crumbs and olive oil. Set aside.

3. *Topping:* In a small bowl, combine minced mini pepper, celery salt, dill and cayenne.

4. Press filling mixture inside each pepper half until completely full. Sprinkle with Parmesan cheese, followed by topping. Place on a baking sheet lined with parchment paper.

5. *Spicy Peach Drizzle:* Meanwhile, in a small bowl, whisk together peach jam, Dijon mustard and hot pepper flakes. Set aside.

MAKE IT NOW Preheat oven to 400°F (200°C). Place baking sheet in preheated oven and bake for 15 to 18 minutes or until topping is golden on top. Meanwhile, microwave peach drizzle on High for 30 seconds. Whisk until smooth. Remove peppers from oven and let cool for 5 minutes. Drizzle about 1 tsp (5 mL) peach sauce over each pepper half.

MAKE IT A FREEZER MEAL Place baking sheet of uncooked peppers in freezer. Freeze for 2 to 3 hours, until solid. Transfer frozen peppers to a labeled gallon-size (4 L) freezer bag. Place peach drizzle in a sandwich-size bag, remove as much air as possible, and freeze. Place peach-drizzle bag in with peppers; seal both together, removing as much air as possible, and freeze.

COOK FROM FROZEN Preheat oven to 400°F (200°C). Place frozen peppers on a baking sheet lined with parchment paper. Bake in preheated oven for 20 minutes or until golden on top. Run hot water over frozen sauce bag until thawed enough to put in a bowl. Microwave sauce on High for 30 seconds or until heated through. Remove peppers from oven and let cool for 5 minutes. Drizzle each pepper half with about 1 tsp (5 mL) peach sauce.

(continued on page 82)

Mini pepper halves	12 (1 batch)	24 (2 batches)	36 (3 batches)	48 (4 batches)	60 (5 batches)
mini peppers	6	12	18	24	30
carrots	¼ cup (60 mL)	½ cup (125 mL)	¾ cup (175 mL)	1 cup (250 mL)	1¼ cups (310 mL)
tomato	2 tbsp (30 mL)	¼ cup (60 mL)	6 tbsp (90 mL)	½ cup (125 mL)	⅔ cup (150 mL)
Italian blend shredded cheese	¼ cup (60 mL)	½ cup (125 mL)	¾ cup (175 mL)	1 cup (250 mL)	1¼ cups (310 mL)
garlic	½ tsp (2 mL)	1 tsp (5 mL)	1½ tsp (7 mL)	2 tsp (10 mL)	2½ tsp (12 mL)
Worcestershire	½ tsp (2 mL)	1 tsp (5 mL)	1½ tsp (7 mL)	2 tsp (10 mL)	2½ tsp (12 mL)
eggs	1	2	3	4	5
Italian bread crumbs	¼ cup (60 mL)	½ cup (125 mL)	¾ cup (175 mL)	1 cup (250 mL)	1¼ cups (310 mL)
olive oil	1 tsp (5 mL)	2 tsp (10 mL)	1 tbsp (15 mL)	4 tsp (20 mL)	5 tsp (25 mL)
Parmesan cheese	1 tbsp (15 mL)	2 tbsp (30 mL)	3 tbsp (45 mL)	¼ cup (60 mL)	⅓ cup (75 mL)
mini peppers for topping	1	2	3	4	5
celery salt	¼ tsp (1 mL)	½ tsp (2 mL)	¾ tsp (3 mL)	1 tsp (5 mL)	1¼ tsp (6 mL)
dried dill	½ tsp (2 mL)	1 tsp (5 mL)	1½ tsp (7 mL)	2 tsp (10 mL)	2½ tsp (12 mL)
cayenne pepper	¼ tsp (1 mL)	½ tsp (2 mL)	¾ tsp (3 mL)	1 tsp (5 mL)	1¼ tsp (6 mL)
peach jam	¼ cup (60 mL)	½ cup (125 mL)	¾ cup (175 mL)	1 cup (250 mL)	1¼ cups (310 mL)
Dijon mustard	1 tbsp (15 mL)	2 tbsp (30 mL)	3 tbsp (45 mL)	¼ cup (60 mL)	⅓ cup (75 mL)
hot pepper flakes	¼ tsp (1 mL)	½ tsp (2 mL)	¾ tsp (3 mL)	1 tsp (5 mL)	1¼ tsp (6 mL)
gallon bags	1	2	3	4	5
sandwich bags	1	2	3	4	5

You know
when you start
craving a food
and can't stop
thinking about it
day after day
until you finally
just have to have it?

Bacon-Wrapped Chicken Bites

When I need a showoff-worthy hot appetizer, I bust out these tempting bites. Sometimes I make them with green beans and sometimes without, but either way they are always a huge hit.
Makes 18 bites.

8 oz (250 g) boneless, skinless chicken breasts

¼ cup (60 mL) tamari sauce

2 tbsp (30 mL) packed brown sugar

2 tbsp (30 mL) unseasoned rice vinegar

½ tsp (2 mL) minced garlic

¼ tsp (1 mL) grated fresh ginger

9 French green beans, trimmed (optional)

6 slices thick-cut bacon, cut crosswise in thirds

1 tsp (5 mL) cornstarch

18 toothpicks

Garnish
Sesame seeds (optional)

1. Slice chicken into pieces ½ inch (1 cm) thick and about 2 inches long (you should have about 18 pieces). Place chicken pieces in a medium bowl.

2. Add tamari sauce, brown sugar, rice vinegar, garlic and ginger to chicken; stir to combine. Cover and marinate in refrigerator for a minimum of 1 hour or up to 24 hours.

3. Meanwhile, if using green beans, bring about 2 cups (500 mL) water to a boil in a small saucepan. Add beans and cook for one minute, then quickly remove with a slotted spoon to an ice-water bath. When cooled, cut each bean in half crosswise; set aside.

4. Place a fine-mesh sieve over a small saucepan; pour chicken and marinade into sieve. Drain chicken so that all the liquid falls into saucepan. Set pan aside.

5. Place each piece of chicken on top of a bacon piece. Add a green bean half (if using) and wrap bacon around both. Pierce through the center with a toothpick to secure. Place on a baking sheet lined with parchment paper, spacing apart.

6. Whisk cornstarch into marinade in saucepan. Bring to a boil, stirring constantly, over medium-high heat. Reduce heat to medium and boil, stirring occasionally, for 6 to 7 minutes, until sauce has thickened. Remove from heat; set aside.

MAKE IT NOW Preheat oven to 375°F (190°C). Bake chicken bites in preheated oven for 15 to 20 minutes, until chicken is no longer pink inside and bacon is crispy and browned. Remove from oven and transfer to a serving platter. Drizzle sauce over bites, then sprinkle with sesame seeds, if using. (You can also serve the sauce on the side for dipping.)

MAKE IT A FREEZER MEAL Using kitchen shears, snip off any pieces of toothpick that are showing. Let sauce cool completely, then place in a labeled quart-size (1 L) freezer bag and seal. Place baking sheet with uncooked bites in freezer; place sauce bag separately in freezer. Freeze for 1 to 2 hours, until solid. Transfer frozen bites to a labeled gallon-size (4 L) freezer bag. Add frozen sauce bag and seal together as a kit, removing as much air as possible. Freeze.

COOK FROM FROZEN Preheat oven to 375°F (190°C). Place frozen bites on a baking sheet lined with parchment paper. Bake in preheated oven for 25 to 30 minutes, until chicken is no longer pink inside and bacon is crispy and browned. Meanwhile, run hot water over frozen sauce bag until thawed enough to pour into a microwave-safe bowl. Heat sauce in microwave on High for 30 seconds or until heated through. Remove chicken from oven and transfer to a serving platter. Drizzle sauce over bites, then sprinkle with sesame seeds, if using. (You can also serve the sauce on the side for dipping.)

(continued on page 85)

Chicken bites	18 (1 batch)	36 (2 batches)	54 (3 batches)	72 (4 batches)	90 (5 batches)
chicken breasts	8 oz (250 g)	1 lb (500 g)	1½ lbs (750 g)	2 lbs (1 kg)	2½ lbs (1.25 kg)
tamari sauce	¼ cup (60 mL)	½ cup (125 mL)	¾ cup (175 mL)	1 cup (250 mL)	1¼ cups (310 mL)
brown sugar	2 tbsp (30 mL)	¼ cup (60 mL)	6 tbsp (90 mL)	½ cup (125 mL)	⅔ cup (150 mL)
rice vinegar	2 tbsp (30 mL)	¼ cup (60 mL)	6 tbsp (90 mL)	½ cup (125 mL)	⅔ cup (150 mL)
garlic	½ tsp (2 mL)	1 tsp (5 mL)	1½ tsp (7 mL)	2 tsp (10 mL)	2½ tsp (12 mL)
fresh ginger	¼ tsp (1 mL)	½ tsp (2 mL)	¾ tsp (3 mL)	1 tsp (5 mL)	1¼ tsp (6 mL)
green beans	9	18	27	36	45
bacon slices	6	12	18	24	30
cornstarch	1 tsp (5 mL)	2 tsp (10 mL)	1 tbsp (15 mL)	4 tsp (20 mL)	5 tsp (25 mL)
toothpicks	18	36	54	72	90
quart bags	1	2	3	4	5
gallon bags	1	2	3	4	5

When I need
a showoff-worthy
hot appetizer,
I bust out these
tempting bites.

Creamy Cilantro Chicken Taquitos

These taquitos are one of the most popular recipes on my blog — and for good reason. With their crunchy outside and perfectly creamy filling with a warm kick, you'll fight over who gets that last one. *Makes about 10 taquitos.*

4 oz (125 g) cream cheese, softened

¾ tsp (3 mL) chili powder

½ tsp (2 mL) onion powder

½ tsp (2 mL) ground cumin

⅛ tsp (0.5 mL) garlic powder

3 cups (750 mL) shredded cooked chicken breast (page 29)

¼ cup (60 mL) mild salsa verde

2 tbsp (30 mL) chopped fresh cilantro

1 tbsp (15 mL) freshly squeezed lime juice

⅓ cup (75 mL) shredded pepper Jack cheese

⅓ cup (75 mL) shredded Monterey Jack cheese

10 6-inch (15 cm) corn tortillas

Cooking spray or olive oil

Salt

1. In a large bowl, combine cream cheese, chili powder, onion powder, cumin and garlic powder. Add chicken, salsa verde, cilantro, lime juice and pepper Jack and Monterey Jack cheeses; gently stir to combine.

2. Place half the tortillas in a slightly damp cloth on a microwave-safe plate. Microwave on High for 35 seconds. Keep covered so they stay warm. Repeat with remaining tortillas.

3. Add about 2 tbsp (30 mL) cream cheese mixture to center of each tortilla. Roll up and place, seam side down, on a baking sheet lined with parchment paper. Spray each taquito with a little cooking spray or brush lightly with olive oil and sprinkle with a little salt.

MAKE IT NOW Preheat oven to 425°F (220°C). Bake taquitos for 12 to 15 minutes, until golden on the edges and hot in the center. Remove from oven and let cool for 5 minutes.

MAKE IT A FREEZER MEAL Place uncooked taquitos in freezer on the baking sheet. Freeze for 2 to 3 hours, until solid. Transfer frozen taquitos to a labeled gallon-size (4 L) freezer bag. Seal, removing as much air as possible, and freeze.

COOK FROM FROZEN Preheat oven to 425°F (220°C). Place frozen taquitos on a baking sheet lined with parchment paper. Bake in preheated oven for 12 to 15 minutes, until golden on the edges and hot in the center. Remove from oven and let cool for 5 minutes.

BULK BATCH GUIDE	Taquitos	10 (1 batch)	20 (2 batches)	30 (3 batches)	40 (4 batches)	50 (5 batches)
	cream cheese	4 oz (125 g)	8 oz (250 g)	12 oz (375 g)	1 lb (500 g)	1¼ lbs (625 g)
	chili powder	¾ tsp (3 mL)	1½ tsp (7 mL)	2¼ tsp (11 mL)	1 tbsp (15 mL)	4 tsp (20 mL)
	onion powder	½ tsp (2 mL)	1 tsp (5 mL)	1½ tsp (7 mL)	2 tsp (10 mL)	2½ tsp (12 mL)
	cumin	½ tsp (2 mL)	1 tsp (5 mL)	1½ tsp (7 mL)	2 tsp (10 mL)	2½ tsp (12 mL)
	garlic powder	⅛ tsp (0.5 mL)	¼ tsp (1 mL)	⅓ tsp (1.5 mL)	½ tsp (2 mL)	¾ tsp (3 mL)
	chicken breast	3 cups (750 mL)	6 cups (1.5 L)	9 cups (2.25 L)	12 cups (3 L)	15 cups (3.75 L)
	salsa verde	¼ cup (60 mL)	½ cup (125 mL)	¾ cup (175 mL)	1 cup (250 mL)	1¼ cups (310 mL)
	cilantro	2 tbsp (30 mL)	¼ cup (60 mL)	6 tbsp (90 mL)	½ cup (125 mL)	⅔ cup (150 mL)
	lime juice	1 tbsp (15 mL)	2 tbsp (30 mL)	3 tbsp (45 mL)	¼ cup (60 mL)	⅓ cup (75 mL)
	pepper Jack cheese	⅓ cup (75 mL)	⅔ cup (150 mL)	1 cup (250 mL)	1⅓ cups (325 mL)	1⅔ cups (400 mL)
	Monterey Jack cheese	⅓ cup (75 mL)	⅔ cup (150 mL)	1 cup (250 mL)	1⅓ cups (325 mL)	1⅔ cups (400 mL)
	tortillas	10	20	30	40	50
	gallon bags	1	2	3	4	5

Homemade Chicken Strips

Everyone has their go-to chicken strip recipe, and this one is mine. These are easy to make, perfectly seasoned, and will have even your pickiest eaters asking for more. They are great to have in your freezer for a quick lunch or last-minute play date. Makes 12 strips.

2 lbs (1 kg) boneless, skinless chicken breasts

½ cup (125 mL) buttermilk

1 cup (250 mL) arrowroot flour (see Tip, below)

¼ cup (60 mL) grated Parmesan cheese

½ tsp (2 mL) dried Italian herb seasoning

½ tsp (2 mL) garlic powder

½ tsp (2 mL) salt

¼ tsp (1 mL) freshly ground black pepper

To Fry
2 cups (500 mL) vegetable oil (approx.)

Tip
You can substitute all-purpose flour for the arrowroot flour if gluten is not a concern.

1. Cut chicken breasts lengthwise into 1-inch (2.5 cm) wide strips.

2. In a medium bowl, combine chicken and buttermilk, stirring to coat chicken.

3. In a small bowl, combine arrowroot flour, Parmesan cheese, Italian seasoning, garlic powder, salt and pepper.

4. Dip both sides of each chicken strip in arrowroot mixture. Set on a baking sheet lined with lightly greased parchment paper. Discard any excess buttermilk and arrowroot mixture.

MAKE IT NOW In a medium, heavy-bottomed saucepan, heat vegetable oil until a candy/deep-fry thermometer registers between 350°F and 375°F (180°C to 190°C). You'll need at least 1½ inches (3.5 cm) oil; if using a deep fryer, fill according to manufacturer's directions. Using tongs, add 3 to 4 chicken strips to the oil at a time. Fry, turning once, for about 2 to 3 minutes per side, until coating is golden and chicken is no longer pink inside. Drain on a plate lined with paper towels. Repeat with remaining chicken strips. Let cool for 5 minutes before serving.

MAKE IT A FREEZER MEAL Place baking sheet with uncooked chicken strips in freezer. Freeze for about 2 to 3 hours, until solid. Transfer frozen strips to a labeled gallon-size (4 L) freezer bag. Seal, removing as much air as possible, and freeze.

COOK FROM FROZEN In a medium, heavy-bottomed saucepan, heat vegetable oil until a candy/deep-fry thermometer registers between 350°F and 375°F (180°C to 190°C). You'll need at least 1½ inches (3.5 cm) oil; if using a deep fryer, follow the manufacturer's directions. Using tongs, add 3 to 4 chicken strips at a time to oil. Fry, turning once, for about 2 to 3 minutes per side, until coating is golden and chicken is no longer pink inside. Drain on a plate lined with paper towels. Repeat with remaining chicken strips. Let cool for 5 minutes before serving.

BULK BATCH GUIDE

Chicken strips	12 (1 batch)	24 (2 batches)	36 (3 batches)	48 (4 batches)	60 (5 batches)
chicken breasts	2 lbs (1 kg)	4 lbs (2 kg)	6 lbs (3 kg)	8 lbs (4 kg)	10 lbs (5 kg)
buttermilk	½ cup (125 mL)	1 cup (250 mL)	1½ cups (375 mL)	2 cups (500 mL)	2½ cups (625 mL)
arrowroot flour	1 cup (250 mL)	2 cups (500 mL)	3 cups (750 mL)	4 cups (1 L)	5 cups (1.25 L)
Parmesan cheese	¼ cup (60 mL)	½ cup (125 mL)	¾ cup (175 mL)	1 cup (250 mL)	1¼ cups (310 mL)
Italian seasoning	½ tsp (2 mL)	1 tsp (5 mL)	1½ tsp (7 mL)	2 tsp (10 mL)	2½ tsp (12 mL)
garlic powder	½ tsp (2 mL)	1 tsp (5 mL)	1½ tsp (7 mL)	2 tsp (10 mL)	2½ tsp (12 mL)
salt	½ tsp (2 mL)	1 tsp (5 mL)	1½ tsp (7 mL)	2 tsp (10 mL)	2½ tsp (12 mL)
pepper	¼ tsp (1 mL)	½ tsp (2 mL)	¾ tsp (3 mL)	1 tsp (5 mL)	1¼ tsp (6 mL)
vegetable oil	2 cups (500 mL)	2 cups (500 mL)	2 cups (500 mL)	2 cups (500 mL)	2 cups (500 mL)
gallon bags	1	2	3	4	5

Empanada Hand Pies

Take delicious homemade Spanish rice, tangy Cheddar cheese and roasted chicken breast, stick it in pie crust, and you'll have my take on handheld pieces of heaven. *Makes 6 hand pies.*

1½ cups (375 mL) cooked Spanish Rice (page 296), cooled

½ cup (125 mL) shredded Cheddar cheese

½ cup (125 mL) shredded cooked chicken breast (page 29)

¼ cup (60 mL) sliced black olives (optional)

1 batch Pie Crust (page 331) or 2 store-bought pie crusts

1 large egg, beaten

1. In a medium bowl, gently combine Spanish rice, Cheddar cheese, chicken, and olives, if using.

2. On a lightly floured surface, roll out pie dough to about 12 inches (30 cm) in diameter and ¼ inch (0.5 cm) thick. Using a small bowl (I like to use a cereal bowl) or a round cutter, cut dough into rounds about 5½ inches (13.5 cm) in diameter. Place ¼ cup (60 mL) rice mixture on one half of each round; fold other half over filling. Seal and crimp edges with a fork. (Or, for a fancy look, take remaining dough scraps, slice into 3 very thin strips, braid, and press around edges of each pie.) Transfer to a baking sheet lined with parchment paper, spacing apart.

3. Using a pastry brush, lightly coat top of each pie with beaten egg.

MAKE IT NOW Preheat oven to 400°F (200°C). Bake empanadas in preheated oven for 15 to 20 minutes, until golden brown and hot in the center. Let cool for 10 minutes.

MAKE IT A FREEZER MEAL Transfer baking sheet with uncooked empanadas to freezer. Freeze for 2 to 3 hours, until solid. Transfer frozen pies to a labeled gallon-size (4 L) freezer bag. Seal, removing as much air as possible, and freeze.

COOK FROM FROZEN Preheat oven to 400°F (200°C). Place frozen pies on a baking sheet lined with parchment paper. Bake for 25 to 30 minutes, until golden brown and hot in the center. Let cool for 10 minutes.

BULK BATCH GUIDE		6 (1 batch)	12 (2 batches)	18 (3 batches)	24 (4 batches)	30 (5 batches)
	Hand pies	6 (1 batch)	12 (2 batches)	18 (3 batches)	24 (4 batches)	30 (5 batches)
	Spanish Rice	1½ cups (375 mL)	3 cups (750 mL)	4½ cups (1.125 L)	6 cups (1.5 L)	7½ cups (1.875 L)
	Cheddar cheese	½ cup (125 mL)	1 cup (250 mL)	1½ cups (375 mL)	2 cups (500 mL)	2½ cups (625 mL)
	chicken breast	½ cup (125 mL)	1 cup (250 mL)	1½ cups (375 mL)	2 cups (500 mL)	2½ cups (625 mL)
	black olives	¼ cup (60 mL)	½ cup (125 mL)	¾ cup (175 mL)	1 cup (250 mL)	1¼ cups (310 mL)
	Pie Crust	1 batch	2 batches	3 batches	4 batches	5 batches
	eggs	1	2	3	4	5
	gallon bags	1	2	3	4	5

Twice-Baked Potatoes

These potatoes are the definition of comfort food with cheesy, bacon-y goodness and just the right flavor to warm your soul. Okay, maybe that was cheesy . . . but not as cheesy as this recipe! Makes 12 potato halves.

6 medium-sized baking potatoes

½ cup (125 mL) butter, softened, divided

¼ tsp (1 mL) salt

8 oz (250 g) cream cheese, softened

1 cup (250 mL) sour cream

⅔ cup (150 mL) milk

1½ cups (375 mL) shredded Cheddar cheese, divided

Additional salt and freshly ground black pepper

12 slices bacon, cooked and finely chopped, divided

1 tsp (5 mL) dried dill

Garnish
¼ cup (60 mL) chopped fresh dill (optional)

1. Preheat oven to 350°F (180°C).

2. Using 2 tbsp (30 mL) butter, grease potatoes on all sides. Sprinkle with salt, dividing equally, then place on a rimmed baking sheet. Bake on middle rack in preheated oven for 1 hour and 15 minutes or until cooked through. Remove potatoes from oven and let stand for about 15 minutes, until cool enough to handle.

3. Cut potatoes in half lengthwise. Carefully scoop cooked potato into a large bowl, leaving ⅛ inch (3 mm) pulp all around inside of potato skin.

4. To cooked potato in bowl, add remaining butter, cream cheese, sour cream, milk, ¾ cup (175 mL) Cheddar cheese and half the bacon. Season to taste with salt and pepper. Using an electric hand mixer or hand masher, mix together until creamy. Do not overmix.

5. Spoon potato mixture back into potato skins. Top with remaining cheese and bacon; sprinkle with dried dill.

MAKE IT NOW Preheat oven to 350°F (180°C). Place potatoes on a baking sheet lined with parchment paper, spacing apart. Bake in preheated oven for 20 to 22 minutes, until cheese is melted and bubbling. Remove from oven and let cool for 15 minutes. Sprinkle with dill, if using.

MAKE IT A FREEZER MEAL Before filling potatoes, let filling cool completely, then fill as directed. Wrap each potato separately in plastic wrap. Place potatoes in 2 labeled gallon-size (4 L) freezer bags. Seal, removing as much air as possible, and freeze.

COOK FROM FROZEN Preheat oven to 350°F (180°C). Remove plastic wrap from potatoes and place on a baking sheet lined with parchment paper. Bake for 35 to 40 minutes, until hot in the center and cheese is bubbly. Sprinkle with dill, if using.

BULK BATCH GUIDE	Potato halves	12 (1 batch)	24 (2 batches)	36 (3 batches)	48 (4 batches)	60 (5 batches)
	baking potatoes	6	12	18	24	30
	butter	½ cup (125 mL)	1 cup (250 mL)	1½ cups (375 mL)	2 cups (500 mL)	2½ cups (625 mL)
	salt	¼ tsp (1 mL)	½ tsp (2 mL)	¾ tsp (3 mL)	1 tsp (5 mL)	1¼ tsp (6 mL)
	cream cheese	8 oz (250 g)	1 lb (500 g)	1½ lbs (750 g)	2 lbs (1 kg)	2½ lbs (1.25 kg)
	sour cream	1 cup (250 mL)	2 cups (500 mL)	3 cups (750 mL)	4 cups (1 L)	5 cups (1.25 L)
	milk	⅔ cup (150 mL)	1⅓ cups (325 mL)	2 cups (500 mL)	2⅔ cups (650 mL)	3⅓ cups (750 mL)
	Cheddar cheese	1½ cups (375 mL)	3 cups (750 mL)	4½ cups (1.125 L)	6 cups (1.5 L)	7½ cups (1.875 L)
	bacon slices	12	24	36	48	60
	dried dill	1 tsp (5 mL)	2 tsp (10 mL)	1 tbsp (15 mL)	4 tsp (20 mL)	5 tsp (25 mL)
	gallon bags	2	4	6	8	10

SOUPS, STEWS & CHILIS

Cauliflower Crave Soup   96

Coconut Cashew Basil Curry Soup   99

Creamy, Cheesy Broccoli Soup   100

Smoky Ham and White Bean Soup   103

Hazelnut Chicken Wild Rice Soup   104

Chicken Tortellini Soup   107

Zesty Tortilla Soup   108

Herbed Chicken and Dumpling Soup   111

Sausage and Gnocchi Soup   112

Sweet & Spicy Pork Carnita Soup   115

Mini Meatball Soup   116

Seriously Good Chili   119

White Bean Chicken Chili   122

Beef Barley Stew   125

Cauliflower Crave Soup

Even people who don't like cauliflower are often pleasantly shocked by this delightfully smooth and satisfying soup that makes your body and soul feel great. Even my kids finish their bowls every time.

Makes 6 servings.

1 head cauliflower, chopped

3 tbsp (45 mL) dried minced onion

1 batch White Sauce (page 336)

2 cups (500 mL) half-and-half (10%) cream

½ tsp (2 mL) salt

¼ tsp (1 mL) freshly ground black pepper

1 cup (250 mL) shredded Monterey Jack cheese (about 4 oz/125 g)

1 cup (250 mL) shredded Cheddar cheese (about 4 oz/125 g)

¼ cup (60 mL) freshly grated Parmesan cheese (about ¾ oz/25 g)

1 tsp (5 mL) Dijon mustard

Garnishes

Olive oil (optional)

Freshly ground black pepper (optional)

Fresh thyme leaves (optional)

Cooked chopped bacon (optional)

1. In a medium saucepan, cover cauliflower and onion with water; bring to a boil over high heat. Immediately reduce heat to low and simmer for 15 minutes, until tender. Remove from heat.

2. Working in batches as necessary, pour saucepan contents into a blender; purée on High until smooth. Pour mixture back into saucepan. Add white sauce, cream, salt, pepper, Monterey Jack cheese, Cheddar cheese, Parmesan cheese and mustard; stir to combine. Heat over medium heat, stirring, for 2 to 3 minutes, until warmed through and cheese is melted.

MAKE IT NOW Ladle into bowls. Drizzle with olive oil and sprinkle with pepper, thyme and bacon, if using.

MAKE IT A FREEZER MEAL Let cooked soup cool completely, about 30 to 40 minutes. Pour into a labeled gallon-size (4 L) freezer bag. Seal, removing as much air as possible, and freeze.

REHEAT Place soup in the refrigerator for at least 12 hours or up to 24 hours to thaw. Pour bag contents into a medium saucepan. Heat over medium heat for about 10 minutes, stirring often, until warmed through. Ladle into bowls. Drizzle with olive oil and sprinkle with pepper, thyme and bacon, if using.

BULK BATCH GUIDE

Servings	6 (1 batch)	12 (2 batches)	18 (3 batches)	24 (4 batches)	30 (5 batches)
cauliflower heads	1	2	3	4	5
dried onion	3 tbsp (45 mL)	6 tbsp (90 mL)	9 tbsp (135 mL)	¾ cup (175 mL)	¾ cup + 3 tbsp (220 mL)
White Sauce	1 batch	2 batches	3 batches	4 batches	5 batches
half-and-half	2 cups (500 mL)	4 cups (1 L)	6 cups (1.5 L)	8 cups (2 L)	10 cups (2.5 L)
salt	½ tsp (2 mL)	1 tsp (5 mL)	1½ tsp (7 mL)	2 tsp (10 mL)	2½ tsp (12 mL)
pepper	¼ tsp (1 mL)	½ tsp (2 mL)	¾ tsp (3 mL)	1 tsp (5 mL)	1¼ tsp (6 mL)
Monterey Jack cheese	1 cup (250 mL)	2 cups (500 mL)	3 cups (750 mL)	4 cups (1 L)	5 cups (1.25 L)
Cheddar cheese	1 cup (250 mL)	2 cups (500 mL)	3 cups (750 mL)	4 cups (1 L)	5 cups (1.25 L)
Parmesan cheese	¼ cup (60 mL)	½ cup (125 mL)	¾ cup (175 mL)	1 cup (250 mL)	1¼ cups (310 mL)
Dijon mustard	1 tsp (5 mL)	2 tsp (10 mL)	1 tbsp (15 mL)	4 tsp (20 mL)	5 tsp (25 mL)
gallon bags	1	2	3	4	5

Coconut Cashew Basil Curry Soup

One of my most requested recipes from family and friends is this coconut cashew curry soup. You will love the rich taste, deep flavors and crunch of the salty cashews. Makes 6 servings.

2 lbs (1 kg) boneless, skinless chicken breasts, diced

½ tsp (2 mL) garlic salt

2 tbsp (30 mL) vegetable oil

1 onion, quartered

1 tbsp (15 mL) minced garlic

1 tsp (5 mL) minced or grated fresh ginger

½ jalapeño pepper

2 cans (each 14 oz/398 mL) coconut milk

2 cups (500 mL) chicken broth or Homemade Chicken Stock (page 349)

2 tbsp (30 mL) curry powder

1 tsp (5 mL) salt

¼ tsp (1 mL) freshly ground black pepper

1½ tsp (7 mL) dried basil

½ cup (125 mL) salted roasted cashews

Garnishes

Chopped fresh cilantro (optional)

Small fresh basil leaves (optional)

Sliced jalapeño pepper (optional)

1. Sprinkle chicken with garlic salt. In a large wok or skillet over high heat, heat vegetable oil until smoking. Working in batches, add chicken and cook for 3 to 4 minutes, stirring constantly, until no longer pink inside and slightly crispy on one or two edges. Using a slotted spoon, transfer chicken to a bowl and set aside.

2. In a blender or food processor, combine onion, garlic, ginger and jalapeño; blend on High until smooth. Add coconut milk, chicken broth, curry powder, salt and pepper; blend until smooth.

MAKE IT NOW In a large saucepan, combine chicken and any accumulated juices, coconut milk mixture and dried basil. Bring to a boil over medium-high heat. Immediately reduce heat to low and simmer for 15 minutes to deepen flavors. Remove from heat. Ladle into bowls and top with cashews, plus cilantro, fresh basil and jalapeño, if using.

MAKE IT A FREEZER MEAL Let chicken cool completely. Pour chicken, coconut milk mixture and dried basil into a labeled gallon-size (4 L) freezer bag. Seal, removing as much air as possible, and freeze. Place cashews in a quart-size (1 L) freezer bag and seal. Place both bags in another gallon bag and seal together.

THAW AND COOK Place soup in refrigerator for at least 12 hours or up to 24 hours to thaw, or run lukewarm water over bag until you can break soup apart. Pour bag contents into a large saucepan and bring to a boil over medium-high heat. Immediately reduce heat to low and simmer for 15 minutes to deepen flavors. Remove from heat. Ladle into bowls and top with cashews, plus cilantro, fresh basil and jalapeño, if using.

BULK BATCH GUIDE	Servings	6 (1 batch)	12 (2 batches)	18 (3 batches)	24 (4 batches)	30 (5 batches)
	chicken breasts	2 lbs (1 kg)	4 lbs (2 kg)	6 lbs (3 kg)	8 lbs (4 kg)	10 lbs (5 kg)
	garlic salt	½ tsp (2 mL)	1 tsp (5 mL)	1½ tsp (7 mL)	2 tsp (10 mL)	2½ tsp (12 mL)
	vegetable oil	2 tbsp (30 mL)	¼ cup (60 mL)	6 tbsp (90 mL)	½ cup (125 mL)	⅔ cup (150 mL)
	onions	1	2	3	4	5
	garlic	1 tbsp (15 mL)	2 tbsp (30 mL)	3 tbsp (45 mL)	¼ cup (60 mL)	⅓ cup (75 mL)
	ginger	1 tsp (5 mL)	2 tsp (10 mL)	1 tbsp (15 mL)	4 tsp (20 mL)	5 tsp (25 mL)
	jalapeño peppers	½	1	1½	2	2½
	coconut milk	28 oz (796 mL)	56 oz (1.592 L)	84 oz (2.388 L)	112 oz (3.184 L)	140 oz (3.98 L)
	chicken broth	2 cups (500 mL)	4 cups (1 L)	6 cups (1.5 L)	8 cups (2 L)	10 cups (2.5 L)
	curry powder	2 tbsp (30 mL)	¼ cup (60 mL)	6 tbsp (90 mL)	½ cup (125 mL)	⅔ cup (150 mL)
	salt	1 tsp (5 mL)	2 tsp (10 mL)	1 tbsp (15 mL)	4 tsp (20 mL)	5 tsp (25 mL)
	pepper	¼ tsp (1 mL)	½ tsp (2 mL)	¾ tsp (3 mL)	1 tsp (5 mL)	1¼ tsp (6 mL)
	dried basil	1½ tsp (7 mL)	1 tbsp (15 mL)	1½ tbsp (22 mL)	2 tbsp (30 mL)	2½ tbsp (37 mL)
	cashews	½ cup (125 mL)	1 cup (250 mL)	1½ cups (375 mL)	2 cups (500 mL)	2½ cups (625 mL)
	gallon bags	2	4	6	8	10
	quart bags	1	2	3	4	5

Creamy, Cheesy Broccoli Soup

The way cheese and broccoli intertwine in a healthy soup makes me believe they are true soulmates. Your addiction to this soup will begin as soon as you taste the melted Gouda, which gives it a creamy, slightly smoky flavor. Makes 6 servings.

1 batch White Sauce (page 336), cooled

1½ cups (375 mL) half-and-half (10%) cream

4 cups (1 L) chicken broth or Homemade Chicken Stock (page 349)

4 cups (1 L) fresh chopped broccoli florets

1 cup (250 mL) puréed or diced onion

1 cup (250 mL) shredded carrots

1½ tsp (7 mL) minced garlic

1 bay leaf

Pinch garlic salt

1 cup (250 mL) shredded smoked Gouda cheese (4 oz/125 g)

½ cup (125 mL) shredded sharp Cheddar cheese (2 oz/60 g)

Salt and freshly ground black pepper

1. In a large bowl, whisk together white sauce and cream. Set aside.

2. In a large stockpot, combine chicken broth, broccoli, onion, carrots, garlic, bay leaf and garlic salt. Bring to a boil over high heat, then immediately reduce heat to low and simmer for 15 minutes, until broccoli is tender. Remove from heat and discard bay leaf.

3. Add white sauce mixture and stir gently to combine. Add Gouda cheese and Cheddar cheese; stir to combine. Heat over medium heat, stirring, for 2 to 3 minutes, until warmed through and cheese is melted.

MAKE IT NOW Season to taste with salt and pepper. Ladle into bowls and serve.

MAKE IT A FREEZER MEAL Let cooked soup cool completely. Pour into a labeled gallon-size (4 L) freezer bag. Seal, removing as much air as possible, and freeze.

THAW AND COOK Place bag in the refrigerator for at least 12 hours or up to 24 hours to thaw. Pour contents into a medium saucepan. Heat over medium heat for about 10 minutes, stirring often, until warmed through. Season to taste with salt and pepper. Ladle into bowls and serve.

Servings	6 (1 batch)	12 (2 batches)	18 (3 batches)	24 (4 batches)	30 (5 batches)
White Sauce	1 batch	2 batches	3 batches	4 batches	5 batches
half-and-half	1½ cups (375 mL)	3 cups (750 mL)	4½ cups (1.125 L)	6 cups (1.5 L)	7½ cups (1.875 L)
chicken broth	4 cups (1 L)	8 cups (2 L)	12 cups (3 L)	16 cups (4 L)	20 cups (5 L)
broccoli	4 cups (1 L)	8 cups (2 L)	12 cups (3 L)	16 cups (4 L)	20 cups (5 L)
onions	1 cup (250 mL)	2 cups (500 mL)	3 cups (750 mL)	4 cups (1 L)	5 cups (1.25 L)
carrots	1 cup (250 mL)	2 cups (500 mL)	3 cups (750 mL)	4 cups (1 L)	5 cups (1.25 L)
garlic	1½ tsp (7 mL)	1 tbsp (15 mL)	1½ tbsp (22 mL)	2 tbsp (30 mL)	2½ tbsp (37 mL)
bay leaves	1	2	3	4	5
smoked Gouda cheese	1 cup (250 mL)	2 cups (500 mL)	3 cups (750 mL)	4 cups (1 L)	5 cups (1.25 L)
Cheddar cheese	½ cup (125 mL)	1 cup (250 mL)	1½ cups (375 mL)	2 cups (500 mL)	2½ cups (625 mL)
gallon bags	1	2	3	4	5

BULK BATCH GUIDE

Smoky Ham and White Bean Soup

This soup always makes me nostalgic. Whenever I eat it I think of cold winter days, fuzzy socks and staying warm by a crackling fire. It's the perfect soup to make when you have leftover ham or ham bones. *Makes 6 servings.*

2 tbsp (30 mL) vegetable oil

1 lb (500 g) ham steak or sliced cooked smoked ham

1 onion, diced

3 celery stalks, chopped

2 tsp (10 mL) minced garlic

½ tsp (2 mL) dried thyme

¼ tsp (1 mL) freshly ground black pepper

1 medium smoked ham hock

2 cans (each 15 oz/425 mL) Great Northern (white kidney) beans, drained and rinsed

8 cups (2 L) low-sodium chicken broth

3 bay leaves

Garnishes

Chopped fresh parsley or chives (optional)

Freshly grated Parmesan cheese (optional)

1. Add vegetable oil to a medium skillet and swirl to coat bottom of skillet. Heat over medium-high heat. Add ham steak and cook, turning once, for about 5 minutes, until browned on each side. Remove ham from skillet and set aside. Return skillet to stove and add onion and celery. Cook for about 4 minutes, stirring occasionally, until softened. Add garlic, thyme and pepper; cook, stirring, for 1 to 2 minutes, until fragrant. Remove from heat.

MAKE IT NOW Chop browned ham and transfer to small bowl. Cover and place in refrigerator. Place onion mixture, ham hock, beans, chicken broth and bay leaves in a large (approx. 5 quart) slow cooker. Cover and cook on Low for 3 to 4 hours. Remove ham hock and bay leaves from slow cooker and pick off any meat from ham hock; discard bone and bay leaves. Stir in ham from hock and chopped ham. Cover and cook for 10 minutes, until ham is heated through. Serve warm, topped with parsley and Parmesan cheese, if using.

MAKE IT A FREEZER MEAL Chop browned ham and place in a labeled quart-size (1 L) freezer bag. Place onion mixture, ham hock, beans, chicken broth and bay leaves in a labeled gallon-size (4 L) freezer bag. Seal, removing as much air as possible, and freeze both bags together as a kit.

THAW AND COOK Place bags in the refrigerator for at least 12 hours or up to 24 hours to thaw. Pour contents of soup-mixture bag into a large (approx. 5 quart) slow cooker (leave bag of cooked ham in the fridge). Cover and cook on Low for 3 to 4 hours. Remove ham hock and bay leaves from slow cooker and pick off any meat from ham hock; discard bone and bay leaves. Stir in ham from hock and chopped ham. Cover and cook for 10 minutes, until ham is heated through. Serve warm, topped with parsley and Parmesan cheese, if using.

	Servings	6 (1 batch)	12 (2 batches)	18 (3 batches)	24 (4 batches)	30 (5 batches)
BULK BATCH GUIDE	vegetable oil	2 tbsp (30 mL)	¼ cup (60 mL)	6 tbsp (90 mL)	½ cup (125 mL)	⅔ cup (150 mL)
	ham steak	1 lb (500 g)	2 lbs (1 kg)	3 lbs (1.5 kg)	4 lbs (2 kg)	5 lbs (2.5 kg)
	onions	1	2	3	4	5
	celery stalks	3	6	9	12	15
	garlic	2 tsp (10 mL)	4 tsp (20 mL)	2 tbsp (30 mL)	8 tsp (40 mL)	10 tsp (50 mL)
	dried thyme	½ tsp (2 mL)	1 tsp (5 mL)	1½ tsp (7 mL)	2 tsp (10 mL)	2½ tsp (12 mL)
	pepper	¼ tsp (1 mL)	½ tsp (2 mL)	¾ tsp (3 mL)	1 tsp (5 mL)	1¼ tsp (6 mL)
	ham hocks	1	2	3	4	5
	Great Northern beans	30 oz (850 mL)	60 oz (1.7 L)	90 oz (2.55 L)	120 oz (3.4 L)	150 oz (4.25 L)
	chicken broth	8 cups (2 L)	16 cups (4 L)	24 cups (6 L)	32 cups (8 L)	40 cups (10 L)
	bay leaves	3	6	9	12	15
	quart bags	1	2	3	4	5
	gallon bags	1	2	3	4	5

Hazelnut Chicken Wild Rice Soup

Feeling wild tonight? Yeah, baby! Okay, calm down now. I'm talking about soup here. This soup is so aromatic and gratifying, with light flavors of sage and garlic in every bite. It is definitely thick and hearty, so put out your strongest spoons and enjoy. *Makes 6 servings.*

½ cup (250 mL) wild rice blend

¾ cup (175 mL) water

⅓ cup (75 mL) butter

1 cup (250 mL) shredded carrots

1½ tbsp (22 mL) dried minced onion

1 tsp (5 mL) minced garlic

⅓ cup (75 mL) all-purpose flour

1 tsp (5 mL) salt

¼ tsp (1 mL) hot pepper flakes (optional)

3 cups (750 mL) chicken broth or Homemade Chicken Stock (page 349), approx.

¾ cup (175 mL) half-and-half (10%) cream

2 cups (500 mL) chopped cooked chicken (see page 29)

¼ cup (60 mL) sliced hazelnuts

⅛ tsp (0.5 mL) dried sage

1. Place rice in a strainer and rinse under cool water until water runs clear. Place rice and water in a small saucepan over high heat. Bring to a boil, then immediately reduce heat to low, cover and simmer 35 to 40 minutes, until water is absorbed. Remove from heat and let sit, covered, for 10 minutes to steam. Fluff with a fork. Set aside to cool.

2. In a large stockpot, melt butter over medium-high heat. Add carrots and dried onion; cook, stirring, until carrots are tender, about 4 minutes. Add garlic and cook, stirring, for about 1 minute, until fragrant.

3. Whisking continuously, add flour, salt and hot pepper flakes, if using. Cook, whisking, for about 3 minutes, until smooth and thick. Reduce heat to medium. Whisking continuously, gradually add chicken broth, followed by the cream; whisk until smooth. Continue to cook, stirring often, for about 3 to 4 minutes, until heated through.

MAKE IT NOW Add chicken, hazelnuts and sage. Cook, stirring often, about 5 minutes longer, until heated through. (Add additional chicken broth if soup is too thick.) Serve.

MAKE IT A FREEZER MEAL Let cooked soup cool completely. Add chicken, hazelnuts and sage; stir to combine. Pour soup into a labeled gallon-size (4 L) freezer bag. Seal, removing as much air as possible, and freeze.

REHEAT Place bag in the refrigerator for at least 12 hours or up to 24 hours to thaw. Pour bag contents into a large stockpot. Stirring often, warm over medium heat for 15 minutes or until heated through. (Add additional chicken broth if soup is too thick.) Serve.

BULK BATCH GUIDE	Servings	6 (1 batch)	12 (2 batches)	18 (3 batches)	24 (4 batches)	30 (5 batches)
	wild rice blend	½ cup (125 mL)	1 cup (250 mL)	1½ cups (375 mL)	2 cups (500 mL)	2½ cups (625 mL)
	water	¾ cup (175 mL)	1½ cups (375 mL)	2¼ cups (560 mL)	3 cups (750 mL)	3¾ cups (925 mL)
	butter	⅓ cup (75 mL)	⅔ cup (150 mL)	1 cup (250 mL)	1⅓ cups (325 mL)	1⅔ cups (400 mL)
	carrots	1 cup (250 mL)	2 cups (500 mL)	3 cups (750 mL)	4 cups (1 L)	5 cups (1.25 L)
	dried onion	1½ tbsp (22 mL)	3 tbsp (45 mL)	4½ tbsp (67 mL)	6 tbsp (90 mL)	7½ tbsp (112 mL)
	garlic	1 tsp (5 mL)	2 tsp (10 mL)	1 tbsp (15 mL)	4 tsp (20 mL)	5 tsp (25 mL)
	all-purpose flour	⅓ cup (75 mL)	⅔ cup (150 mL)	1 cup (250 mL)	1⅓ cups (325 mL)	1⅔ cups (400 mL)
	salt	1 tsp (5 mL)	2 tsp (10 mL)	1 tbsp (15 mL)	4 tsp (20 mL)	5 tsp (25 mL)
	hot pepper flakes	¼ tsp (1 mL)	½ tsp (2 mL)	¾ tsp (3 mL)	1 tsp (5 mL)	1¼ tsp (6 mL)
	chicken broth	3 cups (750 mL)	6 cups (1.5 L)	9 cups (2.25 L)	12 cups (3 L)	15 cups (3.75 L)
	half-and-half	¾ cup (175 mL)	1½ cups (375 mL)	2¼ cups (560 mL)	3 cups (750 mL)	3¾ cups (925 mL)
	cooked chicken	2 cups (500 mL)	4 cups (1 L)	6 cups (1.5 L)	8 cups (2 L)	10 cups (2.5 L)
	hazelnuts	¼ cup (60 mL)	½ cup (125 mL)	¾ cup (175 mL)	1 cup (250 mL)	1¼ cups (310 mL)
	dried sage	⅛ tsp (0.5 mL)	¼ tsp (1 mL)	⅓ tsp (1.5 mL)	½ tsp (2 mL)	¾ tsp (3 mL)
	gallon bags	1	2	3	4	5

Chicken Tortellini Soup

You have to admit, it's fun to say the word "tortellini"! These small rings of pasta are just as much fun to eat as they are to say. The nourishing chicken and savory broth make this a great meal to add to your freezer for busy nights. Makes 6 servings.

6 cups (1.5 L) chicken broth or Homemade Chicken Stock (page 349)

1 celery stalk, diced

1½ cups (375 mL) frozen diced carrots or sliced fresh carrots, blanched (see page 18)

¼ tsp (1 mL) dried rosemary

1 tbsp (15 mL) dried parsley

2 cups (500 mL) chopped cooked chicken breast (see page 29)

2 cups (500 mL) fresh or frozen cheese tortellini (about 7½ oz/215 g)

Salt and freshly ground black pepper

Garnishes

Minced freshly parsley (optional)

Fresh thyme leaves (optional)

MAKE IT NOW In a large pot, combine chicken broth, celery, carrots, rosemary and parsley. Bring to a boil over high heat. Immediately reduce heat to medium-high and boil for 5 minutes, until carrots and celery are tender. Add chicken and tortellini; season to taste with salt and pepper. Simmer, stirring often, for 3 to 4 minutes (7 to 8 minutes for frozen tortellini), until tortellini are tender and filling is hot. Remove from heat. Ladle into bowls. Sprinkle with pepper and parsley and thyme, if using.

MAKE IT A FREEZER MEAL In a labeled gallon-size (4 L) freezer bag, combine chicken broth, celery, carrots, rosemary and parsley. Seal, removing as much air as possible. Place chicken and tortellini in another labeled gallon-size freezer bag. Seal, removing as much air as possible. Place both bags together as a kit, seal and freeze.

THAW AND COOK Place bags in the refrigerator for at least 12 hours or up to 24 hours to thaw. Pour contents of broth bag into a large pot. Bring to a boil over high heat. Immediately reduce heat to medium-high and boil for 5 minutes, until carrots and celery are tender. Add chicken and tortellini; season to taste with salt and pepper. Simmer, stirring, for 3 to 4 minutes, until tortellini are tender and filling is hot. Remove from heat. Ladle into bowls. Sprinkle with pepper and parsley and thyme, if using.

BULK BATCH GUIDE	Servings	6 (1 batch)	12 (2 batches)	18 (3 batches)	24 (4 batches)	30 (5 batches)
	chicken broth	6 cups (1.5 L)	12 cups (3 L)	18 cups (4.5 L)	24 cups (6 L)	30 cups (7.5 L)
	celery stalks	1	2	3	4	5
	carrots	1½ cups (375 mL)	3 cups (750 mL)	4½ cups (1.125 L)	6 cups (1.5 L)	7½ cups (1.875 L)
	dried rosemary	¼ tsp (1 mL)	½ tsp (2 mL)	¾ tsp (3 mL)	1 tsp (5 mL)	1¼ tsp (6 mL)
	dried parsley	1 tbsp (15 mL)	2 tbsp (30 mL)	3 tbsp (45 mL)	¼ cup (60 mL)	⅓ cup (75 mL)
	cooked chicken	2 cups (500 mL)	4 cups (1 L)	6 cups (1.5 L)	8 cups (2 L)	10 cups (2.5 L)
	cheese tortellini	2 cups (500 mL)	4 cups (1 L)	6 cups (1.5 L)	8 cups (2 L)	10 cups (2.5 L)
	gallon bags	2	4	6	8	10

Zesty Tortilla Soup

Want to add a soup with a little flair and zest to your freezer? You will love how these tasty bites of chicken and crunchy tortilla strips tango in your mouth. Okay, maybe that was a little dramatic, but this soup does make me a little *emocionado*. Makes 6 servings.

2 tsp (10 mL) olive oil

½ onion, diced

2 tsp (10 mL) minced garlic

6 cups (1.5 L) chicken broth or Homemade Chicken Stock (page 349)

3 cups (750 mL) shredded cooked chicken (see page 29)

1 can (14 oz/398 mL) diced tomatoes, with juice

2 tbsp (30 mL) tomato paste

1½ cups (375 mL) corn, canned (drained) or frozen

1½ tsp (7 mL) ground cumin

1½ tsp (7 mL) chili powder

Salt and freshly ground black pepper

Garnishes

Corn tortilla strips or crushed tortilla chips

Shredded Cheddar cheese (optional)

Lime wedges (optional)

Chopped fresh cilantro (optional)

Sour cream (optional)

1. In a medium skillet, heat olive oil over medium heat. Add onion and garlic; cook, stirring, for about 2 to 3 minutes, until tender. Remove from heat.

MAKE IT NOW In a large stockpot, combine chicken broth, chicken, onion mixture, tomatoes (with juice), tomato paste, corn, cumin and chili powder. Bring to a boil over medium-high heat, then immediately reduce heat to low. Simmer for 20 to 30 minutes, until flavors are blended. Remove from heat and let cool for 5 minutes. Season to taste with salt and pepper. Serve in bowls topped with tortilla strips, Cheddar cheese, lime wedges, cilantro and sour cream, if using.

MAKE IT A FREEZER MEAL Let onion mixture cool completely. In a large bowl, combine chicken broth, chicken, onion mixture, tomatoes (with juice), tomato paste, corn, cumin and chili powder. Divide equally between two labeled gallon-size (4 L) freezer bags. Gently swish to combine. Seal, removing as much air as possible, and freeze.

THAW AND COOK Place bags in refrigerator for at least 12 hours or up to 24 hours to thaw. Pour contents of both bags into a large stockpot and bring to a boil over medium-high heat. Immediately reduce heat to low and simmer, stirring occasionally, for 20 to 30 minutes, until flavors are blended and soup is hot. Remove from heat and let cool for 5 minutes. Season to taste with salt and pepper. Serve in bowls topped with tortilla strips, Cheddar cheese, lime wedges, cilantro and sour cream, if using.

Servings	6 (1 batch)	12 (2 batches)	18 (3 batches)	24 (4 batches)	30 (5 batches)
olive oil	2 tsp (10 mL)	4 tsp (20 mL)	2 tbsp (30 mL)	8 tsp (40 mL)	10 tsp (50 mL)
onions	½	1	1½	2	2½
garlic	2 tsp (10 mL)	4 tsp (20 mL)	2 tbsp (30 mL)	8 tsp (40 mL)	10 tsp (50 mL)
chicken broth	6 cups (1.5 L)	12 cups (3 L)	18 cups (4.5 L)	24 cups (6 L)	30 cups (7.5 L)
cooked chicken	3 cups (750 mL)	6 cups (1.5 L)	9 cups (2.25 L)	12 cups (3 L)	15 cups (3.75 L)
tomatoes	14 oz (398 mL)	28 oz (796 mL)	42 oz (1.194 L)	56 oz (1.592 L)	70 oz (1.99 L)
tomato paste	2 tbsp (30 mL)	¼ cup (60 mL)	6 tbsp (90 mL)	½ cup (125 mL)	⅔ cup (150 mL)
corn	1½ cups (375 mL)	3 cups (750 mL)	4½ cups (1.125 L)	6 cups (1.5 L)	7½ cups (1.875 L)
cumin	1½ tsp (7 mL)	1 tbsp (15 mL)	1½ tbsp (22 mL)	2 tbsp (30 mL)	2½ tbsp (37 mL)
chili powder	1½ tsp (7 mL)	1 tbsp (15 mL)	1½ tbsp (22 mL)	2 tbsp (30 mL)	2½ tbsp (37 mL)
gallon bags	2	4	6	8	10

BULK BATCH GUIDE

Herbed Chicken and Dumpling Soup

The dumpling can be found almost everywhere in the world in one form or another. In fact, invading Mongols used to pack them wherever they went. You, however, should pack them in your freezer for when family or friends invade your home. This hearty, comforting and nutritious soup, with chicken, carrots and celery infused into a flavorful broth, is fun to eat because of all those delicious and savory dumplings. Makes 6 servings.

Soup

6 cups (1.5 L) chicken broth or Homemade Chicken Stock (page 349)

2 cups (500 mL) chopped cooked chicken (see page 29)

1½ cups (375 mL) frozen diced carrots or sliced fresh carrots, blanched (see page 18)

1 cup (250 mL) chopped celery

½ tsp (2 mL) onion powder

1 tbsp (15 mL) chopped fresh parsley

Dumplings

2 oz (60 g) boneless, skinless chicken breast

1 large egg, beaten

1 tbsp (15 mL) cornstarch

¼ cup (60 mL) heavy or whipping (35%) cream

½ cup (125 mL) all-purpose flour (approx.)

Salt and freshly ground black pepper

1. *Soup:* In a large bowl, combine chicken broth, cooked chicken, carrots, celery, onion powder and parsley. Set aside.

2. *Dumplings:* Place chicken breast in a mini chopper or small food processor fitted with the metal blade. Process until finely puréed.

3. In a small bowl, combine egg and chicken purée. Add cornstarch; stir to combine. Add cream; stir again. Add flour, stirring to make a thick paste (you may need additional flour). Using a spoon, scoop up paste in 1 tsp (5 mL) dollops, roll into balls with your hands and set aside on a plate lightly dusted with flour.

MAKE IT NOW Pour chicken broth mixture into a large stockpot. Bring to a boil over medium-high heat; boil for 5 minutes or until carrots are tender. Season to taste with salt and pepper. Add dumplings and cover. Reduce heat to medium-low and simmer for 10 minutes, until dumplings are firm and no longer pink inside. Serve.

MAKE IT A FREEZER MEAL Pour chicken broth mixture into a labeled gallon-size (4 L) freezer bag. Seal, removing as much air as possible. Place dumplings in a labeled quart-size (1 L) freezer bag. Seal and freeze both bags together as a kit.

THAW AND COOK Place frozen bags in refrigerator for 12 hours to 24 hours to thaw. Empty contents into a large stockpot and bring to a boil over medium-high heat. Boil for 5 minutes or until carrots are tender. Add dumplings. Cover, reduce heat to medium-low and simmer for 10 minutes, until dumplings are firm and no longer pink inside. Serve.

BULK BATCH GUIDE	Servings	6 (1 batch)	12 (2 batches)	18 (3 batches)	24 (4 batches)	30 (5 batches)
	chicken broth	6 cups (1.5 L)	12 cups (3 L)	18 cups (4.5 L)	24 cups (6 L)	30 cups (7.5 L)
	cooked chicken	2 cups (500 mL)	4 cups (1 L)	6 cups (1.5 L)	8 cups (2 L)	10 cups (2.5 L)
	carrots	1½ cups (375 mL)	3 cups (750 mL)	4½ cups (1.125 L)	6 cups (1.5 L)	7½ cups (1.875 L)
	celery	1 cup (250 mL)	2 cups (500 mL)	3 cups (750 mL)	4 cups (1 L)	5 cups (1.25 L)
	onion powder	½ tsp (2 mL)	1 tsp (5 mL)	1½ tsp (7 mL)	2 tsp (10 mL)	2½ tsp (12 mL)
	parsley	1 tbsp (15 mL)	2 tbsp (30 mL)	3 tbsp (45 mL)	¼ cup (60 mL)	⅓ cup (75 mL)
	chicken breast	2 oz (60 g)	4 oz (125 g)	6 oz (175 g)	8 oz (250 g)	10 oz (300 g)
	eggs	1	2	3	4	5
	cornstarch	1 tbsp (15 mL)	2 tbsp (30 mL)	3 tbsp (45 mL)	¼ cup (60 mL)	⅓ cup (75 mL)
	cream	¼ cup (60 mL)	½ cup (125 mL)	¾ cup (175 mL)	1 cup (250 mL)	1¼ cups (310 mL)
	all-purpose flour	½ cup (125 mL)	1 cup (250 mL)	1½ cups (375 mL)	2 cups (500 mL)	2½ cups (625 mL)
	quart bags	1	2	3	4	5
	gallon bags	1	2	3	4	5

Sausage and Gnocchi Soup

Saying I'm obsessed with gnocchi is an understatement — those little balls of potato are just too fun to eat. I am always trying to figure out a way to eat them more often, so I came up with this fantastic soup that combines chickpeas, kale, gnocchi and Italian sausage. And when you take that first bite? Fugget about it! *Makes 6 servings.*

1 lb (500 g) mild Italian sausage

1 tbsp (15 mL) olive oil

¼ cup (60 mL) diced onion

2 tsp (10 mL) minced garlic

1 cup (250 mL) chopped kale

4 cups (1 L) chicken broth or Homemade Chicken Stock (page 349)

1 cup (250 mL) water

1 can (15 oz/425 mL) chickpeas, drained and rinsed

1 tsp (5 mL) dried basil

½ tsp (2 mL) dried oregano

⅛ tsp (0.5 mL) hot pepper flakes

Pinch freshly ground black pepper

1 batch uncooked Gnocchi (page 330)

Tip

If you don't want to make gnocchi from scratch, use 12 oz (375 g) store-bought gnocchi. If you are using frozen gnocchi, it should not be thawed before assembling the freezer meal.

1. In a large skillet, cook sausage over high heat for about 3 to 4 minutes, turning to brown all sides, until crispy and golden. Remove from heat. Transfer to a cutting board and cut into ½-inch (1 cm) slices. Set aside.

2. Place skillet back on stove over medium heat. Add olive oil, onion, garlic and kale. Cook, stirring, for 3 to 5 minutes, until onion is tender.

MAKE IT NOW In a large stockpot, combine sausage, kale mixture, chicken broth, water, chickpeas, basil, oregano, hot pepper flakes and black pepper. Bring to a boil over medium-high heat, then immediately reduce heat to low and simmer for 15 minutes, until flavors intensify. Add gnocchi, increase heat to medium-high and return to a boil. Boil, stirring often, for about 2 to 3 minutes, until gnocchi are al dente and float to the top. Remove from heat and let cool for 5 minutes.

MAKE IT A FREEZER MEAL Let sausage and kale mixture cool completely. Place sausage, kale mixture, chicken broth, water, chickpeas, basil, oregano, hot pepper flakes and black pepper in a labeled gallon-size (4 L) bag. Seal, removing as much air as possible. Place gnocchi in a labeled quart-size (1 L) freezer bag. Seal and freeze both bags together as a kit.

THAW AND COOK Place both bags in the refrigerator for at least 12 hours or up to 24 hours to thaw. Pour soup mixture into a large stockpot and bring to a boil over medium-high heat. Immediately reduce heat to low and simmer for 15 minutes, until flavors intensify. Add gnocchi, increase heat to medium-high and return to a boil. Boil, stirring often, for about 2 to 3 minutes, until gnocchi are al dente and float to the top. Remove from heat and let cool for 5 minutes.

BULK BATCH GUIDE	Servings	6 (1 batch)	12 (2 batches)	18 (3 batches)	24 (4 batches)	30 (5 batches)
	Italian sausage	1 lb (500 g)	2 lbs (1 kg)	3 lbs (1.5 kg)	4 lbs (2 kg)	5 lbs (2.5 kg)
	olive oil	1 tbsp (15 mL)	2 tbsp (30 mL)	3 tbsp (45 mL)	¼ cup (60 mL)	⅓ cup (75 mL)
	onions	¼ cup (60 mL)	½ cup (125 mL)	¾ cup (175 mL)	1 cup (250 mL)	1¼ cups (310 mL)
	garlic	2 tsp (10 mL)	4 tsp (20 mL)	2 tbsp (30 mL)	8 tsp (40 mL)	10 tsp (50 mL)
	kale	1 cup (250 mL)	2 cups (500 mL)	3 cups (750 mL)	4 cups (1 L)	5 cups (1.25 L)
	chicken broth	4 cups (1 L)	8 cups (2 L)	12 cups (3 L)	16 cups (4 L)	20 cups (5 L)
	water	1 cup (250 mL)	2 cups (500 mL)	3 cups (750 mL)	4 cups (1 L)	5 cups (1.25 L)
	chickpeas	15 oz (425 mL)	30 oz (850 mL)	45 oz (1.275 L)	60 oz (1.7 L)	75 oz (2.125 L)
	dried basil	1 tsp (5 mL)	2 tsp (10 mL)	1 tbsp (15 mL)	4 tsp (20 mL)	5 tsp (25 mL)
	dried oregano	½ tsp (2 mL)	1 tsp (5 mL)	1½ tsp (7 mL)	2 tsp (10 mL)	2½ tsp (12 mL)
	hot pepper flakes	⅛ tsp (0.5 mL)	¼ tsp (1 mL)	⅓ tsp (1.5 mL)	½ tsp (2 mL)	¾ tsp (3 mL)
	Gnocchi	1 batch	2 batches	3 batches	4 batches	5 batches
	gallon bags	1	2	3	4	5
	quart bags	1	2	3	4	5

Sweet & Spicy Pork Carnita Soup

Have you ever had carnitas in a soup? Probably not. I make this unique and flavorful recipe when I have leftover pork carnitas, because it comes together in a flash. *Makes 6 servings.*

1 can (15 oz/425 mL) black beans, drained and rinsed, divided

1 can (14 oz/398 mL) diced tomatoes, with juice

½ sweet onion, quartered

1 garlic clove

½ red bell pepper, diced

2 cups (500 mL) shredded cooked pork carnitas (page 203)

4 cups (1 L) beef broth or Homemade Beef Stock (page 350)

1 cup (250 mL) frozen corn

1 can (4½ oz/127 mL) mild green chiles, with juice

1 tsp (5 mL) dried oregano

1 tsp (5 mL) chili powder

1 tsp (5 mL) ground cumin

½ tsp (2 mL) paprika

¼ tsp (1 mL) ground cinnamon

Salt and freshly ground black pepper

Garnishes

⅓ cup (75 mL) crumbled queso fresco

¼ cup (60 mL) chopped fresh cilantro (optional)

1. In a blender, combine half the beans with the tomatoes (with juice), onion and garlic; blend on High until smooth. Pour into a large bowl (to freeze) or a large stockpot (to make it now).

2. Add remaining beans, red pepper, pork, beef broth, corn, green chiles (with juice), oregano, chili powder, cumin, paprika and cinnamon to puréed mixture; stir to combine.

MAKE IT NOW Place stockpot over medium-high heat and bring to a boil. Immediately reduce heat to low and simmer, stirring occasionally, for 15 minutes, to allow flavors to meld. Remove from heat and let cool for 5 minutes. Season to taste with salt and pepper. Ladle into bowls and top with queso fresco and cilantro, if using. Serve immediately.

MAKE IT A FREEZER MEAL Place bowl contents in a labeled gallon-size (4 L) freezer bag. Seal, removing as much air as possible, and freeze.

THAW AND COOK Place bag in the refrigerator for at least 12 hours or up to 24 hours to thaw. Pour contents into a large stockpot and bring to a boil over medium-high heat. Immediately reduce heat to low and simmer, stirring occasionally, for 15 minutes, to allow flavors to meld. Remove from heat and let cool for 5 minutes. Season to taste with salt and pepper. Ladle into bowls and top with queso fresco and cilantro, if using. Serve immediately.

Servings	6 (1 batch)	12 (2 batches)	18 (3 batches)	24 (4 batches)	30 (5 batches)
black beans	15 oz (425 mL)	30 oz (850 mL)	45 oz (1.275 L)	60 oz (1.7 L)	75 oz (2.125 L)
tomatoes	14 oz (398 mL)	28 oz (796 mL)	42 oz (1.194 L)	56 oz (1.59 L)	70 oz (1.99 L)
onions	½	1	1½	2	2½
garlic cloves	1	2	3	4	5
red bell peppers	½	1	1½	2	2½
pork carnitas	2 cups (500 mL)	4 cups (1 L)	6 cups (1.5 L)	8 cups (2 L)	10 cups (2.5 L)
beef broth	4 cups (1 L)	8 cups (2 L)	12 cups (3 L)	16 cups (4 L)	20 cups (5 L)
corn	1 cup (250 mL)	2 cups (500 mL)	3 cups (750 mL)	4 cups (1 L)	5 cups (1.25 L)
mild green chiles	4½ oz (127 mL)	9 oz (254 mL)	13½ oz (381 mL)	18 oz (508 mL)	22½ oz (635 mL)
dried oregano	1 tsp (5 mL)	2 tsp (10 mL)	1 tbsp (15 mL)	4 tsp (20 mL)	5 tsp (25 mL)
chili powder	1 tsp (5 mL)	2 tsp (10 mL)	1 tbsp (15 mL)	4 tsp (20 mL)	5 tsp (25 mL)
cumin	1 tsp (5 mL)	2 tsp (10 mL)	1 tbsp (15 mL)	4 tsp (20 mL)	5 tsp (25 mL)
paprika	½ tsp (2 mL)	1 tsp (5 mL)	1½ tsp (7 mL)	2 tsp (10 mL)	2½ tsp (12 mL)
cinnamon	¼ tsp (1 mL)	½ tsp (2 mL)	¾ tsp (3 mL)	1 tsp (5 mL)	1¼ tsp (6 mL)
gallon bags	1	2	3	4	5

BULK BATCH GUIDE

Mini Meatball Soup

I'll be honest here, I'm weak for any food in mini form. Although this wholesome soup is filled with enticing beans, savory broth and fun mini meatballs, it's definitely not mini in flavor.

Makes 6 servings.

2 cups (500 mL) fusilli pasta (about 12 oz/350 g)

12 oz (375 g) breakfast sausage

2 tbsp (30 mL) Italian-seasoned bread crumbs

2 tbsp (30 mL) freshly grated Parmesan cheese

2 tbsp (30 mL) olive oil

1 small onion, diced

1 cup (250 mL) diced carrots

2 tsp (10 mL) minced garlic

6 cups (1.5 L) chicken broth or Homemade Chicken Stock (page 349)

2 cans (each 15 oz/425 mL) cannellini beans, drained and rinsed

¼ tsp (1 mL) hot pepper flakes

¼ tsp (1 mL) dried thyme

2 tbsp (30 mL) Easy Pesto (page 339)

1 cup (250 mL) chopped kale

Salt and freshly ground black pepper

Garnish

Freshly grated Parmesan cheese (optional)

1. Fill a large stockpot with water and bring to a boil over high heat. Cook pasta for 5 to 6 minutes, stirring occasionally, until just beginning to get soft (it should be starting to get tender but have a firm bite). Drain and rinse with cold water to cool quickly. Set aside.

2. Carefully slit open casings of sausages and peel off, keeping sausage shape intact. Discard casings. Cut sausages crosswise into slices ½ inch (1 cm) thick — these become the "meatballs."

3. In a small bowl, combine bread crumbs and Parmesan cheese. Roll each meatball in mixture, pressing to coat.

4. In a medium skillet, heat olive oil over medium-high heat. Working in batches, fry meatballs, stirring occasionally, for about 4 to 5 minutes, until golden brown on all sides and no longer pink inside. Using a slotted spoon, remove meatballs from skillet and drain on a plate lined with paper towels.

5. Add onion and carrots to skillet. Cook, stirring constantly, for about 3 to 4 minutes, until softened. Add garlic and cook, stirring, for 1 minute, until fragrant. Remove from heat.

MAKE IT NOW In a large stockpot, combine carrot mixture, chicken broth, beans, hot pepper flakes and thyme. Bring to a boil over medium-high heat. Add meatballs, pasta, pesto and kale; season to taste with salt and pepper. Immediately reduce heat to low; simmer, stirring often, for about 5 minutes, until pasta is cooked al dente. Remove from heat and let cool for 5 minutes. Ladle into bowls and sprinkle with Parmesan cheese, if using.

MAKE IT A FREEZER MEAL Let meatballs and carrot mixture cool completely. Place in a labeled gallon-size (4 L) freezer bag. Add chicken broth, beans, hot pepper flakes, thyme, pasta, pesto and kale. Seal, removing as much air as possible, and freeze.

REHEAT Place soup bag in the refrigerator for at least 12 hours or up to 24 hours to thaw. Pour bag contents into a large stockpot and bring to a boil over medium-high heat. Immediately reduce heat to low; simmer, stirring often, for about 5 minutes, until pasta is cooked al dente. Remove from heat and let cool for 5 minutes. Ladle into bowls and sprinkle with Parmesan cheese, if using.

(continued on page 118)

Servings	6 (1 batch)	12 (2 batches)	18 (3 batches)	24 (4 batches)	30 (5 batches)
fusilli	2 cups (500 mL)	4 cups (1 L)	6 cups (1.5 L)	8 cups (2 L)	10 cups (2.5 L)
breakfast sausage	12 oz (375 g)	1½ lbs (750 g)	2¼ lbs (1.125 kg)	3 lbs (1.5 kg)	3¾ lbs (1.875 kg)
Italian bread crumbs	2 tbsp (30 mL)	¼ cup (60 mL)	6 tbsp (90 mL)	½ cup (125 mL)	⅔ cup (150 mL)
Parmesan cheese	2 tbsp (30 mL)	¼ cup (60 mL)	6 tbsp (90 mL)	½ cup (125 mL)	⅔ cup (150 mL)
olive oil	2 tbsp (30 mL)	¼ cup (60 mL)	6 tbsp (90 mL)	½ cup (125 mL)	⅔ cup (150 mL)
onions	1	2	3	4	5
carrots	1 cup (250 mL)	2 cups (500 mL)	3 cups (750 mL)	4 cups (1 L)	5 cups (1.25 L)
garlic	2 tsp (10 mL)	4 tsp (20 mL)	2 tbsp (30 mL)	8 tsp (40 mL)	10 tsp (50 mL)
chicken broth	6 cups (1.5 L)	12 cups (3 L)	18 cups (4.5 L)	24 cups (6 L)	30 cups (7.5 L)
cannellini beans	30 oz (850 mL)	60 oz (1.7 L)	90 oz (2.55 L)	120 oz (3.4 L)	150 oz (4.25 L)
hot pepper flakes	¼ tsp (1 mL)	½ tsp (2 mL)	¾ tsp (3 mL)	1 tsp (5 mL)	1¼ tsp (6 mL)
dried thyme	¼ tsp (1 mL)	½ tsp (2 mL)	¾ tsp (3 mL)	1 tsp (5 mL)	1¼ tsp (6 mL)
Easy Pesto	2 tbsp (30 mL)	¼ cup (60 mL)	6 tbsp (90 mL)	½ cup (125 mL)	⅔ cup (150 mL)
kale	1 cup (250 mL)	2 cups (500 mL)	3 cups (750 mL)	4 cups (1 L)	5 cups (1.25 L)
gallon bags	1	2	3	4	5

Although this wholesome soup is filled with enticing beans, savory broth and fun mini meatballs, it's definitely not mini in flavor.

Seriously Good Chili

When I put the word "serious" in a title, you know I'm not messing around — and neither is this chili! It's kid friendly, meaning heavy on flavor but not too much spice. Well, unless you decide to add a bunch of cayenne . . . Makes 8 servings.

1 tbsp (15 mL) olive oil

2 lbs (1 kg) boneless beef chuck, cut into 1-inch (2.5 cm) cubes

1 lb (500 g) lean ground beef

2 red bell peppers, diced

1 onion, diced or puréed

2 cans (each 15 oz/425 mL) black beans, with liquid

1 can (15 oz/425 mL) red kidney beans, with liquid

1 can (28 oz/796 mL) diced tomatoes, with juice

1 can (8 oz/227 mL) tomato sauce

¼ cup (60 mL) Worcestershire sauce

1½ tsp (7 mL) beef bouillon powder

1 tbsp (15 mL) ground cumin

1 tbsp (15 mL) chili powder

1 tbsp (15 mL) garlic powder

1½ tsp (7 mL) salt

½ tsp (2 mL) freshly ground black pepper

½ tsp (2 mL) unsweetened cocoa powder

¼ tsp (1 mL) cinnamon

1 tsp (5 mL) cayenne pepper (optional)

To Serve

Juice of 1 lime

Chopped fresh cilantro (optional)

Shredded Cheddar cheese (optional)

Chopped onion (optional)

Sour cream (optional)

Radish slices (optional)

Sliced jalapeño peppers (optional)

1. In a large skillet, heat oil over high heat. Add beef chuck; stirring often, sear on all sides for 3 to 4 minutes, until meat is no longer pink inside. Transfer to a large bowl. (To freeze, set aside to cool.)

2. Heat a large skillet over medium-high heat. Once hot, add ground beef, red peppers and onion. Cook, stirring and breaking up beef, for 4 to 5 minutes, until meat is no longer pink and onion is tender. (To freeze, set aside to cool.)

3. To beef chuck in bowl, add cooked ground beef, black beans, kidney beans, diced tomatoes (with juice), tomato sauce, Worcestershire sauce, beef bouillon powder, cumin, chili powder, garlic powder, salt, pepper, cocoa powder, cinnamon and cayenne, if using. Stir to combine.

MAKE IT NOW Transfer bowl contents to a large (approx. 5 quart) slow cooker. Cover and cook on Low for 8 to 10 hours or on High for 4 to 6 hours. Right before serving, add lime juice; stir to combine. Ladle into bowls and top with cilantro, Cheddar cheese, onion, sour cream, radish and jalapeño peppers, if desired.

MAKE IT A FREEZER MEAL Let beef chuck and ground beef mixture cool separately and completely; then add remaining ingredients. Transfer to a labeled gallon-size (4 L) freezer bag. Seal, removing as much air as possible, and freeze.

THAW AND COOK Place bag in the refrigerator for at least 12 hours or up to 24 hours to thaw. Pour contents into a large (approx. 5 quart) slow cooker. Cover and cook on Low for 8 to 10 hours or on High for 4 to 6 hours. Right before serving, add lime juice; stir to combine. Ladle into bowls and top with cilantro, Cheddar cheese, onion, sour cream, radish and jalapeño peppers, if desired.

(continued on page 121)

Servings	8 (1 batch)	16 (2 batches)	24 (3 batches)	32 (4 batches)	40 (5 batches)
olive oil	1 tbsp (15 mL)	2 tbsp (30 mL)	3 tbsp (45 mL)	¼ cup (60 mL)	⅓ cup (75 mL)
beef chuck	2 lbs (1 kg)	4 lbs (2 kg)	6 lbs (3 kg)	8 lbs (4 kg)	10 lbs (5 kg)
ground beef	1 lb (500 g)	2 lbs (1 kg)	3 lbs (1.5 kg)	4 lbs (2 kg)	5 lbs (2.5 kg)
red bell peppers	2	4	6	8	10
onions	1	2	3	4	5
black beans	30 oz (850 mL)	60 oz (1.7 L)	90 oz (2.55 L)	120 oz (3.4 L)	150 oz (4.25 L)
red kidney beans	15 oz (425 mL)	30 oz (850 mL)	45 oz (1.275 L)	60 oz (1.7 L)	75 oz (2.125 L)
diced tomatoes	28 oz (796 mL)	56 oz (1.592 L)	84 oz (2.388 L)	112 oz (3.184 L)	140 oz (3.98 L)
tomato sauce	8 oz (227 mL)	16 oz (454 mL)	24 oz (681 mL)	32 oz (908 mL)	40 oz (1.135 L)
Worcestershire	¼ cup (60 mL)	½ cup (125 mL)	¾ cup (175 mL)	1 cup (250 mL)	1¼ cups (310 mL)
beef bouillon powder	1½ tsp (7 mL)	1 tbsp (15 mL)	1½ tbsp (22 mL)	2 tbsp (30 mL)	2½ tbsp (37 mL)
cumin	1 tbsp (15 mL)	2 tbsp (30 mL)	3 tbsp (45 mL)	¼ cup (60 mL)	⅓ cup (75 mL)
chili powder	1 tbsp (15 mL)	2 tbsp (30 mL)	3 tbsp (45 mL)	¼ cup (60 mL)	⅓ cup (75 mL)
garlic powder	1 tbsp (15 mL)	2 tbsp (30 mL)	3 tbsp (45 mL)	¼ cup (60 mL)	⅓ cup (75 mL)
salt	1½ tsp (7 mL)	1 tbsp (15 mL)	1½ tbsp (22 mL)	2 tbsp (30 mL)	2½ tbsp (37 mL)
pepper	½ tsp (2 mL)	1 tsp (5 mL)	1½ tsp (7 mL)	2 tsp (10 mL)	2½ tsp (12 mL)
cocoa powder	½ tsp (2 mL)	1 tsp (5 mL)	1½ tsp (7 mL)	2 tsp (10 mL)	2½ tsp (12 mL)
cinnamon	¼ tsp (1 mL)	½ tsp (2 mL)	¾ tsp (3 mL)	1 tsp (5 mL)	1¼ tsp (6 mL)
cayenne pepper	1 tsp (5 mL)	2 tsp (10 mL)	1 tbsp (15 mL)	4 tsp (20 mL)	5 tsp (25 mL)
gallon bags	1	2	3	4	5

When I put
the word "serious"
in a title,
you know I'm not
messing around —
and neither is
this chili!

White Bean Chicken Chili

This chicken chili is delicious on its own with its mix of creamy, slightly spicy and hearty flavors, but I adore it even more topped with cheese, corn chips, cilantro and a squeeze of fresh lime juice.
Makes 6 servings.

3 cups (750 mL) chicken broth or Homemade Chicken Stock (page 349)

3 cans (each 15 oz/425 mL) Great Northern (white kidney) beans, drained and rinsed

1 cup (250 mL) mild salsa verde (about 9 oz/250g)

1 lb (500 g) boneless, skinless chicken breasts, chopped

1 large white onion, diced

1½ tsp (7 mL) minced garlic

1 tbsp (15 mL) ground cumin

2 tsp (10 mL) ground coriander

2 tsp (10 mL) dried oregano

½ tsp (2 mL) salt

Hot pepper sauce to taste (I like Tabasco), optional

Garnishes

1 cup (250 mL) sour cream

Shredded Cheddar cheese (optional)

Chopped fresh cilantro (optional)

Corn chips (optional)

Lime wedges (optional)

MAKE IT NOW In a large (approx. 5 quart) slow cooker, combine chicken broth, beans, salsa verde, chicken, onion, garlic, cumin, coriander, oregano, salt and hot pepper sauce, if using; gently stir to combine. Cover and cook on Low for 6 to 8 hours or on High for 3 to 4 hours, until chicken is tender and no longer pink inside. Add sour cream; stir to combine. Ladle into bowls and sprinkle with Cheddar cheese, cilantro and corn chips, if using. Serve with lime wedges on the side, if desired.

MAKE IT A FREEZER MEAL Place chicken broth, beans, salsa verde, chicken, onion, garlic, cumin, coriander, oregano, salt and hot pepper sauce, if using, in a labeled gallon-size (4 L) freezer bag. Seal, removing as much air as possible, and freeze.

THAW AND COOK Place bag in the refrigerator for at least 12 hours or up to 24 hours to thaw. Pour contents into a large (approx. 5 quart) slow cooker and gently stir to combine. Cover and cook on Low for 6 to 8 hours or on High for 3 to 4 hours, until chicken is tender and no longer pink inside. Add sour cream; stir to combine. Ladle into bowls and sprinkle with Cheddar cheese, cilantro and corn chips, if using. Serve with lime wedges on the side, if desired.

BULK BATCH GUIDE	Servings	6 (1 batch)	12 (2 batches)	18 (3 batches)	24 (4 batches)	30 (5 batches)
	chicken broth	3 cups (750 mL)	6 cups (1.5 L)	9 cups (2.25 L)	12 cups (3 L)	15 cups (3.75 L)
	Great Northern beans	45 oz (1.275 L)	90 oz (2.55 L)	135 oz (3.825 L)	180 oz (5.1 L)	225 oz (6.375 L)
	salsa verde	1 cup (250 mL)	2 cups (500 mL)	3 cups (750 mL)	4 cups (1 L)	5 cups (1.25 L)
	chicken breasts	1 lb (500 g)	2 lbs (1 kg)	3 lbs (1.5 kg)	4 lbs (2 kg)	5 lbs (2.5 kg)
	onions	1	2	3	4	5
	garlic	1½ tsp (7 mL)	1 tbsp (15 mL)	1½ tbsp (22 mL)	2 tbsp (30 mL)	2½ tbsp (37 mL)
	cumin	1 tbsp (15 mL)	2 tbsp (30 mL)	3 tbsp (45 mL)	¼ cup (60 mL)	⅓ cup (75 mL)
	coriander	2 tsp (10 mL)	4 tsp (20 mL)	2 tbsp (30 mL)	8 tsp (40 mL)	10 tsp (50 mL)
	oregano	2 tsp (10 mL)	4 tsp (20 mL)	2 tbsp (30 mL)	8 tsp (40 mL)	10 tsp (50 mL)
	salt	½ tsp (2 mL)	1 tsp (5 mL)	1½ tsp (7 mL)	2 tsp (10 mL)	2½ tsp (12 mL)
	gallon bags	1	2	3	4	5

Beef Barley Stew

Looking for the food equivalent of a warm blanket? Look no further. The smell of this rich, deep soup and the flavors of the hearty beef and stock will make everyone's mouths water. I just need to lift the lid and stir the pot a few times and the soup bowls start showing up. *Makes 6 servings.*

1 lb (500 g) stewing beef, trimmed and diced

1¼ cups (310 mL) frozen diced carrots or sliced fresh carrots, blanched (see page 18)

1¼ cups (310 mL) chopped onions

¾ cup (175 mL) chopped celery

1 can (15 oz/425 mL) tomato sauce

½ cup (125 mL) pearl barley, rinsed

2 tbsp (30 mL) beef bouillon powder

1 tsp (5 mL) granulated sugar

1 tsp (5 mL) dried parsley

5 cups (1.25 L) water

Garnishes

Chopped fresh parsley (optional)

Freshly ground black pepper (optional)

MAKE IT NOW Place beef, carrots, onions, celery, tomato sauce, barley, bouillon powder, sugar, parsley and water in a large (approx. 5 quart) slow cooker; stir to combine. Cover and cook on Low for 8 to 10 hours or on High for 4 to 5 hours, until beef is tender. Serve topped with fresh parsley and pepper, if using.

MAKE IT A FREEZER MEAL Place beef, carrots, onions, celery, tomato sauce, barley, bouillon powder, sugar and parsley in a labeled gallon-size (4 L) freezer bag. (Do not add water until cooking day.) Seal, removing as much air as possible, and freeze.

THAW AND COOK Place bag in the refrigerator for at least 12 hours or up to 24 hours to thaw. Pour contents into a large (approx. 5 quart) slow cooker. Add 5 cups (1.25 L) water and stir. Cover and cook on Low for 8 to 10 hours or on High 4 to 5 hours, until beef is fork-tender. Serve topped with fresh parsley and pepper, if using.

BULK BATCH GUIDE	Servings	6 (1 batch)	12 (2 batches)	18 (3 batches)	24 (4 batches)	30 (5 batches)
	beef	1 lb (500 g)	2 lbs (1 kg)	3 lbs (1.5 kg)	4 lbs (2 kg)	5 lbs (2.5 kg)
	carrots	1¼ cups (310 mL)	2½ cups (625 mL)	3¾ cups (925 mL)	5 cups (1.25 L)	6¼ cups (1.56 L)
	onions	1¼ cups (310 mL)	2½ cups (625 mL)	3¾ cups (925 mL)	5 cups (1.25 L)	6¼ cups (1.56 L)
	celery	¾ cup (175 mL)	1½ cups (375 mL)	2¼ cups (560 mL)	3 cups (750 mL)	3¾ cups (925 mL)
	tomato sauce	15 oz (425 mL)	30 oz (850 mL)	45 oz (1.275 L)	60 oz (1.7 L)	75 oz (2.125 L)
	barley	½ cup (125 mL)	1 cup (250 mL)	1½ cups (375 mL)	2 cups (500 mL)	2½ cups (625 mL)
	beef bouillon powder	2 tbsp (30 mL)	¼ cup (60 mL)	6 tbsp (90 mL)	½ cup (125 mL)	⅔ cup (150 mL)
	sugar	1 tsp (5 mL)	2 tsp (10 mL)	1 tbsp (15 mL)	4 tsp (20 mL)	5 tsp (25 mL)
	dried parsley	1 tsp (5 mL)	2 tsp (10 mL)	1 tbsp (15 mL)	4 tsp (20 mL)	5 tsp (25 mL)
	water	5 cups (1.125 L)	10 cups (2.5 L)	15 cups (3.75 L)	20 cups (5 L)	25 cups (6.25 L)
	gallon bags	1	2	3	4	5

POULTRY

Buttermilk Dill Chicken Sandwiches 128

Cashew Basil Chicken 131

Sun-Dried Tomato and Bacon Chicken 132

Crescent Chicken Divine 135

Hazelnut Pear Chicken 136

Chicken Parmigiana 139

Herbes de Provence Chicken 140

Honey Lime Chicken 143

Lemon Tarragon Chicken 144

Maple Dijon Chicken 147

Smoky Grilled Louisiana Turkey Legs 148

Broccoli Chicken Alfredo Bake 151

Chicken Pesto Parmesan Shells 152

Old-Fashioned Chicken Pot Pie 155

Cilantro Lime Chicken Tacos 156

Killer Chicken Enchiladas 159

Asian Chicken Lettuce Wraps 160

Amazing Chicken Satay with Peanut Sauce 163

Chicken Tikka Masala 164

Peanut Perfection Pad Thai 167

Teriyaki Chicken 170

Buttermilk Dill Chicken Sandwiches

I don't know what I love more about this sandwich, the fresh zing of dill or the delightful crunch of crispy chicken. I am so glad I don't have to choose! Makes 8 servings.

2 lbs (1 kg) boneless, skinless chicken breasts (about 4 breasts total)

1 cup (250 mL) buttermilk

½ tsp (2 mL) dried dill

¼ cup (60 mL) olive oil

3 cups (750 mL) panko bread crumbs

2 tsp (10 mL) dried Italian seasoning

3 large eggs

⅓ cup (75 mL) all-purpose flour

1 tsp (5 mL) salt

¼ tsp (1 mL) freshly ground black pepper

Garnishes

8 buns or rolls, split

Fresh lettuce leaves

Pickle slices (optional)

Ranch dressing or mayonnaise (optional)

1. With the blade of a sharp knife parallel to the cutting board, cut chicken breasts in half horizontally. Place chicken between two pieces of plastic wrap and, using a mallet or heavy skillet, pound to ¼-inch (0.5 cm) thickness. You should have 8 cutlets.

2. Place chicken in a gallon-size (4 L) freezer bag. Add buttermilk and dill; swish around until all sides are coated. Place bag in the refrigerator and marinate for at least 15 minutes or up to 2 hours.

3. In a large skillet, heat olive oil over medium heat. Once oil is hot and shimmering, add panko crumbs and Italian seasoning; cook, stirring constantly, for 1 to 2 minutes, until crumbs are barely starting to turn light golden brown (you do not want the panko to become a deep golden brown). Transfer to a shallow dish and let cool.

4. In a small bowl, whisk eggs until well beaten.

5. In another small bowl, combine flour, salt and pepper.

6. Working with one cutlet at a time, remove chicken from marinade. Coat in flour mixture, shaking off excess. Dip in egg mixture, then coat with panko crumbs, patting gently to help them adhere. Place on a baking sheet lined with greased parchment paper, spacing apart. Spray tops of cutlets lightly with cooking spray. Discard marinade and leftover egg, flour and crumb mixtures.

MAKE IT NOW Preheat oven to 400°F (200°C). Bake chicken in preheated oven for 8 minutes. Flip cutlets and bake for an additional 7 to 10 minutes, until crust is golden brown and chicken is no longer pink inside. Remove from oven and let cool for 5 minutes; serve each on a bun with lettuce, pickles and ranch dressing, if using.

MAKE IT A FREEZER MEAL Place coated chicken, on baking sheet, in freezer for 2 to 3 hours, until solid. Transfer to a labeled gallon-size (4 L) freezer bag. Seal, removing as much air as possible, and freeze.

COOK FROM FROZEN Preheat oven to 400°F (200°C). Place chicken on a baking sheet lined with lightly greased parchment paper. Bake in preheated oven for 10 minutes. Flip cutlets and bake for an additional 10 to 15 minutes, until crust is golden brown and chicken is no longer pink inside. Remove from oven and let cool for 5 minutes; serve on a bun with lettuce, pickles and ranch dressing, if using.

Servings	8 (1 batch)	16 (2 batches)	24 (3 batches)	32 (4 batches)	40 (5 batches)
chicken breasts	2 lbs (1 kg)	4 lbs (2 kg)	6 lbs (3 kg)	8 lbs (4 kg)	10 lbs (5 kg)
buttermilk	1 cup (250 mL)	2 cups (500 mL)	3 cups (750 mL)	4 cups (1 L)	5 cups (1.25 L)
dried dill	½ tsp (2 mL)	1 tsp (5 mL)	1½ tsp (7 mL)	2 tsp (10 mL)	2½ tsp (12 mL)
olive oil	¼ cup (60 mL)	½ cup (125 mL)	¾ cup (175 mL)	1 cup (250 mL)	1¼ cups (310 mL)
panko	3 cups (750 mL)	6 cups (1.5 L)	9 cups (2.25 L)	12 cups (3 L)	15 cups (3.75 L)
Italian seasoning	2 tsp (10 mL)	4 tsp (20 mL)	2 tbsp (30 mL)	8 tsp (40 mL)	10 tsp (50 mL)
eggs	3	6	9	12	15
all-purpose flour	⅓ cup (75 mL)	⅔ cup (150 mL)	1 cup (250 mL)	1⅓ cups (325 mL)	1⅔ cups (400 mL)
salt	1 tsp (5 mL)	2 tsp (10 mL)	1 tbsp (15 mL)	4 tsp (20 mL)	5 tsp (25 mL)
pepper	¼ tsp (1 mL)	½ tsp (2 mL)	¾ tsp (3 mL)	1 tsp (5 mL)	1¼ tsp (6 mL)
gallon bags	2	3	4	5	6

BULK BATCH GUIDE

Cashew Basil Chicken

I stand by the motto that wrapping anything in bacon makes it great, especially chicken. Once you add fragrant basil and sprinkle in some cashews, you've got yourself a masterpiece. I keep this dish in my freezer for dinner guests who show up at the last minute. Makes 6 servings.

1 cup (250 mL) raw cashews

1 cup (250 mL) grated Parmesan cheese (about 3½ oz/100 g)

1 tsp (5 mL) garlic salt

5 fresh basil leaves

6 boneless, skinless chicken breasts (each 5 oz/150 g)

1 lb (500 g) thick-cut sliced bacon

Garnish

Fresh basil leaves (optional)

1. In a food processor fitted with the metal blade, combine cashews, Parmesan cheese, garlic salt and basil leaves; process until superfine and crumbly. Set aside.

2. Place one chicken breast flat on a cutting board with the smooth side up and the thin end pointing toward you. Place one hand flat on top of the meat, pressing down slightly to hold it steady. Starting at the top, in the thickest part of the breast, with knife blade parallel to the cutting board, carefully cut horizontally through the breast down its length, cutting it almost in half but stopping ½ inch (1 cm) from the other side. Open up the chicken breast like a book. Repeat with remaining chicken.

3. On a cutting board, lay out 6 to 7 pieces of bacon crosswise, slightly overlapping the edges, to make a rough rectangle. (The bacon rectangle should be long enough to wrap around the length of one chicken breast.) Place a chicken breast, cut side up, lengthwise in center of the bacon, perpendicular to the slices.

4. Spread one-sixth of the cashew mixture over chicken. Starting with the right side, roll up bacon, chicken and spread all together, jelly-roll style, ending with the seam side down. Repeat with remaining chicken, bacon and cashew mixture.

MAKE IT NOW Preheat oven to 300°F (150°C). Place chicken rolls in a lightly greased 13- by 9-inch (33 by 23 cm) baking dish, spacing them apart. Bake in preheated oven for 1½ hours, until internal temperature reaches 165°F (74°C). If necessary, turn broiler to High to crisp bacon for the last 2 to 3 minutes of cooking. Remove from oven and serve sprinkled with fresh basil leaves, if using.

MAKE IT A FREEZER MEAL Wrap each uncooked rolled chicken breast, with the bacon seam side down, in plastic wrap. Place in 2 labeled gallon-size (4 L) freezer bags. Seal, removing as much air as possible, and freeze.

COOK FROM FROZEN Preheat oven to 300°F (150°C). Remove chicken rolls from freezer, unwrap and place in a lightly greased 13- by 9-inch (33 by 23 cm) baking dish, spacing apart. Bake in preheated oven for 2 hours, until internal temperature reaches 165°F (74°C). If necessary, turn broiler to High to crisp bacon for the last 2 to 3 minutes of cooking. Remove from oven and serve sprinkled with fresh basil leaves, if using.

	Servings	6 (1 batch)	12 (2 batches)	18 (3 batches)	24 (4 batches)	30 (5 batches)
BULK BATCH	cashews	1 cup (250 mL)	2 cups (500 mL)	3 cups (750 mL)	4 cups (1 L)	5 cups (1.25 L)
	Parmesan cheese	1 cup (250 mL)	2 cups (500 mL)	3 cups (750 mL)	4 cups (1 L)	5 cups (1.25 L)
	garlic salt	1 tsp (5 mL)	2 tsp (10 mL)	1 tbsp (15 mL)	4 tsp (20 mL)	5 tsp (25 mL)
	basil leaves	5	10	15	20	25
	chicken breasts	6	12	18	24	30
	bacon	1 lb (500 g)	2 lbs (1 kg)	3 lbs (1.5 kg)	4 lbs (2 kg)	5 lbs (2.5 kg)
	gallon bags	2	4	6	8	10

Sun-Dried Tomato and Bacon Chicken

Does anyone else want to run away to the Tuscan sun anytime you bite into a sun-dried tomato? Yeah, me too. That is why I love my fragrant and smoky sun-dried tomato and bacon chicken. I put a little North American spin on it by throwing in some cream cheese, which gives this recipe just the right velvety smooth flavor. It's one of my favorites! Makes 6 servings.

4 slices bacon

1 batch White Sauce (page 336), cooled

8 oz (250 g) cream cheese, softened

½ cup (125 mL) sliced dry-packed sun-dried tomatoes

1 tbsp (15 mL) dried Italian seasoning

2 lbs (1 kg) boneless, skinless chicken breasts

Garnish

Chopped fresh parsley (optional)

1. Heat a large skillet over medium-high heat. Add bacon and cook for about 6 to 7 minutes, flipping occasionally, until crispy. Remove from skillet and place on a plate lined with paper towels. Let cool and then chop.

2. In a large bowl, combine white sauce and cream cheese. Add chopped bacon, sun-dried tomatoes and Italian seasoning; stir to combine.

MAKE IT NOW Place chicken and sauce mixture in a large (approx. 5 quart) slow cooker. Cook on Low for 5 to 6 hours or on High for 3 to 4 hours, until chicken is very tender. Sprinkle with parsley, if using; serve.

MAKE IT A FREEZER MEAL Combine chicken and sauce mixture in a labeled gallon-size (4 L) freezer bag; swish to coat. Seal, removing as much air as possible, and freeze.

THAW AND COOK Place bag in the refrigerator for at least 12 hours or up to 24 hours to thaw. Empty contents into a large (approx. 5 quart) slow cooker. Cook on Low for 5 to 6 hours or on High for 3 to 4 hours until chicken is very tender. Sprinkle with parsley, if using; serve.

Servings	6 (1 batch)	12 (2 batches)	18 (3 batches)	24 (4 batches)	30 (5 batches)
bacon slices	4	8	12	16	20
White Sauce	1 batch	2 batches	3 batches	4 batches	5 batches
cream cheese	8 oz (250 g)	1 lb (500 g)	1½ lbs (750 g)	2 lbs (1 kg)	2½ lbs (1.25 kg)
sun-dried tomatoes	½ cup (125 mL)	1 cup (250 mL)	1½ cups (375 mL)	2 cups (500 mL)	2½ cups (625 mL)
Italian seasoning	1 tbsp (15 mL)	2 tbsp (30 mL)	3 tbsp (45 mL)	¼ cup (60 mL)	⅓ cup (75 mL)
chicken breasts	2 lbs (1 kg)	4 lbs (2 kg)	6 lbs (3 kg)	8 lbs (4 kg)	10 lbs (5 kg)
gallon bags	1	2	3	4	5

BULK BATCH

Crescent Chicken Divine

Want to show a neighbor, a new mom or a sick friend that you care? Try giving them these buttery crescent rolls filled with cheese and chicken, then baked in a creamy white sauce and encircled with bright green peas. The recipients of this gift will be ever thankful, and so will their taste buds! Makes 6 servings.

1 batch White Sauce (page 336), cooled

¼ cup (60 mL) sour cream

½ tsp (2 mL) dried Italian seasoning

1½ cups (375 mL) diced cooked chicken (see page 29)

¾ cup (175 mL) shredded Cheddar cheese (about 3 oz/90 g)

1 can (12 oz/375 g) large-size refrigerated crescent rolls (8 rolls)

1 cup (250 mL) frozen peas

Additional dried Italian seasoning

1. In a large bowl, combine white sauce, sour cream and Italian seasoning; whisk until smooth. Set aside.

2. In another large bowl, combine chicken and cheese; stir well.

3. Separate crescent roll dough and place each piece on work surface. Place a heaping ¼ cup (60 mL) chicken-cheese mixture at the wide end of each piece. Roll up and pinch edges to seal. Place in a greased 13- by 9-inch (33 by 23 cm) baking dish, spacing at least 2 inches (5 cm) apart.

4. Carefully pour frozen peas around rolls. Pour sauce over everything. Sprinkle with a few more dashes of Italian seasoning.

MAKE IT NOW Preheat oven to 350°F (180°C). Bake in preheated oven for 30 to 35 minutes or until tops of rolls are golden brown and sauce is bubbling. Let cool for 5 minutes, then serve.

MAKE IT A FREEZER MEAL Wrap baking dish tightly with plastic wrap, pressing down gently to remove air. Cover with foil. Label and freeze.

THAW AND COOK Place dish in the refrigerator for at least 12 hours or up to 24 hours to thaw. Preheat oven to 350°F (180°C). Remove foil and plastic wrap. Bake in preheated oven for 35 to 40 minutes, until tops of rolls are golden brown and sauce is bubbling. Let cool for 5 minutes, then serve.

BULK BATCH GUIDE	Servings	6 (1 batch)	12 (2 batches)	18 (3 batches)	24 (4 batches)	30 (5 batches)
	White Sauce	1 batch	2 batches	3 batches	4 batches	5 batches
	sour cream	¼ cup (60 mL)	½ cup (125 mL)	¾ cup (175 mL)	1 cup (250 mL)	1¼ cups (310 mL)
	Italian seasoning	½ tsp (2 mL)	1 tsp (5 mL)	1½ tsp (7 mL)	2 tsp (10 mL)	2½ tsp (12 mL)
	cooked chicken	1½ cups (375 mL)	3 cups (750 mL)	4½ cups (1.125 L)	6 cups (1.5 L)	7½ cups (1.875 L)
	Cheddar cheese	¾ cup (175 mL)	1½ cups (375 mL)	2¼ cups (560 mL)	3 cups (750 mL)	3¾ cups (925 mL)
	crescent rolls	12 oz (375 g)	1½ lbs (750 g)	2¼ lbs (1.125 kg)	3 lbs (1.5 kg)	3.75 lbs (1.875 kg)
	peas	1 cup (250 mL)	2 cups (500 mL)	3 cups (750 mL)	4 cups (1 L)	5 cups (1.25 L)
	13x9 dishes	1	2	3	4	5

Hazelnut Pear Chicken

After years of my husband letting me know at the last minute that someone was coming over for dinner, then frantically running to the store to get ingredients for a nice meal, I'm now a bit wiser. I make ahead a bunch of these pretty little chicken breasts packed with sweet pears, blue cheese and hazelnuts, and within 35 minutes I have a fancy meal ready to go. This recipe will have you looking like a rock-star cook even on short notice. Makes 6 servings.

1 cup (250 mL) minced drained canned or peeled fresh pears

2 tbsp (30 mL) grated Parmesan cheese (about ½ oz/15 g)

6 tbsp + 2 tsp (100 mL) crumbled blue cheese (about 2 oz/60 g), divided

2 tbsp (30 mL) coarsely chopped hazelnuts

6 boneless, skinless chicken breasts (each 5 oz/150 g)

¼ cup (60 mL) all-purpose flour

½ tsp (2 mL) salt

¼ tsp (1 mL) freshly ground pepper

To Cook

2 tbsp (30 mL) olive oil

Garnishes

Additional minced pears (optional)

Additional chopped hazelnuts (optional)

1. In a small bowl, combine pears, Parmesan cheese, 2 tsp (10 mL) blue cheese and hazelnuts; stir gently.

2. On a cutting board, starting at the thickest part of one long side, cut a pocket horizontally into each chicken breast, stopping ¼ inch (0.5 cm) from the opposite side. Stuff each chicken breast with one-sixth of the pear mixture. Use toothpicks to close each opening.

3. In a small bowl, combine flour, salt and pepper.

4. Coat each chicken breast with the flour mixture; discard any excess mixture.

MAKE IT NOW Preheat oven to 375°F (190°C). In a large skillet, heat olive oil over medium-high heat. Add chicken, in batches as necessary, and cook for about 2 minutes on each side, until lightly golden brown. Transfer chicken to a rimmed baking sheet lined with parchment paper. Bake in preheated oven for 12 to 15 minutes or until chicken is no longer pink inside. Remove from oven and sprinkle 1 tbsp (15 mL) blue cheese over each breast; return to oven for 2 to 3 minutes, until melted. Sprinkle with additional minced pears and hazelnuts, if using; serve.

MAKE IT A FREEZER MEAL Wrap each breast individually in plastic wrap and place in a labeled gallon-size (4 L) freezer bag. Seal, removing as much air as possible, and freeze.

COOK FROM FROZEN Preheat oven to 375°F (190°C). Remove plastic wrap from breasts. In a large skillet, heat olive oil over medium-high heat. Add chicken and cook for about 2 minutes on each side, until lightly golden brown. Transfer chicken to a rimmed baking sheet lined with parchment paper. Bake in preheated oven for 30 to 35 minutes or until no longer pink inside. Remove from oven and sprinkle 1 tbsp (15 mL) blue cheese on each breast; return to oven for 2 to 3 minutes, until melted. Sprinkle with additional minced pears and hazelnuts, if using; serve.

BULK BATCH GUIDE	Servings	6 (1 batch)	12 (2 batches)	18 (3 batches)	24 (4 batches)	30 (5 batches)
	pears	1 cup (250 mL)	2 cups (500 mL)	3 cups (750 mL)	4 cups (1 L)	5 cups (1.25 L)
	Parmesan cheese	2 tbsp (30 mL)	¼ cup (60 mL)	6 tbsp (90 mL)	½ cup (125 mL)	⅔ cup (150 mL)
	blue cheese	6 tbsp + 2 tsp (100 mL)	¾ cup + 4 tsp (200 mL)	1¼ cups (310 mL)	1⅔ cups (400 mL)	2 cups + 4 tsp (520 mL)
	hazelnuts	2 tbsp (30 mL)	¼ cup (60 mL)	6 tbsp (90 mL)	½ cup (125 mL)	⅔ cup (150 mL)
	chicken breasts	6	12	18	24	30
	all-purpose flour	¼ cup (60 mL)	½ cup (125 mL)	¾ cup (175 mL)	1 cup (250 mL)	1¼ cups (310 mL)
	salt	½ tsp (2 mL)	1 tsp (5 mL)	1½ tsp (7 mL)	2 tsp (10 mL)	2½ tsp (12 mL)
	pepper	¼ tsp (1 mL)	½ tsp (2 mL)	¾ tsp (3 mL)	1 tsp (5 mL)	1¼ tsp (6 mL)
	gallon bags	1	2	3	4	5

Chicken Parmigiana

This popular Italian-American dish is well loved for a reason. Crispy chicken smothered in homemade tomato sauce and topped with bubbling provolone cheese is simply *magnifico*! I think I just died and went to Italy. Makes 8 servings.

½ cup (125 mL) grated Parmesan cheese (about 1¾ oz/50 g), divided

½ cup (125 mL) Italian-seasoned bread crumbs

⅓ cup (75 mL) all-purpose flour

¾ cup (175 mL) melted butter, divided

2 lbs/1 kg boneless, skinless chicken breasts (about 4 breasts total)

2 cups (500 mL) Red Sauce (page 334)

4 slices provolone cheese

Garnish

Chopped fresh parsley (optional)

Tip

If you're making this recipe right away, you can use a glass or ceramic baking dish.

1. Preheat oven to 450°F (230°C).

2. In a medium bowl, combine Parmesan cheese and bread crumbs.

3. Place flour in a small bowl.

4. Place ½ cup (125 mL) melted butter in a second small bowl. Spread remaining melted butter on a rimmed baking sheet lined with parchment paper.

5. With the blade of a sharp knife parallel to the cutting board, cut chicken breasts in half horizontally. Place chicken pieces between two pieces of plastic wrap and, using a mallet or heavy skillet, pound to ¼-inch (0.5 cm) thickness. You should have 8 cutlets.

6. Working with one cutlet at a time, dip in flour, turning to coat. Dip in melted butter, then into bread crumbs. Dip again in butter, then again in bread crumbs, patting gently to adhere. Place on prepared baking sheet, spacing apart.

7. Bake chicken in preheated oven for 9 minutes or until bottoms are golden brown. Flip cutlets and bake for an additional 8 to 9 minutes, until golden brown and chicken is no longer pink inside. Remove from oven.

8. Pour red sauce into a 13- by 9-inch (33 by 23 cm) metal or foil pan. Place chicken on top. Cut cheese slices in half and arrange evenly over cutlets.

MAKE IT NOW Reduce oven heat to 350°F (180°C). Bake for 15 minutes or until sauce is bubbling all over and cheese is melted and golden. Sprinkle with parsley, if using; serve.

MAKE IT A FREEZER MEAL Let chicken cool completely. Wrap the pan tightly with plastic wrap, pressing down gently to remove as much air as possible. Cover with foil. Label and freeze.

COOK FROM FROZEN Preheat oven to 350°F (180°C). Remove plastic wrap and foil. Cover pan with new foil. Bake for 1 hour. Remove foil and continue baking for 10 to 15 minutes, until chicken is no longer pink, sauce is bubbling all over and cheese is melted and golden. Sprinkle with parsley, if using; serve.

BULK BATCH GUIDE	Servings	8 (1 batch)	16 (2 batches)	24 (3 batches)	32 (4 batches)	40 (5 batches)
	Parmesan cheese	½ cup (125 mL)	1 cup (250 mL)	1½ cups (375 mL)	2 cups (500 mL)	2½ cups (625 mL)
	Italian bread crumbs	½ cup (125 mL)	1 cup (250 mL)	1½ cups (375 mL)	2 cups (500 mL)	2½ cups (625 mL)
	all-purpose flour	⅓ cup (75 mL)	⅔ cup (150 mL)	1 cup (250 mL)	1⅓ cups (325 mL)	1⅔ cups (400 mL)
	butter	¾ cup (175 mL)	1½ cups (375 mL)	2¼ cups (560 mL)	3 cups (750 mL)	3¾ cups (925 mL)
	chicken breasts	2 lbs (1 kg)	4 lbs (2 kg)	6 lbs (3 kg)	8 lbs (4 kg)	10 lbs (5 kg)
	Red Sauce	2 cups (500 mL)	4 cups (1 L)	6 cups (1.5 L)	8 cups (2 L)	10 cups (2.5 L)
	provolone cheese slices	4	8	12	16	20
	13x9 pans	1	2	3	4	5

Herbes de Provence Chicken

In just minutes you can prepare a savory French-inspired freezer meal that is healthy and lovely to set in the center of your family dinner table. I like to serve this recipe with Wild Rice Pilaf (page 299), freshly cooked asparagus and buttered crusty bread. Makes 6 servings.

1 tbsp (15 mL) red wine vinegar

1 tbsp (15 mL) olive oil

½ tsp (2 mL) freshly squeezed lemon juice

½ tsp (2 mL) minced garlic

2 tsp (10 mL) Dijon mustard

1½ tsp (7 mL) herbes de Provence

1 tsp (5 mL) salt

¼ tsp (1 mL) freshly ground black pepper

6 bone-in, skin-on chicken thighs (each about 6 oz/175 g)

1 onion, thinly sliced

1. In a medium bowl, combine red wine vinegar, olive oil, lemon juice, garlic, mustard, herbes de Provence, salt and pepper. Add chicken thighs and stir to coat completely.

2. Place onion slices on the bottom of a 13- by 9-inch (33 by 23 cm) baking dish. Place chicken thighs, skin side up, on top of onion slices, spacing apart. Pour marinade overtop.

MAKE IT NOW Preheat oven to 375°F (190°C). Bake in preheated oven for 50 minutes or until juices run clear when chicken is pierced.

MAKE IT A FREEZER MEAL Wrap the baking dish tightly with plastic wrap, pressing down gently to remove air. Cover with foil. Label and freeze.

THAW AND COOK Place baking dish in the refrigerator for at least 24 hours or up to 48 hours to thaw. Remove plastic wrap and foil. Preheat oven to 375°F (190°C). Bake in preheated oven for 50 minutes or until juices run clear when chicken is pierced.

BULK BATCH GUIDE — Servings	6 (1 batch)	12 (2 batches)	18 (3 batches)	24 (4 batches)	30 (5 batches)
red wine vinegar	1 tbsp (15 mL)	2 tbsp (30 mL)	3 tbsp (45 mL)	¼ cup (60 mL)	⅓ cup (75 mL)
olive oil	1 tbsp (15 mL)	2 tbsp (30 mL)	3 tbsp (45 mL)	¼ cup (60 mL)	⅓ cup (75 mL)
lemon juice	½ tsp (2 mL)	1 tsp (5 mL)	1½ tsp (7 mL)	2 tsp (10 mL)	2½ tsp (12 mL)
garlic	½ tsp (2 mL)	1 tsp (5 mL)	1½ tsp (7 mL)	2 tsp (10 mL)	2½ tsp (12 mL)
Dijon mustard	2 tsp (10 mL)	4 tsp (20 mL)	2 tbsp (30 mL)	8 tsp (40 mL)	10 tsp (50 mL)
herbes de Provence	1½ tsp (7 mL)	1 tbsp (15 mL)	1½ tbsp (22 mL)	2 tbsp (30 mL)	2½ tbsp (37 mL)
salt	1 tsp (5 mL)	2 tsp (10 mL)	1 tbsp (15 mL)	4 tsp (20 mL)	5 tsp (25 mL)
pepper	¼ tsp (1 mL)	½ tsp (2 mL)	¾ tsp (3 mL)	1 tsp (5 mL)	1¼ tsp (6 mL)
chicken thighs	6	12	18	24	30
onions	1	2	3	4	5
13x9 dishes	1	2	3	4	5

Honey Lime Chicken

Honey lime chicken is a family favorite around these parts, and one of the few dishes that I know my youngest child will eat. Every. Single. Time. Maybe it's the delicate citrus tang of the sauce, or perhaps it's the perfectly tender chicken paired with the bright pop of pineapple, but either way, he loves it, and that's good enough for me! *Makes 6 servings.*

2 lbs (1 kg) boneless, skinless chicken breasts, diced

1 tsp (5 mL) garlic salt

1 can (20 oz/600 mL) pineapple tidbits, with juice

1 tbsp (15 mL) vegetable oil

¼ cup (60 mL) honey

3 tbsp (45 mL) freshly squeezed lime juice

1½ tbsp (22 mL) tamari sauce

2½ tsp (12 mL) cornstarch

1. In a bowl, sprinkle diced chicken breasts with garlic salt; toss to combine. Set aside.

2. Drain pineapple juice into a small bowl; set aside.

3. In a large skillet, heat vegetable oil over medium-high heat until shimmering. Add chicken and cook for 4 to 5 minutes, stirring constantly, until edges are golden brown and chicken is no longer pink inside. Add 1/4 cup (60 mL) pineapple juice. Immediately reduce heat to low, cover and simmer for 4 to 5 minutes, until most of the juice has been absorbed.

4. In a small bowl, whisk together remaining pineapple juice, honey, lime juice, tamari sauce and cornstarch, until smooth. Pour over chicken in skillet; cook, stirring constantly, for about 1 minute, until sauce has thickened. Add pineapple tidbits to skillet; heat for about 1 minute, stirring, until warm. Remove from heat and serve.

MAKE IT A FREEZER MEAL Let cool completely. Place chicken and pineapple sauce in a labeled gallon-size (4 L) freezer bag. Seal, removing as much air as possible, and freeze.

REHEAT Place bag in the refrigerator for at least 12 hours or up to 24 hours to thaw, or run lukewarm water over bag until you can break the food apart slightly. Heat a large skillet over medium-high heat. Add chicken and heat for about 4 to 5 minutes, stirring constantly, until heated through.

Servings	6 (1 batch)	12 (2 batches)	18 (3 batches)	24 (4 batches)	30 (5 batches)
chicken breasts	2 lbs (1 kg)	4 lbs (2 kg)	6 lbs (3 kg)	8 lbs (4 kg)	10 lbs (5 kg)
garlic salt	1 tsp (5 mL)	2 tsp (10 mL)	1 tbsp (15 mL)	4 tsp (20 mL)	5 tsp (25 mL)
pineapple tidbits	20 oz (600 mL)	40 oz (1.2 L)	60 oz (1.8 L)	80 oz (2.4 L)	100 oz (3 L)
vegetable oil	1 tbsp (15 mL)	2 tbsp (30 mL)	3 tbsp (45 mL)	¼ cup (60 mL)	⅓ cup (75 mL)
honey	¼ cup (60 mL)	½ cup (125 mL)	¾ cup (175 mL)	1 cup (250 mL)	1¼ cups (310 mL)
lime juice	3 tbsp (45 mL)	6 tbsp (90 mL)	9 tbsp (135 mL)	¾ cup (175 mL)	¾ cup + 3 tbsp (220 mL)
tamari sauce	1½ tbsp (22 mL)	3 tbsp (45 mL)	4½ tbsp (67 mL)	6 tbsp (90 mL)	7½ tbsp (112 mL)
cornstarch	2½ tsp (12 mL)	5 tsp (25 mL)	2½ tbsp (37 mL)	10 tsp (50 mL)	¼ cup (60 mL)
gallon bags	1	2	3	4	5

BULK BATCH GUIDE

Lemon Tarragon Chicken

The bold, enticing flavors of lemon, tarragon and garlic will waft their way through your house as this dish bakes in the oven. It's one of the easiest and most refreshing freezer meals in this book. I love to serve this with my Wild Rice Pilaf (page 299) and steamed Brussels sprouts. Makes 8 servings.

2 lbs (1 kg) boneless, skinless chicken breasts (about 4 breasts total)

½ tsp (2 mL) garlic salt

1 cup (250 mL) chicken broth or Homemade Chicken Stock (page 349)

¼ cup (60 mL) freshly squeezed lemon juice

1 tbsp (15 mL) honey

1 tbsp (15 mL) cornstarch

1 tsp (5 mL) minced garlic

2 tsp (10 mL) dried tarragon

1 tbsp (15 mL) melted butter

1 tbsp (15 mL) olive oil or butter

1 lemon, thinly sliced (optional)

Garnish

Fresh tarragon (optional)

1. With the blade of a sharp knife parallel to the cutting board, cut chicken breasts in half horizontally. Place chicken pieces between two pieces of plastic wrap and, using a mallet or heavy skillet, pound to ¼-inch (0.5 cm) thickness. You should end up with 8 cutlets.

2. Sprinkle both sides of chicken cutlets with garlic salt.

3. In a small bowl, whisk together chicken broth, lemon juice, honey, cornstarch, garlic, dried tarragon and melted butter. Set aside.

MAKE IT NOW Preheat oven to 350°F (180°C). In a large skillet, heat olive oil over medium-high heat. Add chicken, in batches, and cook for about 2 minutes on each side, until lightly golden brown. Transfer chicken to a 13- by 9-inch (33 by 23 cm) baking dish, overlapping as necessary, and pour lemon sauce overtop. Arrange lemon slices over chicken, if using. Cover with foil and bake for 20 to 25 minutes, until sauce is slightly thickened and chicken is no longer pink inside. Let stand for 5 minutes, then serve garnished with fresh tarragon, if using.

MAKE IT A FREEZER MEAL Place chicken cutlets in a labeled gallon-size (4 L) freezer bag. Place lemon sauce in a quart-size (1 L) freezer bag. Seal bag, removing as much air as possible. Place sliced lemon, if using, in another quart-size (1 L) freezer bag; seal. Place lemon sauce and sliced lemon in gallon bag with chicken. Seal together as a kit and freeze.

THAW AND COOK Place bags in the refrigerator for at least 12 hours or up to 24 hours to thaw. Preheat oven to 350°F (180°C). In a large skillet, heat olive oil over medium-high heat. Add chicken, in batches, and cook for about 2 minutes on each side, until lightly golden brown. Transfer chicken to a 13- by 9-inch (33 by 23 cm) baking dish, overlapping as necessary. Gently whisk bag contents to combine lemon sauce, then pour overtop. Arrange lemon slices over chicken, if using. Cover with foil and bake for 20 to 25 minutes, until sauce is slightly thickened and chicken is no longer pink inside. Let stand for 5 minutes, then serve garnished with fresh tarragon, if using.

Servings	8 (1 batch)	16 (2 batches)	24 (3 batches)	32 (4 batches)	40 (5 batches)
chicken breast	2 lbs (1 kg)	4 lbs (2 kg)	6 lbs (3 kg)	8 lbs (4 kg)	10 lbs (5 kg)
garlic salt	½ tsp (2 mL)	1 tsp (5 mL)	1½ tsp (7 mL)	2 tsp (10 mL)	2½ tsp (12 mL)
chicken broth	1 cup (250 mL)	2 cups (500 mL)	3 cups (750 mL)	4 cups (1 L)	5 cups (1.25 L)
lemon juice	¼ cup (60 mL)	½ cup (125 mL)	¾ cup (175 mL)	1 cup (250 mL)	1¼ cups (310 mL)
honey	1 tbsp (15 mL)	2 tbsp (30 mL)	3 tbsp (45 mL)	¼ cup (60 mL)	⅓ cup (75 mL)
cornstarch	1 tbsp (15 mL)	2 tbsp (30 mL)	3 tbsp (45 mL)	¼ cup (60 mL)	⅓ cup (75 mL)
garlic	1 tsp (5 mL)	2 tsp (10 mL)	1 tbsp (15 mL)	4 tsp (20 mL)	5 tsp (25 mL)
dried tarragon	2 tsp (10 mL)	4 tsp (20 mL)	2 tbsp (30 mL)	8 tsp (40 mL)	10 tsp (50 mL)
butter	1 tbsp (15 mL)	2 tbsp (30 mL)	3 tbsp (45 mL)	¼ cup (60 mL)	⅓ cup (75 mL)
olive oil or butter	1 tbsp (15 mL)	2 tbsp (30 mL)	3 tbsp (45 mL)	¼ cup (60 mL)	⅓ cup (75 mL)
lemons	1	2	3	4	5
gallon bags	1	2	3	4	5
quart bags	2	4	6	8	10

BULK BATCH GUIDE

Maple Dijon Chicken

Sounds strange, right? Who would have thought that maple and mustard would go together, but believe you me it does. The Dijon mustard has an almost nutty, spicy bite that is somehow tamed but not muted by the sweet natural perfection that is maple syrup. I love serving this slow-cooked chicken with buttery mashed potatoes (page 292) and steamed carrots. Makes 6 servings.

2 lbs (1 kg) boneless, skinless chicken tenders

1 cup (250 mL) Dijon mustard

¼ cup (60 mL) pure maple syrup

2 tbsp (30 mL) unseasoned rice vinegar

½ tsp (2 mL) dried rosemary

Salt and freshly ground black pepper

1. In a large bowl, combine chicken, Dijon mustard, maple syrup, rice vinegar and rosemary. Season with salt and pepper.

MAKE IT NOW Transfer chicken to a large (approx. 5 quart) slow cooker. Cook on Low for 4 to 6 hours or on High for 3 to 4 hours, until chicken is tender and no longer pink inside. Serve.

MAKE IT A FREEZER MEAL Place chicken mixture in a labeled gallon-size (4 L) freezer bag. Seal, removing as much air as possible, and freeze.

THAW AND COOK Place bag in the refrigerator for at least 12 hours or up to 24 hours to thaw. Transfer chicken mixture to a large (approx. 5 quart) slow cooker. Cook on Low for 4 to 6 hours or on High for 3 to 4 hours, until chicken is tender and no longer pink inside. Serve.

BULK BATCH	Servings	6 (1 batch)	12 (2 batches)	18 (3 batches)	24 (4 batches)	30 (5 batches)
	chicken tenders	2 lbs (1 kg)	4 lbs (2 kg)	6 lbs (3 kg)	8 lbs (4 kg)	10 lbs (5 kg)
	Dijon mustard	1 cup (250 mL)	2 cups (500 mL)	3 cups (750 mL)	4 cups (1 L)	5 cups (1.25 L)
	maple syrup	¼ cup (60 mL)	½ cup (125 mL)	¾ cup (175 mL)	1 cup (250 mL)	1¼ cups (310 mL)
	rice vinegar	2 tbsp (30 mL)	¼ cup (60 mL)	6 tbsp (90 mL)	½ cup (125 mL)	⅔ cup (150 mL)
	dried rosemary	½ tsp (2 mL)	1 tsp (5 mL)	1½ tsp (7 mL)	2 tsp (10 mL)	2½ tsp (12 mL)
	gallon bags	1	2	3	4	5

Smoky Grilled Louisiana Turkey Legs

Who says you have to go all the way to Louisiana to get fall-apart, smoky and fragrant grilled turkey legs? All you need is this recipe, which will give you all the flavors of turkey legs slow-smoked on a hot grill without ever having to leave your hometown. Makes 4 servings.

4 turkey legs

1 cup (250 mL) chicken broth or Homemade Chicken Stock (page 349)

¼ cup (60 mL) freshly squeezed lime juice

2 tsp (10 mL) liquid smoke

¼ cup (60 mL) diced onion

1 tsp (5 mL) minced garlic

1 tsp (5 mL) dried oregano

1 tsp (5 mL) salt

½ tsp (2 mL) paprika

¼ tsp (1 mL) dried thyme

¼ tsp (1 mL) cayenne pepper

2 tsp (10 mL) Creole seasoning (optional, spicy)

1. Place turkey legs in a gallon-size (4 L) freezer bag. Add chicken broth, lime juice, liquid smoke, onion, garlic, oregano, salt, paprika, thyme, cayenne and Creole seasoning, if using. Seal bag, shake, and then reseal, removing as much air as possible.

MAKE IT NOW Place bag in refrigerator and marinate for a minimum of 4 hours or up to 24 hours. Preheat a greased barbecue grill to High. Place turkey legs on grill over indirect heat and close lid. Discard marinade. Cook for 40 to 50 minutes, turning every 10 minutes, until golden and tender and internal temperature registers 180°F (90°C). Serve hot.

MAKE IT A FREEZER MEAL Label bag containing turkey legs and marinade and freeze.

THAW AND COOK Place bag in the refrigerator for at least 24 hours or up to 48 hours to thaw. Preheat a greased barbecue grill to High. Place turkey legs on grill over indirect heat and close lid. Discard marinade. Cook for 40 to 50 minutes, turning every 10 minutes, until golden and tender and internal temperature registers 180°F (90°C). Serve hot.

Tip

If you don't have a grill you can place the turkey legs in a large (approx. 5 quart) slow cooker (discard marinade) and cook on High for 3 to 4 hours or on Low for 6 to 8 hours. Then place legs on a baking sheet under the broiler and broil for 3 to 5 minutes, turning halfway, until skin is crisp and a few places begin to char. Serve hot.

BULK BATCH GUIDE	Servings	4 (1 batch)	8 (2 batches)	12 (3 batches)	16 (4 batches)	20 (5 batches)
	turkey legs	4	8	12	16	20
	chicken broth	1 cup (250 mL)	2 cups (500 mL)	3 cups (750 mL)	4 cups (1 L)	5 cups (1.25 L)
	lime juice	¼ cup (60 mL)	½ cup (125 mL)	¾ cup (175 mL)	1 cup (250 mL)	1¼ cups (310 mL)
	liquid smoke	2 tsp (10 mL)	4 tsp (20 mL)	2 tbsp (30 mL)	8 tsp (40 mL)	10 tsp (50 mL)
	onion	¼ cup (60 mL)	½ cup (125 mL)	¾ cup (175 mL)	1 cup (250 mL)	1¼ cups (310 mL)
	garlic	1 tsp (5 mL)	2 tsp (10 mL)	1 tbsp (15 mL)	4 tsp (20 mL)	5 tsp (25 mL)
	oregano	1 tsp (5 mL)	2 tsp (10 mL)	1 tbsp (15 mL)	4 tsp (20 mL)	5 tsp (25 mL)
	salt	1 tsp (5 mL)	2 tsp (10 mL)	1 tbsp (15 mL)	4 tsp (20 mL)	5 tsp (25 mL)
	paprika	½ tsp (2 mL)	1 tsp (5 mL)	1½ tsp (7 mL)	2 tsp (10 mL)	2½ tsp (12 mL)
	dried thyme	¼ tsp (1 mL)	½ tsp (2 mL)	¾ tsp (3 mL)	1 tsp (5 mL)	1¼ tsp (6 mL)
	cayenne pepper	¼ tsp (1 mL)	½ tsp (2 mL)	¾ tsp (3 mL)	1 tsp (5 mL)	1¼ tsp (6 mL)
	Creole seasoning	2 tsp (10 mL)	4 tsp (20 mL)	2 tbsp (30 mL)	8 tsp (40 mL)	10 tsp (50 mL)
	gallon bags	1	2	3	4	5

Broccoli Chicken Alfredo Bake

When I want to feel like Supermom, I make a bunch of these beautiful bakes ahead of time to pull out on those crazy-busy nights. These babies are delicious, comforting and full of healthy broccoli, which makes my mama heart happy when my kids happily finish their plates. It's win-win all around.
Makes 6 servings.

1 batch Alfredo Sauce (page 333)

2 cups (500 mL) whole milk or half-and-half (10%) cream

1 lb (500 g) fusilli pasta

1 package (1 lb/500 g) frozen broccoli florets

2 cups (500 mL) shredded cooked chicken breast (see page 29)

Salt and freshly ground black pepper

1 cup (250 mL) freshly grated Parmesan cheese (about 3½ oz/100 g)

Tip
If you're making this recipe right away, you can use a glass or ceramic baking dish.

1. In a large bowl, combine Alfredo sauce and milk. Set aside.

2. Fill a large stockpot with water and bring to a boil over high heat. Add fusilli and cook for 5 to 6 minutes, stirring occasionally, until just beginning to get soft (the pasta should be starting to get tender but have a firm bite). Drain and rinse with cold water to cool quickly.

3. Pour drained pasta into sauce mixture; add broccoli and chicken. Stir to combine. Season to taste with salt and pepper. Pour mixture into a 13- by 9-inch (33 by 23 cm) metal or foil pan. Sprinkle Parmesan cheese overtop.

MAKE IT NOW Preheat oven to 350°F (180°C). Bake in preheated oven for 30 to 40 minutes, until sauce is bubbling all over and topping is golden brown.

MAKE IT A FREEZER MEAL Wrap the pan tightly with plastic wrap, pressing down gently to remove air. Cover with foil. Label and freeze.

THAW AND COOK Place pan in the refrigerator for at least 12 hours or up to 24 hours to thaw. Preheat oven to 350°F (180°C). Remove plastic wrap and foil. Bake in preheated oven for 40 to 50 minutes, until sauce is bubbling all over and topping is golden brown. (You can also cook from frozen: Remove foil and plastic wrap and cover with new foil. Bake for 1 hour. Remove foil and bake for an additional 15 to 20 minutes or until bubbling all over and top is slightly golden brown.)

BULK BATCH GUIDE	Servings	6 (1 batch)	12 (2 batches)	18 (3 batches)	24 (4 batches)	30 (5 batches)
	Alfredo Sauce	1 batch	2 batches	3 batches	4 batches	5 batches
	whole milk	2 cups (500 mL)	4 cups (1 L)	6 cups (1.5 L)	8 cups (2 L)	10 cups (2.5 L)
	fusilli	1 lb (500 g)	2 lbs (1 kg)	3 lbs (1.5 kg)	4 lbs (2 kg)	5 lbs (2.5 kg)
	broccoli	1 lb (500 g)	2 lbs (1 kg)	3 lbs (1.5 kg)	4 lbs (2 kg)	5 lbs (2.5 kg)
	cooked chicken	2 cups (500 mL)	4 cups (1 L)	6 cups (1.5 L)	8 cups (2 L)	10 cups (2.5 L)
	Parmesan cheese	1 cup (250 mL)	2 cups (500 mL)	3 cups (750 mL)	4 cups (1 L)	5 cups (1.25 L)
	13x9 pans	1	2	3	4	5

Chicken Pesto Parmesan Shells

I truly can't get enough of the nutty, bright, fresh taste of pesto, and this dish sure has it in spades! Each shell is stuffed with delectable cheeses, chicken and, of course, pesto. Then they are topped with a luscious, rich Alfredo sauce that makes you wonder why store-bought Alfredo even exists! Makes 6 servings.

Topping

¼ cup (60 mL) panko bread crumbs

¼ cup (60 mL) freshly grated Parmesan cheese

½ tsp (2 mL) seasoned salt

Chicken Parmesan Shells

1 batch Alfredo Sauce (page 333)

1 cup (250 mL) milk

30 jumbo pasta shells (about 9 oz/255 g)

8 oz (250 g) cream cheese, softened

3 cups (750 mL) shredded cooked chicken breast (see page 29)

1½ cups (375 mL) freshly grated Parmesan cheese (about 5¼ oz/167 g)

½ cup (125 mL) Easy Pesto (page 339)

1½ tsp (7 mL) minced garlic

Salt and freshly ground black pepper to taste

Tip

If you're making this recipe right away, you can use a glass or ceramic baking dish.

1. *Topping:* In a small bowl, combine panko crumbs, Parmesan cheese and seasoned salt; set aside.

2. *Chicken Parmesan Shells:* In a large bowl, combine Alfredo sauce and milk. Pour into a lightly greased 13- by 9-inch (33 by 23 cm) metal or foil pan and spread evenly.

3. Fill a large stockpot with water and bring to a boil over high heat. Add shells and cook for 5 to 6 minutes, stirring occasionally, until just beginning to get soft (the pasta should be starting to get tender but have a firm bite). Drain and rinse with cold water to cool quickly.

4. In a large bowl, combine cream cheese, chicken, Parmesan cheese, pesto and garlic. Fill each of the shells with mixture and place, open side up, in pan. After filling all the shells, gently turn over each to coat with sauce, then flip back over so open sides face up. Sprinkle crumb topping evenly overtop.

MAKE IT NOW Preheat oven to 400°F (200°C). Bake in preheated oven for about 25 to 30 minutes, until sauce is bubbling all over and topping is golden brown.

MAKE IT A FREEZER MEAL Wrap the pan tightly with plastic wrap, pressing down gently to remove air. Cover with foil. Label and freeze.

THAW AND COOK Place pan in the refrigerator for at least 12 hours or up to 24 hours to thaw. Preheat oven to 400°F (200°C). Remove plastic wrap and foil. Cover with new foil. Bake in preheated oven for 30 minutes, until bubbling all over. Remove foil and bake for an additional 5 to 10 minutes, until topping is golden brown. (You can also cook from frozen: Remove plastic wrap and foil and cover with new foil. Bake for 50 minutes, until bubbling all over. Remove foil and continue baking for 5 to 10 minutes, until topping is golden brown.)

BULK BATCH GUIDE Servings	6 (1 batch)	12 (2 batches)	18 (3 batches)	24 (4 batches)	30 (5 batches)
panko	¼ cup (60 mL)	½ cup (125 mL)	¾ cup (175 mL)	1 cup (250 mL)	1¼ cups (310 mL)
Parmesan cheese	¼ cup (60 mL)	½ cup (125 mL)	¾ cup (175 mL)	1 cup (250 mL)	1¼ cups (310 mL)
seasoned salt	½ tsp (2 mL)	1 tsp (5 mL)	1½ tsp (7 mL)	2 tsp (10 mL)	2½ tsp (12 mL)
Alfredo Sauce	1 batch	2 batches	3 batches	4 batches	5 batches
milk	1 cup (250 mL)	2 cups (500 mL)	3 cups (750 mL)	4 cups (1 L)	5 cups (1.25 L)
jumbo pasta shells	30	60	90	120	150
cream cheese	8 oz (250 g)	1 lb (500 g)	1½ lbs (750 g)	2 lbs (1 kg)	2½ lbs (1.25 kg)
cooked chicken	3 cups (750 mL)	6 cups (1.5 L)	9 cups (2.25 L)	12 cups (3 L)	15 cups (3.75 L)
Parmesan cheese	1½ cups (375 mL)	3 cups (750 mL)	4½ cups (1.125 L)	6 cups (1.5 L)	7½ cups (1.875 L)
Easy Pesto	½ cup (125 mL)	1 cup (250 mL)	1½ cups (375 mL)	2 cups (500 mL)	2½ cups (625 mL)
garlic	1½ tsp (7 mL)	1 tbsp (15 mL)	1½ tbsp (22 mL)	2 tbsp (30 mL)	2½ tbsp (37 mL)
13x9 pans	1	2	3	4	5

Old-Fashioned Chicken Pot Pie

"Rustic perfection" may be an understatement when talking about this dish. Every bite is filled with moist chicken, hearty veggies and all the delicate, creamy delight you crave when you think of traditional chicken pot pie. It sorta makes me wanna throw on some cowboy boots and yell, "Yee-haw!" Makes 8 servings.

2 batches White Sauce (page 336), cooled

¼ tsp (1 mL) poultry seasoning

1 tbsp (15 mL) dried parsley

1 tsp (5 mL) celery salt

1 tsp (5 mL) onion powder

½ cup (125 mL) heavy or whipping (35%) cream

Salt and freshly ground black pepper

5 cups (1.25 L) frozen diced hash browns (about 20 oz/565 g)

4 cups (1 L) chopped cooked chicken (see page 29)

2 cups (500 mL) frozen peas and carrots (about 12 oz/375 g)

1 batch Pie Crust (page 331) or 2 store-bought pie crusts

Garnish

Fresh thyme sprigs (optional)

1. In a large bowl, combine white sauce, poultry seasoning, parsley, celery salt and onion powder. Add cream; stir gently to combine. Add salt and pepper to taste. Add hash browns, chicken and peas and carrots; stir gently to combine. Pour into two 10-inch (25 cm) metal or foil deep-dish pie plates.

2. Place pie crusts over tops of pies. Cut away excess dough, leaving a ¾-inch (2 cm) overhang. Fold overhanging dough under itself and, using the tines of a fork, press all along the edges or flute with your fingers.

MAKE IT NOW Preheat oven to 375°F (190°C). Make several slits in the tops of the pies to allow steam to escape. Place on a large rimmed baking sheet and bake in preheated oven for 45 minutes, until tops are golden and filling is bubbly. (If crust starts to brown too quickly during baking, cover it loosely with foil.) Let cool for 15 minutes. Place thyme sprigs on tops of pies, if using. Serve.

MAKE IT A FREEZER MEAL Wrap unbaked pies tightly with several layers of plastic wrap. Cover with foil. Label and freeze.

COOK FROM FROZEN Preheat oven to 375°F (190°C). Remove foil and plastic wrap. Make several slits in the tops of the pies to allow steam to escape. Place on a large rimmed baking sheet and bake in preheated oven for 1 hour and 30 minutes, until tops are golden and insides are bubbly. (If crust starts to brown too quickly during baking, cover it loosely with foil.) Let cool for 15 minutes. Place thyme sprigs on tops of pies, if using. Serve.

> HELPFUL TIPS: You can use one 13- by 9-inch (33 by 23 cm) metal or foil pan or 6 mini (5-inch/1.25 cm) soup crocks instead of 2 pie plates for this recipe.
>
> Instead of using frozen diced hash browns, use cooked and cooled diced potatoes instead.

BULK BATCH GUIDE	Servings	8 (1 batch)	16 (2 batches)	24 (3 batches)	32 (4 batches)	40 (5 batches)
	White Sauce	2 batches	4 batches	6 batches	8 batches	10 batches
	poultry seasoning	¼ tsp (1 mL)	½ tsp (2 mL)	¾ tsp (3 mL)	1 tsp (5 mL)	1¼ tsp (6 mL)
	dried parsley	1 tbsp (15 mL)	2 tbsp (30 mL)	3 tbsp (45 mL)	¼ cup (60 mL)	⅓ cup (75 mL)
	celery salt	1 tsp (5 mL)	2 tsp (10 mL)	1 tbsp (15 mL)	4 tsp (20 mL)	5 tsp (25 mL)
	onion powder	1 tsp (5 mL)	2 tsp (10 mL)	1 tbsp (15 mL)	4 tsp (20 mL)	5 tsp (25 mL)
	cream	½ cup (125 mL)	1 cup (250 mL)	1½ cups (375 mL)	2 cups (500 mL)	2½ cups (625 mL)
	hash browns	5 cups (1.25 L)	10 cups (2.5 L)	15 cups (3.75 L)	20 cups (5 L)	25 cups (6.25 L)
	cooked chicken	4 cups (1 L)	8 cups (2 L)	12 cups (3 L)	16 cups (4 L)	20 cups (5 L)
	peas and carrots	2 cups (500 mL)	4 cups (1 L)	6 cups (1.5 L)	8 cups (2 L)	10 cups (2.5 L)
	Pie Crust	1 batch	2 batches	3 batches	4 batches	5 batches
	10-inch pie plates	2	4	6	8	10

Cilantro Lime Chicken Tacos

Yes, friends, these tacos are unique — and green! They're made with shredded chicken that has been blended with fresh cilantro, refreshing lime juice and savory Parmesan cheese. You may find yourself eating two, three or even five. Meh, who's counting anyway? Makes 6 servings.

⅓ cup (75 mL) chicken broth or Homemade Chicken Stock (page 349)

2½ tbsp (37 mL) olive oil

2 tbsp (30 mL) minced garlic

2 tsp (10 mL) freshly squeezed lime juice

½ cup (125 mL) freshly grated Parmesan cheese (about 1¾ oz/50 g)

2 tbsp (30 mL) sliced almonds (optional)

1 tsp (5 mL) salt

1 cup (250 mL) fresh cilantro leaves

3 cups (750 mL) shredded cooked chicken breast (see page 29)

To Serve
12 corn tortillas (6 inches/15 cm), warmed

½ cup (125 mL) crumbled queso fresco (optional)

Chopped fresh cilantro (optional)

Lime wedges (optional)

1. In a blender or food processor, combine chicken broth, olive oil, garlic, lime juice, Parmesan cheese, almonds, if using, and salt; pulse until a coarse paste forms. Add cilantro and pulse 3 to 4 times, until leaves are broken up but paste is still chunky.

2. Place chicken in a medium bowl. Pour in cilantro mixture and stir until combined.

MAKE IT NOW In a medium skillet, heat chicken-and-cilantro mixture over medium heat, stirring occasionally, for about 3 to 4 minutes. Remove from heat, cover and set aside. In a small, dry, nonstick skillet over medium heat, heat tortillas for about 30 seconds on each side, until warmed through. (Or, using tongs, char the tortillas directly over a gas stove flame for a few seconds on each side.) Spoon chicken onto tortillas, then add red cabbage, queso fresco and cilantro, if using. Serve with lime wedges to squeeze over tacos, if desired.

MAKE IT A FREEZER MEAL Place chicken-and-cilantro mixture in a gallon-size (4 L) freezer bag. Seal, removing as much air as possible, and freeze.

REHEAT Place bag in the refrigerator for at least 12 hours or up to 24 hours to thaw. In a medium skillet, heat bag contents over medium heat, stirring occasionally, for about 3 to 4 minutes. Remove from heat, cover and set aside. In a small, dry, nonstick skillet over medium heat, heat tortillas for about 30 seconds on each side, until warmed through. (Or, using tongs, char the tortillas directly over a gas stove flame for a few seconds on each side.) Spoon chicken onto tortillas, then add queso fresco and cilantro, if using. Serve with lime wedges to squeeze over tacos, if desired.

Servings	6 (1 batch)	12 (2 batches)	18 (3 batches)	24 (4 batches)	30 (5 batches)
chicken broth	⅓ cup (75 mL)	⅔ cup (150 mL)	1 cup (250 mL)	1⅓ cups (325 mL)	1⅔ cups (400 mL)
olive oil	2½ tbsp (37 mL)	⅓ cup (75 mL)	½ cup (125 mL)	⅔ cup (150 mL)	¾ cup + 1½ tsp (182 mL)
garlic	2 tbsp (30 mL)	¼ cup (60 mL)	6 tbsp (90 mL)	½ cup (125 mL)	⅔ cup (150 mL)
lime juice	2 tsp (10 mL)	4 tsp (20 mL)	2 tbsp (30 mL)	8 tsp (40 mL)	10 tsp (50 mL)
Parmesan cheese	½ cup (125 mL)	1 cup (250 mL)	1½ cups (375 mL)	2 cups (500 mL)	2½ cups (625 mL)
sliced almonds	2 tbsp (30 mL)	¼ cup (60 mL)	6 tbsp (90 mL)	½ cup (125 mL)	⅔ cup (150 mL)
salt	1 tsp (5 mL)	2 tsp (10 mL)	1 tbsp (15 mL)	4 tsp (20 mL)	5 tsp (25 mL)
cilantro	1 cup (250 mL)	2 cups (500 mL)	3 cups (750 mL)	4 cups (1 L)	5 cups (1.25 L)
cooked chicken	3 cups (750 mL)	6 cups (1.5 L)	9 cups (2.25 L)	12 cups (3 L)	15 cups (3.75 L)
gallon bags	1	2	3	4	5

BULK BATCH GUIDE

Killer Chicken Enchiladas

Once you dig into these enchiladas, you will toss every other enchilada recipe out the window — guaranteed! Not only does my enchilada sauce have a special yet mild kick to it, I have found the absolute best way to ensure no soggy tortillas in your enchiladas, ever again! This recipe, inspired by my brother Jordan, kills it every time. Makes 6 servings.

2 cups (500 mL) shredded cooked chicken breast (see page 29)

2 cups (500 mL) shredded Monterey Jack cheese (about 8 oz/ 250 g), divided

1 batch Enchilada Sauce (page 346), cooled, divided

9 corn tortillas (8 inches/20 cm)

Cooking spray or 1 tsp (5 mL) olive oil

Garnishes

Crumbled queso fresco (optional)

Chopped fresh cilantro (optional)

Avocado slices (optional)

Tip

If you're making this recipe right away, you can use a glass or ceramic baking dish.

1. Preheat oven to 300°F (150°C).

2. In a medium bowl, combine chicken, ¼ cup (60 mL) Monterey Jack cheese and ¼ cup (60 mL) enchilada sauce.

3. Spray tortillas on both sides with cooking spray or brush with olive oil. Place in a single layer on 2 baking sheets lined with parchment paper. Bake in preheated oven for 3 to 4 minutes, or until soft and workable.

4. Spoon about ¼ cup (60 mL) chicken mixture into center of each tortilla and roll up tightly. Place seam side down, in a single layer, in a greased 13- by 9-inch (33 by 23 cm) metal or foil pan.

MAKE IT NOW Increase oven temperature to 400°F (200°C). Bake enchiladas for 10 to 15 minutes or until tops are lightly golden. Pour remaining enchilada sauce over enchiladas, sprinkle with remaining Monterey Jack cheese and cover with lightly greased foil. Bake for about 15 to 20 minutes longer, until sauce is bubbly and cheese on top is melted. Remove from oven and serve on individual plates. Sprinkle with queso fresco, cilantro and avocado slices, if using.

MAKE IT A FREEZER MEAL Wrap the pan tightly with plastic wrap, pressing down gently to remove air. Cover with foil. Pour remaining enchilada sauce into a quart-size (1 L) freezer bag. Seal, removing as much air as possible, and place on top of plastic-wrapped pan. Place remaining shredded Monterey Jack cheese in another quart-size (1 L) freezer bag. Seal, removing as much air as possible, and place on top of pan. Cover everything with foil, label and freeze.

COOK FROM FROZEN Preheat oven to 400°F (200°C). Remove foil, sauce bag, cheese bag and plastic wrap. Spray tops of enchiladas with cooking spray or brush with olive oil. Bake in preheated oven for 10 to 15 minutes or until lightly golden. Meanwhile, run hot water over bag of enchilada sauce until it is broken up enough to pour into a microwave-safe bowl. Microwave on High for 1 to 2 minutes, until all frozen chunks are melted and sauce is warmed through. Remove pan from oven and pour sauce overtop. Gently break up frozen shredded cheese and sprinkle overtop. Cover with lightly greased foil. Bake for about 20 to 25 minutes longer, until sauce is bubbly and cheese on top is melted. Remove from oven and serve on individual plates. Sprinkle with queso fresco, cilantro and avocado slices, if using.

	Servings	6 (1 batch)	12 (2 batches)	18 (3 batches)	24 (4 batches)	30 (5 batches)
BULK BATCH	cooked chicken	2 cups (500 mL)	4 cups (1 L)	6 cups (1.5 L)	8 cups (2 L)	10 cups (2.5 L)
	Monterey Jack cheese	2 cups (500 mL)	4 cups (1 L)	6 cups (1.5 L)	8 cups (2 L)	10 cups (2.5 L)
	Enchilada Sauce	1 batch	2 batches	3 batches	4 batches	5 batches
	tortillas	9	18	27	36	45
	quart bags	2	4	6	8	10
	13x9 pans	1	2	3	4	5

Asian Chicken Lettuce Wraps

Are you looking for a lighter meal option? I love this recipe for the times when I am trying to make both satisfying and healthier choices but don't want to sacrifice flavor. I love guilt-free recipes, don't you? Makes 6 servings.

1 tbsp (15 mL) vegetable oil

1 lb (500 g) ground chicken

½ cup (125 mL) Blistered Roasted Peppers (page 353), puréed

½ cup (125 mL) Time-Saving Roasted Garlic and Onion Purée (page 355)

¼ cup (60 mL) hoisin sauce

2 tbsp (30 mL) tamari sauce

1 tbsp (15 mL) unseasoned rice vinegar

1 tsp (5 mL) minced ginger

¼ tsp (1 mL) hot pepper flakes

1 can (8 oz/227 g) water chestnuts, drained and diced

To Serve

1 head butter or iceberg lettuce

Shredded carrots (optional)

Chopped fresh cilantro (optional)

Sliced green onions (optional)

Sesame seeds (optional)

Sriracha sauce (optional)

1. In a large skillet, heat vegetable oil over medium-high heat. Add chicken and cook, stirring and chopping with a wooden spoon, for about 7 to 8 minutes, until crumbled and no longer pink. Drain off any fat. Return chicken to skillet over medium heat.

2. Add puréed peppers, garlic and onion purée, hoisin sauce, tamari sauce, rice vinegar, ginger and hot pepper flakes; stir to combine. Add water chestnuts and cook, stirring, for about 1 to 2 minutes, until heated through.

MAKE IT NOW Spoon warm chicken mixture into lettuce leaves. Top with shredded carrots, cilantro, green onions and sesame seeds, if using. Then fold up the lettuce, taco style. Dip into Sriracha sauce, if desired.

MAKE IT A FREEZER MEAL Let cooked chicken mixture cool completely. Place in a labeled gallon-size (4 L) freezer bag. Seal, removing as much air as possible, and freeze.

THAW AND COOK Place bag in the refrigerator for 12 to 24 hours to thaw. Transfer to a medium, microwave-safe bowl and microwave on High for 1 to 2 minutes, until warmed through. (You can also reheat the chicken in a large skillet over medium-high heat, stirring often, until warmed through.) Spoon warm chicken mixture into lettuce leaves. Top with shredded carrots, cilantro, green onions and sesame seeds, if using. Then fold up the lettuce, taco style. Dip into Sriracha sauce, if desired.

BULK BATCH GUIDE	Servings	6 (1 batch)	12 (2 batches)	18 (3 batches)	24 (4 batches)	30 (5 batches)
	vegetable oil	1 tbsp (15 mL)	2 tbsp (30 mL)	3 tbsp (45 mL)	¼ cup (60 mL)	⅓ cup (75 mL)
	ground chicken	1 lb (500 g)	2 lbs (1 kg)	3 lbs (1.5 kg)	4 lbs (2 kg)	5 lbs (2.5 kg)
	Blistered Peppers	½ cup (125 mL)	1 cup (250 mL)	1½ cups (375 mL)	2 cups (500 mL)	2½ cups (625 mL)
	Garlic and Onion Purée	½ cup (125 mL)	1 cup (250 mL)	1½ cups (375 mL)	2 cups (500 mL)	2½ cups (625 mL)
	hoisin sauce	¼ cup (60 mL)	½ cup (125 mL)	¾ cup (175 mL)	1 cup (250 mL)	1¼ cups (310 mL)
	tamari sauce	2 tbsp (30 mL)	¼ cup (60 mL)	6 tbsp (90 mL)	½ cup (125 mL)	⅔ cup (150 mL)
	rice vinegar	1 tbsp (15 mL)	2 tbsp (30 mL)	3 tbsp (45 mL)	¼ cup (60 mL)	⅓ cup (75 mL)
	ginger	1 tsp (5 mL)	2 tsp (10 mL)	1 tbsp (15 mL)	4 tsp (20 mL)	5 tsp (25 mL)
	hot pepper flakes	¼ tsp (1 mL)	½ tsp (2 mL)	¾ tsp (3 mL)	1 tsp (5 mL)	1¼ tsp (6 mL)
	water chestnuts	8 oz (227 g)	16 oz (454 g)	24 oz (681 g)	32 oz (908 g)	40 oz (1.135 kg)
	gallon bags	1	2	3	4	5

Amazing Chicken Satay with Peanut Sauce

When you bite into this amazing chicken satay, you get a flavor-burst of fresh cilantro and lime followed by a hint of curry and creamy, buttery coconut milk. Take it to the next level and dip them in peanut sauce: your senses will be flooded with fresh ginger and the subtle fire of Sriracha sauce. Total yum! Makes 6 servings (12 skewers).

2 lbs (1 kg) boneless, skinless chicken breasts

1 tbsp (15 mL) finely chopped fresh cilantro

½ cup (125 mL) coconut milk

1 tbsp (15 mL) fish sauce (nam pla)

2 tsp (10 mL) curry powder

1½ tsp (7 mL) granulated sugar

¼ tsp (1 mL) salt

¼ tsp (1 mL) freshly ground black pepper

1 batch Peanut Sauce (page 345)

To Serve

12 bamboo skewers, soaked in water for 30 minutes

¼ cup (60 mL) chopped peanuts (optional)

Finely chopped fresh cilantro (optional)

1. Cut chicken breasts lengthwise into ¼-inch (0.5 cm) strips about 5 to 6 inches (12 to 15 cm) long.

2. Place cilantro, coconut milk, fish sauce, curry powder, sugar, salt and pepper in a gallon-size (4 L) freezer bag or large bowl. (Label the bag if freezing for later.) Seal the bag and shake or stir until all ingredients are thoroughly combined. Add sliced chicken and shake or stir until coated. Reseal bag, removing all the air, or cover bowl.

MAKE IT NOW Place chicken in the refrigerator to marinate for at least 2 hours or up to 24 hours. Remove from marinade and thread one strip of chicken lengthwise on each skewer. If you're using a barbecue grill to cook the skewers, preheat greased grill to High. Cook for 4 to 5 minutes, turning every 1 to 2 minutes, until no longer pink inside. If you're using the oven to cook the skewers, set to Broil. Place skewers on a baking sheet lined with foil, spacing them apart. Broil for 4 to 5 minutes, turning every 1 to 2 minutes, until no longer pink inside. Garnish with peanuts and cilantro, if using, and serve with a side of peanut sauce.

MAKE IT A FREEZER MEAL Place peanut sauce in a quart-size (1 L) freezer bag; seal bag, removing as much air as possible, and freeze alongside satay bag as a kit.

THAW AND COOK Place bags in the refrigerator for at least 12 hours or up to 24 hours to thaw. Remove chicken from marinade and thread one strip lengthwise on each skewer. If you're using a barbecue grill to cook the skewers, preheat greased grill to High. Cook for 4 to 5 minutes, turning every 1 to 2 minutes, until no longer pink inside. If you're using the oven to cook the skewers, set to Broil. Place skewers on a baking sheet lined with foil, spacing them apart. Broil for 4 to 5 minutes, turning every 1 to 2 minutes, until no longer pink inside. Transfer peanut sauce to a small, microwave-safe bowl; microwave on High for 30 to 45 seconds, until warmed through. Garnish with peanuts and cilantro, if using, and serve with a side of peanut sauce.

BULK BATCH GUIDE						
Servings	6 (1 batch)	12 (2 batches)	18 (3 batches)	24 (4 batches)	30 (5 batches)
chicken breasts	2 lbs (1 kg)	4 lbs (2 kg)	6 lbs (3 kg)	8 lbs (4 kg)	10 lbs (5 kg)
cilantro	1 tbsp (15 mL)	2 tbsp (30 mL)	3 tbsp (45 mL)	¼ cup (60 mL)	⅓ cup (75 mL)
coconut milk	½ cup (125 mL)	1 cup (250 mL)	1½ cups (375 mL)	2 cups (500 mL)	2½ cups (625 mL)
fish sauce	1 tbsp (15 mL)	2 tbsp (30 mL)	3 tbsp (45 mL)	¼ cup (60 mL)	⅓ cup (75 mL)
curry powder	2 tsp (10 mL)	4 tsp (20 mL)	2 tbsp (30 mL)	8 tsp (40 mL)	10 tsp (50 mL)
sugar	1½ tsp (7 mL)	1 tbsp (15 mL)	1½ tbsp (22 mL)	2 tbsp (30 mL)	2½ tbsp (37 mL)
salt	¼ tsp (1 mL)	½ tsp (2 mL)	¾ tsp (3 mL)	1 tsp (5 mL)	1¼ tsp (6 mL)
pepper	¼ tsp (1 mL)	½ tsp (2 mL)	¾ tsp (3 mL)	1 tsp (5 mL)	1¼ tsp (6 mL)
Peanut Sauce	1 batch	2 batches	3 batches	4 batches	5 batches
gallon bags	1	2	3	4	5
quart bags	1	2	3	4	5

Chicken Tikka Masala

Every time I eat Indian food, the velvety smooth masalas and curries dance in my mouth all night, leaving me wanting more. I am so excited to share my favorite tikka masala recipe. Makes 6 servings.

Chicken Tikka

2 lbs (1 kg) skinless, boneless chicken thighs or breasts, cut into 1-inch (2.5 cm) chunks

3 tbsp (45 mL) freshly squeezed lemon juice

1¼ tsp (6 mL) salt

6 tbsp (90 mL) heavy or whipping (35%) cream

1 tbsp (15 mL) grated or puréed ginger

1 tsp (5 mL) minced garlic

1 tsp (5 mL) ground cumin

1 tsp (5 mL) paprika

½ tsp (2 mL) chili powder

½ tsp (2 mL) garam masala

Masala Sauce

3 tbsp (45 mL) vegetable oil

1 large onion, finely chopped

1 tbsp (15 mL) minced garlic

1 tbsp (15 mL) grated or puréed ginger

2 cans (each 28 oz/796 mL) tomato sauce

1 tbsp (15 mL) granulated sugar

3 tbsp (45 mL) garam masala

1 tsp (5 mL) salt

½ tsp (2 mL) hot pepper flakes

1½ cups (375 mL) heavy or whipping (35%) cream

To Serve

Additional heavy or whipping (35%) cream (optional)

Chopped fresh cilantro (optional)

Rice (optional)

Lip-Smackin' Chutney (page 344) (optional)

1. *Chicken Tikka:* In a gallon-size (4 L) freezer bag or large bowl, combine chicken, lemon juice and salt. (Label the bag if freezing for later.) Toss to coat chicken on all sides. Let stand for 2 minutes. Add cream, ginger, garlic, cumin, paprika, chili powder and garam masala; swish the chicken around in the bag or stir to combine. Place in refrigerator to marinate for 10 minutes.

2. *Masala Sauce:* In a large stockpot, heat vegetable oil over medium-high heat. Once oil is hot and shimmering, add onion and cook, stirring often, for about 7 to 8 minutes, until brown. Add garlic and ginger and cook, stirring, for 1 minute, until fragrant. Add tomato sauce, sugar, garam masala, salt and hot pepper flakes; stir to combine. Bring to a boil, then cover and immediately reduce heat to low. Simmer for 15 minutes, stirring occasionally, until flavors have deepened. Remove from heat, add cream and stir.

MAKE IT NOW Preheat oven to Broil. Place marinated chicken pieces on a rimmed baking sheet lined with foil, spacing them apart. Broil on middle rack of oven for 9 minutes. Flip chicken and broil for an additional 9 minutes, until slightly charred in spots and meat is no longer pink inside. Ladle sauce into a deep serving dish and place chicken on top. Drizzle with additional cream and sprinkle cilantro overtop, if using. Serve with a side of rice and chutney, if desired, to make it a whole meal.

MAKE IT A FREEZER MEAL Let sauce cool completely and pour into a labeled gallon-size (4 L) freezer bag. Seal, removing as much air as possible. Reseal marinade bag (if you used a bowl, place the chicken in a fresh bag), removing as much air as possible. Freeze the two bags together as a kit.

THAW AND COOK Place bags in the refrigerator for at least 12 hours or up to 24 hours to thaw. Preheat oven to Broil. Place marinated chicken pieces on a baking sheet lined with foil, spacing them apart. Broil on middle rack of oven for 9 minutes. Flip chicken and broil for an additional 9 minutes, until slightly charred in spots and meat is no longer pink inside. Pour sauce into a large stockpot. Heat over medium heat, stirring often, for 5 to 6 minutes, until sauce barely comes to a simmer; immediately remove from heat. Ladle sauce into a deep serving dish and place chicken on top. Drizzle with additional cream and sprinkle cilantro overtop, if using. Serve with a side of rice and chutney, if desired, to make it a whole meal.

(continued on page 166)

Servings	6 (1 batch)	12 (2 batches)	18 (3 batches)	24 (4 batches)	30 (5 batches)
chicken	2 lbs (1 kg)	4 lbs (2 kg)	6 lbs (3 kg)	8 lbs (4 kg)	10 lbs (5 kg)
lemon juice	3 tbsp (45 mL)	6 tbsp (90 mL)	9 tbsp (135 mL)	¾ cup (175 mL)	¾ cup + 3 tbsp (220 mL)
salt	1¼ tsp (6 mL)	2½ tsp (12 mL)	3¾ tsp (18 mL)	5 tsp (25 mL)	6¼ tsp (31 mL)
cream	6 tbsp (90 mL)	¾ cup (175 mL)	1 cup + 2 tbsp (280 mL)	1½ cups (375 mL)	1¾ cups + 2 tbsp (455 mL)
ginger	1 tbsp (15 mL)	2 tbsp (30 mL)	3 tbsp (45 mL)	¼ cup (60 mL)	⅓ cup (75 mL)
garlic	1 tsp (5 mL)	2 tsp (10 mL)	1 tbsp (15 mL)	4 tsp (20 mL)	5 tsp (25 mL)
cumin	1 tsp (5 mL)	2 tsp (10 mL)	1 tbsp (15 mL)	4 tsp (20 mL)	5 tsp (25 mL)
paprika	1 tsp (5 mL)	2 tsp (10 mL)	1 tbsp (15 mL)	4 tsp (20 mL)	5 tsp (25 mL)
chili powder	½ tsp (2 mL)	1 tsp (5 mL)	1½ tsp (7 mL)	2 tsp (10 mL)	2½ tsp (12 mL)
garam masala	½ tsp (2 mL)	1 tsp (5 mL)	1½ tsp (7 mL)	2 tsp (10 mL)	2½ tsp (12 mL)
vegetable oil	3 tbsp (45 mL)	6 tbsp (90 mL)	9 tbsp (135 mL)	¾ cup (175 mL)	¾ cup + 3 tbsp (220 mL)
onions	1	2	3	4	5
garlic for sauce	1 tbsp (15 mL)	2 tbsp (30 mL)	3 tbsp (45 mL)	¼ cup (60 mL)	⅓ cup (75 mL)
ginger for sauce	1 tbsp (15 mL)	2 tbsp (30 mL)	3 tbsp (45 mL)	¼ cup (60 mL)	⅓ cup (75 mL)
tomato sauce	56 oz (1.592 L)	112 oz (3.184 L)	168 oz (4.776 L)	224 oz (6.368 L)	280 oz (7.96 L)
sugar	1 tbsp (15 mL)	2 tbsp (30 mL)	3 tbsp (45 mL)	¼ cup (60 mL)	⅓ cup (75 mL)
garam masala	3 tbsp (45 mL)	6 tbsp (90 mL)	9 tbsp (135 mL)	¾ cup (175 mL)	¾ cup + 3 tbsp (220 mL)
salt for sauce	1 tsp (5 mL)	2 tsp (10 mL)	1 tbsp (15 mL)	4 tsp (20 mL)	5 tsp (25 mL)
hot pepper flakes	½ tsp (2 mL)	1 tsp (5 mL)	1½ tsp (7 mL)	2 tsp (10 mL)	2½ tsp (12 mL)
cream	1½ cups (375 mL)	3 cups (750 mL)	4½ cups (1.125 L)	6 cups (1.5 L)	7½ cups (1.875 L)
gallon bags	2	4	6	8	10

I am so excited
to share my favorite
tikka masala recipe,
and I hope you
delight in it as much
as I do.

Peanut Perfection Pad Thai

My love affair with pad thai began one happy evening when my husband and I were out celebrating our wedding anniversary at a local Thai restaurant. I kept filling my plate with creamy, peanutty rice noodles and knew I needed to recreate it as a freezer meal. You'll love how the coconut milk, delicate curry flavors and peanut sauce dance with the crunch of peanuts, the kick of cilantro and the tang of freshly squeezed lime juice. Makes 6 servings.

Peanutty Sauce

1 batch Peanut Sauce (page 345)

½ cup (125 mL) coconut milk

1 tsp (5 mL) fish sauce (nam pla)

¼ tsp (1 mL) hot pepper flakes, approx. (optional)

Noodles

1 large egg

1 small white onion, minced

1 cup (250 mL) shredded carrots

2 cloves garlic, minced

¼ tsp (1 mL) ground white pepper

2 tsp (10 mL) curry powder

8 oz (250 g) Thai-style rice noodles

1 tbsp (15 mL) toasted sesame oil

3 tbsp (45 mL) canola oil, divided

1 lb (500 g) skinless, boneless chicken breasts, cut into ⅛-inch (3 mm) strips

Garnishes

¼ cup (60 mL) chopped roasted peanuts

¼ cup (60 mL) chopped fresh cilantro

1 lime, cut into wedges

1. *Peanutty Sauce:* In a blender, combine peanut sauce, coconut milk, fish sauce and hot pepper flakes, if using. Blend on High until smooth. Taste and add more hot pepper flakes, if desired. Set aside.

2. *Noodles:* In a small bowl, whisk egg; set aside.

3. In another small bowl, combine onion, carrots, garlic, white pepper and curry powder; set aside.

4. Fill a large stockpot with water and bring to a boil over high heat. Add noodles and cook for about 1 minute, stirring often, until undercooked but just beginning to soften. Drain and rinse with cold water to cool, then return noodles to pot. Add sesame oil and gently toss to coat. Set aside.

5. In a large wok or skillet, heat 1½ tsp (7 mL) canola oil over high heat until hot and shimmering. Add egg and cook, scrambling with a chopstick or spoon, for about 2 minutes, until set but still moist and soft. Transfer egg to a clean small bowl; set aside.

6. Return wok to high heat and add remaining canola oil. Once hot and smoking, add chicken. Cook, stirring constantly, for about 5 minutes, until chicken is no longer pink inside and is golden and crispy around the edges. Add vegetable mixture; cook, stirring, for 3 to 4 minutes or until carrots and onions are tender.

7. Add noodles to wok and combine gently, being careful not to break them. Add egg and sauce; stir gently until combined. Remove from heat.

MAKE IT NOW Top with chopped peanuts and fresh cilantro. Serve with lime wedges on the side.

MAKE IT A FREEZER MEAL Let pad thai cool to room temperature. Place in a labeled gallon-size (4 L) freezer bag. Seal, removing as much air as possible, and freeze.

REHEAT Place bag in the refrigerator for at least 6 hours or up to 8 hours to thaw. To reheat in the microwave, pour contents into a large, microwave-safe bowl and microwave on High for 1 to 2 minutes. Or heat 1 tsp (5 mL) canola oil in a large wok or skillet over high heat; add pad thai and cook, stirring gently, for 1 to 2 minutes or until heated through. Top with chopped peanuts and fresh cilantro. Serve with lime wedges on the side.

(continued on page 169)

Servings	6 (1 batch)	12 (2 batches)	18 (3 batches)	24 (4 batches)	30 (5 batches)
Peanut Sauce	1 batch	2 batches	3 batches	4 batches	5 batches
coconut milk	½ cup (125 mL)	1 cup (250 mL)	1½ cups (375 mL)	2 cups (500 mL)	2½ cups (625 mL)
fish sauce	1 tsp (5 mL)	2 tsp (10 mL)	1 tbsp (15 mL)	4 tsp (20 mL)	5 tsp (25 mL)
hot pepper flakes	¼ tsp (1 mL)	½ tsp (2 mL)	¾ tsp (3 mL)	1 tsp (5 mL)	1¼ tsp (6 mL)
eggs	1	2	3	4	5
onions	1	2	3	4	5
carrots	1 cup (250 mL)	2 cups (500 mL)	3 cups (750 mL)	4 cups (1 L)	5 cups (1.25 L)
garlic cloves	2	4	6	8	10
white pepper	¼ tsp (1 mL)	½ tsp (2 mL)	¾ tsp (3 mL)	1 tsp (5 mL)	1¼ tsp (6 mL)
curry powder	2 tsp (10 mL)	4 tsp (20 mL)	2 tbsp (30 mL)	8 tsp (40 mL)	10 tsp (50 mL)
rice noodles	8 oz (250 g)	1 lb (500 g)	1½ lbs (750 g)	2 lbs (1 kg)	2½ lbs (1.25 kg)
sesame oil	1 tbsp (15 mL)	2 tbsp (30 mL)	3 tbsp (45 mL)	¼ cup (60 mL)	⅓ cup (75 mL)
canola oil	3 tbsp (45 mL)	6 tbsp (90 mL)	½ cup (125 mL)	¾ cup (175 mL)	¾ cup + 3 tbsp (220 mL)
chicken breasts	1 lb (500 g)	2 lbs (1 kg)	3 lbs (1.5 kg)	4 lbs (2 kg)	5 lbs (2.5 kg)
gallon bags	1	2	3	4	5

My love affair
with pad thai began
one happy evening
when my husband and I
were out celebrating
our wedding anniversary
at a local Thai restaurant.

Teriyaki Chicken

Move over, store-bought teriyaki sauce. This recipe is so easy and simple to make it will totally open your eyes to how good a homemade teriyaki sauce can be. The tender chicken is baked to perfection and will leave even the biggest restaurant addict running home to make this recipe.
Makes 6 servings.

2 cups (500 mL) water

1½ cups (375 mL) packed brown sugar

2 tbsp (30 mL) cornstarch

½ cup (125 mL) tamari sauce

2 tbsp (30 mL) minced garlic

2 tsp (10 mL) sesame seeds

6 cups (1.5 L) chopped cooked chicken (see page 29)

1. In a medium bowl, whisk together water, brown sugar, cornstarch, tamari sauce, garlic and sesame seeds, until sugar is dissolved. Add chicken and stir to combine.

MAKE IT NOW Preheat oven to 400°F (200°C). Pour chicken mixture into a 13- by 9-inch (33 by 23 cm) baking dish. Bake for 45 minutes or until sauce is dark and slightly thickened.

MAKE IT A FREEZER MEAL Pour chicken mixture into a labeled gallon-size (4 L) freezer bag. Seal, removing as much air as possible, and freeze.

REHEAT Place bag in the refrigerator for at least 12 hours or up to 24 hours to thaw, or run lukewarm water over it until you can break apart the contents. Preheat oven to 400°F (200°C). Pour chicken mixture into a 13- by 9-inch (33 by 23 cm) baking dish. Bake for 45 minutes or until sauce is dark and slightly thickened. (The cooking time will be slightly longer if you use the quick-thaw method.)

BULK BATCH GUIDE	Servings	6 (1 batch)	12 (2 batches)	18 (3 batches)	24 (4 batches)	30 (5 batches)
	water	2 cups (500 mL)	4 cups (1 L)	6 cups (1.5 L)	8 cups (2 L)	10 cups (2.5 L)
	brown sugar	1½ cups (375 mL)	3 cups (750 mL)	4½ cups (1.125 L)	6 cups (1.5 L)	7½ cups (1.875 L)
	cornstarch	2 tbsp (30 mL)	¼ cup (60 mL)	6 tbsp (90 mL)	½ cup (125 mL)	⅔ cup (150 mL)
	tamari sauce	½ cup (125 mL)	1 cup (250 mL)	1½ cups (375 mL)	2 cups (500 mL)	2½ cups (625 mL)
	garlic	2 tbsp (30 mL)	¼ cup (60 mL)	6 tbsp (90 mL)	½ cup (125 mL)	⅔ cup (150 mL)
	sesame seeds	2 tsp (10 mL)	4 tsp (20 mL)	2 tbsp (30 mL)	8 tsp (40 mL)	10 tsp (50 mL)
	cooked chicken	6 cups (1.5 L)	12 cups (3 L)	18 cups (4.5 L)	24 cups (6 L)	30 cups (7.5 L)
	gallon bags	1	2	3	4	5

PORK

Bacon Love Pork Tenderloin 174

Cranberry Pork Roast 177

Honey Pork Chops 178

Island Pork 181

Rosemary Brown Sugar Pork Chops 182

Rio-Style Sweet Pork Salad 185

Pork 'n' Pepper Stir-Fry 186

Boneless BBQ Pork Ribs 189

Bacon Carbonara Pasta Pie 190

Stromboli 193

Perfect Pizza Any Way You Top It 194

Hash-Brown Casserole 199

Smoky Pulled Pork Sandwiches 200

Perfect Pork Carnitas Tacos 203

Bacon Love Pork Tenderloin

No, you're not dreaming. Every single bite of this crispy, gorgeous bacon-wrapped pork will make you ooh and aah with delight. The bacon gives the pork the perfect smoky depth and keeps it juicy and tender. It's what I like to call bacon perfection. *Makes 6 servings.*

¼ cup (60 mL) packed brown sugar

1 tbsp (15 mL) paprika

1 tbsp (15 mL) salt

1 tsp (5 mL) freshly ground black pepper

¼ tsp (1 mL) cayenne pepper

2 tsp (10 mL) onion powder

2 tsp (10 mL) garlic powder

2 large pork tenderloins (about 3 lbs/1.5 kg total), each cut crosswise into 3 pieces

1 lb (500 g) sliced bacon

1 cup (250 mL) Smoky BBQ Sauce (page 341) or store-bought smoky barbecue sauce

Tip
If you are making this recipe right away, you can use two smaller baking dishes, if desired.

1. In a small bowl, combine brown sugar, paprika, salt, pepper, cayenne, onion powder and garlic powder.

2. Lay out a large piece of aluminum foil.

3. Dip pork into spice mixture, coating all sides. Wrap bacon around pork pieces, overlapping slightly and making sure they fit snugly around the meat. Tightly tuck ends underneath pieces to hold them in place.

4. Spread barbecue sauce evenly over tops with a brush or the back of a spoon.

MAKE IT NOW Preheat oven to 300°F (150°C). Lift pork pieces from foil and place in a lightly greased 13- by 9-inch (33 by 23 cm) baking dish, spacing evenly apart; discard foil. Bake in preheated oven for 1½ hours, until internal temperature reaches 155°F (70°C). To crisp the bacon, turn broiler to High for the last 2 to 3 minutes of cooking. Remove from oven, cover with foil and let rest for 10 minutes. Slice across the grain and enjoy.

MAKE IT A FREEZER MEAL Cut out six 8-inch (20 cm) square pieces of foil. Wrap foil tightly around bacon-wrapped tenderloin pieces. Place all pieces in a labeled gallon-size (4 L) freezer bag. Seal, removing as much air as possible, and freeze.

THAW AND COOK Place bag in the refrigerator for at least 24 hours or up to 48 hours to thaw. Preheat oven to 300°F (150°C). Unwrap pork and place in a lightly greased 13- by 9-inch (33 by 23 cm) baking dish, spacing evenly apart; discard foil. Bake in preheated oven for 1½ hours, until internal temperature reaches 155°F (70°C). To crisp bacon, turn broiler to High for last 2 to 3 minutes of cooking. Remove from oven, cover with foil and let rest for 10 minutes. Slice across the grain and enjoy.

BULK BATCH GUIDE	Servings	6 (1 batch)	12 (2 batches)	18 (3 batches)	24 (4 batches)	30 (5 batches)
	brown sugar	¼ cup (60 mL)	½ cup (125 mL)	¾ cup (175 mL)	1 cup (250 mL)	1¼ cups (310 mL)
	paprika	1 tbsp (15 mL)	2 tbsp (30 mL)	3 tbsp (45 mL)	¼ cup (60 mL)	⅓ cup (75 mL)
	salt	1 tbsp (15 mL)	2 tbsp (30 mL)	3 tbsp (45 mL)	¼ cup (60 mL)	⅓ cup (75 mL)
	pepper	1 tsp (5 mL)	2 tsp (10 mL)	1 tbsp (15 mL)	4 tsp (20 mL)	5 tsp (25 mL)
	cayenne pepper	¼ tsp (1 mL)	½ tsp (2 mL)	¾ tsp (3 mL)	1 tsp (5 mL)	1¼ tsp (6 mL)
	onion powder	2 tsp (10 mL)	4 tsp (20 mL)	2 tbsp (30 mL)	8 tsp (40 mL)	10 tsp (50 mL)
	garlic powder	2 tsp (10 mL)	4 tsp (20 mL)	2 tbsp (30 mL)	8 tsp (40 mL)	10 tsp (50 mL)
	pork tenderloin	3 lbs (1.5 kg)	6 lbs (3 kg)	9 lbs (4.5 kg)	12 lbs (6 kg)	15 lbs (7.5 kg)
	bacon	1 lb (500 g)	2 lbs (1 kg)	3 lbs (1.5 kg)	4 lbs (2 kg)	5 lbs (2.5 kg)
	BBQ Sauce	1 cup (250 mL)	2 cups (500 mL)	3 cups (750 mL)	4 cups (1 L)	5 cups (1.25 L)
	gallon bags	1	2	3	4	5

Cranberry Pork Roast

Get a little holiday feeling throughout the year with this juicy pork roast recipe. Just find all those unused cranberry sauce cans from Thanksgiving and make up a batch to share. Makes 6 servings.

3 lbs (1.5 kg) boneless pork sirloin roast, trimmed

1 tsp (5 mL) dried rosemary

½ tsp (2 mL) ground marjoram

½ tsp (2 mL) salt

¼ tsp (1 mL) freshly ground black pepper

1 can (14 oz/398 mL) cranberry sauce

½ cup (125 mL) orange juice

Pinch ground nutmeg

1. Prick roast all over with the tip of a knife. Place in a large bowl.

2. In a small bowl, combine rosemary, marjoram, salt and pepper. Pour seasoning mixture over roast and, using your hands, rub it in very well on all sides.

3. In a medium bowl, combine cranberry sauce, orange juice and nutmeg. Set aside 1 cup (250 mL) of the mixture for serving over the meat.

MAKE IT NOW Preheat oven to 350°F (180°C). In a large Dutch oven or 13- by 9-inch (33 by 23 cm) baking dish, combine roast and cranberry sauce mixture; spoon sauce over meat. Bake for 50 to 55 minutes or until internal temperature reaches 145°F (63°C) for medium, or to desired doneness. Remove from oven, cover with foil and let rest for 15 minutes. Meanwhile, in a small saucepan over medium heat, heat reserved cranberry sauce for 3 to 4 minutes, until warmed. Slice roast across the grain. Pour reserved cranberry sauce overtop and serve.

MAKE IT A FREEZER MEAL Place reserved 1 cup (250 mL) cranberry sauce mixture in a quart-size (1 L) freezer bag. Seal, removing as much air as possible. Place uncooked roast in a labeled gallon-size (4 L) freezer bag with remaining cranberry sauce mixture. Seal, removing as much air as possible. Place both bags in a gallon-size freezer bag and seal together. Label and freeze.

THAW AND COOK Place bags in the refrigerator for at least 24 hours or up to 48 hours to thaw. Preheat oven to 350°F (180°C). Pour roast and sauce into a large Dutch oven or 13- by 9-inch (33 by 23 cm) baking dish; spoon sauce over meat. Bake for 50 to 55 minutes or until internal temperature registers 145°F (63°C) for medium, or to desired doneness. Remove from oven, cover with foil and let rest for 15 minutes. Meanwhile, in a small saucepan over medium heat, heat reserved cranberry sauce for 3 to 4 minutes, until warmed. Slice roast across the grain. Pour reserved cranberry sauce overtop and serve.

BULK BATCH GUIDE	Servings	6 (1 batch)	12 (2 batches)	18 (3 batches)	24 (4 batches)	30 (5 batches)
	pork roast	3 lbs (1.5 kg)	6 lbs (3 kg)	9 lbs (4.5 kg)	12 lbs (6 kg)	15 lbs (7.5 kg)
	dried rosemary	1 tsp (5 mL)	2 tsp (10 mL)	1 tbsp (15 mL)	4 tsp (20 mL)	5 tsp (25 mL)
	marjoram	½ tsp (2 mL)	1 tsp (5 mL)	1½ tsp (7 mL)	2 tsp (10 mL)	2½ tsp (12 mL)
	salt	½ tsp (2 mL)	1 tsp (5 mL)	1½ tsp (7 mL)	2 tsp (10 mL)	2½ tsp (12 mL)
	pepper	¼ tsp (1 mL)	½ tsp (2 mL)	¾ tsp (3 mL)	1 tsp (5 mL)	1¼ tsp (6 mL)
	cranberry sauce	14 oz (398 mL)	28 oz (696 mL)	42 oz (1.044 L)	56 oz (1.392 L)	70 oz (1.74 L)
	orange juice	½ cup (125 mL)	1 cup (250 mL)	1½ cups (375 mL)	2 cups (500 mL)	2½ cups (625 mL)
	quart bags	1	2	3	4	5
	gallon bags	2	4	6	8	10

Honey Pork Chops

Pork chops smothered in a marvelous full-flavored honey-ginger sauce — what more could you ask for? I like to make this meal a few times a month and serve it with Garlic Herb Smashed Potatoes (page 291) and warm Brown 'n' Serve Rolls (page 284). Makes 6 servings.

¼ cup (60 mL) honey

2 tbsp (30 mL) tamari sauce

1 shallot, quartered

½ tsp (2 mL) minced or grated garlic

½ tsp (2 mL) grated ginger

⅛ tsp (0.5 mL) freshly ground black pepper

1 tsp (5 mL) olive oil

6 medium boneless pork loin chops (each about 3 oz/90 g)

1. In a blender, combine honey, tamari sauce, shallot, garlic, ginger and pepper; blend on High until smooth.

MAKE IT NOW Preheat oven to 350°F (180°C). Heat a large skillet over medium-high heat. Once it is hot but not smoking, add olive oil. Sear pork chops, in batches as necessary, for about 1 minute per side, until browned (if you are really pressed for time, skip this step). Place chops in a greased 13- by 9-inch (33 by 23 cm) baking dish. Pour sauce overtop. Bake in preheated oven for 25 to 30 minutes or until tender. Spoon sauce over pork to serve.

MAKE IT A FREEZER MEAL Place uncooked pork chops in a labeled gallon-size (4 L) freezer bag and add sauce. Seal bag, removing as much air as possible, and freeze.

THAW AND COOK Place bag in the refrigerator for at least 24 hours or up to 48 hours to thaw. Preheat oven to 350°F (180°C). Pour pork and sauce into a greased 13- by 9-inch (33 by 23 cm) baking dish. Bake in preheated oven for 25 to 30 minutes or until tender. Spoon sauce over pork to serve.

Servings	6 (1 batch)	12 (2 batches)	18 (3 batches)	24 (4 batches)	30 (5 batches)
honey	¼ cup (60 mL)	½ cup (125 mL)	¾ cup (175 mL)	1 cup (250 mL)	1¼ cups (310 mL)
tamari sauce	2 tbsp (30 mL)	¼ cup (60 mL)	6 tbsp (90 mL)	½ cup (125 mL)	⅔ cup (150 mL)
shallots	1	2	3	4	5
garlic	½ tsp (2 mL)	1 tsp (5 mL)	1½ tsp (7 mL)	2 tsp (10 mL)	2½ tsp (12 mL)
ginger	½ tsp (2 mL)	1 tsp (5 mL)	1½ tsp (7 mL)	2 tsp (10 mL)	2½ tsp (12 mL)
pepper	⅛ tsp (0.5 mL)	¼ tsp (1 mL)	⅓ tsp (1.5 mL)	½ tsp (2 mL)	¾ tsp (3 mL)
olive oil	1 tsp (5 mL)	2 tsp (10 mL)	1 tbsp (15 mL)	4 tsp (20 mL)	5 tsp (25 mL)
pork chops	6	12	18	24	30
gallon bags	1	2	3	4	5

BULK BATCH GUIDE

Island Pork

Close your eyes and let this pineapple-flavored pork take you away to the tropics. I love how quickly I can get this recipe into the slow cooker and then enjoy the amazing smell of it cooking all day. I like to serve it with rice and fresh sliced pineapple for a delicious whole meal — grass skirt and coconut bra optional. *Makes 6 servings.*

1 tsp (5 mL) onion powder

2½ tsp (12 mL) salt

1 tsp (5 mL) dried oregano

1 tsp (5 mL) ground ginger

1 tsp (5 mL) whole cumin seeds

¼ tsp (1 mL) ground cloves

1 tsp (5 mL) garam masala

3½ lbs (1.75 kg) boneless pork shoulder roast, trimmed and cut into 4-inch (10 cm) chunks

1 onion, thinly sliced

To Cook

1 whole pineapple

1. In a medium bowl, combine onion powder, salt, oregano, ginger, cumin, cloves and garam masala.

2. Using your hands, rub mixture over pork, making sure to coat it completely.

MAKE IT NOW Wash and dry pineapple skin. Slice off top and bottom of pineapple. Cut off skin in about 6 big pieces; set aside. Cut pineapple in half lengthwise. Remove core and set it aside with skin. Slice pineapple crosswise into ½-inch (1 cm) slices; place in refrigerator to serve later along with cooked pork. Layer sliced onion in bottom of a large (approx. 5 quart) slow cooker. Add pork pieces; then lay pineapple cores and skins on top of pork, skin side up. Cook on Low for 10 to 12 hours. Using tongs, transfer pork to a bowl or serving platter. Using two forks, shred into pieces. Skim fat from juices remaining in the slow cooker; ladle juices over shredded pork. Serve with cooked pineapple skins to squeeze over pork, sliced fresh pineapple and a side of rice, if desired.

MAKE IT A FREEZER MEAL Place sliced onion in a labeled quart-size (1 L) freezer bag. Seal, removing as much air as possible. Place uncooked pork in a labeled gallon-size (4 L) freezer bag. Seal together and freeze.

THAW AND COOK Place bags in refrigerator for at least 12 hours or up to 24 hours to thaw. Wash and dry pineapple skin. Slice off top and bottom of pineapple. Cut off skin in about 6 big pieces; set aside. Cut pineapple in half lengthwise. Remove core and set it aside with skin. Slice pineapple crosswise into ½-inch (1 cm) slices; place in refrigerator to serve later along with cooked pork. Layer sliced onion in bottom of a large (approx. 5 quart) slow cooker. Add pork pieces; then lay pineapple cores and skins on top of pork, skin side up. Cook on Low for 10 to 12 hours. Using tongs, transfer pork to a bowl or serving platter. Using two forks, shred into pieces. Skim fat from juices remaining in the slow cooker; ladle juices over shredded pork. Serve with cooked pineapple skins to squeeze over pork, sliced fresh pineapple and a side of rice, if desired.

BULK BATCH GUIDE	Servings	6 (1 batch)	12 (2 batches)	18 (3 batches)	24 (4 batches)	30 (5 batches)
	onion powder	1 tsp (5 mL)	2 tsp (10 mL)	1 tbsp (15 mL)	4 tsp (20 mL)	5 tsp (25 mL)
	salt	2½ tsp (12 mL)	5 tsp (25 mL)	7½ tsp (37 mL)	10 tsp (50 mL)	¼ cup (60 mL)
	dried oregano	1 tsp (5 mL)	2 tsp (10 mL)	1 tbsp (15 mL)	4 tsp (20 mL)	5 tsp (25 mL)
	ground ginger	1 tsp (5 mL)	2 tsp (10 mL)	1 tbsp (15 mL)	4 tsp (20 mL)	5 tsp (25 mL)
	cumin seeds	1 tsp (5 mL)	2 tsp (10 mL)	1 tbsp (15 mL)	4 tsp (20 mL)	5 tsp (25 mL)
	cloves	¼ tsp (1 mL)	½ tsp (2 mL)	¾ tsp (3 mL)	1 tsp (5 mL)	1¼ tsp (6 mL)
	garam masala	1 tsp (5 mL)	2 tsp (10 mL)	1 tbsp (15 mL)	4 tsp (20 mL)	5 tsp (25 mL)
	pork roast	3½ lbs (1.75 kg)	7 lbs (3.5 kg)	10½ lbs (5.25 kg)	14 lbs (7 kg)	17½ lbs (8.75 kg)
	onions	1	2	3	4	5
	quart bags	1	2	3	4	5
	gallon bags	1	2	3	4	5

Rosemary Brown Sugar Pork Chops

Dinner guests?! No problem. With this simple but decadent freezer meal at the ready you are sure to impress the fanciest of guests without slaving away all day in the kitchen. It's perfect served with my Wild Rice Pilaf (page 299) and some roasted Brussels sprouts. Makes 6 servings.

1 tsp (5 mL) finely minced fresh rosemary

1 tsp (5 mL) cayenne pepper

1 tsp (5 mL) garlic powder

1 tsp (5 mL) paprika

1 tsp (5 mL) salt

½ tsp (2 mL) freshly ground black pepper

6 medium boneless pork loin chops (each about 3 oz/90 g)

2 tbsp (30 mL) olive oil

½ cup (125 mL) packed brown sugar

¼ cup (60 mL) water

Garnish

1 to 2 sprigs fresh rosemary

1. In a small bowl, combine rosemary, cayenne, garlic powder, paprika, salt and pepper. Divide mixture in half; set one half aside.

2. Rub pork chops with remaining seasoning mixture.

3. Heat a large skillet over medium heat. Once it is hot but not smoking, add olive oil. Cook pork chops, in batches as necessary, for about 4 minutes in total, flipping once, or until golden brown on each side and pork is cooked through (you may need to reduce the heat if the meat is browning too quickly). Transfer to a plate and cook remaining chops. Once all are cooked, return chops to skillet. Remove from heat, cover skillet with a lid and let stand for 10 minutes. Transfer pork chops to a clean plate and set aside.

4. Heat skillet over medium-high heat; add brown sugar, reserved seasoning mixture and water. Bring to a boil, stirring constantly, and boil for 1 minute, until slightly thickened. Remove from heat.

MAKE IT NOW Return pork to skillet and coat completely with sauce. Place skillet over low heat until meat is warmed through. Sprinkle leaves from 1 or 2 fresh rosemary sprigs over pork and serve.

MAKE IT A FREEZER MEAL Let cooked pork and sauce cool separately and completely. Place chops in a labeled gallon-size (4 L) freezer bag. Pour sauce overtop. Seal bag, removing as much air as possible, and freeze.

REHEAT Place bag in the refrigerator for at least 12 hours or up to 24 hours to thaw. Preheat oven to 425°F (220°C). Place pork and sauce in a 9-inch (23 cm) square baking dish, overlapping chops as necessary. Bake in preheated oven for 15 minutes or until sauce is bubbly and pork is heated through.

BULK BATCH GUIDE	Servings	6 (1 batch)	12 (2 batches)	18 (3 batches)	24 (4 batches)	30 (5 batches)
	rosemary	1 tsp (5 mL)	2 tsp (10 mL)	1 tbsp (15 mL)	4 tsp (20 mL)	5 tsp (25 mL)
	cayenne pepper	1 tsp (5 mL)	2 tsp (10 mL)	1 tbsp (15 mL)	4 tsp (20 mL)	5 tsp (25 mL)
	garlic powder	1 tsp (5 mL)	2 tsp (10 mL)	1 tbsp (15 mL)	4 tsp (20 mL)	5 tsp (25 mL)
	paprika	1 tsp (5 mL)	2 tsp (10 mL)	1 tbsp (15 mL)	4 tsp (20 mL)	5 tsp (25 mL)
	salt	1 tsp (5 mL)	2 tsp (10 mL)	1 tbsp (15 mL)	4 tsp (20 mL)	5 tsp (25 mL)
	pepper	½ tsp (2 mL)	1 tsp (5 mL)	1½ tsp (7 mL)	2 tsp (10 mL)	2½ tsp (12 mL)
	pork chops	6	12	18	24	30
	olive oil	2 tbsp (30 mL)	¼ cup (60 mL)	6 tbsp (90 mL)	½ cup (125 mL)	⅔ cup (150 mL)
	brown sugar	½ cup (125 mL)	1 cup (250 mL)	1½ cups (375 mL)	2 cups (500 mL)	2½ cups (625 mL)
	water	¼ cup (60 mL)	½ cup (125 mL)	¾ cup (175 mL)	1 cup (250 mL)	1¼ cups (310 mL)
	gallon bags	1	2	3	4	5

Rio-Style Sweet Pork Salad

This is exactly the kind of freezer meal I love to have on hand when I am in the mood for a healthy salad for dinner. The pork is so juicy and flavorful, served on top of a bed of crisp lettuce and sprinkled with tortilla strips and queso fresco. Salad paradise, I tell you! *Makes 6 servings.*

3 lbs (1.5 kg) boneless pork shoulder roast, trimmed

2 cups (500 mL) packed brown sugar

1 cup (250 mL) Worcestershire sauce

1 tsp (5 mL) salt

1 tsp (5 mL) chili powder

1 tsp (5 mL) garlic powder

1 tsp (5 mL) onion powder

1 cup (250 mL) Enchilada Sauce (page 346)

To Serve

2 heads romaine lettuce, chopped

1 cup (250 mL) cooked or canned black beans, drained and rinsed

Queso fresco (optional)

Tortilla strips (optional)

Chopped fresh cilantro (optional)

Avocado Crema (page 348; optional)

Lime wedges

1. In a large (approx. 5 quart) slow cooker, combine pork, brown sugar, Worcestershire sauce, salt, chili powder, garlic powder and onion powder. Cook on Low for 8 to 10 hours.

2. Remove pork from slow cooker. Transfer to a cutting board and, using two forks, shred into pieces, discarding excess fat. Reserve 1 cup (250 mL) liquid from slow cooker, discarding excess. Return pork to slow cooker; add enchilada sauce and reserved cup of liquid, stirring gently to combine. Increase heat to High and cook for 20 to 30 minutes with the lid off to infuse flavors.

MAKE IT NOW Divide chopped lettuce and black beans equally among serving plates. Using tongs, pick up pork, letting the juices drain a little, and place equal amounts on top of each salad. Sprinkle with queso fresco, tortilla strips and cilantro, if using. Top with avocado crema, if using, and a squeeze of fresh lime juice.

MAKE IT A FREEZER MEAL Let pork cool in sauce to room temperature. Pour into a labeled gallon-size (4 L) freezer bag. Seal, removing as much air as possible, and freeze.

REHEAT Place bag in the refrigerator for 12 to 24 hours to thaw. Add contents of bag to a large stockpot; bring to a boil over medium-high heat, stirring often. Boil for 2 to 3 minutes, until heated through. Remove from heat. Divide chopped lettuce and black beans equally among serving plates. Using tongs, pick up pork, letting the juices drain a little, and place equal amounts on top of each salad. Sprinkle with queso fresco, tortilla strips and cilantro, if using. Top with avocado crema, if using, and a squeeze of fresh lime juice.

BULK BATCH GUIDE	Servings	6 (1 batch)	12 (2 batches)	18 (3 batches)	24 (4 batches)	30 (5 batches)
	pork roast	3 lbs (1.5 kg)	6 lbs (3 kg)	9 lbs (4.5 kg)	12 lbs (6 kg)	15 lbs (7.5 kg)
	brown sugar	2 cups (500 mL)	4 cups (1 L)	6 cups (1.5 L)	8 cups (2 L)	10 cups (2.5 L)
	Worcestershire	1 cup (250 mL)	2 cups (500 mL)	3 cups (750 mL)	4 cups (1 L)	5 cups (1.25 L)
	salt	1 tsp (5 mL)	2 tsp (10 mL)	1 tbsp (15 mL)	4 tsp (20 mL)	5 tsp (25 mL)
	chili powder	1 tsp (5 mL)	2 tsp (10 mL)	1 tbsp (15 mL)	4 tsp (20 mL)	5 tsp (25 mL)
	garlic powder	1 tsp (5 mL)	2 tsp (10 mL)	1 tbsp (15 mL)	4 tsp (20 mL)	5 tsp (25 mL)
	onion powder	1 tsp (5 mL)	2 tsp (10 mL)	1 tbsp (15 mL)	4 tsp (20 mL)	5 tsp (25 mL)
	Enchilada Sauce	1 cup (250 mL)	2 cups (500 mL)	3 cups (750 mL)	4 cups (1 L)	5 cups (1.25 L)
	gallon bags	1	2	3	4	5

Pork 'n' Pepper Stir-Fry

My youngest daughter has a wheat allergy, so I am always on the lookout for great gluten-free family recipes. I was thrilled when my sister Tiffany shared this colorful and delicious stir-fry with me. Thanks, sis! *Makes 6 servings.*

1 lb (500 g) pork tenderloin, sliced into ¼-inch (0.5 cm) strips

2 tbsp + 1 tsp (35 mL) tamari sauce, divided

½ tsp (2 mL) minced garlic

1 can (20 oz/600 mL) pineapple tidbits, with juice

1 tbsp (15 mL) cornstarch

1 tsp (5 mL) packed brown sugar

¾ cup (175 mL) water

2 tbsp (30 mL) vegetable oil

2 bell peppers, cut lengthwise into strips

1 small onion, thinly sliced

Garnish

Sesame seeds (optional)

1. In a medium bowl, combine pork, 2 tbsp (30 mL) tamari sauce and garlic. Cover and place in the refrigerator for 15 minutes to marinate.

2. Drain juice from pineapple into a small bowl. Set pineapple aside.

3. Add cornstarch, brown sugar, 1 tsp (5 mL) tamari sauce and water to pineapple juice. Whisk to combine.

MAKE IT NOW In a wok or large skillet, heat vegetable oil over high heat. Pour pork and marinade into wok and cook, stirring, for 4 to 5 minutes, until cooked through. Transfer to a bowl. Add bell peppers and onion to wok; cook, stirring, for 2 to 3 minutes, until tender-crisp. Add pineapple, pork with accumulated juices, and pineapple sauce; cook, stirring constantly, for about 5 minutes, until sauce has thickened. Sprinkle with sesame seeds, if using, and serve.

MAKE IT A FREEZER MEAL Spread bell peppers and onion on 2 large parchment-covered baking sheets. Place in freezer and freeze until solid, about 1 hour. Transfer marinated pork mixture to a labeled gallon-size (4 L) freezer bag. Place pineapple in a quart-size (1 L) freezer bag. Place pineapple sauce mixture in another labeled quart-size freezer bag. Seal all bags, removing as much air as possible. Remove onion and peppers from freezer and place in another labeled gallon-size freezer bag. Put labeled pork, sauce and pineapple bags into bag with peppers and onion. Seal, removing as much air as possible, and freeze.

THAW AND COOK Place pork, pineapple and sauce bags in refrigerator for at least 6 hours or up to 8 hours to thaw (keep the peppers-and-onion bag frozen until ready to stir-fry). In a wok or large skillet, heat vegetable oil over high heat. Pour contents of pork bag into wok and cook, stirring, for 4 to 5 minutes, until cooked through. Transfer to a bowl. Add bell peppers and onion to wok; cook, stirring, for 3 to 4 minutes, until tender-crisp. Add pineapple, pork with accumulated juices, and pineapple sauce; cook, stirring constantly, for about 5 minutes, until sauce has thickened. Sprinkle with sesame seeds, if using, and serve.

BULK BATCH GUIDE

Servings	6 (1 batch)	12 (2 batches)	18 (3 batches)	24 (4 batches)	30 (5 batches)
pork tenderloin	1 lb (500 g)	2 lbs (1 kg)	3 lbs (1.5 kg)	4 lbs (2 kg)	5 lbs (2.5 kg)
tamari sauce	2 tbsp + 1 tsp (35 mL)	¼ cup + 2 tsp (70 mL)	7 tbsp (105 mL)	½ cup + 1 tbsp (140 mL)	⅔ cup + 4 tsp (170 mL)
garlic	½ tsp (2 mL)	1 tsp (5 mL)	1½ tsp (7 mL)	2 tsp (10 mL)	2½ tsp (12 mL)
pineapple tidbits	20 oz (600 mL)	40 oz (1.2 mL)	60 oz (1.8 mL)	80 oz (2.4 L)	100 oz (3 L)
cornstarch	1 tbsp (15 mL)	2 tbsp (30 mL)	3 tbsp (45 mL)	¼ cup (60 mL)	⅓ cup (75 mL)
brown sugar	1 tsp (5 mL)	2 tsp (10 mL)	1 tbsp (15 mL)	4 tsp (20 mL)	5 tsp (25 mL)
water	¾ cup (175 mL)	1½ cups (375 mL)	2¼ cups (560 mL)	3 cups (750 mL)	3¾ cups (925 mL)
vegetable oil	2 tbsp (30 mL)	¼ cup (60 mL)	6 tbsp (90 mL)	½ cup (125 mL)	⅔ cup (150 mL)
bell peppers	2	4	6	8	10
onions	1	2	3	4	5
gallon bags	2	4	6	8	10
quart bags	2	4	6	8	10

Boneless BBQ Pork Ribs

Tender, fall-off-the-bone pork ribs slathered in barbecue sauce? Yes, please. Served with a side of fresh corn on the cob and buttery mashed potatoes? Oh, heck to the yeah! Makes 6 servings.

3 lbs (1.5 kg) boneless pork country-style ribs

⅓ cup (75 mL) packed brown sugar

½ tsp (2 mL) salt

¼ tsp (1 mL) freshly ground black pepper

2 cups (500 mL) Smoky BBQ Sauce (page 341) or store-bought smoky barbecue sauce

Tip

If you don't want to cook the ribs before freezing, place raw ribs and seasonings in a labeled gallon-size (4 L) freezer bag. Pour 2 cups (500 mL) barbecue sauce into a quart-size (1 L) freezer bag. Seal bags, removing as much air as possible, and freeze together. Thaw for 12 to 24 hours, then cook as directed in the slow cooker.

1. Place ribs in a large (approx. 5 quart) slow cooker. Add brown sugar, salt and pepper. Cover and cook on Low for 8 to 10 hours or on High for 5 to 6 hours, until ribs are fork-tender.

2. Remove ribs from slow cooker and transfer to a large bowl. Discard liquid from slow cooker and wipe inside with a paper towel to remove any grease.

3. Return ribs to slow cooker. Add barbecue sauce; stir gently to coat. Cook on High for 1 hour, until heated through.

MAKE IT NOW Serve warm with buttery mashed potatoes (page 292) and/or corn on the cob. You can also serve the meat on buns as sandwiches.

MAKE IT A FREEZER MEAL Let cooked ribs cool completely in sauce. Transfer to a labeled gallon-size (4 L) freezer bag. Seal, removing as much air as possible, and freeze.

REHEAT Place bag in the refrigerator for at least 12 hours or up to 24 hours, or run lukewarm water over it until you can break the ribs apart. Empty bag contents into a microwave-safe bowl; microwave on High for 1-minute intervals until warmed through. Alternatively, empty bag into a medium saucepan and heat over medium-low heat, occasionally stirring gently, for about 5 minutes, until heated through. Serve warm with buttery Mashed Potatoes (page 292) and/or corn on the cob. You can also serve the meat on buns as sandwiches.

	Servings	6 (1 batch)	12 (2 batches)	18 (3 batches)	24 (4 batches)	30 (5 batches)
BULK BATCH	pork ribs	3 lbs (1.5 kg)	6 lbs (3 kg)	9 lbs (4.5 kg)	12 lbs (6 kg)	15 lbs (7.5 kg)
	brown sugar	⅓ cup (75 mL)	⅔ cup (150 mL)	1 cup (250 mL)	1⅓ cups (325 mL)	1⅔ cups (400 mL)
	salt	½ tsp (2 mL)	1 tsp (5 mL)	1½ tsp (7 mL)	2 tsp (10 mL)	2½ tsp (12 mL)
	pepper	¼ tsp (1 mL)	½ tsp (2 mL)	¾ tsp (3 mL)	1 tsp (5 mL)	1¼ tsp (6 mL)
	BBQ Sauce	2 cups (500 mL)	4 cups (1 L)	6 cups (1.5 L)	8 cups (2 L)	10 cups (2.5 L)
	gallon bags	1	2	3	4	5

Bacon Carbonara Pasta Pie

I'm serious about two things: creamy Alfredo sauce and crispy bacon. While this meal may seem unusual, it's probably one of my family's favorite freezer meal of all time. Makes 6 servings.

8 oz (250 g) sliced bacon

8 oz (250 g) spaghetti

2 large eggs, lightly beaten

½ cup (125 mL) freshly grated Parmesan cheese (about 1½ oz/45 g)

½ tsp (2 mL) dried Italian seasoning or dried parsley

1 batch Alfredo Sauce (page 333), cooled

½ cup (125 mL) shredded mozzarella cheese (about 1½ oz/45 g), optional

Garnish

Minced fresh flat-leaf (Italian) parsley, optional

1. In a large skillet, arrange bacon pieces close together and cook for 5 to 6 minutes, turning often, until evenly crispy throughout (do not burn!). Drain on a plate lined with paper towels; set aside to cool. Once cool, chop into ½-inch (1 cm) pieces.

2. Fill a large stockpot with water and bring to a boil over high heat. Cook pasta for 5 to 6 minutes, stirring occasionally, until just beginning to get soft (it should be starting to get tender but have a firm bite). Drain and rinse with cold water to cool quickly. Transfer to a large bowl.

3. Add eggs, Parmesan cheese and Italian seasoning to pasta; stir gently to combine.

4. Press pasta mixture into a lightly greased 9-inch (23 cm) baking dish, so that it covers the bottom and goes all the way up the sides of the dish.

5. Spread Alfredo sauce overtop, then sprinkle with bacon bits and mozzarella cheese, if using.

MAKE IT NOW Preheat oven to 350°F (180°C). Bake in preheated oven for 35 to 40 minutes or until sauce is bubbly on top. Sprinkle with fresh parsley, if using.

MAKE IT A FREEZER MEAL Let unbaked dish cool completely. Wrap baking dish tightly with plastic wrap, pressing down gently to remove as much air as possible. Cover with foil. Label and place in the freezer.

THAW AND COOK Place dish in the refrigerator for at least 24 hours or up to 48 hours to thaw. Preheat oven to 350°F (180°C). Remove plastic wrap and foil. Bake in preheated oven for 40 to 45 minutes, until sauce is bubbly on top. Sprinkle with fresh parsley, if using.

Servings	6 (1 batch)	12 (2 batches)	18 (3 batches)	24 (4 batches)	30 (5 batches)
bacon	8 oz (250 g)	1 lb (500 g)	1½ lbs (750 g)	2 lbs (1 kg)	2½ lbs (1.25 kg)
spaghetti	8 oz (250 g)	1 lb (500 g)	1½ lbs (750 g)	2 lbs (1 kg)	2½ lbs (1.25 kg)
eggs	2	4	6	8	10
Parmesan cheese	½ cup (125 mL)	1 cup (250 mL)	1½ cups (375 mL)	2 cups (500 mL)	2½ cups (625 mL)
Italian seasoning	½ tsp (2 mL)	1 tsp (5 mL)	1½ tsp (7 mL)	2 tsp (10 mL)	2½ tsp (12 mL)
Alfredo Sauce	1 batch	2 batches	3 batches	4 batches	5 batches
mozzarella cheese	½ cup (125 mL)	1 cup (250 mL)	1½ cups (375 mL)	2 cups (500 mL)	2½ cups (625 mL)
9x9 dishes	1	2	3	4	5

BULK BATCH GUIDE

Stromboli

Stromboli is one of the best freezer meals to pull out when lots of extended family or friends come to visit. The thin slices of savory meat, the perfectly light Tuscan-inspired sauce and bold, gooey cheese nestled inside its perfect rustic crust are sure to get the whole group running into the kitchen, all the while cheering your name! *Makes 6 servings.*

1 batch Pizza Dough (page 332), fresh (never frozen)

1 lb (500 g) mozzarella cheese, shredded

½ cup (125 mL) Thirty-Minute Pizza Sauce (page 340)

1 lb (500 g) thinly sliced ham (see Tip, below)

Tip

You can also fill the stromboli with 8 oz (250 g) thinly sliced ham plus 8 oz (250 g) sliced pepperoni, if you prefer.

1. Cut 2 pieces of parchment paper into 16- by 12-inch (40 by 30 cm) rectangles. (If you plan to freeze the stromboli, skip the parchment paper.)

2. After the dough has risen, divide into 2 equal pieces and dump each onto a separate parchment rectangle. Working with one at a time, spread dough into a rectangle about 14 by 10 inches (35 by 25 cm). Layer one-quarter of the mozzarella cheese and half of the ham along one long side of the rectangle, leaving the other side bare. Spread ¼ cup (60 mL) pizza sauce over ham. Layer one-quarter of the mozzarella cheese on top of the sauce, leaving a 1-inch (2.5 cm) border. Fold bare side over toppings and pinch the seam together to seal. Repeat with remaining dough and fillings.

MAKE IT NOW Preheat oven to 375°F (190°C), placing a pizza stone on middle rack. Slide parchment paper with stromboli onto preheated pizza stone. Bake for 30 to 35 minutes or until dough is golden brown and filling is hot. Remove from oven and let cool for 10 minutes, then slice and eat.

MAKE IT A FREEZER MEAL Wrap each unbaked stromboli tightly with plastic wrap. Cover with foil and freeze.

THAW AND COOK Place stromboli in the refrigerator for at least 12 hours or up to 24 hours to thaw. Remove foil and plastic wrap and place each on a piece of parchment paper. Cover with lightly greased plastic wrap. Let dough come to room temperature, about 30 minutes to 1 hour. Meanwhile, preheat oven to 375°F (190°C), positioning a pizza stone on the middle rack. Slide parchment with stromboli onto preheated pizza stone. Bake for 30 to 35 minutes or until dough is golden brown and filling is hot. Remove from oven and let cool for 10 minutes, then slice and eat.

BULK BATCH	Servings	6 (1 batch)	12 (2 batches)	18 (3 batches)	24 (4 batches)	30 (5 batches)
	Pizza Dough	1 batch	2 batches	3 batches	4 batches	5 batches
	mozzarella cheese	1 lb (500 g)	2 lbs (1 kg)	3 lbs (1.5 kg)	4 lbs (2 kg)	5 lbs (2.5 kg)
	Pizza Sauce	½ cup (125 mL)	1 cup (250 mL)	1½ cups (375 mL)	2 cups (500 mL)	2½ cups (625 mL)
	ham	1 lb (500 g)	2 lbs (1 kg)	3 lbs (1.5 kg)	4 lbs (2 kg)	5 lbs (2.5 kg)

Perfect Pizza Any Way You Top It

This recipe has been tried and tested on my family for week after week, making the best homemade pizza every single time. Having these freezer-meal pizza kits on hand means that on busy nights all I have to do is pull out a kit, let the dough rise for a few hours, and add toppings. After 10 minutes of baking we can enjoy the perfect crust, zesty sauce and all our favorite toppings. Makes two 12-inch (40 cm) pizzas or 6 servings.

¼ cup (60 mL) olive oil

1 batch Pizza Dough (page 332), prepared through Step 2

½ cup (125 mL) Thirty-Minute Pizza Sauce (page 340) or store-bought pizza sauce

2 cups (500 mL) shredded mozzarella cheese (about 6 oz/175 g)

30 pepperoni slices (about 3 oz/90 g)

MAKE IT NOW

1. Pour 2 tbsp (30 mL) olive oil each into 2 separate large bowls. Divide pizza dough in half and place in bowls, turning to coat in oil. Cover bowls with greased plastic wrap and let rise for about 45 minutes, until doubled in size.

2. Preheat oven to 500°F (260°C), placing a pizza stone on the middle rack.

3. Working with one piece of dough at a time, dump dough out of bowl onto a large sheet of parchment paper. Very gently, use two fingers to spread it out into a 12-inch (30 cm) circle. If you prefer a thinner crust, press down more firmly and spread out into a 14- to 16-inch (35 to 40 cm) circle.

4. Spread ¼ cup (60 mL) pizza sauce over each dough circle, leaving a ½-inch (1 cm) border. Sprinkle each pizza with 1 cup (250 mL) mozzarella cheese and evenly arrange about 15 pieces of pepperoni.

5. Slide entire pizza, including parchment paper, onto preheated stone. Bake for 8 to 10 minutes, until bottom of crust is starting to turn golden brown and cheese is melted. Remove and let cool for 5 minutes before cutting. Repeat to make second pizza.

MAKE IT A FREEZER MEAL Add 2 tbsp (30 ml) olive oil to a labeled gallon-size (4 L) freezer bag and manipulate to coat all sides. Place one shaped dough (before it rises the first time) in bag, coating all sides with oil. Place half the pizza sauce, shredded mozzarella and pepperoni slices in separate sandwich bags. Seal all the bags, removing as much air as possible, and place in a labeled gallon-size freezer bag. Seal and freeze together as a kit. Repeat with remaining dough, toppings and bags.

THAW AND COOK Remove dough from freezer 3 to 4 hours before making. Let dough thaw and rise at room temperature in sealed bag on the counter. Meanwhile, let topping ingredients thaw at room temperature for up to 30 minutes, then place in the refrigerator while dough rises. Once dough has thawed and doubled in size, about 3 to 4 hours, cook as directed, starting with Step 2 above.

FAMILY-FAVORITE PIZZA VARIATIONS
BBQ Chicken: Spread 2 to 3 tbsp (30 to 45 mL) Smoky BBQ Sauce (page 341) over each circle of dough, leaving a ½-inch (1 cm) border. Then sprinkle each pizza evenly with 1 cup (250 mL) mozzarella cheese, ½ cup (125 mL) shredded cooked chicken, ¼ cup (60 mL) cooked chopped bacon and ¼ cup (60 mL) pineapple tidbits. Bake as directed.

(continued on page 196)

Ham and Pineapple: Spread ¼ cup (60 mL) Thirty-Minute Pizza Sauce over each circle of dough, leaving a ½-inch (1 cm) border. Then sprinkle each pizza evenly with 1 cup (250 mL) mozzarella cheese, 8 to 10 pieces (about 6 oz/175 g) sliced cooked ham and 1/4 cup (60 mL) pineapple tidbits. Bake as directed.

Alfredo Bacon: Spread ½ cup (125 mL) Alfredo Sauce (page 333) over each circle of dough, leaving a ½-inch (1 cm) border. Then sprinkle each pizza evenly with 1 cup (250 mL) mozzarella cheese, ½ cup (125 mL) shredded cooked chicken and ¼ cup (60 mL) cooked chopped bacon. Bake as directed. Garnish with fresh chopped parsley.

Basil Pesto: Spread ¼ cup (60 mL) Easy Pesto (page 339) over each circle of dough, leaving a ½-inch (1 cm) border. Then sprinkle each pizza evenly with 1 cup (250 mL) mozzarella cheese. Bake as directed. Garnish with 7 to 8 fresh basil leaves.

Servings	**6** (1 batch)	**12** (2 batches)	**18** (3 batches)	**24** (4 batches)	**30** (5 batches)
olive oil	¼ cup (60 mL)	½ cup (125 mL)	¾ cup (175 mL)	1 cup (250 mL)	1¼ cup (310 mL)
Pizza Dough	1 batch	2 batches	3 batches	4 batches	5 batches
Pizza Sauce	½ cup (125 mL)	1 cup (250 mL)	1½ cups (375 mL)	2 cups (500 mL)	2½ cups (625 mL)
mozzarella cheese	2 cups (500 mL)	4 cups (1 L)	6 cups (1.5 L)	8 cups (2 L)	10 cups (2.5 L)
pepperoni slices	30	60	90	120	150
gallon bags	4	8	12	16	20
sandwich bags	6	12	18	24	30

This recipe has been tried and tested on my family for week after week, making the best homemade pizza every single time.

Hash-Brown Casserole

Right before I die, I want this to be my last meal. With its creamy cheese, filling potatoes and inviting bites of smoky ham, this is comfort food at its finest. Did I just hear you say you want to eat some right now? Well, me too. Makes 6 servings.

¼ cup (60 mL) butter

2 cups (500 mL) sour cream

3 cups (750 mL) shredded Cheddar cheese (about 12 oz/375 g)

1 tsp (5 mL) salt

¼ tsp (1 mL) onion powder

¼ tsp (1 mL) freshly ground black pepper

1 package (1½ lbs/750 g) frozen diced hash browns (see Tip, below)

2 cups (500 mL) diced cooked ham (about 10 oz/300 g)

1 tsp (5 mL) dried parsley

Tip

If you don't want to use frozen hash browns, you can use 6 medium potatoes that have been boiled, cooled and diced.

1. In a medium, microwave-safe bowl, microwave butter on High for 20 to 30 seconds, until melted. Add sour cream and stir to combine. Add Cheddar cheese, salt, onion powder and pepper; stir well to combine.

2. Break up frozen hash browns, then place in a large bowl. Add sour cream mixture and ham; stir to combine.

3. Place in a 13- by 9-inch (33 by 23 cm) baking dish and spread out with the back of a large spoon until top is smooth. Sprinkle with parsley.

MAKE IT NOW Preheat oven to 350°F (180°C). Bake casserole in preheated oven for 45 to 55 minutes or until bubbly all over and top is golden brown.

MAKE IT A FREEZER MEAL Cover assembled dish with plastic wrap, pressing down gently to remove air. Cover with foil, label and freeze.

THAW AND COOK Place dish in the refrigerator for at least 12 hours or up to 24 hours to thaw. Preheat oven to 350°F (180°C). Remove foil and plastic wrap. Bake casserole in preheated oven for 55 to 60 minutes or until bubbly all over and top is golden brown.

BULK BATCH GUIDE

Servings	6 (1 batch)	12 (2 batches)	18 (3 batches)	24 (4 batches)	30 (5 batches)
butter	¼ cup (60 mL)	½ cup (125 mL)	¾ cup (175 mL)	1 cup (250 mL)	1¼ cups (310 mL)
sour cream	2 cups (500 mL)	4 cups (1 L)	6 cups (1.5 L)	8 cups (2 L)	10 cups (2.5 L)
Cheddar cheese	3 cups (750 mL)	6 cups (1.5 L)	9 cups (2.25 L)	12 cups (3 L)	15 cups (3.75 L)
salt	1 tsp (5 mL)	2 tsp (10 mL)	1 tbsp (15 mL)	4 tsp (20 mL)	5 tsp (25 mL)
onion powder	¼ tsp (1 mL)	½ tsp (2 mL)	¾ tsp (3 mL)	1 tsp (5 mL)	1¼ tsp (6 mL)
pepper	¼ tsp (1 mL)	½ tsp (2 mL)	¾ tsp (3 mL)	1 tsp (5 mL)	1¼ tsp (6 mL)
hash browns	1½ lbs (750 g)	3 lbs (1.5 kg)	4½ lbs (2.25 kg)	6 lbs (3 kg)	7½ lbs (3.75 kg)
ham	2 cups (500 mL)	4 cups (1 L)	6 cups (1.5 L)	8 cups (2 L)	10 cups (2.5 L)
dried parsley	1 tsp (5 mL)	2 tsp (10 mL)	1 tbsp (15 mL)	4 tsp (20 mL)	5 tsp (25 mL)
13x9 dishes	1	2	3	4	5

Smoky Pulled Pork Sandwiches

Pulled pork sandwiches seem to be a huge hit at many restaurants these days, and I can see why. What's not to love about that juicy, fall-apart pork that has been slathered with the perfect blend of hickory-inspired sweetness? Once you take a bite of these sandwiches, you will never want to go out to eat again . . . at least, not for pulled pork sandwiches. Makes 6 servings.

2 cups (500 mL) store-bought smoky barbecue sauce or Smoky BBQ Sauce (page 341), divided

1 can (12 oz/355 mL) root beer or 1 cup (250 mL) water

3 lbs (1.5 kg) boneless pork shoulder roast, trimmed

To Serve
Cabbage slaw (optional)

6 buns, split

1. In a medium bowl, combine 1 cup (250 mL) barbecue sauce and the root beer.

MAKE IT NOW Place pork roast in a large (approx. 5 quart) slow cooker. Pour sauce mixture overtop. Cook on Low for 8 to 10 hours, until pork is fork-tender. Remove from slow cooker, discarding juices. Transfer pork to a cutting board and, using two forks, shred into pieces, discarding excess fat. Return meat to slow cooker. Pour remaining 1 cup (250 mL) barbecue sauce over shredded pork, stir, and cook for 30 minutes on High, until warmed through. Serve in buns, topped with slaw, if using.

MAKE IT A FREEZER MEAL Place pork roast in a labeled gallon-size (4 L) freezer bag. Add sauce mixture to bag. Place remaining 1 cup (250 mL) barbecue sauce in a quart-size (1 L) freezer bag. Seal both, removing as much air as possible, and freeze together as a kit.

THAW AND COOK Place bags in the refrigerator for at least 12 hours or up to 24 hours to thaw. Place pork and sauce in a large (approx. 5 quart) slow cooker. Cook on Low for 8 to 10 hours, until tender and juicy. Remove pork from slow cooker, discarding juices. Transfer to a cutting board and, using two forks, shred into pieces, discarding excess fat. Return meat to slow cooker. Pour remaining 1 cup (250 mL) barbecue sauce over shredded pork, stir, and cook on High for 30 minutes, until heated through. Serve in buns, topped with slaw, if using.

BULK BATCH	Servings	6 (1 batch)	12 (2 batches)	18 (3 batches)	24 (4 batches)	30 (5 batches)
	smoky barbecue sauce	2 cups (500 mL)	4 cups (1 L)	6 cups (1.5 L)	8 cups (2 L)	10 cups (2.5 L)
	root beer	12 oz (355 mL)	24 oz (710 mL)	36 oz (1.065 L)	48 oz (1.42 L)	60 oz (1.775 L)
	pork roast	3 lbs (1.5 kg)	6 lbs (3 kg)	9 lbs (4.5 kg)	12 lbs (6 kg)	15 lbs (7.5 kg)
	gallon bags	1	2	3	4	5
	quart bags	1	2	3	4	5

Perfect Pork Carnitas Tacos

Ground beef, fish or chicken tacos seem to get all the attention, but what about poor, oft-forgotten pork? These carnitas are sweet and spicy yet have a refreshing citrus undertone. Once you add toppings, I guarantee that this is the taco you will be forever craving. Makes 6 servings.

1 tbsp (15 mL) garlic powder

1 tbsp (15 mL) chili powder

¼ tsp (1 mL) salt

⅛ tsp (0.5 mL) freshly ground black pepper

2 lbs (1 kg) boneless pork shoulder, cut into 3-inch (7.5 cm) cubes

2 tbsp (30 mL) olive oil

¾ cup (175 mL) water (approx.)

½ cup (125 mL) orange juice

¼ cup (60 mL) freshly squeezed lime juice

¼ cup (60 mL) packed brown sugar

1 bay leaf

To Serve

12 6-inch (10 cm) corn tortillas, warmed

Crumbled Cotija cheese (optional)

Shredded red cabbage (optional)

Salsa (optional)

Sour cream (optional)

Avocado, sliced or diced (optional)

Fresh cilantro leaves (optional)

1. In a medium bowl, combine garlic powder, chili powder, salt and pepper. Add pork and toss until meat is completely coated.

2. In a large Dutch oven or heavy-bottomed saucepan, heat olive oil over medium-high heat. Add pork and cook for about 1 minute on each side, until browned. Reduce heat to low and add water, orange juice, lime juice, brown sugar and bay leaf. Add more water if necessary, to just barely cover the meat.

3. Bring liquid to a boil over high heat, stirring often. Cover and immediately reduce heat to low. Simmer for 1½ hours, until meat is fairly tender. Remove lid, increase heat to medium and continue cooking for 30 minutes or until liquid has evaporated. Discard bay leaf. Transfer pork to a cutting board, discarding liquid. Using two forks, shred into pieces, discarding excess fat.

MAKE IT NOW Fill tortillas with shredded pork. Add Cotija cheese, cabbage, salsa, sour cream, avocado and/or cilantro, if using. Serve.

MAKE IT A FREEZER MEAL Let shredded pork cool, then transfer to a labeled gallon-size (4 L) freezer bag. Seal, removing as much air as possible, and freeze. If desired, place tortillas in a separate gallon-size freezer bag and freeze alongside pork as a kit.

REHEAT Place pork in refrigerator for 12 hours to thaw, or run lukewarm or hot water over bag until you can break the meat apart. Place meat in a microwave-safe bowl; microwave on High for 1-minute intervals, until warmed through. Alternatively, place pork in a medium saucepan and heat over medium-low heat, frequently stirring gently, for about 4 minutes, until heated through. Fill tortillas with shredded pork and add Cotija cheese, cabbage, salsa, sour cream, avocado and/or cilantro, if using.

BULK BATCH GUIDE	Servings	6 (1 batch)	12 (2 batches)	18 (3 batches)	24 (4 batches)	30 (5 batches)
	garlic powder	1 tbsp (15 mL)	2 tbsp (30 mL)	3 tbsp (45 mL)	¼ cup (60 mL)	⅓ cup (75 mL)
	chili powder	1 tbsp (15 mL)	2 tbsp (30 mL)	3 tbsp (45 mL)	¼ cup (60 mL)	⅓ cup (75 mL)
	salt	¼ tsp (1 mL)	½ tsp (2 mL)	¾ tsp (3 mL)	1 tsp (5 mL)	1¼ tsp (6 mL)
	pepper	⅛ tsp (0.5 mL)	¼ tsp (1 mL)	⅓ tsp (1.5 mL)	½ tsp (2 mL)	¾ tsp (3 mL)
	pork shoulder	2 lbs (1 kg)	4 lbs (2 kg)	6 lbs (3 kg)	8 lbs (4 kg)	10 lbs (5 kg)
	olive oil	2 tbsp (30 mL)	¼ cup (60 mL)	6 tbsp (90 mL)	½ cup (125 mL)	⅔ cup (150 mL)
	water	¾ cup (175 mL)	1½ cups (375 mL)	2¼ cups (560 mL)	3 cups (750 mL)	3¾ cups (925 mL)
	orange juice	½ cup (125 mL)	1 cup (250 mL)	1½ cups (375 mL)	2 cups (500 mL)	2½ cups (625 mL)
	lime juice	¼ cup (60 mL)	½ cup (125 mL)	¾ cup (175 mL)	1 cup (250 mL)	1¼ cups (310 mL)
	brown sugar	¼ cup (60 mL)	½ cup (125 mL)	¾ cup (175 mL)	1 cup (250 mL)	1¼ cups (310 mL)
	bay leaves	1	2	3	4	5
	gallon bags	1	2	3	4	5

BEEF

Rosemary Pot Roast 205

Steak with Gorgonzola Butter 209

Brown Sugar Meatloaf 210

Balsamic Short Ribs 213

BBQ Beef Brisket 214

Mongolian Beef and Green Beans 217

Thai Beef Stir-Fry 218

Venezuelan Steak 221

Baked Ziti 222

Momma's Lasagna 225

Tempting Taco Pasta Shell Casserole 226

Mole Tamale Pie 229

Sizzlin' Steak Fajitas 232

French Dip Sandwiches 235

Rosemary Pot Roast

This pot roast is anything but boring. I find that a bit of rosemary goes a long way when it comes to adding bold flavor with little effort. Add a fresh garden salad and warmed Brown 'n' Serve Rolls (page 284) and you've got a five-star meal. Makes 6 servings.

1 tsp (5 mL) salt

¼ tsp (1 mL) freshly ground black pepper

1½ tsp (7 mL) onion powder

3 lbs (1.5 kg) boneless beef chuck roast

½ cup (125 mL) freshly squeezed lemon juice (about 2 large lemons)

¼ cup (60 mL) balsamic vinegar

2 tsp (10 mL) minced garlic

1 tsp (5 mL) dried rosemary

½ tsp (2 mL) celery salt

To Serve

2 tbsp (30 mL) canola oil

1 tbsp (15 mL) butter, softened

2 lbs (1 kg) yellow-fleshed baby potatoes

Salt and freshly ground black pepper

1 lb (500 g) baby carrots

3 to 4 fresh rosemary sprigs

1. In a small bowl, combine salt, pepper and onion powder. Using your hands, rub mixture onto all sides of roast.

2. In another small bowl, combine lemon juice, balsamic vinegar, garlic, rosemary and celery salt. Stir to combine.

MAKE IT NOW In a large skillet, heat oil over high heat. Add roast and cook on each side for 2 to 3 minutes, until brown. Remove meat from skillet. Add balsamic mixture to skillet; stir to combine, scraping up any brown bits on bottom of pan. Remove from heat. Use butter to grease the bottom of a large (approx. 5 quart) slow cooker. Place potatoes in bottom of slow cooker; sprinkle with salt and pepper to taste. Place roast on top. Arrange carrots around roast. Pour balsamic mixture over meat. Cover and cook on Low for 8 to 10 hours or on High for 4 to 5 hours, until meat is very tender. Serve.

MAKE IT A FREEZER MEAL Transfer seasoned roast to a labeled gallon-size (4 L) freezer bag. Pour balsamic mixture over meat. Seal, removing as much air as possible, and freeze.

THAW AND COOK Place bag in the refrigerator for 24 hours to thaw. In a large skillet, heat canola oil over high heat. Add roast and cook on each side for 2 to 3 minutes, until brown. Remove meat from skillet. Add balsamic marinade to skillet; stir to combine, scraping up any brown bits on bottom of pan. Remove from heat. Use butter to grease the bottom of a large (approx. 5 quart) slow cooker. Place potatoes in bottom of slow cooker; sprinkle with salt and pepper to taste. Place roast on top. Arrange carrots around roast. Pour balsamic mixture over meat. Cover and cook on Low for 8 to 10 hours or on High for 4 to 5 hours, until meat is very tender. Serve.

	Servings	6 (1 batch)	12 (2 batches)	18 (3 batches)	24 (4 batches)	30 (5 batches)
BULK BATCH GUIDE	salt	1 tsp (5 mL)	2 tsp (10 mL)	1 tbsp (15 mL)	4 tsp (20 mL)	5 tsp (25 mL)
	pepper	¼ tsp (1 mL)	½ tsp (2 mL)	¾ tsp (3 mL)	1 tsp (5 mL)	1¼ tsp (6 mL)
	onion powder	1½ tsp (7 mL)	1 tbsp (15 mL)	1½ tbsp (22 mL)	2 tbsp (30 mL)	2½ tbsp (37 mL)
	chuck roast	3 lbs (1.5 kg)	6 lbs (3 kg)	9 lbs (4.5 kg)	12 lbs (6 kg)	15 lbs (7.5 kg)
	lemon juice	½ cup (125 mL)	1 cup (250 mL)	1½ cups (375 mL)	2 cups (500 mL)	2½ cups (625 mL)
	balsamic vinegar	¼ cup (60 mL)	½ cup (125 mL)	¾ cup (175 mL)	1 cup (250 mL)	1¼ cups (310 mL)
	garlic	2 tsp (10 mL)	4 tsp (20 mL)	2 tbsp (30 mL)	8 tsp (40 mL)	10 tsp (50 mL)
	dried rosemary	1 tsp (5 mL)	2 tsp (10 mL)	1 tbsp (15 mL)	4 tsp (20 mL)	5 tsp (25 mL)
	celery salt	½ tsp (2 mL)	1 tsp (5 mL)	1½ tsp (7 mL)	2 tsp (10 mL)	2½ tsp (12 mL)
	gallon bags	1	2	3	4	5

Steak with Gorgonzola Butter

Give your steak a makeover with this delicious Gorgonzola butter sauce. Gorgonzola is an Italian blue cheese made from full-fat cow's milk that makes a great topping to a beautifully seared steak. Tuck this stout, earthy recipe into your back pocket for the next time you want to impress an especially important dinner guest. Makes 6 servings.

Gorgonzola Butter

¼ cup (60 mL) butter

2 tbsp (30 mL) Gorgonzola cheese

½ tsp (2 mL) dried thyme

½ tsp (2 mL) dried parsley

Steaks

1 tbsp (15 mL) garlic powder

1 tsp (5 mL) onion salt

1 tsp (5 mL) paprika

¼ tsp (1 mL) freshly ground black pepper

6 New York strip beef steaks or skirt steaks (each about 8 oz/250 g)

To Serve

2 tbsp (30 mL) canola oil

Fresh thyme leaves (optional)

1. *Gorgonzola Butter:* In a small, microwave-safe bowl, microwave butter on High for about 20 seconds, until melted. Add Gorgonzola, thyme and parsley. Using a fork, mash cheese until mixture is well incorporated, with no large chunks.

2. *Steaks:* In a small bowl, combine garlic powder, onion salt, paprika and pepper. Using your hands, rub onto both sides of each steak.

MAKE IT NOW In a large skillet, heat canola oil over medium-high heat. Once oil is smoking, add steaks, in batches as necessary, and cook for 3 minutes; flip and cook for another 3 minutes. Flip once more and cook for 1 minute on each side, until steaks are seared but still slightly pink inside (medium-rare). Cook for 1 minute longer on each side for medium doneness. Transfer steaks to a plate, put 1 tbsp (15 mL) Gorgonzola butter on each steak, then cover with foil and let rest for 6 to 7 minutes. Sprinkle fresh thyme overtop, if using; serve.

MAKE IT A FREEZER MEAL Place seasoned steaks in a labeled gallon-size (4 L) freezer bag. Place Gorgonzola butter in a sandwich-size bag; seal, removing as much air as possible, and place in gallon bag with steaks. Seal together, removing as much air as possible, and freeze.

THAW AND COOK Place bags in the refrigerator for at least 24 hours or up to 48 hours to thaw. In a large skillet, heat oil over medium-high heat. Once oil is smoking, add steaks, in batches as necessary, and cook for 3 minutes; flip and cook for another 3 minutes. Flip once more and cook for 1 minute on each side, until steaks are seared but still slightly pink inside (medium-rare). Cook for 1 minute longer on each side for medium doneness. Transfer steaks to a plate, put 1 tbsp (15 mL) Gorgonzola butter on each steak, then cover with foil and let rest for 6 to 7 minutes. Sprinkle fresh thyme overtop, if using; serve.

BULK BATCH GUIDE

Servings	6 (1 batch)	12 (2 batches)	18 (3 batches)	24 (4 batches)	30 (5 batches)
butter	¼ cup (60 mL)	½ cup (125 mL)	¾ cup (175 mL)	1 cup (250 mL)	1¼ cups (310 mL)
Gorgonzola cheese	2 tbsp (30 mL)	¼ cup (60 mL)	6 tbsp (90 mL)	½ cup (125 mL)	⅔ cup (150 mL)
dried thyme	½ tsp (2 mL)	1 tsp (5 mL)	1½ tsp (7 mL)	2 tsp (10 mL)	2½ tsp (12 mL)
dried parsley	½ tsp (2 mL)	1 tsp (5 mL)	1½ tsp (7 mL)	2 tsp (10 mL)	2½ tsp (12 mL)
garlic powder	1 tbsp (15 mL)	2 tbsp (30 mL)	3 tbsp (45 mL)	¼ cup (60 mL)	⅓ cup (75 mL)
onion salt	1 tsp (5 mL)	2 tsp (10 mL)	1 tbsp (15 mL)	4 tsp (20 mL)	5 tsp (25 mL)
paprika	1 tsp (5 mL)	2 tsp (10 mL)	1 tbsp (15 mL)	4 tsp (20 mL)	5 tsp (25 mL)
pepper	¼ tsp (1 mL)	½ tsp (2 mL)	¾ tsp (3 mL)	1 tsp (5 mL)	1¼ tsp (6 mL)
beef steaks	6	12	18	24	30
gallon bags	1	2	3	4	5
sandwich bags	1	2	3	4	5

Brown Sugar Meatloaf

Meatloaf is a classic that gets moaned and groaned about on the regular. Well, that is all about to change when your family tries this kid-tested-for-years, perfectly sweet in just the right way meatloaf. This is such a hit that it is always devoured in just a few minutes! Makes 6 servings.

Meatloaf

1½ lbs (750 g) ground beef

½ cup (125 mL) panko bread crumbs

¼ cup (60 mL) Smoky BBQ Sauce (page 341) or store-bought smoky barbecue sauce

1 tbsp (15 mL) Dijon mustard

1 tbsp (15 mL) honey

½ tsp (2 mL) salt

½ tsp (2 mL) freshly ground black pepper

Sauce

⅓ cup (75 mL) packed brown sugar

½ cup (125 mL) ketchup

1 tbsp (15 mL) Worcestershire sauce

1. *Meatloaf:* In a large bowl, using your hands, squish together ground beef, panko crumbs, barbecue sauce, mustard, honey, salt and pepper, just until combined. Do not overmix.

2. *Sauce:* In a small bowl, stir together brown sugar, ketchup and Worcestershire sauce until smooth.

MAKE IT NOW Preheat oven to 350°F (180°C). Pack ground beef mixture into a 9- by 5-inch (23 cm by 12.5 cm) loaf pan. Spread sauce over meat. Place baking dish on a rimmed baking sheet to catch drips. Bake in preheated oven for 50 minutes, until internal temperature registers 160°F (71°C). Drain off fat and let cool for 5 to 10 minutes; serve.

MAKE IT A FREEZER MEAL Pack ground beef mixture into a a 9- by 5-inch (23 cm by 12.5 cm) loaf pan. Wrap with several layers of plastic wrap, pressing down gently to remove as much air as possible. Place sauce mixture in a quart-size (1 L) freezer bag, seal and place on top of wrapped meatloaf. Wrap both completely with aluminum foil, label and freeze.

THAW AND COOK Place meatloaf and sauce bag in refrigerator for 24 hours to thaw. Preheat oven to 350°F (180°C). Remove foil, sauce bag and plastic wrap. Spread sauce evenly over meat. Place loaf pan on a rimmed baking sheet to catch drips. Bake in preheated oven for 50 minutes, until internal temperature registers 160°F (71°C). Drain off fat and let cool for 5 to 10 minutes; serve.

BULK BATCH GUIDE	Servings	6 (1 batch)	12 (2 batches)	18 (3 batches)	24 (4 batches)	30 (5 batches)
	ground beef	1½ lbs (750 g)	3 lbs (1.5 kg)	4½ lbs (2.25 kg)	6 lbs (3 kg)	7½ lbs (3.75 kg)
	panko	½ cup (125 mL)	1 cup (250 mL)	1½ cups (375 mL)	2 cups (500 mL)	2½ cups (625 mL)
	BBQ Sauce	¼ cup (60 mL)	½ cup (125 mL)	¾ cup (175 mL)	1 cup (250 mL)	1¼ cups (310 mL)
	Dijon mustard	1 tbsp (15 mL)	2 tbsp (30 mL)	3 tbsp (45 mL)	¼ cup (60 mL)	⅓ cup (75 mL)
	honey	1 tbsp (15 mL)	2 tbsp (30 mL)	3 tbsp (45 mL)	¼ cup (60 mL)	⅓ cup (75 mL)
	salt	½ tsp (2 mL)	1 tsp (5 mL)	1½ tsp (7 mL)	2 tsp (10 mL)	2½ tsp (12 mL)
	pepper	½ tsp (2 mL)	1 tsp (5 mL)	1½ tsp (7 mL)	2 tsp (10 mL)	2½ tsp (12 mL)
	brown sugar	⅓ cup (75 mL)	⅔ cup (150 mL)	1 cup (250 mL)	1⅓ cups (325 mL)	1⅔ cups (400 mL)
	ketchup	½ cup (125 mL)	1 cup (250 mL)	1½ cups (375 mL)	2 cups (500 mL)	2½ cups (625 mL)
	Worcestershire	1 tbsp (15 mL)	2 tbsp (30 mL)	3 tbsp (45 mL)	¼ cup (60 mL)	⅓ cup (75 mL)
	9x5 loaf pans	1	2	3	4	5
	quart bags	1	2	3	4	5

Balsamic Short Ribs

Did you know that when you cook down balsamic vinegar you are left with all the aromatics from the wood barrels in which it's aged? Add some amazing herbs and that, my friends, is what makes these short ribs so unbelievably good. The acids in the vinegar break down the beef so the ribs are tender and perfect, every time. I am not exaggerating when I tell you this dish is nothing short of melt-in-your-mouth, falling-off-the-bone, tender, juicy culinary perfection. Makes 6 servings.

1 tsp (5 mL) dried oregano

½ tsp (2 mL) paprika

½ tsp (2 mL) garlic powder

½ tsp (2 mL) onion powder

¼ tsp (1 mL) dried sage

¼ tsp (1 mL) dried rosemary

3 lbs (1.5 kg) beef short ribs

2 tbsp (30 mL) vegetable oil

1 tsp (5 mL) minced garlic

1 can (15 oz/425 mL) tomato sauce

1 cup (250 mL) balsamic vinegar

½ cup (125 mL) packed brown sugar

To Serve

2 tbsp (30 mL) vegetable oil

Salt

1. In a small bowl, combine oregano, paprika, garlic powder, onion powder, sage and rosemary.

2. Using your hands, rub herb mixture evenly onto all sides of the ribs.

3. In a large skillet over medium heat, heat 2 tbsp (30 mL) vegetable oil. Once hot, add garlic; cook, stirring often, for 2 minutes, until fragrant. Add tomato sauce, balsamic vinegar and brown sugar; stir constantly until it comes to a boil. Immediately remove from heat. Continue stirring until all the sugar has dissolved.

MAKE IT NOW In another large skillet, heat 2 tbsp (30 mL) oil over high heat. Once oil is hot and shimmering, add ribs. Cook meat on all sides for about 4 minutes total, turning as each side is browned. Place ribs and sauce in a large (approx. 5 quart) slow cooker. Cover and cook on Low for 6 to 8 hours or on High for 3 to 4 hours, until ribs are tender. Season to taste with salt.

MAKE IT A FREEZER MEAL Place seasoned ribs in a labeled gallon-size (4 L) freezer bag; seal, removing as much air as possible, and refrigerate immediately. Meanwhile, let sauce cool completely. Transfer to a quart-size (1 L) freezer bag. Seal bag, removing as much air as possible, and freeze bags together.

THAW AND COOK Place bags in refrigerator for at least 12 hours or up to 24 hours to thaw. In a large skillet, heat 2 tbsp (30 mL) vegetable oil over high heat. Once oil is hot and shimmering, add ribs. Cook ribs on all sides for about 4 minutes total, turning as each side is browned. Place ribs and sauce in a large (approx. 5 quart) slow cooker. Cover and cook on Low for 6 to 8 hours or on High for 3 to 4 hours, until ribs are tender. Season to taste with salt.

BULK BATCH GUIDE Servings	6 (1 batch)	12 (2 batches)	18 (3 batches)	24 (4 batches)	30 (5 batches)
dried oregano	1 tsp (5 mL)	2 tsp (10 mL)	1 tbsp (15 mL)	4 tsp (20 mL)	5 tsp (25 mL)
paprika	½ tsp (2 mL)	1 tsp (5 mL)	1½ tsp (7 mL)	2 tsp (10 mL)	2½ tsp (12 mL)
garlic powder	½ tsp (2 mL)	1 tsp (5 mL)	1½ tsp (7 mL)	2 tsp (10 mL)	2½ tsp (12 mL)
onion powder	½ tsp (2 mL)	1 tsp (5 mL)	1½ tsp (7 mL)	2 tsp (10 mL)	2½ tsp (12 mL)
dried sage	¼ tsp (1 mL)	½ tsp (2 mL)	¾ tsp (3 mL)	1 tsp (5 mL)	1¼ tsp (6 mL)
dried rosemary	¼ tsp (1 mL)	½ tsp (2 mL)	¾ tsp (3 mL)	1 tsp (5 mL)	1¼ tsp (6 mL)
beef short ribs	3 lbs (1.5 kg)	6 lbs (3 kg)	9 lbs (4.5 kg)	12 lbs (6 kg)	15 lbs (7.5 kg)
vegetable oil	2 tbsp (30 mL)	¼ cup (60 mL)	6 tbsp (90 mL)	½ cup (125 mL)	⅔ cup (150 mL)
garlic	1 tsp (5 mL)	2 tsp (10 mL)	1 tbsp (15 mL)	4 tsp (20 mL)	5 tsp (25 mL)
tomato sauce	15 oz (425 mL)	30 oz (850 mL)	45 oz (1.275 L)	60 oz (1.7 L)	75 oz (2.125 L)
balsamic vinegar	1 cup (250 mL)	2 cups (500 mL)	3 cups (750 mL)	4 cups (1 L)	5 cups (1.25 L)
brown sugar	½ cup (125 mL)	1 cup (250 mL)	1½ cups (375 mL)	2 cups (500 mL)	2½ cups (625 mL)
gallon bags	1	2	3	4	5
quart bags	1	2	3	4	5

BBQ Beef Brisket

Yes, I know, just thinking about making brisket can be intimidating. But trust me, this recipe is so easy to make, and it turns out beautifully every time — you'll have your family wondering if a professional cooked dinner! I usually wait for the meat to go on sale, then freeze it for a special night. Makes 6 servings.

½ cup (125 mL) packed brown sugar

¼ cup (60 mL) paprika

2 tbsp (30 mL) salt

2 tbsp (30 mL) garlic powder

2 tbsp (30 mL) onion powder

1 tbsp (15 mL) freshly ground black pepper

½ tsp (2 mL) chili powder

3 lb (1.5 kg) piece beef brisket, trimmed

1 tbsp (15 mL) liquid smoke

1 cup (250 mL) Smoky BBQ Sauce (page 341) or store-bought smoky barbecue sauce (optional)

1. In a small bowl, combine brown sugar, paprika, salt, garlic powder, onion powder, pepper and chili powder.

2. Place a large piece of foil, about 16 by 24 inches (40 by 60 cm), in a 13- by 9-inch (33 by 23 cm) baking dish. Place brisket on top of foil. Using your hands, season both sides of meat with seasoning mixture. Pour liquid smoke over brisket and, using your hands, rub it all over meat. Arrange brisket fat side up and wrap completely in foil. Cover baking dish with additional foil. Refrigerate for a minimum of 8 hours or up to 2 days.

3. Preheat oven to 275°F (140°C). Bake brisket in preheated oven for 3 hours; if you are cooking a larger piece, calculate about 1 hour per pound (500 g). Turn off heat and let covered brisket sit in the oven (with the door tightly closed) for 1 hour, until tender. Remove from oven. Preheat broiler. Remove foil and brush top of brisket with any drippings from bottom of baking dish. Broil meat until lightly browned and fat is crispy.

MAKE IT NOW Let brisket cool for 10 minutes. Cut across the grain into ½-inch (1 cm) slices. Serve with barbecue sauce on the side, if using.

MAKE IT A FREEZER MEAL Let cooked brisket cool at room temperature for up to 30 minutes, then refrigerate to cool completely. Cut across the grain into ½-inch (1 cm) slices. Pour barbecue sauce over meat, if using. Place in a labeled gallon-size (4 L) freezer bag. Seal, removing as much air as possible, and freeze.

REHEAT Place bag in the refrigerator for at least 12 hours or up to 24 hours prior to thaw. Preheat oven to 350°F (180°C). Pour bag contents into a 13- by 9-inch (33 by 23 cm) baking dish, cover with foil and place in preheated oven for about 30 minutes, until heated through.

Servings	6 (1 batch)	12 (2 batches)	18 (3 batches)	24 (4 batches)	30 (5 batches)
brown sugar	½ cup (125 mL)	1 cup (250 mL)	1½ cups (375 mL)	2 cups (500 mL)	2½ cups (625 mL)
paprika	¼ cup (60 mL)	½ cup (125 mL)	¾ cup (175 mL)	1 cup (250 mL)	1¼ cups (310 mL)
salt	2 tbsp (30 mL)	¼ cup (60 mL)	6 tbsp (90 mL)	½ cup (125 mL)	⅔ cup (150 mL)
garlic powder	2 tbsp (30 mL)	¼ cup (60 mL)	6 tbsp (90 mL)	½ cup (125 mL)	⅔ cup (150 mL)
onion powder	2 tbsp (30 mL)	¼ cup (60 mL)	6 tbsp (90 mL)	½ cup (125 mL)	⅔ cup (150 mL)
pepper	1 tbsp (15 mL)	2 tbsp (30 mL)	3 tbsp (45 mL)	¼ cup (60 mL)	⅓ cup (75 mL)
chili powder	½ tsp (2 mL)	1 tsp (5 mL)	1½ tsp (7 mL)	2 tsp (10 mL)	2½ tsp (12 mL)
beef brisket	3 lbs (1.5 kg)	6 lbs (3 kg)	9 lbs (4.5 kg)	12 lbs (6 kg)	15 lbs (7.5 kg)
liquid smoke	1 tbsp (15 mL)	2 tbsp (30 mL)	3 tbsp (45 mL)	¼ cup (60 mL)	⅓ cup (75 mL)
BBQ Sauce	1 cup (250 mL)	2 cups (500 mL)	3 cups (750 mL)	4 cups (1 L)	5 cups (1.25 L)
gallon bags	1	2	3	4	5

BULK BATCH GUIDE

Mongolian Beef and Green Beans

I used to go for dinner to a certain restaurant and found myself ordering their Mongolian beef at every visit. After some time and some very real late-night cravings, I decided I could not only make it myself but do it better. This dish is absolutely to die for! Makes 6 servings.

½ cup (125 mL) tamari sauce

½ cup (125 mL) water

½ cup (125 mL) packed dark brown sugar

1½ cups + 1 tbsp (390 mL) vegetable oil (approx.), divided

2 tbsp (30 mL) minced garlic

1 tsp (5 mL) minced or grated ginger

½ cup (125 mL) cornstarch

2 lbs (1 kg) beef flank steak, sliced across the grain into ¼-inch (0.5 cm) strips

1 lb (500 g) frozen whole green beans

To Serve

1 tbsp (15 mL) vegetable oil

1. In a medium bowl, combine tamari sauce, water and brown sugar.

2. In a medium saucepan, heat 1 tbsp (15 mL) vegetable oil over medium heat. Add garlic and ginger; cook, stirring, for 1 to 2 minutes, until garlic begins to brown. Add tamari sauce mixture and bring to a boil, stirring constantly. Boil for 2 to 3 minutes, until sauce has thickened slightly. Remove from heat and set aside.

3. In a medium, heavy-bottomed saucepan or wok, heat 1½ cups (375 mL) vegetable oil to 350°F (180°C) — you'll need at least 1 inch (2.5 cm) oil.

4. Place cornstarch in a small bowl. In batches, lightly dip each piece of beef in cornstarch to coat. Discard any excess cornstarch.

5. Working in batches of about ten at a time, deep-fry beef for 30 seconds to 1 minute per side, until edges are light brown and crispy. Drain on a plate lined with paper towels. Safely discard oil.

MAKE IT NOW Add 1 tbsp (15 mL) vegetable oil to wok or saucepan and return to medium-high heat. Add green beans; cook, stirring constantly, for 2 to 3 minutes, until tender-crisp. Add beef strips and sauce mixture; cook, stirring, for 2 to 3 minutes, until beef is heated through and sauce has thickened. Serve immediately.

MAKE IT A FREEZER MEAL Spread fried beef on a baking sheet lined with parchment paper, leaving space between pieces. Freeze for 30 minutes to 1 hour, until solid. Meanwhile, let sauce cool completely. Transfer beef to a labeled gallon-size (4 L) freezer bag. If necessary, transfer frozen green beans to another labeled gallon-size freezer bag and seal, removing as much air as possible. Pour cooled sauce into a labeled quart-size (1 L) freezer bag and seal, removing as much air as possible. Place sauce and green bean bags into beef bag and seal as a kit, removing as much air as possible. Freeze.

COOK FROM FROZEN Run hot water over sauce bag until thawed. In a wok or large skillet, heat 1 tbsp (15 mL) vegetable oil over high heat. Add green beans; cook, stirring constantly, for 3 to 4 minutes, until tender-crisp. Add beef strips and sauce mixture; cook, stirring, for 2 to 3 minutes, until beef is heated through and evenly coated with sauce. Serve immediately.

BULK BATCH GUIDE	Servings	6 (1 batch)	12 (2 batches)	18 (3 batches)	24 (4 batches)	30 (5 batches)
	tamari sauce	½ cup (125 mL)	1 cup (250 mL)	1½ cups (375 mL)	2 cups (500 mL)	2½ cups (625 mL)
	water	½ cup (125 mL)	1 cup (250 mL)	1½ cups (375 mL)	2 cups (500 mL)	2½ cups (625 mL)
	brown sugar	½ cup (125 mL)	1 cup (250 mL)	1½ cups (375 mL)	2 cups (500 mL)	2½ cups (625 mL)
	vegetable oil	1½ cups + 1 tbsp (390 mL)	1½ cups + 1 tbsp (390 mL)	1½ cups + 1 tbsp (390 mL)	1½ cups + 1 tbsp (390 mL)	1½ cups + 1 tbsp (390 mL)
	garlic	2 tbsp (30 mL)	¼ cup (60 mL)	6 tbsp (90 mL)	½ cup (125 mL)	⅔ cup (150 mL)
	ginger	1 tsp (5 mL)	2 tsp (10 mL)	1 tbsp (15 mL)	4 tsp (20 mL)	5 tsp (25 mL)
	cornstarch	½ cup (125 mL)	1 cup (250 mL)	1½ cups (375 mL)	2 cups (500 mL)	2½ cups (625 mL)
	flank steak	2 lb (1 kg)	4 lbs (2 kg)	6 lbs (3 kg)	8 lbs (4 kg)	10 lbs (5 kg)
	green beans	1 lb (500 g)	2 lbs (1 kg)	3 lbs (1.5 kg)	4 lbs (2 kg)	5 lbs (2.5 kg)
	quart bags	1	2	3	4	5
	gallon bags	2	4	6	8	10

Thai Beef Stir-Fry

Instead of going out, why not stay home and cook up a delectable Thai-inspired beef stir-fry? The tender beef slices have just the right crunch around the edges and the garlic and vinegar combine perfectly with the lightly sweet bell peppers. This stir-fry is so stellar that I am certain my husband would eat it every day if he could. *Makes 6 servings.*

2 lbs (1 kg) beef flank steak, sliced across the grain into ¼-inch (0.5 cm) strips

2 tbsp (30 mL) unseasoned rice vinegar

2 tbsp (30 mL) water

1 tbsp (15 mL) fish sauce

1 tbsp (15 mL) tamari sauce

1 tbsp (15 mL) packed brown sugar

¼ tsp (1 mL) hot pepper flakes

2 tsp (10 mL) minced garlic

1 medium onion, thinly sliced

1½ red bell peppers, sliced

To Serve

3 tbsp (45 mL) vegetable oil

Garnishes

Chopped fresh cilantro (optional)

Sesame seeds (optional)

1. In a large bowl, combine flank steak, rice vinegar, water, fish sauce, tamari sauce, brown sugar, hot pepper flakes and garlic.

MAKE IT NOW In a wok or large skillet, heat vegetable oil over high heat. Add beef and marinade; cook, stirring constantly, for 3 to 4 minutes, or until meat is no longer pink inside. Add onion and bell peppers; cook, stirring, for 2 to 3 minutes, until tender. Remove from heat and sprinkle with cilantro and sesame seeds, if using.

MAKE IT A FREEZER MEAL Line a baking sheet with parchment paper. Spread sliced onion and bell peppers on baking sheet, separating them as much as possible. Place in freezer for 30 to 45 minutes, until onion and peppers are frozen solid. Transfer to a gallon-size (4 L) freezer bag. Pour beef and marinade into another gallon-size freezer bag. Seal, removing as much air as possible, and freeze bags together as a kit.

THAW AND COOK Place meat bag in refrigerator for at least 12 hours or up to 24 hours to thaw (leave vegetable bag in freezer). In a wok or large skillet, heat vegetable oil over high heat. Add beef and marinade; cook, stirring constantly, for 3 to 4 minutes, until meat is no longer pink inside. Add frozen onion and peppers; cook, stirring, for 3 minutes, until tender. Remove from heat and sprinkle with cilantro and sesame seeds, if using.

BULK BATCH GUIDE	Servings	6 (1 batch)	12 (2 batches)	18 (3 batches)	24 (4 batches)	30 (5 batches)
	flank steak	2 lbs (1 kg)	4 lbs (2 kg)	6 lbs (3 kg)	8 lbs (4 kg)	10 lbs (5 kg)
	rice vinegar	2 tbsp (30 mL)	¼ cup (60 mL)	6 tbsp (90 mL)	½ cup (125 mL)	⅔ cup (150 mL)
	water	2 tbsp (30 mL)	¼ cup (60 mL)	6 tbsp (90 mL)	½ cup (125 mL)	⅔ cup (150 mL)
	fish sauce	1 tbsp (15 mL)	2 tbsp (30 mL)	3 tbsp (45 mL)	¼ cup (60 mL)	⅓ cup (75 mL)
	tamari sauce	1 tbsp (15 mL)	2 tbsp (30 mL)	3 tbsp (45 mL)	¼ cup (60 mL)	⅓ cup (75 mL)
	brown sugar	1 tbsp (15 mL)	2 tbsp (30 mL)	3 tbsp (45 mL)	¼ cup (60 mL)	⅓ cup (75 mL)
	hot pepper flakes	¼ tsp (1 mL)	½ tsp (2 mL)	¾ tsp (3 mL)	1 tsp (5 mL)	1¼ tsp (6 mL)
	garlic	2 tsp (10 mL)	4 tsp (20 mL)	2 tbsp (30 mL)	8 tsp (40 mL)	10 tsp (50 mL)
	onions	1	2	3	4	5
	red bell peppers	1½	3	4½	6	7½
	gallon bags	2	4	6	8	10

Venezuelan Steak

Go international and make this rich, juicy Venezuelan slow cooker meal. This unique and flavorful steak is made as a celebratory dish in Venezuela, and it is just the right thing to eat before you spend your Sunday afternoon napping in the hammock. Okay, I don't have a hammock, but a girl can dream. *Makes 6 servings.*

2 lbs (1 kg) beef flank steak, cut across the grain into 1-inch (2.5 cm) slices

2 cups (500 mL) beef broth or Homemade Beef Stock (page 350)

1 can (8 oz/227 mL) tomato sauce

⅓ cup (75 mL) tomato paste (about 3 oz/90 g)

1 tbsp (15 mL) Worcestershire sauce

1 red bell pepper, thinly sliced

½ medium onion, thinly sliced

1 tsp (5 mL) minced garlic

2 tbsp (30 mL) olive oil

1 tsp (5 mL) dried oregano

1 bay leaf

½ tsp (2 mL) salt

⅛ tsp (0.5 mL) freshly ground black pepper

1. In a large bowl, combine flank steak, beef broth, tomato sauce, tomato paste, Worcestershire sauce, bell pepper, onion, garlic, olive oil, oregano, bay leaf, salt and pepper; stir well.

MAKE IT NOW Pour beef and sauce into a large (approx. 5 quart) slow cooker. Cover and cook on Low for 7 to 8 hours or on High for 5 to 6 hours, until meat is tender. Remove bay leaf and serve.

MAKE IT A FREEZER MEAL Pour contents of bowl into a labeled gallon-size (4 L) freezer bag. Seal, removing as much air as possible, and freeze.

THAW AND COOK Place bag in refrigerator for at least 12 hours or up to 24 hours to thaw. Pour beef and sauce into a large (approx. 5 quart) slow cooker. Cook on Low for 8 to 9 hours or on High for 5 to 6 hours, until meat is tender. Remove bay leaf and serve.

BULK BATCH GUIDE	Servings	6 (1 batch)	12 (2 batches)	18 (3 batches)	24 (4 batches)	30 (5 batches)
	flank steak	2 lbs (1 kg)	4 lbs (2 kg)	6 lbs (3 kg)	8 lbs (4 kg)	10 lbs (5 kg)
	beef broth	2 cups (500 mL)	4 cups (1 L)	6 cups (1.5 L)	8 cups (2 L)	10 cups (2.5 L)
	tomato sauce	8 oz (227 mL)	16 oz (454 mL)	24 oz (681 mL)	32 oz (908 mL)	40 oz (1.135 L)
	tomato paste	⅓ cup (75 mL)	⅔ cup (150 mL)	1 cup (250 mL)	1⅓ cups (325 mL)	1⅔ cups (400 mL)
	Worcestershire	1 tbsp (15 mL)	2 tbsp (30 mL)	3 tbsp (45 mL)	¼ cup (60 mL)	⅓ cup (75 mL)
	red bell peppers	1	2	3	4	5
	onions	½	1	1½	2	2½
	garlic	1 tsp (5 mL)	2 tsp (10 mL)	1 tbsp (15 mL)	4 tsp (20 mL)	5 tsp (25 mL)
	olive oil	2 tbsp (30 mL)	¼ cup (60 mL)	6 tbsp (90 mL)	½ cup (125 mL)	⅔ cup (150 mL)
	dried oregano	1 tsp (5 mL)	2 tsp (10 mL)	1 tbsp (15 mL)	4 tsp (20 mL)	5 tsp (25 mL)
	bay leaves	1	2	3	4	5
	salt	½ tsp (2 mL)	1 tsp (5 mL)	1½ tsp (7 mL)	2 tsp (10 mL)	2½ tsp (12 mL)
	pepper	⅛ tsp (0.5 mL)	¼ tsp (1 mL)	⅓ tsp (1.5 mL)	½ tsp (2 mL)	¾ tsp (3 mL)
	gallon bags	1	2	3	4	5

Baked Ziti

Little Italy ain't got nothin' on my baked ziti. The sauce is as robust and rich as a bolognese without all the sweat and tears that can come with cooking it. Mild, cheesy goodness complements this dish perfectly, and it is sure to please even the pickiest of eaters! Makes 6 servings.

1 lb (500 g) ziti or penne pasta

1 tsp (5 mL) salt

15 oz (450 g) ricotta cheese

1 lb (500 g) mozzarella cheese, shredded, divided

½ cup (125 mL) freshly grated Parmesan cheese (about 1¾ oz/50 g)

1 large egg, beaten

4 cups (1 L) Red Sauce (page 334), cooled

Garnish

Chopped fresh parsley (optional)

1. Fill a large stockpot with water and bring to a boil over high heat. Add ziti and cook for 5 to 6 minutes, stirring occasionally, until just beginning to get soft (the pasta should be starting to get tender but have a firm bite). Drain and rinse with cold water to cool quickly.

2. In a large bowl, combine ricotta cheese, 2 cups (500 mL) mozzarella, Parmesan cheese and egg. Add ziti and stir gently to combine.

3. Spread 1½ cups (375 mL) red sauce in bottom of a 13- by 9-inch (33 by 23 cm) baking dish. Pour half of the ziti mixture into dish. Spread 1 cup (250 mL) red sauce overtop, followed by 1 cup (250 mL) mozzarella. Top with remaining ziti mixture and remaining red sauce. Sprinkle remaining mozzarella cheese overtop.

MAKE IT NOW Preheat oven to 375°F (190°C). Bake in preheated oven for 20 to 30 minutes, until sauce is bubbling all over and topping is golden brown. Sprinkle with fresh parsley, if using; serve.

MAKE IT A FREEZER MEAL Wrap baking dish tightly with plastic wrap, pressing down gently to remove air. Cover with foil. Label and freeze.

THAW AND COOK Place dish in refrigerator for at least 12 hours or up to 24 hours to thaw. Preheat oven to 375°F (190°C). Remove foil and plastic wrap. Bake in preheated oven for 35 to 45 minutes, until sauce is bubbling all over and topping is golden brown. Sprinkle with fresh parsley, if using; serve. (You can also cook the baked ziti from frozen. Preheat oven to 375°F/190°C. Remove foil and plastic wrap. Cover with new foil. Bake in preheated oven for 1 hour. Remove foil and bake for an additional 15 to 20 minutes, until bubbling all over and topping is golden brown. Sprinkle with fresh parsley, if using, and serve.)

BULK BATCH GUIDE	Servings	6 (1 batch)	12 (2 batches)	18 (3 batches)	24 (4 batches)	30 (5 batches)
	ziti	1 lb (500 g)	2 lbs (1 kg)	3 lbs (1.5 kg)	4 lbs (2 kg)	5 lbs (2.5 kg)
	salt	1 tsp (5 mL)	2 tsp (10 mL)	1 tbsp (15 mL)	4 tsp (20 mL)	5 tsp (25 mL)
	ricotta cheese	15 oz (450 g)	30 oz (900 g)	45 oz (1.35 kg)	60 oz (1.8 kg)	75 oz (2.25 kg)
	mozzarella cheese	1 lb (500 g)	2 lbs (1 kg)	3 lbs (1.5 kg)	4 lbs (2 kg)	5 lbs (2.5 kg)
	Parmesan cheese	½ cup (125 mL)	1 cup (250 mL)	1½ cups (375 mL)	2 cups (500 mL)	2½ cups (625 mL)
	eggs	1	2	3	4	5
	Red Sauce	4 cups (1 L)	8 cups (2 L)	12 cups (3 L)	16 cups (4 L)	20 cups (5 L)
	13x9 dishes	1	2	3	4	5

Momma's Lasagna

Growing up, we had a tradition of a great big Sunday dinner after church, and lasagna was always the most popular dish. This is the exact same recipe my mom used to make, in all its cheesy noodle glory! It has become everyone's favorite lasagna recipe among all our friends and extended family.

Makes 6 servings.

12 oz (375 g) lasagna noodles

1 tsp (5 mL) salt

2 cups (500 mL) cottage cheese

¼ cup (60 mL) freshly grated Parmesan cheese (about ¾ oz/22 g)

2 tbsp (30 mL) dried parsley

4 cups (1 L) Red Sauce (page 334), cooled (see Tip, below)

1 lb (500 g) mozzarella cheese, shredded, divided

Garnish

Fresh thyme leaves (optional)

Tip

If you don't have time to make Red Sauce from scratch, you can use 1 jar (26 oz/700 mL) of your favorite tomato sauce combined with 1 lb (500 g) cooked ground beef.

1. Fill a large stockpot with water and bring to a boil over high heat. Add lasagna noodles and salt; cook, stirring occasionally, until just beginning to get soft (the noodles should be starting to get tender but have a firm bite). Drain and rinse with cold water to cool quickly.

2. In a medium bowl, combine cottage cheese, Parmesan cheese and parsley.

3. Spread 1 cup (250 mL) red sauce evenly over bottom of a 13- by 9-inch (33 by 23 cm) baking dish. Add a layer of lasagna noodles. Spread 1 cup (250 mL) red sauce evenly overtop. Using a spoon, drop one-third of the cottage cheese mixture evenly overtop, followed by an even sprinkling of one-third of the mozzarella. Repeat the layers twice more, starting with lasagna noodles and ending with mozzarella cheese.

MAKE IT NOW Preheat oven to 350°F (180°C). Cover baking dish with foil and bake in preheated oven for 30 to 35 minutes. Remove foil and cook for an additional 10 to 12 minutes, until bubbly and golden on top. Let stand for 15 minutes before serving; top with fresh thyme, if using.

MAKE IT A FREEZER MEAL Wrap baking dish tightly with plastic wrap, pressing down gently to remove air. Cover with foil, label and freeze.

THAW AND COOK Place dish in refrigerator for at least 24 hours or up to 48 hours to thaw. Preheat oven to 350°F (180°C). Remove plastic wrap and foil. Cover with new foil. Bake in preheated oven for 45 minutes. Remove foil and bake for about 10 minutes more, until bubbly and golden on top. Let stand for 15 minutes before serving; top with fresh thyme, if using.

BULK BATCH GUIDE	Servings	6 (1 batch)	12 (2 batches)	18 (3 batches)	24 (4 batches)	30 (5 batches)
	lasagna noodles	12 oz (375 g)	1½ lbs (750 g)	2¼ lbs (1.125 kg)	3 lbs (1.5 kg)	3.75 lbs (1.875 kg)
	salt	1 tsp (5 mL)	2 tsp (10 mL)	1 tbsp (15 mL)	4 tsp (20 mL)	5 tsp (25 mL)
	cottage cheese	2 cups (500 mL)	4 cups (1 L)	6 cups (1.5 L)	8 cups (2 L)	10 cups (2.5 L)
	Parmesan cheese	¼ cup (60 mL)	½ cup (125 mL)	¾ cup (175 mL)	1 cup (250 mL)	1¼ cups (310 mL)
	dried parsley	2 tbsp (30 mL)	¼ cup (60 mL)	6 tbsp (90 mL)	½ cup (125 mL)	⅔ cup (150 mL)
	Red Sauce	4 cups (1 L)	8 cups (2 L)	12 cups (3 L)	16 cups (4 L)	20 cups (5 L)
	mozzarella cheese	1 lb (500 g)	2 lbs (1 kg)	3 lbs (1.5 kg)	4 lbs (2 kg)	5 lbs (2.5 kg)
	13x9 dishes	1	2	3	4	5

Tempting Taco Pasta Shell Casserole

Are you constantly torn between having pasta or tacos for dinner? Yeah, me too. Cue this amazing fusion of Italian and Tex-Mex that will satisfy both your taco and pasta cravings. The perfectly al dente pasta shells are stuffed with all the vibrant flavors you think of when you are craving tacos. From cilantro to cumin, your taste buds will be groovin'. Makes 6 servings.

2 lbs (1 kg) ground beef

¼ cup (60 mL) taco seasoning

1 cup (250 mL) water

24 jumbo pasta shells (half of a 12 oz/375 g box)

1½ cups (375 mL) shredded mozzarella cheese (about 6 oz/175 g), divided

1½ cups (375 mL) shredded Cheddar cheese (about 6 oz/175 g), divided

1 batch Enchilada Sauce (page 346)

Garnishes

½ cup (125 mL) chopped tomato (optional)

2 tbsp (30 mL) chopped fresh cilantro (optional)

Sour cream (optional)

Tip

If you are short on time, you can substitute for my homemade enchilada sauce recipe with 1 can (28 oz/796 mL) of your favorite enchilada sauce.

1. In a large skillet over medium-high heat, cook beef, breaking up with a spoon, for 4 to 5 minutes, until browned. Drain off fat and return meat to pan. Add taco seasoning and water; bring to a boil. Immediately reduce heat to medium and simmer, stirring occasionally, for 5 to 6 minutes, until all the liquid has evaporated. Remove from heat. Add ½ cup (125 mL) mozzarella cheese and ½ cup (125 mL) Cheddar cheese; stir to combine. Set aside (let cool completely before assembling for freezing).

2. Fill a large stockpot with water and bring to a boil over high heat. Add pasta shells and cook for 6 to 7 minutes, stirring occasionally, until just beginning to get soft (the pasta should be starting to get tender but have a firm bite). Drain and rinse with cold water to cool quickly.

3. Spread ½ cup (125 mL) enchilada sauce in bottom of a 13- by 9-inch (33 by 23 cm), or a similar-sized, baking dish. Spoon about 3 tbsp (45 mL) meat mixture into each pasta shell. Place shells, open side up, in baking dish, just barely touching each other. Evenly pour remaining enchilada sauce over shells. Sprinkle with remaining mozzarella and Cheddar cheese.

MAKE IT NOW Preheat oven to 375°F (190°C). Bake in preheated oven for 30 to 35 minutes, until sauce is bubbling all over and topping is golden. Remove from oven and let cool for 5 minutes. Sprinkle with tomato and fresh cilantro and add a dollop of sour cream, if using.

MAKE IT A FREEZER MEAL Let baking dish cool completely. Wrap dish tightly with plastic wrap, pressing down gently to remove air. Cover with foil. Label and freeze.

THAW AND COOK Place baking dish in refrigerator for 24 hours to thaw. Preheat oven to 350°F (180°C). Remove foil and plastic wrap. Cover with new foil. Bake in preheated oven for 40 minutes. Remove foil and bake for an additional 5 minutes, until sauce is bubbling all over and topping is golden. Remove from oven and let cool for 5 minutes. Sprinkle with fresh tomato and cilantro and add a dollop of sour cream, if using.

BULK BATCH GUIDE	Servings	6 (1 batch)	12 (2 batches)	18 (3 batches)	24 (4 batches)	30 (5 batches)
	ground beef	2 lbs (1 kg)	4 lbs (2 kg)	6 lbs (3 kg)	8 lbs (4 kg)	10 lbs (5 kg)
	taco seasoning	¼ cup (60 mL)	½ cup (125 mL)	¾ cup (175 mL)	1 cup (250 mL)	1¼ cups (310 mL)
	water	1 cup (250 mL)	2 cups (500 mL)	3 cups (750 mL)	4 cups (1 L)	5 cups (1.25 L)
	jumbo pasta shells	24	48	72	96	120
	mozzarella cheese	1½ cups (375 mL)	3 cups (750 mL)	4½ cups (1.125 L)	6 cups (1.5 L)	7½ cups (1.875 L)
	Cheddar cheese	1½ cups (375 mL)	3 cups (750 mL)	4½ cups (1.125 L)	6 cups (1.5 L)	7½ cups (1.875 L)
	Enchilada Sauce	1 batch	2 batches	3 batches	4 batches	5 batches
	13x9 dishes	1	2	3	4	5

Mole Tamale Pie

What's better than a tasty tamale? How about a whole pie of tamale! This warm, inviting pie (a.k.a. casserole) is a Southwestern favorite. It's hard to mess with a meal made with spicy meat, rich mole sauce, warm cornbread and tasty vegetables. Can we give a big *ole!* to the mole? I think we should. Makes 6 servings.

Filling

1½ lbs (750 g) ground beef

1 can (8 oz/227 mL) tomato sauce

½ cup (125 mL) mole sauce

1 can (14 oz/398 mL) diced tomatoes, with juice

1 can (15 oz/425 mL) black beans, drained and rinsed

8 oz (250 g) frozen corn kernels

2 tbsp (30 mL) freshly squeezed lime juice

1 can (4½ oz/127 mL) mild green chiles or ¼ cup (60 mL) salsa verde

3 tbsp (45 mL) taco seasoning

1½ tsp (7 mL) dried minced onion

¼ cup (60 mL) minced fresh cilantro

½ tsp (2 mL) minced garlic

2 cups (500 mL) shredded Mexican-blend cheese (about 8 oz/250 g), divided

Crust

1 large egg

1 cup (250 mL) milk

1 cup + 2 tbsp (280 mL) cornmeal

¾ cup (175 mL) all-purpose flour

½ cup (125 mL) honey

2 tbsp (30 mL) butter, softened

1 tbsp (15 mL) baking powder

½ tsp (2 mL) salt

1. *Filling:* In a large skillet, cook beef over medium-high heat, breaking up with a spoon, for 4 to 5 minutes, until browned. Drain off fat. (Let cool completely before assembling for freezing.)

2. In a 13- by 9-inch (33 by 23 cm), or a similar-sized, baking dish, combine beef, tomato sauce, mole sauce, tomatoes (with juice), black beans, corn, lime juice, green chiles, taco seasoning, dried onion, cilantro, garlic and 1 cup (250 mL) Mexican-blend cheese. Using the back of a wooden spoon, press down until it's even and smooth. Sprinkle remaining shredded cheese overtop.

3. *Crust:* Using a stand mixer fitted with the wire whisk attachment, beat egg until fluffy. Add milk, cornmeal, flour, honey, butter, baking powder and salt; mix at low speed just until moistened (it should look a little lumpy). Spread mixture evenly over meat filling.

MAKE IT NOW Preheat oven to 375°F (190°C). Cover baking dish with foil. Bake in preheated oven for 20 minutes. Remove foil and bake for an additional 15 to 20 minutes, until golden brown on top.

MAKE IT A FREEZER MEAL Wrap baking dish tightly with plastic wrap, pressing down gently to remove air. Cover with foil. Label and freeze.

THAW AND COOK Place baking dish in refrigerator for at least 12 hours or up to 24 hours to thaw. Preheat oven to 375°F (190°C). Remove foil and plastic wrap, then cover with new foil. Bake in preheated oven for 30 minutes. Remove foil and bake for 25 to 30 minutes, until golden brown on top and cooked through.

> HELPFUL TIP: If you can't get Mexican cheese blend, substitute an equal amount of sharp (old) Cheddar cheese, Colby cheese or Monterey Jack cheese, or a combination of the three.

(continued on page 230)

Servings	6 (1 batch)	12 (2 batches)	18 (3 batches)	24 (4 batches)	30 (5 batches)
ground beef	1½ lbs (750 g)	3 lbs (1.5 kg)	4½ lbs (2.25 kg)	6 lbs (3 kg)	7½ lbs (3.75 kg)
tomato sauce	8 oz (227 mL)	16 oz (454 mL)	24 oz (681 mL)	32 oz (908 mL)	40 oz (1.135 L)
mole sauce	½ cup (125 mL)	1 cup (250 mL)	1½ cups (375 mL)	2 cups (500 mL)	2½ cups (625 mL)
diced tomatoes	14 oz (398 mL)	28 oz (796 mL)	42 oz (1.194 L)	56 oz (1.592 L)	70 oz (1.99 L)
black beans	15 oz (425 mL)	30 oz (850 mL)	45 oz (1.275 L)	60 oz (1.7 L)	75 oz (2.125 L)
corn	8 oz (250 g)	1 lb (500 g)	1½ lbs (750 g)	2 lbs (1 kg)	2½ lbs (1.25 kg)
lime juice	2 tbsp (30 mL)	¼ cup (60 mL)	6 tbsp (90 mL)	½ cup (125 mL)	⅔ cup (150 mL)
green chiles	4½ oz (127 mL)	9 oz (254 mL)	13½ oz (381 mL)	18 oz (508 mL)	22½ oz (635 mL)
taco seasoning	3 tbsp (45 mL)	6 tbsp (90 mL)	½ cup (125 mL)	¾ cup (175 mL)	¾ cup + 3 tbsp (220 mL)
dried onion	1½ tsp (7 mL)	1 tbsp (15 mL)	1½ tbsp (22 mL)	2 tbsp (30 mL)	2½ tbsp (37 mL)
cilantro	¼ cup (60 mL)	½ cup (125 mL)	¾ cup (175 mL)	1 cup (250 mL)	1¼ cups (310 mL)
garlic	½ tsp (2 mL)	1 tsp (5 mL)	1½ tsp (7 mL)	2 tsp (10 mL)	2½ tsp (12 mL)
Mexican-blend cheese	2 cups (500 mL)	4 cups (1 L)	6 cups (1.5 L)	8 cups (2 L)	10 cups (2.5 L)
eggs	1	2	3	4	5
milk	1 cup (250 mL)	2 cups (500 mL)	3 cups (750 mL)	4 cups (1 L)	5 cups (1.25 L)
cornmeal	1 cup + 2 tbsp (280 mL)	2¼ cups (560 mL)	3 cups + 6 tbsp (840 mL)	4½ cups (1.125 L)	5⅔ cups (1.4 L)
all-purpose flour	¾ cup (175 mL)	1½ cups (375 mL)	2¼ cups (560 mL)	3 cups (750 mL)	3¾ cups (925 mL)
honey	½ cup (125 mL)	1 cup (250 mL)	1½ cups (375 mL)	2 cups (500 mL)	2½ cups (625 mL)
butter	2 tbsp (30 mL)	¼ cup (60 mL)	6 tbsp (90 mL)	½ cup (125 mL)	⅔ cup (150 mL)
baking powder	1 tbsp (15 mL)	2 tbsp (30 mL)	3 tbsp (45 mL)	¼ cup (60 mL)	⅓ cup (75 mL)
salt	½ tsp (2 mL)	1 tsp (5 mL)	1½ tsp (7 mL)	2 tsp (10 mL)	2½ tsp (12 mL)
13x9 dishes	1	2	3	4	5

It's hard to mess with
a meal made with
spicy meat, rich mole sauce,
warm cornbread
and tasty vegetables.

Sizzlin' Steak Fajitas

Oh, how I love fajitas. These simply seasoned, tender strips of steak paired with fragrant peppers, spicy onions and the tart pop of lime create one of the tastiest and easiest freezer meals you will ever make. Makes 6 servings.

2 lbs (1 kg) beef flank steak, cut across the grain into ¼-inch (0.5 cm) strips

½ jalapeño pepper, finely chopped

¼ cup (60 mL) chopped fresh cilantro

2 tbsp (30 mL) freshly squeezed lime juice

1 tsp (5 mL) minced garlic

½ tsp (2 mL) ground cumin

2 tbsp (30 mL) olive oil

1 medium onion, thinly sliced

3 bell peppers, thinly sliced

To Serve

Sliced green onions, green part only (optional)

Chopped fresh cilantro (optional)

6 corn tortillas (6 inches/30 cm), warmed

1. In a labeled quart-size (1 L) freezer bag or large bowl, combine flank steak, jalapeño pepper, cilantro, lime juice, garlic and cumin. Seal and mix gently (or stir in the bowl) so meat is evenly coated. Cover bowl, if necessary. Transfer to the refrigerator to marinate for 15 minutes.

MAKE IT NOW In a wok or large skillet, heat olive oil over high heat. Add beef and marinade; cook, stirring, for 4 to 5 minutes, until meat is no longer pink inside. Add onion and bell peppers; cook, stirring, for 2 to 3 minutes, until tender-crisp. Sprinkle with green onions and cilantro, if using. Serve in warm corn tortillas.

MAKE IT A FREEZER MEAL On a baking sheet lined with parchment paper, spread out flank steak and marinade and freeze for about 1 hour, until solid. Spread sliced onion and bell peppers on two more baking sheets lined with parchment paper; freeze for about 1 hour, until solid. Place beef and frozen marinade pieces in a labeled quart-size (1 L) freezer bag; seal, removing as much air as possible. Place peppers and onion in a labeled gallon-size (4 L) freezer bag. Place meat bag in vegetable bag. Seal, removing as much air as possible, and freeze.

COOK FROM FROZEN In a wok or large skillet, heat olive oil over high heat. Add beef and marinade; cook, stirring, for 5 to 6 minutes, until no longer pink inside. Add onion and bell peppers; cook, stirring, for 4 to 5 minutes, until tender-crisp. Sprinkle with green onions and cilantro, if using. Serve in warm corn tortillas.

BULK BATCH GUIDE	Servings	6 (1 batch)	12 (2 batches)	18 (3 batches)	24 (4 batches)	30 (5 batches)
	flank steak	2 lbs (1 kg)	4 lbs (2 kg)	6 lbs (3 kg)	8 lbs (4 kg)	10 lbs (5 kg)
	jalapeño peppers	½	1	1½	2	2½
	cilantro	¼ cup (60 mL)	½ cup (125 mL)	¾ cup (175 mL)	1 cup (250 mL)	1¼ cups (310 mL)
	lime juice	2 tbsp (30 mL)	¼ cup (60 mL)	6 tbsp (90 mL)	½ cup (125 mL)	⅔ cup (150 mL)
	garlic	1 tsp (5 mL)	2 tsp (10 mL)	1 tbsp (15 mL)	4 tsp (20 mL)	5 tsp (25 mL)
	cumin	½ tsp (2 mL)	1 tsp (5 mL)	1½ tsp (7 mL)	2 tsp (10 mL)	2½ tsp (12 mL)
	olive oil	2 tbsp (30 mL)	1/4 cup (60 mL)	6 tbsp (90 mL)	½ cup (125 mL)	⅔ cup (150 mL)
	onions	1	2	3	4	5
	bell peppers	3	6	9	12	15
	quart bags	1	2	3	4	5
	gallon bags	1	2	3	4	5

French Dip Sandwiches

After years of trying to figure out the perfect blend of seasonings and flavors for homemade French dip sandwiches, I finally got it right. Dipping the tender beef sandwich into this delightfully flavorful jus is out of this world. Even though I say all my recipes are good, this one is really amazing — seriously, try it. *Makes 8 servings.*

1 tsp (5 mL) salt

1 tsp (5 mL) freshly ground black pepper

3 lbs (1.5 kg) boneless beef shoulder roast, trimmed

4 cups (1 L) beef broth or Homemade Beef Stock (page 350)

1½ onions, puréed or minced

½ cup (125 mL) tamari sauce

⅓ cup (75 mL) Worcestershire sauce

2 tbsp (30 mL) yellow mustard

1½ tsp (7 mL) minced garlic

4 bay leaves

To Serve

8 buns or rolls

Cooking spray or olive oil

8 slices provolone cheese

1. Using your hands, rub salt and pepper generously all over the roast.

2. In a labeled gallon-size (4 L) freezer bag, combine broth, onions, tamari sauce, Worcestershire sauce, mustard, garlic and bay leaves. Add roast and seal, removing as much air as possible.

MAKE IT NOW Marinate beef in refrigerator for a minimum of 1 hour or up to 12 hours. Pour contents of bag into a large (approx. 5 quart) slow cooker. Cook on Low for 7 hours, until beef is tender. Remove roast, reserving jus left in slow cooker. Discard bay leaves. Transfer roast to a cutting board and, using two forks, shred. Preheat broiler. Slice buns in half, spray with a little cooking spray or brush with olive oil, and place on a baking sheet lined with aluminum foil. Broil for 1 minute or until golden and toasted. Remove from oven, place shredded meat on bottom half of bun and add a slice of provolone cheese. Broil for 30 seconds to 1 minute, until cheese is melted. Remove from oven and cover with top half of bun. Skim any fat off top of jus in slow cooker and ladle liquid into small bowls. Serve sandwiches with jus on the side for dipping.

MAKE IT A FREEZER MEAL Freeze roast and marinade in bag.

THAW AND COOK Place bag in refrigerator for at least 24 hours or up to 48 hours to thaw. Transfer contents to a large (approx. 5 quart) slow cooker. Cook on Low for 7 to 8 hours, until beef is tender. Remove roast, reserving jus left in slow cooker. Discard bay leaves. Transfer roast to a cutting board and, using two forks, shred. Preheat broiler. Slice buns in half, spray with a little cooking spray or brush with olive oil, and place on a baking sheet lined with aluminum foil. Broil for 1 minute or until golden and toasted. Remove from oven, place shredded meat on bottom half of bun and add a slice of provolone cheese. Broil for 30 seconds to 1 minute, until cheese is melted. Remove from oven and cover with top half of bun. Skim any fat off top of jus in slow cooker and ladle liquid into small bowls. Serve sandwiches with jus on the side for dipping.

BULK BATCH GUIDE	Servings	8 (1 batch)	16 (2 batches)	24 (3 batches)	32 (4 batches)	40 (5 batches)
	salt	1 tsp (5 mL)	2 tsp (10 mL)	1 tbsp (15 mL)	4 tsp (20 mL)	5 tsp (25 mL)
	pepper	1 tsp (5 mL)	2 tsp (10 mL)	1 tbsp (15 mL)	4 tsp (20 mL)	5 tsp (25 mL)
	shoulder roast	3 lbs (1.5 kg)	6 lbs (3 kg)	9 lbs (4.5 kg)	12 lbs (6 kg)	15 lbs (7.5 kg)
	beef broth	4 cups (1 L)	8 cups (2 L)	12 cups (3 L)	16 cups (4 L)	20 cups (5 L)
	onions	1½	3	4½	6	7½
	tamari sauce	½ cup (125 mL)	1 cup (250 mL)	1½ cups (375 mL)	2 cups (500 mL)	2½ cups (625 mL)
	Worcestershire	⅓ cup (75 mL)	⅔ cup (150 mL)	1 cup (250 mL)	1⅓ cups (325 mL)	1⅔ cups (400 mL)
	yellow mustard	2 tbsp (30 mL)	¼ cup (60 mL)	6 tbsp (90 mL)	½ cup (125 mL)	⅔ cup (150 mL)
	garlic	1½ tsp (7 mL)	1 tbsp (15 mL)	1½ tbsp (22 mL)	2 tbsp (30 mL)	2½ tbsp (37 mL)
	bay leaves	4	8	12	16	20
	gallon bags	1	2	3	4	5

SEAFOOD

Savory Salmon in Foil   238

Baked Shrimp Scampi   241

Easy Tuna Casserole   242

Lemon Dill Tilapia Tacos   245

Flower's Seafood Gumbo   246

Shrimp Jambalaya   251

Savory Salmon in Foil

My picky son, who swears that he hates salmon, will devour two of these fillets in minutes. This recipe takes no time to prepare, and the individually wrapped packets are perfect for busy nights — which is every night in my house! When you tear open one of these savory salmon packages, you will be hit with an aroma that will take you to the breezy northwestern coast and fill your senses with a kiss of peppery heat and lemony wonderment. *Makes 6 servings.*

2 lbs (1 kg) salmon fillet, cut into 6 equal pieces

2 medium lemons

1 tbsp (15 mL) olive oil

1 tsp (5 mL) sea salt

1 tsp (5 mL) dried rosemary

1 tsp (5 mL) dried dill

12 to 15 whole pink peppercorns (optional)

1½ tsp (7 mL) butter

1. Cut six 12-inch (30 cm) squares of foil. Lay out squares on a flat surface and place one salmon piece in center of each.

2. Cut six ¼-inch (1 cm) thick slices crosswise out of center of each lemon. Using ends of the lemons, squeeze equal amounts of juice over each fillet. Then drizzle each fillet with ½ tsp (2 mL) olive oil.

3. In a small bowl, combine sea salt, rosemary and dill. Sprinkle equally over fillets. Top each fillet with 2 lemon slices, 2 to 3 peppercorns, if using, and ¼ tsp (1 mL) butter.

4. Wrap foil tightly around each fillet by folding in two sides, then bringing top and bottom ends together in the center. Roll ends together, gently pressing out any air. Seal tightly.

MAKE IT NOW Preheat oven to 400°F (200°C). Place sealed packets directly on oven rack. Bake in preheated oven for 15 minutes for 1-inch (2.5 cm) thick fillets; cooking time will vary depending on the thickness of the fish. Check the thinnest piece first: you want the fish to be just opaque and flaky. If necessary, reseal packet and return to oven for up to 7 minutes longer. Do not overcook!

MAKE IT A FREEZER MEAL Label a gallon-size (4 L) freezer bag. Place sealed packets in bag. Seal, removing as much air as possible, and freeze.

THAW AND COOK Place packets in the refrigerator for at least 12 hours or up to 24 hours to thaw. Preheat oven to 400°F (200°C). Place sealed packets directly on oven rack. Bake in preheated oven for 15 minutes for 1-inch (2.5 cm) thick fillets; cooking time will vary depending on the thickness of the fish. Check the thinnest piece first: you want the fish to be just opaque and flaky. If necessary, reseal packet and return to oven for up to 7 minutes longer. Do not overcook!

Servings	6 (1 batch)	12 (2 batches)	18 (3 batches)	24 (4 batches)	30 (5 batches)
salmon	2 lbs (1 kg)	4 lbs (2 kg)	6 lbs (3 kg)	8 lbs (4 kg)	10 lbs (5 kg)
lemons	2	4	6	8	10
olive oil	1 tbsp (15 mL)	2 tbsp (30 mL)	3 tbsp (45 mL)	¼ cup (60 mL)	⅓ cup (75 mL)
salt	1 tsp (5 mL)	2 tsp (10 mL)	1 tbsp (15 mL)	4 tsp (20 mL)	5 tsp (25 mL)
dried rosemary	1 tsp (5 mL)	2 tsp (10 mL)	1 tbsp (15 mL)	4 tsp (20 mL)	5 tsp (25 mL)
dried dill	1 tsp (5 mL)	2 tsp (10 mL)	1 tbsp (15 mL)	4 tsp (20 mL)	5 tsp (25 mL)
peppercorns	12	24	36	48	60
butter	1½ tsp (7 mL)	1 tbsp (15 mL)	1½ tbsp (22 mL)	2 tbsp (30 mL)	2½ tbsp (37 mL)
gallon bags	1	2	3	4	5

BULK BATCH GUIDE

Baked Shrimp Scampi

Seriously, is there anything better than shrimp scampi? The answer is NO. This freezer meal recipe is as beautiful as it is delicious. There is nothing better than making everyone think you've spent hours in the kitchen cooking when the meal really took only minutes to throw together. You'll especially love the fresh, lemony zing that hits your palate when you bite into this dish. Makes 6 servings.

¼ cup (60 mL) unsalted butter

1 tbsp (15 mL) minced garlic

½ cup (125 mL) chicken broth or Homemade Chicken Stock (page 349)

Grated zest and juice of 1 large lemon

10 oz (300 g) angel hair pasta

2 tbsp (30 mL) olive oil

2 tbsp (30 mL) minced fresh parsley

1¾ lbs (875 g) frozen peeled and deveined raw shrimp (41/50 size)

½ tsp (2 mL) salt

¼ tsp (1 mL) freshly ground black pepper

¼ tsp (1 mL) hot pepper flakes (optional)

Lemon slices (optional)

2 tbsp (30 mL) cold unsalted butter

Additional minced fresh parsley (optional)

Garnish
Freshly grated Parmesan cheese (optional)

1. In a large skillet over medium-high heat, heat ¼ cup (60 mL) butter until melted. Add garlic; cook, stirring, for about 3 minutes, until just beginning to brown. Add chicken broth, lemon zest and lemon juice; bring to a boil. Remove from heat and let cool.

2. Fill a large stockpot with water and bring to a boil over high heat. Add pasta and cook for 3 minutes, stirring occasionally, until just beginning to get soft (it should be starting to get tender but have a firm bite). Drain and rinse with cold water to cool quickly. Place back in pot. Add olive oil and parsley; toss until well combined.

3. Carefully twist about 9 small portions of noodles into 3- to 4-inch (7.5 to 10 cm) mounds and place snugly side by side in a lightly greased 13- by 9-inch (33 by 23 cm) baking dish. Arrange frozen shrimp over noodles. Pour cooled sauce evenly overtop; sprinkle with salt, pepper and hot pepper flakes, if using. Evenly arrange lemon slices over the top, if using. Grate cold butter evenly overtop. Sprinkle with additional parsley, if using.

MAKE IT NOW Preheat oven to 350°F (180°C). Bake in preheated oven for 30 to 35 minutes, until shrimp just turn pink and opaque. Preheat broiler. Place baking dish on middle rack and broil for 3 minutes, until shrimp are lightly golden. Serve with a sprinkling of Parmesan cheese, if using.

MAKE IT A FREEZER MEAL Wrap baking dish tightly with plastic wrap, pressing down gently to remove air. Cover with foil. Label and place in freezer.

THAW AND COOK Place baking dish in the refrigerator for at least 12 hours or up to 24 hours to thaw. Preheat oven to 350°F (180°C). Remove foil and plastic wrap; cover with new foil. Bake in preheated oven for 35 to 40 minutes, until shrimp just turn pink and opaque. Preheat broiler. Place dish on middle rack and broil for 3 minutes, until shrimp are lightly golden. Serve with a sprinkling of Parmesan cheese, if using.

BULK BATCH GUIDE	Servings	6 (1 batch)	12 (2 batches)	18 (3 batches)	24 (4 batches)	30 (5 batches)
	unsalted butter	¼ cup (60 mL)	½ cup (125 mL)	¾ cup (175 mL)	1 cup (250 mL)	1¼ cups (310 mL)
	garlic	1 tbsp (15 mL)	2 tbsp (30 mL)	3 tbsp (45 mL)	¼ cup (60 mL)	⅓ cup (75 mL)
	chicken broth	½ cup (125 mL)	1 cup (250 mL)	1½ cups (375 mL)	2 cups (500 mL)	2½ cups (625 mL)
	lemons	1	2	3	4	5
	angel hair pasta	10 oz (300 g)	20 oz (600 g)	30 oz (900 g)	40 oz (1.13 kg)	50 oz (1.5 kg)
	olive oil	2 tbsp (30 mL)	¼ cup (60 mL)	6 tbsp (90 mL)	½ cup (125 mL)	⅔ cup (150 mL)
	parsley	2 tbsp (30 mL)	¼ cup (60 mL)	6 tbsp (90 mL)	½ cup (125 mL)	⅔ cup (150 mL)
	shrimp	1¾ lbs (875 g)	3½ lbs (1.75 kg)	5¼ lbs (2.625 kg)	7 lbs (3.5 kg)	8¾ lbs (4.375 kg)
	salt	½ tsp (2 mL)	1 tsp (5 mL)	1½ tsp (7 mL)	2 tsp (10 mL)	2½ tsp (12 mL)
	pepper	¼ tsp (1 mL)	½ tsp (2 mL)	¾ tsp (3 mL)	1 tsp (5 mL)	1¼ tsp (6 mL)
	hot pepper flakes	¼ tsp (1 mL)	½ tsp (2 mL)	¾ tsp (3 mL)	1 tsp (5 mL)	1¼ tsp (6 mL)
	lemon for topping	1	2	3	4	5
	cold butter	2 tbsp (30 mL)	¼ cup (60 mL)	6 tbsp (90 mL)	½ cup (125 mL)	⅔ cup (150 mL)
	13x9 dishes	1	2	3	4	5

Easy Tuna Casserole

This is my sister Ashleigh's favorite freezer meal of all time. I know tuna noodle casserole sounds old-fashioned, but this isn't your typical can-of-soup version. My recipe is a creamy, comforting and more flavorful version that works really well for giving to a family or friend in need. Make it extra fun by baking in individual containers! Makes 6 servings.

1 batch White Sauce (page 336)

1 can (6 oz/170 g) tuna, drained

1 lb (500 g) macaroni

½ cup (125 mL) mayonnaise

2 cups (500 mL) shredded Cheddar cheese (about 8 oz/250 g), divided

½ tsp (2 mL) onion powder

1 cup (250 mL) frozen peas (optional)

Salt and freshly ground black pepper

Tip

If you're making this recipe right away, you can use a glass or ceramic baking dish.

1. In a medium bowl, combine white sauce and tuna. Set aside.

2. Fill a large stockpot with water and bring to a boil over high heat. Cook macaroni for 5 to 6 minutes, stirring occasionally, until just beginning to get soft (it should be starting to get tender but have a firm bite). Drain and rinse with cold water to cool quickly. Return macaroni to pot.

3. Add white sauce mixture, mayonnaise, 1 cup (250 mL) Cheddar cheese and onion powder. Gently mix in frozen peas, if using. Season to taste with salt and pepper; stir gently to combine. Pour mixture into a 13- by 9-inch (33 by 23 cm) metal or foil pan or six 12 oz (375 mL) individual metal or foil baking containers. Sprinkle remaining cheese overtop.

MAKE IT NOW Preheat oven to 350°F (180°C). Bake in preheated oven for 35 to 40 minutes, until sauce is bubbling all over and cheese is melted. Remove from oven and let cool for 10 minutes; serve.

MAKE IT A FREEZER MEAL Cover pan with plastic wrap, pressing down gently to remove air. Cover with foil, label and freeze.

COOK FROM FROZEN Preheat oven to 350°F (180°C). Remove plastic wrap and foil; cover with new foil. Place pan in preheated oven and bake for 1 hour. Remove foil and bake for an additional 20 minutes, until sauce is bubbling all over and cheese is melted. Remove from oven and let cool for 10 minutes; serve.

BULK BATCH GUIDE

Servings	6 (1 batch)	12 (2 batches)	18 (3 batches)	24 (4 batches)	30 (5 batches)
White Sauce	1 batch	2 batches	3 batches	4 batches	5 batches
tuna	6 oz (170 g)	12 oz (340 g)	18 oz (510 g)	24 oz (680 g)	30 oz (850 g)
macaroni	1 lb (500 g)	2 lbs (1 kg)	3 lbs (1.5 kg)	4 lbs (2 kg)	5 lbs (2.5 kg)
mayonnaise	½ cup (125 mL)	1 cup (250 mL)	1½ cups (375 mL)	2 cups (500 mL)	2½ cups (625 mL)
Cheddar cheese	2 cups (500 mL)	4 cups (1 L)	6 cups (1.5 L)	8 cups (2 L)	10 cups (2.5 L)
onion powder	½ tsp (2 mL)	1 tsp (5 mL)	1½ tsp (7 mL)	2 tsp (10 mL)	2½ tsp (12 mL)
peas	1 cup (250 mL)	2 cups (500 mL)	3 cups (750 mL)	4 cups (1 L)	5 cups (1.25 L)
13x9 pans	1	2	3	4	5

Lemon Dill Tilapia Tacos

"Girl, what have you done?" Those were my husband's first words after he laid eyes on these tacos the first night I made them. With all their delightful flavors of garlic, lively lemon and dill, I'm certain you too will swoon over these, especially when you realize how fast they are to make!

Makes 6 servings.

¼ cup (60 mL) melted butter

¼ cup (60 mL) chicken broth or Homemade Chicken Stock (page 349)

Grated zest and juice of 2 large lemons

1½ tsp (7 mL) dried dill

½ tsp (2 mL) minced garlic

2 lbs (1 kg) skinless tilapia fillets (about six 6 oz/175 g pieces)

To serve

2 tbsp (30 mL) olive oil

12 6-inch (15 cm) corn tortillas, warmed

Toppings

1 cup (250 mL) shredded lettuce

1 cup (250 mL) canned or cooked black beans, drained and rinsed (optional)

¼ cup (60 mL) salsa or pico de gallo (optional)

Tip
You can also make a dilly sauce, if desired. In a small saucepan, combine 2 tsp (10 mL) cornstarch and the marinade from the bag. Bring to a boil over medium-high heat, stirring constantly, until thickened, about 3 to 5 minutes. Remove from heat. Build your tacos and then drizzle a little lemon dill sauce overtop.

1. In a small bowl, whisk together melted butter, chicken broth, lemon zest, lemon juice, dill and garlic.

2. Place marinade mixture and tilapia fillets in a gallon-size (4 L) freezer bag or bowl. (Label the bag if freezing for later.) Seal bag, removing as much air as possible, or cover bowl. Transfer to refrigerator to marinate for 15 minutes.

MAKE IT NOW Preheat oven to 400°F (200°C). Drizzle olive oil over a rimmed baking sheet. Transfer baking sheet to oven while it preheats. Once oven is preheated, remove baking sheet from oven, add fillets and return it to oven. Bake for 10 to 12 minutes, until fish is flaky and lightly crisped on the edges. Remove from oven and chop into chunks. Arrange tortillas on a work surface. Evenly divide fish and lettuce, plus beans and salsa (if using), among tortillas. Serve.

MAKE IT A FREEZER MEAL Freeze bag.

THAW AND COOK Place bag in the refrigerator for 12 to 24 hours to thaw. Preheat oven to 400°F (200°C). Drizzle olive oil over a rimmed baking sheet. Transfer baking sheet to oven while it preheats. Once oven is preheated, remove baking sheet from oven, add fillets and return it to oven. Bake for 10 to 12 minutes, until fish is flaky and lightly crisped on the edges. Remove from oven and chop into chunks. Arrange tortillas on a work surface. Evenly divide fish and lettuce, plus beans and salsa, if using, among tortillas. Serve.

BULK BATCH	Servings	6 (1 batch)	12 (2 batches)	18 (3 batches)	24 (4 batches)	30 (5 batches)
	butter	¼ cup (60 mL)	½ cup (125 mL)	¾ cup (175 mL)	1 cup (250 mL)	1¼ cups (310 mL)
	chicken broth	¼ cup (60 mL)	½ cup (125 mL)	¾ cup (175 mL)	1 cup (250 mL)	1¼ cups (310 mL)
	lemons	2	4	6	8	10
	dried dill	1½ tsp (7 mL)	1 tbsp (15 mL)	1½ tbsp (22 mL)	2 tbsp (30 mL)	2½ tbsp (37 mL)
	garlic	½ tsp (2 mL)	1 tsp (5 mL)	1½ tsp (7 mL)	2 tsp (10 mL)	2½ tsp (12 mL)
	tilapia	2 lbs (1 kg)	4 lbs (2 kg)	6 lbs (3 kg)	8 lbs (4 kg)	10 lbs (5 kg)
	gallon bags	1	2	3	4	5

Flower's Seafood Gumbo

This recipe comes from my friend Flower, who was given the recipe by a friend who grew up in Louisiana, learning Creole cuisine from his great-grandmother. This gumbo takes your taste buds right down to the salty waters of the bayou. I can even hear the zydeco music in the distance.

Makes 6 servings.

1 celery stalk, cut into chunks

½ medium onion, cut into chunks

1 red bell pepper, cut into chunks

1 clove garlic

6 oz (175 g) andouille sausage

⅓ cup (75 mL) butter

⅓ cup (75 mL) all-purpose flour

6 cups (1.5 L) beef broth or Homemade Beef Stock (page 350)

2 tbsp (30 mL) beef bouillon powder

1 cup (250 mL) stewed tomatoes (about 8 oz/250 g)

⅓ cup (75 mL) tomato sauce

1 tbsp (15 mL) hot pepper sauce

2 tbsp (30 mL) Worcestershire sauce

10 oz (300 g) frozen sliced okra

1 can (8 oz/250 g) lump crab meat, drained

½ tsp (2 mL) Cajun seasoning

2 bay leaves

¼ tsp (1 mL) dried thyme

2 tsp (10 mL) gumbo filé powder, divided

1½ lbs (750 g) frozen peeled, deveined raw shrimp (41/50 size)

1. In a blender or food processor, blend celery, onion, bell pepper and garlic on High until smooth. Set aside.

2. Slice each sausage in half lengthwise, then slice crosswise into ½-inch (1 cm) pieces. In a large Dutch oven or heavy-bottomed saucepan, heat butter over medium-high heat until melted. Add sausage and cook, stirring, for about 4 minutes, until browned. Using a slotted spoon, transfer sausage to a bowl and set aside.

3. Reduce heat to medium-low. Add flour; cook, whisking constantly, for 15 to 20 minutes, until a dark mahogany color. Do not burn.

4. Gradually add beef broth, whisking constantly until smooth. Add beef bouillon powder, stewed tomatoes, tomato sauce, hot sauce, Worcestershire sauce, okra, crab meat, celery mixture, Cajun seasoning, bay leaves, thyme and 1 tsp (5 mL) filé powder. Stir well to combine.

MAKE IT NOW Increase heat to medium-high and bring to a boil, stirring occasionally. Immediately reduce heat to low; simmer for 10 minutes, until flavors have deepened and vegetables are tender. Add shrimp and simmer for an additional 5 minutes, until shrimp just turn pink and opaque. Remove bay leaves and stir in remaining filé powder; serve hot.

MAKE IT A FREEZER MEAL Let soup cool completely. Place frozen shrimp in a labeled quart-size (1 L) freezer bag. Pour cooled soup mixture into a labeled gallon-size (4 L) freezer bag. Seal, removing as much air as possible, and freeze both bags together.

THAW AND COOK Place bags in the refrigerator for at least 12 hours or up to 24 hours to thaw. Pour contents of soup bag into a large Dutch oven or heavy-bottomed saucepan. Bring to a boil over medium-high heat, stirring occasionally. Immediately reduce heat to low; simmer for 10 minutes, until flavors have deepened and vegetables are tender. Drain shrimp, add to saucepan and simmer for additional 5 minutes, until shrimp just turn pink and opaque. Remove bay leaves and stir in remaining filé powder; serve hot.

(continued on page 248)

Servings	6 (1 batch)	12 (2 batches)	18 (3 batches)	24 (4 batches)	30 (5 batches)
celery stalks	1	2	3	4	5
onions	½	1	1½	2	2½
red bell peppers	1	2	3	4	5
garlic cloves	1	2	3	4	5
andouille sausage	6 oz (175 g)	12 oz (375 g)	1 lb 2 oz (560 g)	1½ lbs (750 g)	1 lb 14 oz (900 g)
butter	⅓ cup (75 mL)	⅔ cup (150 mL)	1 cup (250 mL)	1⅓ cups (325 mL)	1⅔ cups (400 mL)
all-purpose flour	⅓ cup (75 mL)	⅔ cup (150 mL)	1 cup (250 mL)	1⅓ cups (325 mL)	1⅔ cups (400 mL)
beef broth	6 cups (1.5 L)	12 cups (3 L)	18 cups (4.5 L)	24 cups (6 L)	30 cups (7.5 L)
beef bouillon powder	2 tbsp (30 mL)	¼ cup (60 mL)	6 tbsp (90 mL)	½ cup (125 mL)	⅔ cup (150 mL)
stewed tomatoes	1 cup (250 mL)	2 cups (500 mL)	3 cups (750 mL)	4 cups (1 L)	5 cups (1.25 L)
tomato sauce	⅓ cup (75 mL)	⅔ cup (150 mL)	1 cup (250 mL)	1⅓ cups (325 mL)	1⅔ cups (400 mL)
hot pepper sauce	1 tbsp (15 mL)	2 tbsp (30 mL)	3 tbsp (45 mL)	¼ cup (60 mL)	⅓ cup (75 mL)
Worcestershire	2 tbsp (30 mL)	¼ cup (60 mL)	6 tbsp (90 mL)	½ cup (125 mL)	⅔ cup (150 mL)
okra	10 oz (300 g)	1¼ lbs (625 g)	1 lb 14 oz (900 g)	2½ lbs (1.5 kg)	3 lbs 2 oz (1.56 kg)
crab meat	8 oz (250 g)	1 lb (500 g)	1½ lbs (750 g)	2 lbs (1 kg)	2½ lbs (1.25 kg)
Cajun seasoning	½ tsp (2 mL)	1 tsp (5 mL)	1½ tsp (7 mL)	2 tsp (10 mL)	2½ tsp (12 mL)
bay leaves	2	4	6	8	10
dried thyme	¼ tsp (1 mL)	½ tsp (2 mL)	¾ tsp (3 mL)	1 tsp (5 mL)	1¼ tsp (6 mL)
gumbo filé powder	2 tsp (10 mL)	4 tsp (20 mL)	2 tbsp (30 mL)	8 tsp (40 mL)	10 tsp (50 mL)
shrimp	1½ lbs (750 g)	3 lbs (1.5 kg)	4½ lbs (2.25 kg)	6 lbs (3 kg)	7½ lbs (3.75 kg)
quart bags	1	2	3	4	5
gallon bags	1	2	3	4	5

This gumbo takes your taste buds right down to the salty waters of the bayou.

Shrimp Jambalaya

With its tasty andouille sausage, tender spicy chicken breast and freshly cooked shrimp, all seasoned with a masterpiece of Cajun flavors, you will be ecstatic that you made this freezer meal — and so will anyone else who tries it. *Makes 6 servings.*

2 cups (500 mL) long-grain white rice

2 tbsp (30 mL) butter

8 oz (250 g) andouille sausage, cut into ¼-inch (0.5 cm) slices

1 lb (500 g) boneless, skinless chicken breasts, cut into 1-inch (2.5 cm) pieces

1 medium white onion, diced

1 bell pepper, diced

1 celery stalk, cut into ¼-inch (0.5 cm) slices

1 can (14 oz/398 mL) diced tomatoes, drained

1 tsp (5 mL) hot pepper sauce

1 cup (250 mL) chicken broth or Homemade Chicken Stock (page 349)

1 tsp (5 mL) dried oregano

1½ tsp (7 mL) Cajun seasoning

1/2 tsp (2 mL) dried thyme

1 lb (500 g) frozen peeled and deveined raw shrimp (41/50 size)

1. Cook rice according to package instructions, reducing water by ¼ cup (60 mL). Set aside to cool.

2. In a large skillet, melt butter over medium-high heat. Add sausage and cook, stirring occasionally, for 4 to 5 minutes, until golden. Using a slotted spoon, transfer sausage to a bowl and set aside.

3. Add chicken to skillet and cook, stirring occasionally, for 5 to 6 minutes, until golden and no longer pink inside. Using a slotted spoon, transfer chicken to a separate bowl and set aside.

4. Add onion, bell pepper and celery to skillet. Cook, stirring, for about 3 to 4 minutes, until tender. Remove skillet from heat.

5. In a 13- by 9-inch (33 by 23 cm) baking dish, combine rice, sausage, chicken, cooked vegetables, tomatoes, hot pepper sauce, chicken broth, oregano, Cajun seasoning, thyme and shrimp. Gently stir until combined. (If you're making a freezer meal, let ingredients cool separately and completely before assembling in baking dish.)

MAKE IT NOW Preheat oven to 350°F (180°C). Cover baking dish with foil and bake in preheated oven for 15 to 20 minutes, until heated through and shrimp are pink and opaque. Serve.

MAKE IT A FREEZER MEAL Wrap baking dish tightly with plastic wrap, pressing down gently to remove air. Cover with foil. Label and place in freezer.

THAW AND COOK Place baking dish in the refrigerator for 12 to 24 hours to thaw. Preheat oven to 350°F (180°C). Remove plastic wrap and foil; cover with new foil. Bake for 35 to 40 minutes, until heated through and shrimp are pink and opaque. Serve.

BULK BATCH GUIDE	Servings	6 (1 batch)	12 (2 batches)	18 (3 batches)	24 (4 batches)	30 (5 batches)
	white rice	2 cups (500 mL)	4 cups (1 L)	6 cups (1.5 L)	8 cups (2 L)	10 cups (2.5 L)
	butter	2 tbsp (30 mL)	¼ cup (60 mL)	6 tbsp (90 mL)	½ cup (125 mL)	⅔ cup (150 mL)
	andouille sausage	8 oz (250 g)	1 lb (500 g)	1½ lbs (750 g)	2 lbs (1 kg)	2½ lbs (1.25 kg)
	chicken breast	1 lb (500 g)	2 lbs (1 kg)	3 lbs (1.5 kg)	4 lbs (2 kg)	5 lbs (2.5 kg)
	onions	1	2	3	4	5
	bell peppers	1	2	3	4	5
	celery stalks	1	2	3	4	5
	diced tomatoes	14 oz (398 mL)	28 oz (796 mL)	42 oz (1.194 L)	56 oz (1.592 L)	70 oz (1.99 L)
	hot pepper sauce	1 tsp (5 mL)	2 tsp (10 mL)	1 tbsp (15 mL)	4 tsp (20 mL)	5 tsp (25 mL)
	chicken broth	1 cup (250 mL)	2 cups (500 mL)	3 cups (750 mL)	4 cups (1 L)	5 cups (1.25 L)
	dried oregano	1 tsp (5 mL)	2 tsp (10 mL)	1 tbsp (15 mL)	4 tsp (20 mL)	5 tsp (25 mL)
	Cajun seasoning	1½ tsp (7 mL)	1 tbsp (15 mL)	1½ tbsp (22 mL)	2 tbsp (30 mL)	2½ tbsp (37 mL)
	dried thyme	½ tsp (2 mL)	1 tsp (5 mL)	1½ tsp (7 mL)	2 tsp (10 mL)	2½ tsp (12 mL)
	shrimp	1 lb (500 g)	2 lbs (1 kg)	3 lbs (1.5 kg)	4 lbs (2 kg)	5 lbs (2.5 kg)
	13x9 dishes	1	2	3	4	5

MEATLESS MAINS

Amazing Macaroni and Cheese   254

Cauliflower Chickpea Curry Bake   257

Spinach Gnocchi Alfredo   258

Deep-Dish Cheesy Broccoli Brown Rice   261

Lentil Supreme Shepherd's Pie   262

Cashew Mushroom Fried Rice   265

Cheesy Eggplant Parmigiana   266

Cilantro Black Bean Taco Salad   269

Smashed Bean and Red Pepper Quesadillas   270

Sun-Dried Tomato Basil Pesto Quiche   273

Great Northern Enchiladas   274

Hazelnut Mushroom Potatoes au Gratin   277

Buffalo Ranch Roasted Cauliflower and Broccoli   280

Amazing Macaroni and Cheese

You know that question, "If you had to pick one thing to eat for the rest of your life, what would it be?" For me, this would be it. I never tire of this gooey, creamy, cheesy baked pasta and crispy Parmesan topping. It's even good as leftovers — if there are any. Makes 6 servings.

Topping

1 cup (250 mL) dry Italian seasoned bread crumbs

1 cup (250 mL) freshly grated Parmesan cheese (3½ oz/100 g)

1 tsp (5 mL) seasoned salt

Pasta

1 batch Vegetarian White Sauce (page 337), warmed

1 cup (250 mL) milk

Pinch dry mustard

1 cup (250 mL) shredded Colby cheese (about 4 oz/125 g)

1 cup (250 mL) shredded Gruyère cheese (about 4 oz/125 g)

1 cup (250 mL) shredded extra-sharp white Cheddar cheese (about 4 oz/ 125 g)

1 lb (500 g) elbow macaroni

Salt and freshly ground black pepper

1. *Topping:* In a small bowl, combine bread crumbs, Parmesan cheese and seasoned salt; set aside.

2. *Pasta:* In a large bowl, combine white sauce, milk and dry mustard. Add Colby, Gruyère and Cheddar cheeses; stir until melted and smooth. Set aside.

3. Fill a large stockpot with water and bring to a boil over high heat. Cook macaroni for 5 to 6 minutes, stirring occasionally, until just beginning to get soft (the pasta should be starting to get tender but have a firm bite). Drain and rinse with cold water to cool quickly. Set aside.

MAKE IT NOW Preheat oven to 400°F (200°C). Return macaroni to stockpot, add cheese sauce and gently mix together. Season to taste with salt and pepper. Transfer to a 13- by 9-inch (33 by 23 cm) baking dish. Sprinkle topping over macaroni. Bake in preheated oven for 25 to 30 minutes, until golden on top and bubbly on the inside. Let cool for 10 minutes, then serve.

MAKE IT A FREEZER MEAL Let cheese sauce cool to room temperature. Return macaroni to stockpot, add sauce and gently mix together. Season to taste with salt and pepper. Transfer to a 13- by 9-inch (33 by 23 cm) baking dish. Wrap baking dish tightly with plastic wrap, pressing down gently to remove air. Place topping mix in a quart-size (1 L) freezer bag and place on top of baking dish. Cover both with foil. Label and place in freezer.

THAW AND COOK Place baking dish in refrigerator for at least 12 hours or up to 24 hours to thaw. Preheat oven to 400°F (200°C). Remove foil, topping packet and plastic wrap. Sprinkle topping mixture over macaroni. Cover with new foil. Bake in preheated oven for 45 minutes. Remove foil and bake for an additional 10 minutes or until golden on top and bubbly on the inside. Let cool for 10 minutes, then serve.

	Servings	6 (1 batch)	12 (2 batches)	18 (3 batches)	24 (4 batches)	30 (5 batches)
BULK BATCH GUIDE	Italian bread crumbs	1 cup (250 mL)	2 cups (500 mL)	3 cups (750 mL)	4 cups (1 L)	5 cups (1.5 L)
	Parmesan cheese	1 cup (250 mL)	2 cups (500 mL)	3 cups (750 mL)	4 cups (1 L)	5 cups (1.25 L)
	seasoned salt	1 tsp (5 mL)	2 tsp (10 mL)	1 tbsp (15 mL)	4 tsp (20 mL)	5 tsp (25 mL)
	Vegetarian White Sauce	1 batch	2 batches	3 batches	4 batches	5 batches
	milk	1 cup (250 mL)	2 cups (500 mL)	3 cups (750 mL)	4 cups (1 L)	5 cups (1.25 L)
	Colby cheese	1 cup (250 mL)	2 cups (500 mL)	3 cups (750 mL)	4 cups (1 L)	5 cups (1.25 L)
	Gruyère cheese	1 cup (250 mL)	2 cups (500 mL)	3 cups (750 mL)	4 cups (1 L)	5 cups (1.25 L)
	Cheddar cheese	1 cup (250 mL)	2 cups (500 mL)	3 cups (750 mL)	4 cups (1 L)	5 cups (1.25 L)
	macaroni	1 lb (500 g)	2 lbs (1 kg)	3 lbs (1.5 kg)	4 lbs (2 kg)	5 lbs (2.5 kg)
	13x9 dishes	1	2	3	4	5
	quart bags	1	2	3	4	5

Cauliflower Chickpea Curry Bake

This one! I've made a lot of freezer meals in my life, but this one is truly special. It's a fun, Indian-inspired twist on a classic casserole. The combination of pasta, chickpeas and cauliflower with a distinctive creamy curry sauce will make your taste buds squeal with delight. *Makes 6 servings.*

8 oz (250 g) radiatori pasta

1 batch Vegetarian White Sauce (page 337), cooled

1 cup (250 mL) coconut milk

1½ tsp (7 mL) curry powder

1 tsp (5 mL) garlic powder

½ tsp (2 mL) ground cardamom

2 tbsp (30 mL) freshly squeezed lemon juice

3 cups (750 mL) frozen cauliflower florets

1 can (14 oz/398 mL) chickpeas, drained and rinsed

1 cup (250 mL) shredded Cheddar cheese (about 4 oz/125 g)

¼ tsp (1 mL) cayenne pepper (optional)

Tip
If you're making this recipe right away, you can use a glass or ceramic baking dish.

1. Fill a large stockpot with water and bring to a boil over high heat. Cook pasta for 3 to 4 minutes, stirring occasionally, until just beginning to get soft (the pasta should be starting to get tender but have a firm bite). Drain and rinse with cold water to cool quickly. Set aside.

2. In a large bowl, combine white sauce, coconut milk, curry powder, garlic powder, cardamom and lemon juice. Add cauliflower, chickpeas and cooked pasta; mix gently until well combined. Pour into a lightly greased 13- by 9-inch (33 by 23 cm) metal or foil pan. Sprinkle with Cheddar cheese and cayenne pepper, if using.

MAKE IT NOW Preheat oven to 350°F (180°C). Cover pan with foil and bake in preheated oven for 40 minutes. Remove foil and bake for an additional 10 to 15 minutes, until bubbling and cheese is melted and golden.

MAKE IT A FREEZER MEAL Wrap the pan tightly with plastic wrap, pressing down gently to remove air. Cover with foil, label and freeze.

COOK FROM FROZEN Preheat oven to 350°F (180°C). Remove plastic wrap and foil. Cover with new foil. Bake in preheated oven for 1½ hours. Remove foil and bake for an additional 10 to 15 minutes, until bubbling and cheese is melted and golden.

BULK BATCH GUIDE Servings	6 (1 batch)	12 (2 batches)	18 (3 batches)	24 (4 batches)	30 (5 batches)
radiatori	8 oz (250 g)	1 lb (500 g)	1½ lbs (750 g)	2 lbs (1 kg)	2½ lbs (1.25 kg)
Vegetarian White Sauce	1 batch	2 batches	3 batches	4 batches	5 batches
coconut milk	1 cup (250 mL)	2 cups (500 mL)	3 cups (750 mL)	4 cups (1 L)	5 cups (1.25 L)
curry powder	1½ tsp (7 mL)	1 tbsp (15 mL)	1½ tbsp (22 mL)	2 tbsp (30 mL)	2½ tbsp (37 mL)
garlic powder	1 tsp (5 mL)	2 tsp (10 mL)	1 tbsp (15 mL)	4 tsp (20 mL)	5 tsp (25 mL)
cardamom	½ tsp (2 mL)	1 tsp (5 mL)	1½ tsp (7 mL)	2 tsp (10 mL)	2½ tsp (12 mL)
lemon juice	2 tbsp (30 mL)	¼ cup (60 mL)	6 tbsp (90 mL)	½ cup (125 mL)	⅔ cup (150 mL)
cauliflower	3 cups (750 mL)	6 cups (1.5 L)	9 cups (2.25 L)	12 cups (3 L)	15 cups (3.75 L)
chickpeas	14 oz (398 mL)	28 oz (796 mL)	42 oz (1.194 L)	56 oz (1.592 L)	70 oz (1.99 L)
Cheddar cheese	1 cup (250 mL)	2 cups (500 mL)	3 cups (750 mL)	4 cups (1 L)	5 cups (1.25 L)
cayenne pepper	¼ tsp (1 mL)	½ tsp (2 mL)	¾ tsp (3 mL)	1 tsp (5 mL)	1¼ tsp (6 mL)
13x9 pans	1	2	3	4	5

Spinach Gnocchi Alfredo

I don't host a lot of dinner parties, but when I do, it's for people I really adore. This wholesome, creamy gourmet recipe is one I pull out only for those special occasions. It's my way of saying "I love you" through food. For a fun and fancier way to serve this, consider baking it in individual-size containers. Makes 6 servings.

1½ lbs (750 g) store-bought gnocchi or 2 batches Gnocchi (page 330)

1 tbsp (15 mL) unsalted butter

1 tsp (5 mL) minced garlic

4 cups (1 L) lightly packed trimmed fresh spinach (about 4 oz/125 g)

1 tsp (5 mL) onion powder

1 batch Alfredo Sauce (page 333), cooled

¼ cup (60 mL) freshly grated Parmesan cheese (about ¾ oz/22 g)

½ cup (125 mL) Italian-seasoned bread crumbs

Tip

If you're making this recipe right away, you can use a glass or ceramic baking dish.

1. Fill a large stockpot with water and bring to a boil over high heat. Add gnocchi and cook for 2 to 3 minutes, stirring occasionally, until they float to the top and are al dente. Drain and rinse with cold water to cool quickly. Set aside.

2. In a large saucepan, melt butter over medium-high heat. Add garlic and cook, stirring, for 10 to 15 seconds, until fragrant. Add spinach and onion powder; cook for about 3 to 4 minutes, stirring constantly, until spinach is wilted. Remove from heat and let cool completely.

3. Combine gnocchi, spinach and Alfredo sauce in a 13- by 9-inch (33 by 23 cm) metal or foil pan. Sprinkle Parmesan cheese and bread crumbs overtop.

MAKE IT NOW Preheat oven to 350°F (180°C). Cover pan with foil and bake in preheated oven for 25 minutes. Remove foil and bake for 7 to 8 minutes more, until bubbly and golden on top.

MAKE IT A FREEZER MEAL Let pan cool completely. Wrap pan tightly with plastic wrap, pressing down gently to remove air. Cover with foil. Label and freeze.

COOK FROM FROZEN Preheat oven to 350°F (180°C). Remove plastic wrap and foil. Cover with new foil. Bake in preheated oven for 1 hour and 20 minutes. Remove foil and bake for 7 to 8 minutes more, until bubbly and golden on top.

	Servings	6 (1 batch)	12 (2 batches)	18 (3 batches)	24 (4 batches)	30 (5 batches)
BULK BATCH GUIDE	gnocchi	1½ lbs (750 g)	3 lbs (1.5 kg)	4½ lbs (2.25 kg)	6 lbs (3 kg)	7½ lbs (3.75 kg)
	unsalted butter	1 tbsp (15 mL)	2 tbsp (30 mL)	3 tbsp (45 mL)	¼ cup (60 mL)	⅓ cup (75 mL)
	garlic	1 tsp (5 mL)	2 tsp (10 mL)	1 tbsp (15 mL)	4 tsp (20 mL)	5 tsp (25 mL)
	spinach	4 cups (1 L)	8 cups (2 L)	12 cups (3 L)	16 cups (4 L)	20 cups (5 L)
	onion powder	1 tsp (5 mL)	2 tsp (10 mL)	1 tbsp (15 mL)	4 tsp (20 mL)	5 tsp (25 mL)
	Alfredo Sauce	1 batch	2 batches	3 batches	4 batches	5 batches
	Parmesan cheese	¼ cup (60 mL)	½ cup (125 mL)	¾ cup (175 mL)	1 cup (250 mL)	1¼ cups (310 mL)
	Italian bread crumbs	½ cup (125 mL)	1 cup (250 mL)	1½ cups (375 mL)	2 cups (500 mL)	2½ cups (625 mL)
	13x9 pans	1	2	3	4	5

Deep-Dish Cheesy Broccoli Brown Rice

You will fall head over heels for this dish made with bold and hearty brown rice, rich and decadent cheese sauce, and perfectly cooked broccoli. I bake this in deep-dish pans, individual bowls or sometimes even a big pot, but no matter which way you cook it, you are definitely going to love it!
Makes 6 servings.

1 cup (250 mL) long-grain brown rice

1½ cups (375 mL) water

3 cups (750 mL) frozen broccoli

1 batch Vegetarian White Sauce (page 337)

2 cups (500 mL) shredded Cheddar cheese (about 8 oz/250 g)

½ tsp (2 mL) dry mustard

¼ tsp (1 mL) salt

½ tsp (2 mL) garlic powder

½ cup (125 mL) freshly grated Parmesan cheese (about 1¾ oz/50 g)

Garnish

Additional freshly grated Parmesan cheese (optional)

Freshly ground pepper

Tip
If you're making this recipe right away, you can use a glass or ceramic baking dish.

1. Place rice in a strainer and rinse under cool water until water runs clear. In a small saucepan, combine rice and water. Bring to a boil over high heat. Immediately reduce heat to low, cover and simmer for 35 to 40 minutes, until rice is tender and water is absorbed. Remove from heat and let stand for 10 minutes longer. Fluff with a fork. Set aside to cool.

2. In a large bowl, combine rice, broccoli, white sauce, Cheddar cheese, mustard, salt and garlic powder; stir until well combined.

3. Pour into a lightly greased 13- by 9-inch (33 by 23 cm) metal or foil pan. Sprinkle Parmesan cheese overtop and pepper to taste.

MAKE IT NOW Preheat oven to 400°F (200°C). Cover pan with foil. Bake in preheated oven for 30 minutes. Remove foil and bake for about 10 minutes more, until bubbly and golden on top. Serve with additional Parmesan cheese, if using, and pepper sprinkled overtop.

MAKE IT A FREEZER MEAL Let rice mixture cool completely in pan. Wrap pan tightly with plastic wrap, pressing down to remove air. Cover with foil, label and freeze.

COOK FROM FROZEN Preheat oven to 400°F (200°C). Remove plastic wrap and foil. Cover with new foil. Bake in preheated oven for 50 minutes. Remove foil and bake for about 10 minutes more, until bubbly and golden on top. Serve with additional Parmesan cheese, if using, and pepper sprinkled overtop.

	Servings	6 (1 batch)	12 (2 batches)	18 (3 batches)	24 (4 batches)	30 (5 batches)
BULK BATCH GUIDE	brown rice	1 cup (250 mL)	2 cups (500 mL)	3 cups (750 mL)	4 cups (1 L)	5 cups (1.25 L)
	water	1½ cups (375 mL)	3 cups (750 mL)	4½ cups (1.125 L)	6 cups (1.5 L)	7½ cups (1.875 L)
	broccoli	3 cups (750 mL)	6 cups (1.5 L)	9 cups (2.25 L)	12 cups (3 L)	15 cups (3.75 L)
	Vegetarian White Sauce	1 batch	2 batches	3 batches	4 batches	5 batches
	Cheddar cheese	2 cups (500 mL)	4 cups (1 L)	6 cups (1.5 L)	8 cups (2 L)	10 cups (2.5 L)
	dry mustard	½ tsp (2 mL)	1 tsp (5 mL)	1½ tsp (7 mL)	2 tsp (10 mL)	2½ tsp (12 mL)
	salt	¼ tsp (1 mL)	½ tsp (2 mL)	¾ tsp (3 mL)	1 tsp (5 mL)	1¼ tsp (6 mL)
	garlic powder	½ tsp (2 mL)	1 tsp (5 mL)	1½ tsp (7 mL)	2 tsp (10 mL)	2½ tsp (12 mL)
	Parmesan cheese	½ cup (125 mL)	1 cup (250 mL)	1½ cups (375 mL)	2 cups (500 mL)	2½ cups (625 mL)
	13x9 pans	1	2	3	4	5

Lentil Supreme Shepherd's Pie

A lovely twist on traditional shepherd's pie, this hearty lentil and vegetable filling topped with a mashed potato crust is a wholesome way to enjoy a lovely dinner together. *Makes 6 servings.*

1 tbsp (15 mL) olive oil

1 onion, diced

1 tsp (5 mL) minced garlic

¾ cup (175 mL) dried brown lentils

2 cups (500 mL) Homemade Vegetable Stock (page 351)

1 tsp (5 mL) vegan Worcestershire sauce

1 tsp (5 mL) ketchup

½ tsp (2 mL) dried thyme

2 lbs (1 kg) yellow-fleshed potatoes, quartered

½ cup (125 mL) butter, divided

¼ cup (60 mL) half-and-half (10%) cream

Salt and freshly ground black pepper

2 cups (500 mL) frozen peas, diced carrots or mixed vegetables

Cooking spray or olive oil

1. In a large saucepan, heat olive oil over medium heat. Add onion and garlic and cook, stirring, for about 3 to 4 minutes, until golden. Add lentils, vegetable stock, Worcestershire sauce, ketchup and thyme; bring to a boil. Immediately reduce heat to low and simmer for 35 to 40 minutes, until lentils are tender.

2. Meanwhile, in a large stockpot, cover potatoes with water and bring to a boil over high heat. Reduce heat and boil gently for 20 minutes or until soft; drain. Transfer to bowl of a stand mixer fitted with the wire whisk attachment (you can also use a hand mixer). Add ¼ cup (60 mL) butter and cream and sprinkle with salt and pepper. Beat on Low for 30 to 45 seconds, just until combined and most of the big lumps are gone.

3. Remove lentil mixture from heat and stir in frozen peas. If sauce is very thin, add 1 tsp (5 mL) mashed potato at a time to thicken, until texture resembles gravy. Season to taste with salt and pepper.

4. Pour lentil mixture into a lightly greased 13- by 9-inch (33 by 23 cm) baking dish. Spoon mashed potatoes overtop. Slice remaining butter and scatter over potato layer.

MAKE IT NOW Preheat oven to 425°F (220°C). Bake in preheated oven for 15 to 20 minutes, until golden on top and you can hear it bubbling inside. Remove from oven, let cool for 5 minutes, then serve.

MAKE IT A FREEZER MEAL Let baking dish cool to room temperature. Wrap dish tightly with plastic wrap, pressing down gently to remove air. Cover with foil. Label and freeze.

THAW AND COOK Place baking dish in the refrigerator for at least 12 hours or up to 24 hours to thaw. Preheat oven to 425°F (220°C). Remove plastic wrap and foil. Cover with new foil. Bake in preheated oven for 30 minutes. Remove foil and bake for an additional 10 minutes, or until golden on top and bubbly on the inside.

Servings	6 (1 batch)	12 (2 batches)	18 (3 batches)	24 (4 batches)	30 (5 batches)
olive oil	1 tbsp (15 mL)	2 tbsp (30 mL)	3 tbsp (45 mL)	¼ cup (60 mL)	⅓ cup (75 mL)
onions	1	2	3	4	5
garlic	1 tsp (5 mL)	2 tsp (10 mL)	1 tbsp (15 mL)	4 tsp (20 mL)	5 tsp (25 mL)
lentils	¾ cup (175 mL)	1½ cups (375 mL)	2¼ cups (560 mL)	3 cups (750 mL)	3¾ cups (925 mL)
Vegetable Stock	2 cups (500 mL)	4 cups (1 L)	6 cups (1.5 L)	8 cups (2 L)	10 cups (2.5 L)
Worcestershire	1 tsp (5 mL)	2 tsp (10 mL)	1 tbsp (15 mL)	4 tsp (20 mL)	5 tsp (25 mL)
ketchup	1 tsp (5 mL)	2 tsp (10 mL)	1 tbsp (15 mL)	4 tsp (20 mL)	5 tsp (25 mL)
dried thyme	½ tsp (2 mL)	1 tsp (5 mL)	1½ tsp (7 mL)	2 tsp (10 mL)	2½ tsp (12 mL)
yellow-fleshed potatoes	2 lbs (1 kg)	4 lbs (2 kg)	6 lbs (3 kg)	8 lbs (4 kg)	10 lbs (5 kg)
butter	½ cup (125 mL)	1 cup (250 mL)	1½ cups (375 mL)	2 cups (500 mL)	2½ cups (625 mL)
half-and-half	¼ cup (60 mL)	½ cup (125 mL)	¾ cup (175 mL)	1 cup (250 mL)	1¼ cups (310 mL)
peas	2 cups (500 mL)	4 cups (1 L)	6 cups (1.5 L)	8 cups (2 L)	10 cups (2.5 L)
13x9 dishes	1	2	3	4	5

BULK BATCH GUIDE

Cashew Mushroom Fried Rice

Here it is — my favorite homemade fried rice recipe. This is a pleasant blend of savory mushrooms, filling rice, flavorful vegetables and crunchy cashews. Confession: I often make this recipe without mushrooms, because I'm the picky eater in my family! Don't worry, though; it's still as delicious.

Makes 6 servings.

2 cups (500 mL) long-grain brown rice

3 cups (750 mL) water

2 tbsp (30 mL) olive oil

6 white mushrooms, thinly sliced

½ cup (125 mL) shredded carrot

1½ cups (375 mL) thinly sliced, trimmed asparagus

1 red bell pepper, diced

½ onion, puréed or diced

2 tsp (10 mL) minced garlic

1 cup (250 mL) halved raw cashews

2 tbsp (30 mL) tamari sauce

Freshly ground black pepper

Garnish

Chopped green onions (optional)

1. Place rice in a strainer and rinse under cool water until water runs clear. In a small saucepan, combine rice and water. Bring to a boil over high heat. Immediately reduce heat to low, cover and simmer for 35 to 40 minutes, until rice is tender and water is absorbed. Remove from heat and let stand, covered, for 10 minutes longer. Fluff with a fork. Set aside to cool.

2. In a large wok or skillet, heat olive oil over high heat. Once it is smoking, add mushrooms and cook, stirring, for 2 to 3 minutes, until evenly browned. Add carrot, asparagus, bell pepper, onion, garlic and cashews; cook, stirring, for 2 minutes, until vegetables are tender.

3. Add rice and stir constantly for 1 to 2 minutes, separating any clumps, until well combined and heated through. Add tamari sauce, sprinkle with pepper to taste, and stir to combine.

MAKE IT NOW Serve sprinkled with green onions, if using.

MAKE IT A FREEZER MEAL Let fried rice cool completely. Transfer to a gallon-size (4 L) freezer bag. Seal, removing as much air as possible, and freeze.

REHEAT Place bag in the refrigerator for at least 12 hours or up to 24 hours to thaw. Transfer contents to a large, microwave-safe bowl and cover with plastic wrap. Microwave on High for 5 to 6 minutes, stirring once a minute, until heated through. Serve sprinkled with green onions, if using.

BULK BATCH GUIDE	Servings	6 (1 batch)	12 (2 batches)	18 (3 batches)	24 (4 batches)	30 (5 batches)
	brown rice	2 cups (500 mL)	4 cups (1 L)	6 cups (1.5 L)	8 cups (2 L)	10 cups (2.5 L)
	water	3 cups (750 mL)	6 cups (1.5 L)	9 cups (2. 25 L)	12 cups (3 L)	15 cups (3.75 L)
	olive oil	2 tbsp (30 mL)	¼ cup (60 mL)	6 tbsp (90 mL)	½ cup (125 mL)	⅔ cup (150 mL)
	mushrooms	6	12	18	24	30
	carrots	½ cup (125 mL)	1 cup (250 mL)	1½ cups (375 mL)	2 cups (500 mL)	2½ cups (625 mL)
	asparagus	1½ cups (375 mL)	3 cups (750 mL)	4½ cups (1.125 L)	6 cups (1.5 L)	7½ cups (1.875 L)
	red bell peppers	1	2	3	4	5
	onions	½	1	1½	2	2½
	garlic	2 tsp (10 mL)	4 tsp (20 mL)	2 tbsp (30 mL)	8 tsp (40 mL)	10 tsp (50 mL)
	cashews	1 cup (250 mL)	2 cups (500 mL)	3 cups (750 mL)	4 cups (1 L)	5 cups (1.25 L)
	tamari sauce	2 tbsp (30 mL)	¼ cup (60 mL)	6 tbsp (90 mL)	½ cup (125 mL)	⅔ cup (150 mL)
	gallon bags	1	2	3	4	5

Cheesy Eggplant Parmigiana

Warning: this silky eggplant parmigiana recipe is so good that people will be begging you for the recipe. Some have even told me it's the best eggplant parmigiana they've ever had!

Makes 6 servings.

2 large eggplants (each about 2 lbs/ 1 kg)

4 large eggs

¼ cup (60 mL) milk

3 cups (750 mL) Italian-seasoned bread crumbs

¼ cup (60 mL) vegetable oil

2 cups (500 mL) shredded mozzarella cheese (about 8 oz/250 g)

1 cup (250 mL) freshly grated Parmesan cheese (about 3½ oz/100 g)

8 oz (250 g) ricotta cheese

6 cups (1.5 L) Marinara Sauce (page 338) or favorite marinara sauce

---

Tip

If you're making this recipe right away, you can use a glass or ceramic baking dish.

1. Peel eggplants and slice crosswise into ¼-inch (0.5 cm) thick rounds.

2. In a medium bowl, whisk together eggs and milk.

3. Pour bread crumbs into a shallow pan.

4. Heat a large skillet over medium-high heat. Once it is hot, add vegetable oil. Working with 4 to 5 slices at a time, dip eggplant in egg mixture, then bread crumbs. Add to skillet and fry for 1 to 2 minutes on each side, until golden. Drain on a plate lined with paper towels. Discard any excess egg mixture and bread crumbs.

5. In a medium bowl, combine mozzarella, Parmesan and ricotta cheeses.

6. Spread 2 cups (500 mL) marinara sauce evenly across bottom of a 13- by 9-inch (33 by 23 cm) metal or foil pan. Place eggplant on top, overlapping slightly to avoid gaps. Sprinkle one-third of the cheese mixture overtop. Repeat the layers twice more, starting with marinara sauce and ending with the cheese mixture.

MAKE IT NOW Preheat oven to 350°F (180°C). Cover pan with foil. Bake in preheated oven for 30 to 35 minutes, until bubbly and cheese on top is melted. Remove from oven and let cool for 15 minutes; serve.

MAKE IT A FREEZER MEAL Let contents of pan cool completely. Wrap pan tightly with plastic wrap, pressing down gently to remove air. Cover with foil. Label and place in freezer.

COOK FROM FROZEN Preheat oven to 350°F (180°C). Remove plastic wrap and foil. Cover with new foil. Bake in preheated oven for 1½ hours. Remove foil and cook for about 20 minutes more, until bubbly all over and cheese on top is melted. Remove from oven and let cool for 15 minutes; serve.

Servings	6 (1 batch)	12 (2 batches)	18 (3 batches)	24 (4 batches)	30 (5 batches)
eggplants	2	4	6	8	10
eggs	4	8	12	16	20
milk	¼ cup (60 mL)	½ cup (125 mL)	¾ cup (175 mL)	1 cup (250 mL)	1¼ cups (310 mL)
Italian bread crumbs	3 cups (750 mL)	6 cups (1.5 L)	9 cups (2.25 L)	12 cups (3 L)	15 cups (3.75 L)
vegetable oil	¼ cup (60 mL)	½ cup (125 mL)	¾ cup (175 mL)	1 cup (250 mL)	1¼ cups (310 mL)
mozzarella cheese	2 cups (500 mL)	4 cups (1 L)	6 cups (1.5 L)	8 cups (2 L)	10 cups (2.5 L)
Parmesan cheese	1 cup (250 mL)	2 cups (500 mL)	3 cups (750 mL)	4 cups (1 L)	5 cups (1.25 L)
ricotta cheese	8 oz (250 g)	1 lb (500 g)	1½ lbs (750 g)	2 lbs (1 kg)	2½ lbs (1.25 kg)
Marinara Sauce	6 cups (1.5 L)	12 cups (3 L)	18 cups (4.5 L)	24 cups (6 L)	30 cups (7.5 L)
13x9 pans	1	2	3	4	5

BULK BATCH GUIDE

Cilantro Black Bean Taco Salad

This is a perfect meat-free salad, and I love eating it outside on lazy summer nights. Layer your plate with crispy tortilla chips and fresh, crisp lettuce, then toss on this zesty Southwest-inspired bean and corn mixture and let the fiesta in your mouth begin. Makes 6 servings.

    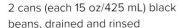

2 cans (each 15 oz/425 mL) black beans, drained and rinsed

1 can (15 oz/425 mL) kidney beans, drained and rinsed

1 can (15 oz/425 mL) corn kernels, drained and rinsed

1 can (14 oz/398 mL) diced tomatoes, with juice

½ cup (125 mL) salsa verde

3 tbsp (45 mL) gluten-free taco seasoning

Garnishes

1 head romaine lettuce, chopped

Sliced avocado or Avocado Crema (page 348), optional

Corn chips or tortilla strips (optional)

Chopped fresh cilantro

Lime wedges (optional)

1. In a medium bowl, combine black beans, kidney beans, corn, tomatoes (with juice), salsa verde and taco seasoning.

MAKE IT NOW Place mixture in a medium saucepan. Bring to a boil over medium-high heat, stirring often. Immediately reduce heat to low and simmer, stirring often, for 15 minutes, until flavors have deepened. Serve over fresh lettuce topped with avocado and corn chips, if using, and sprinkle with cilantro. Serve with lime wedges on the side, if desired.

MAKE IT A FREEZER MEAL Place bean mixture in a labeled gallon-size (4 L) freezer bag. Seal, removing as much air as possible, and freeze.

THAW AND COOK Place bag in the refrigerator for 12 to 24 hours to thaw, or run lukewarm water over bag until you can break apart the contents. Pour into a medium saucepan. Bring to a boil over medium-high heat, stirring often. Immediately reduce heat to low and simmer, stirring often, for 15 minutes, until flavors have deepened. Serve over fresh lettuce topped with avocado and corn chips, if using, and sprinkle with cilantro. Serve with lime wedges on the side, if desired.

BULK BATCH GUIDE	Servings	6 (1 batch)	12 (2 batches)	18 (3 batches)	24 (4 batches)	30 (5 batches)
	black beans	30 oz (850 mL)	60 oz (1.7 L)	90 oz (2.55 L)	120 oz (3.4 L)	150 oz (4.25 L)
	kidney beans	15 oz (425 mL)	30 oz (850 mL)	45 oz (1.275 L)	60 oz (1.7 L)	75 oz (2.125 L)
	corn	15 oz (425 mL)	30 oz (850 mL)	45 oz (1.275 L)	60 oz (1.7 L)	75 oz (2.125 L)
	tomatoes	14 oz (398 mL)	28 oz (796 mL)	42 oz (1.194 L)	56 oz (1.592 L)	70 oz (1.99 L)
	salsa verde	½ cup (125 mL)	1 cup (250 mL)	1½ cups (375 mL)	2 cups (500 mL)	2½ cups (625 mL)
	taco seasoning	3 tbsp (45 mL)	6 tbsp (90 mL)	9 tbsp (135 mL)	¾ cup (175 mL)	¾ cup + 3 tbsp (220 mL)
	gallon bags	1	2	3	4	5

Smashed Bean and Red Pepper Quesadillas

File this recipe under "quick and tasty." All you need to do is pull these quesadillas out of the freezer, heat them in the oven for 20 minutes, add a side salsa and sour cream and you're a dinnertime hero. The roasted peppers add just enough kick to make you want to reach for more. Makes 6 servings.

2 cans (each 15 oz/425 mL) butter beans, drained and rinsed

12 flour tortillas (10 inches/30 cm)

¼ cup (60 mL) Lip-Smackin' Chutney (page 344)

1 can (15 oz/425 mL) black beans, drained and rinsed

½ batch Blistered Roasted Peppers (page 353), sliced

1½ cups (375 mL) shredded Cheddar cheese (about 6 oz/175 g)

Cooking spray or olive oil

Garnishes

Sour cream (optional)

Chopped fresh cilantro (optional)

1. In a medium bowl, mash butter beans until mostly smooth but some chunks remain.

2. Using a fork, evenly spread a heaping ¼ cup (60 mL) smashed beans over each tortilla, making sure to go all the way to the edges.

3. Spoon about 1 tsp (5 mL) chutney evenly over bean layer, followed by about ⅓ cup (75 mL) black beans. Arrange 6 to 8 roasted pepper slices overtop, then sprinkle with about ¼ cup (60 mL) Cheddar cheese. Cover with a second tortilla.

4. Heat a large, nonstick skillet over medium heat. Once it is hot, spray skillet with cooking spray or brush with olive oil. Flip tortilla stack into skillet with the cheese side down. Cover skillet with a lid and cook for 2 minutes or until golden. Remove lid, flip stack and cook, uncovered, for 1 to 2 minutes. Transfer to a cutting board (or a wire rack to cool for freezing) and repeat with remaining quesadillas. Slice each into 4 quarters.

MAKE IT NOW Serve immediately, topped with sour cream and cilantro, if desired.

MAKE IT A FREEZER MEAL Let cooked quesadillas cool. Wrap in foil, including up to 4 pieces per package. Place in a labeled gallon-size (4 L) freezer bag. Seal, removing as much air as possible, and freeze.

COOK FROM FROZEN Preheat oven to 400°F (200°C). Place foil-wrapped quesadillas directly on center oven rack. Bake for 20 minutes or until crispy and heated through. (You can also remove the foil and microwave the quesadillas on a microwave-safe plate: microwave on High for 1 minute at a time, until heated through.) Serve immediately, topped with sour cream and cilantro, if using.

BULK BATCH GUIDE	Servings	6 (1 batch)	12 (2 batches)	18 (3 batches)	24 (4 batches)	30 (5 batches)
	butter beans	30 oz (850 mL g)	60 oz (1.7 L)	90 oz (2.55 L)	120 oz (3.4 L)	150 oz (4.25 L)
	tortillas	12	24	36	48	60
	chutney	¼ cup (60 mL)	½ cup (125 mL)	¾ cup (175 mL)	1 cup (250 mL)	1¼ cups (310 mL)
	black beans	15 oz (425 mL)	30 oz (850 mL)	45 oz (1.275 L)	60 oz (1.7 L)	75 oz (2.125 L)
	Blistered Peppers	½ batch	1 batch	1½ batches	2 batches	2½ batches
	Cheddar cheese	1½ cups (375 mL)	3 cups (750 mL)	4½ cups (1.125 L)	6 cups (1.5 L)	7½ cups (1.875 L)
	gallon bags	1	2	3	4	5

Sun-Dried Tomato Basil Pesto Quiche

Confession: this is the first quiche I've ever liked in my entire life. Filled with my favorite things, like Gouda cheese and sun-dried tomatoes, then drizzled with a swirl of pesto and baked in a crispy, buttery hash-brown crust, it's easy to see why it changed my mind. Makes 6 servings.

3 cups (750 mL) frozen shredded hash browns (about 11 oz/312 g)

¼ cup (60 mL) melted butter

1 tsp (5 mL) garlic powder

4 large eggs

1 cup (250 mL) half-and-half (10%) cream

2 tbsp (30 mL) basil pesto or Easy Pesto (page 339)

1 cup (250 mL) shredded smoked Gouda cheese (about 4 oz/125 g)

2 tbsp (30 mL) minced dry-packed sun-dried tomatoes

Tip
If you're making this recipe right away, you can use a glass or ceramic baking dish.

1. Preheat oven to 450°F (230°C).

2. In a 9-inch (23 cm) metal or foil pie plate or 9-inch (23 cm) metal or foil square pan, combine hash browns, melted butter and garlic powder. Using a fork, press mixture up the sides of the dish and along the bottom, forming a crust.

3. Bake in preheated oven for 20 to 25 minutes or until golden. Remove from oven.

4. In a medium bowl, whisk together eggs and cream. Set aside.

5. Scoop pesto into a piping bag or small resealable bag. Set aside.

MAKE IT NOW Reduce oven temperature to 350°F (180°C). Sprinkle Gouda cheese along bottom and up sides of baked crust. Pour in egg mixture. Sprinkle sun-dried tomatoes evenly overtop. Pipe on pesto in a spiral, starting from the middle and working your way to the outer edge. Place on a rimmed baking sheet and bake in preheated oven for 40 to 45 minutes, or until a tester inserted in the center comes out clean. Let cool for 5 minutes, then serve.

MAKE IT A FREEZER MEAL Allow baked crust to cool completely. Sprinkle Gouda cheese along bottom and up sides of crust. Pour in egg mixture. Sprinkle sun-dried tomatoes evenly overtop. Pipe on pesto in a spiral, starting from the middle and working your way to the outer edge. Freeze for 1 to 2 hours or until frozen solid. Wrap baking dish tightly with plastic wrap, pressing down gently to remove air. Cover with foil. Label and freeze.

COOK FROM FROZEN Preheat oven to 350°F (180°C). Remove foil and plastic wrap from quiche. Place on a rimmed baking sheet. Bake for 1 hour, or until a tester inserted in the center comes out clean. Let cool for 5 minutes, then serve.

BULK BATCH GUIDE	Servings	6 (1 batch)	12 (2 batches)	18 (3 batches)	24 (4 batches)	30 (5 batches)
	hash browns	3 cups (750 mL)	6 cups (1.5 L)	9 cups (2.25 L)	12 cups (3 L)	15 cups (3.75 L)
	butter	¼ cup (60 mL)	½ cup (125 mL)	¾ cup (175 mL)	1 cup (250 mL)	1¼ cups (310 mL)
	garlic powder	1 tsp (5 mL)	2 tsp (10 mL)	1 tbsp (15 mL)	4 tsp (20 mL)	5 tsp (25 mL)
	eggs	4	8	12	16	20
	half-and-half	1 cup (250 mL)	2 cups (500 mL)	3 cups (750 mL)	4 cups (1 L)	5 cups (1.25 L)
	pesto	2 tbsp (30 mL)	¼ cup (60 mL)	6 tbsp (90 mL)	½ cup (125 mL)	⅔ cup (150 mL)
	Smoked Gouda cheese	1 cup (250 mL)	2 cups (500 mL)	3 cups (750 mL)	4 cups (1 L)	5 cups (1.25 L)
	sun-dried tomatoes	2 tbsp (30 mL)	¼ cup (60 mL)	6 tbsp (90 mL)	½ cup (125 mL)	⅔ cup (150 mL)
	9-inch pie plates	1	2	3	4	5

Great Northern Enchiladas

My husband likes to remind me that all great things come from the north (he's Canadian). This is such a wonderful vegetarian recipe, with spiced Great Northern beans topped with smooth homemade enchilada sauce and sprinkled with queso fresco. Makes 6 servings.

1 can (15 oz/425 mL) Great Northern beans, drained and rinsed

1 cup (250 mL) frozen corn kernels

1 cup (250 mL) crumbled queso fresco (about 4 oz/125 g)

1 cup (250 mL) shredded Monterey Jack cheese (about 4 oz/125 g), divided

½ fresh jalapeño pepper, thinly sliced (see Tip, below)

1 batch Enchilada Sauce (page 346), divided

9 corn tortillas (8 inches/20 cm)

Cooking spray or olive oil

Garnishes

Avocado Crema (page 348), optional

Salsa (optional)

Sour cream (optional)

Additional crumbled queso fresco (optional)

Chopped fresh cilantro (optional)

Tips

If spice is your thing, increase the quantity of jalapeño!

If you're making this recipe right away, you can use a glass or ceramic baking dish.

1. Preheat oven to 300°F (150°C).

2. In a medium bowl, gently combine beans, corn, queso fresco, ¼ cup (60 mL) Monterey Jack cheese, jalapeño and ¼ cup (60 mL) enchilada sauce.

3. Spray tortillas on both sides with cooking spray or brush with olive oil. Place in a single layer on 2 baking sheets lined with parchment paper. Bake in preheated oven for 3 to 4 minutes, or until soft and workable. Remove from oven.

4. Place about ⅓ cup (75 mL) bean mixture in center of each warm tortilla and roll up tightly. Place, seam side down, in a lightly greased 13- by 9-inch (33 by 23 cm) metal or foil pan, in a single layer.

MAKE IT NOW Increase oven temperature to 400°F (200°C). Bake enchiladas for 10 to 15 minutes or until tops are lightly golden. Pour remaining enchilada sauce overtop, sprinkle with remaining Monterey Jack cheese and cover with lightly greased foil. Bake for about 15 to 20 minutes longer, until sauce is bubbly and cheese on top is melted. Remove from oven and top with avocado crema, salsa, sour cream, queso fresco and/or cilantro, if using.

MAKE IT A FREEZER MEAL Wrap pan tightly with plastic wrap, pressing down gently to remove air. Place enchilada sauce in a quart-size (1 L) bag; seal, removing as much air as possible, and place on top of plastic-wrapped baking dish. Place remaining ¾ cup (175 mL) Monterey Jack cheese in another quart-size bag; seal and place on top of pan. Cover all with foil, label and freeze.

COOK FROM FROZEN Preheat oven to 400°F (200°C). Remove foil, sauce bag, cheese bag and plastic wrap. Spray tops of enchiladas with cooking spray or brush with olive oil. Bake in preheated oven for 10 to 15 minutes or until tops are lightly golden. Run hot water over bag of enchilada sauce until broken up enough to pour into a microwave-safe bowl. Microwave on High for 1 to 2 minutes, until all frozen chunks are melted and sauce is warmed through. Remove toasted enchiladas from oven and pour sauce over to cover completely. Gently break up frozen shredded cheese and sprinkle overtop. Cover with lightly greased foil. Bake for about 25 to 30 minutes longer, until sauce is bubbly and cheese on top is melted. Remove from oven and top with avocado crema, salsa, sour cream, queso fresco and/or cilantro, if using.

(continued on page 276)

Servings	6 (1 batch)	12 (2 batches)	18 (3 batches)	24 (4 batches)	30 (5 batches)
Great Northern beans	15 oz (425 mL)	30 oz (850 mL)	45 oz (1.275 L)	60 oz (1.7 L)	75 oz (2.125 L)
corn	1 cup (250 mL)	2 cups (500 mL)	3 cups (750 mL)	4 cups (1 L)	5 cups (1.25 L)
queso fresco	1 cup (250 mL)	2 cups (500 mL)	3 cups (750 mL)	4 cups (1 L)	5 cups (1.25 L)
Monterey Jack cheese	1 cup (250 mL)	2 cups (500 mL)	3 cups (750 mL)	4 cups (1 L)	5 cups (1.25 L)
jalapeño peppers	½	1	1½	2	2½
Enchilada Sauce	1 batch	2 batches	3 batches	4 batches	5 batches
tortillas	9	18	27	36	45
13x9 pans	1	2	3	4	5
quart bags	2	4	6	8	10

My husband likes to
remind me that
all great things come
from the north
(he's Canadian).

Hazelnut Mushroom Potatoes au Gratin

For all you folks holding on to that mandoline you bought but never use, here's your chance to finally use it! This is such a beautiful dish, filled with thinly sliced potatoes, mushrooms and Swiss cheese covered in creamy sauce. Oh, and let's not forget about the enticing crunch of hazelnuts in every bite. Makes 6 servings.

6 medium red potatoes (about 1½ lbs/750 g)

Cooking spray or olive oil

1 batch Vegetarian White Sauce (page 337), cooled

1 cup (250 mL) milk

1 tbsp (15 mL) olive oil

1 tbsp (15 mL) minced garlic

1 tbsp (15 mL) dried minced onion

2 cups (500 mL) sliced mushrooms

¼ cup (60 mL) ground hazelnuts, divided

8 slices Swiss cheese

1. Preheat oven to 400°F (200°C).

2. Using a mandoline slicer, cut potatoes into ⅛-inch (3 mm) slices. Place on a baking sheet lined with lightly greased parchment paper, overlapping slightly. Spray tops of potatoes lightly with cooking spray or brush with olive oil. Bake in preheated oven for 6 to 7 minutes or until tender. Remove from oven and set aside.

3. Place white sauce in a large bowl. Slowly whisk in milk. Set aside.

4. In a medium skillet, heat olive oil over medium-high heat. Add garlic and dried onion; cook, stirring, for 1 minute, until fragrant. Remove from heat and scrape half into sauce mixture. Return skillet with remaining garlic and onion to medium-high heat. Add mushrooms and cook, stirring, for 4 to 5 minutes, until onion is golden and mushrooms are lightly browned. Remove from heat and set aside.

5. Pour ½ cup (125 mL) sauce mixture over bottom of a greased 9-inch (23 cm) baking dish, spreading evenly. Arrange about half of the cooked potato slices in 2 layers, overlapping slightly, then spread another ½ cup (125 mL) sauce mixture evenly overtop. Sprinkle with 1 tbsp (15 mL) ground hazelnuts and top with 4 slices of Swiss cheese. Layer mushrooms evenly overtop. Repeat with ½ cup (125 mL) sauce mixture, 1 tbsp (15 mL) ground hazelnuts and 4 slices of cheese. Add remaining sliced potatoes in 2 layers and pour remaining ½ cup (125 mL) sauce mixture overtop. Sprinkle remaining ground hazelnuts around edges of dish.

MAKE IT NOW Preheat oven to 425°F (220°C). Bake in preheated oven for 10 minutes. Reduce heat to 350°F (180°C) and continue baking for 45 to 60 minutes, until top is golden brown and sauce is bubbling all over. Remove from oven and let cool for 10 minutes before serving.

MAKE IT A FREEZER MEAL Wrap baking dish tightly with plastic wrap, pressing down gently to remove air. Cover with foil. Label and freeze.

THAW AND COOK Place baking dish in the refrigerator for at least 12 hours or up to 24 hours to thaw. Preheat oven to 425°F (220°C). Remove foil and plastic wrap from dish. Bake in preheated oven for 10 minutes. Reduce heat to 350°F (180°C) and continue baking for 55 to 60 minutes, until golden brown and sauce is bubbling all over. Remove from oven and let cool for 10 minutes before serving.

(continued on page 279)

Servings	6 (1 batch)	12 (2 batches)	18 (3 batches)	24 (4 batches)	30 (5 batches)
red potatoes	6	12	18	24	30
White Sauce	1 batch	2 batches	3 batches	4 batches	5 batches
milk	1 cup (250 mL)	2 cups (500 mL)	3 cups (750 mL)	4 cups (1 L)	5 cups (1.25 L)
olive oil	1 tbsp (15 mL)	2 tbsp (30 mL)	3 tbsp (45 mL)	¼ cup (60 mL)	⅓ cup (75 mL)
garlic	1 tbsp (15 mL)	2 tbsp (30 mL)	3 tbsp (45 mL)	¼ cup (60 mL)	⅓ cup (75 mL)
dried onion	1 tbsp (15 mL)	2 tbsp (30 mL)	3 tbsp (45 mL)	¼ cup (60 mL)	⅓ cup (75 mL)
mushrooms	2 cups (500 mL)	4 cups (1 L)	6 cups (1.5 L)	8 cups (2 L)	10 cups (2.5 L)
ground hazelnuts	¼ cup (60 mL)	½ cup (125 mL)	¾ cup (175 mL)	1 cup (250 mL)	1¼ cups (310 mL)
Swiss cheese slices	8	16	24	32	40
9x9 dishes	1	2	3	4	5

For all you folks holding on to that mandoline you bought but never use, here's your chance to finally use it!

Buffalo Ranch Roasted Cauliflower and Broccoli

These simple ingredients may not seem like much, but put them together and you have a symphony of savory goodness. The sharp and distinctive "hot wings" flavor of this meal makes it a fun dish that is guaranteed to please the whole crowd, from chicken lovers to vegetarians alike!

Makes 6 servings.

3 cups (750 mL) frozen cauliflower (9 oz/255 g)

2 tbsp (30 mL) Buffalo wing sauce, such as Frank's RedHot

4 cups (1 L) frozen broccoli florets (9.5 oz/270 g)

2 tbsp (30 mL) olive oil

3 tbsp (45 mL) powdered ranch dressing mix

1. In a large bowl, toss cauliflower with wing sauce.

2. In another large bowl, toss broccoli with olive oil, ensuring that all pieces are evenly coated. Add ranch dressing mix and toss to coat.

MAKE IT NOW Preheat oven to 425°F (220°C). Combine cauliflower and broccoli on a rimmed baking sheet lined with parchment paper, spreading into a single layer. Bake in preheated oven for 10 minutes, stir once, then bake for an additional 15 minutes, until vegetables begin to crisp on top but are not burned. Remove from oven and serve.

MAKE IT A FREEZER MEAL Spread cauliflower mixture on a rimmed baking sheet lined with parchment paper, spacing pieces so they aren't touching. Spread broccoli mixture on another rimmed baking sheet lined with parchment paper, spacing pieces so they aren't touching. Place both baking sheets in the freezer and freeze for about 30 minutes, until solid. Transfer frozen vegetables to a labeled gallon-size (4 L) freezer bag. Seal, removing as much air as possible, and freeze.

COOK FROM FROZEN Preheat oven to 425°F (220°C). Transfer bag contents to a rimmed baking sheet lined with parchment paper, spreading into a single layer. Bake in preheated oven for 13 minutes, stir once, then bake for an additional 15 to 17 minutes, until vegetables begin to crisp on top but are not burned. Remove from oven and serve.

BULK BATCH GUIDE

Servings	6 (1 batch)	12 (2 batches)	18 (3 batches)	24 (4 batches)	30 (5 batches)
cauliflower	3 cups (750 mL)	6 cups (1.5 L)	9 cups (2.25 L)	12 cups (3 L)	15 cups (3.75 L)
Buffalo wing sauce	2 tbsp (30 mL)	¼ cup (60 mL)	6 tbsp (90 mL)	½ cup (125 mL)	⅔ cup (150 mL)
broccoli	4 cups (1 L)	8 cups (2 L)	12 cups (3 L)	16 cups (4 L)	20 cups (5 L)
olive oil	2 tbsp (30 mL)	¼ cup (60 mL)	6 tbsp (90 mL)	½ cup (125 mL)	⅔ cup (150 mL)
ranch dressing mix	3 tbsp (45 mL)	6 tbsp (90 mL)	9 tbsp (135 mL)	¾ cup (175 mL)	¾ cup + 3 tbsp (220 mL)
gallon bags	1	2	3	4	5

SIDE DISHES

Brown 'n' Serve Rolls   284

Cheesy Potatoes   287

Roasted Candied Sweet Potatoes   288

Garlic Herb Smashed Potatoes   291

Mashed Potatoes   292

Dirty Rice   295

Spanish Rice   296

Wild Rice Pilaf   299

Cilantro Lime Corn   300

Brown 'n' Serve Rolls

Haven't you always wanted a homemade roll recipe that you could make ahead and freeze? Well, I've got you covered! Tender, buttery and perfect for all your big holiday or family gatherings, this recipe will save you lots of time, helping you produce fresh, steaming-hot rolls out of the oven on short notice. Makes 18 rolls.

1 large egg

Lukewarm water

¼ cup (60 mL) granulated sugar

1½ tsp (7 mL) active dry yeast

½ cup (125 mL) melted butter, slightly cooled

¾ tsp (3 mL) salt

4 to 4½ cups (1 to 1.125 L) bread flour

Additional ¼ cup (60 mL) melted butter

Tip

If you're making this recipe right away, you can use a glass or ceramic baking dish.

1. In a large measuring cup, whisk egg. Add enough lukewarm water to total 1½ cups (375 mL) liquid; whisk until combined.

2. Pour egg mixture into bowl of a stand mixer fitted with the dough hook. Add sugar and yeast; beat on Low for 1 minute, until sugar has dissolved. Add ½ cup (125 mL) melted butter, salt and 4 cups (1 L) flour. Once they are combined, increase speed to High and knead for 6 minutes, until dough is smooth and elastic and comes away cleanly from sides of bowl. You may need to gradually add up to ½ cup (125 mL) more flour. The dough should be sticky when you remove it from the bowl.

3. Place dough in a large greased bowl and cover bowl with greased plastic wrap. Let dough rise for about 60 minutes, or until doubled in size. Punch down dough and cover again; let rise for 30 minutes or until doubled in size again.

4. Punch down dough again. Cut into thirds and then cut each piece into 3 equal pieces. Cut each of those pieces in half to make 18 pieces of dough.

5. With lightly floured hands, roll each piece of dough into a ball. Place dough balls in two greased 9-inch (23 cm) metal or foil pans (9 rolls in each). Brush lightly with additional melted butter. Cover with greased plastic wrap. Let rise for about 30 minutes, or until doubled in size.

MAKE IT NOW Preheat oven to 400°F (200°C). Remove plastic wrap and place rolls in preheated oven. Bake for 15 to 20 minutes, until cooked through and golden brown. Remove from oven and let cool.

MAKE IT A FREEZER MEAL Preheat oven to 400°F (200°C). Remove plastic wrap and place rolls in preheated oven. Bake for 10 to 11 minutes, or just until beginning to turn light golden brown. Remove from oven and let cool. Place pans in freezer and freeze for about 1 hour, until rolls are firm. Remove from freezer and cover each pan with plastic wrap, gently pressing down to remove air. Cover with foil, label and freeze.

COOK FROM FROZEN Preheat oven to 400°F (200°C). Remove pan from freezer and remove foil and plastic wrap. Bake in preheated oven for 15 to 20 minutes, until cooked through and golden brown.

BULK BATCH GUIDE Rolls	18 (1 batch)	36 (2 batches)	54 (3 batches)	72 (4 batches)	90 (5 batches)
eggs	1	2	3	4	5
sugar	¼ cup (60 mL)	½ cup (125 mL)	¾ cup (175 mL)	1 cup (250 mL)	1¼ cups (310 mL)
active dry yeast	1½ tsp (7 mL)	1 tbsp (15 mL)	1½ tbsp (22 mL)	2 tbsp (30 mL)	2½ tbsp (37 mL)
butter	½ cup (125 mL)	1 cup (250 mL)	1½ cups (375 mL)	2 cups (500 mL)	2½ cups (625 mL)
salt	¾ tsp (3 mL)	1½ tsp (7 mL)	2¼ tsp (11 mL)	1 tbsp (15 mL)	3¾ tsp (18 mL)
bread flour	4 to 4½ cups (1 to 1.125 L)	8 to 9 cups (2 to 2.25 L)	12 to 13½ cups (3 to 3.375 L)	16 to 18 cups (4 to 4.5 L)	20 to 22½ cups (5 to 5.625 L)
butter for brushing	¼ cup (60 mL)	½ cup (125 mL)	¾ cup (175 mL)	1 cup (250 mL)	1¼ cups (310 mL)
9x9 pans	2	4	6	8	10

Cheesy Potatoes

Everyone needs a good comforting and cheesy potato side dish ready to go in the freezer. I love serving these buttery, tender potatoes alongside my savory and bold bacon-wrapped Cashew Basil Chicken (page 131) or as a perfect partner to my BBQ Beef Brisket (page 214). Sometimes when I make these cheesy potatoes, they get eaten more than the main. When you consider all that gooey golden greatness, how could anyone resist, right? *Makes 8 servings.*

1 batch White Sauce (page 336), cooled

1 cup (250 mL) sour cream

1 cup (250 mL) milk

2 cups (500 mL) shredded Colby cheese (about 8 oz/250 g)

2 cups (500 mL) shredded sharp Cheddar cheese (about 8 oz/250 g)

1 tsp (5 mL) onion powder

Pinch garlic salt

Salt and freshly ground black pepper

1 bag (1 lb/500 g) frozen shredded hash browns

Tip
If you're making this recipe right away, you can use a glass or ceramic baking dish.

1. In a large bowl, combine white sauce, sour cream and milk. Add Colby cheese, Cheddar cheese, onion powder and garlic salt; stir to combine. Season to taste with salt and pepper. Add frozen hash browns and stir gently until well incorporated.

2. Spread mixture in a lightly greased 13- by 9-inch (33 by 23 cm) metal or foil pan.

MAKE IT NOW Preheat oven to 350°F (180°C). Bake in preheated oven for about 45 minutes, until bubbling all over and top is golden brown.

MAKE IT A FREEZER MEAL Wrap pan tightly with plastic wrap, pressing down gently to remove air. Cover with foil. Label and freeze.

COOK FROM FROZEN Preheat oven to 350°F (180°C). Remove plastic wrap and foil. Bake in preheated oven for about 1 hour and 15 minutes, until sauce is bubbling all over and topping is golden brown.

BULK BATCH GUIDE					
Servings	8 (1 batch)	16 (2 batches)	24 (3 batches)	32 (4 batches)	40 (5 batches)
White Sauce	1 batch	2 batches	3 batches	4 batches	5 batches
sour cream	1 cup (250 mL)	2 cups (500 mL)	3 cups (750 mL)	4 cups (1 L)	5 cups (1.25 L)
milk	1 cup (250 mL)	2 cups (500 mL)	3 cups (750 mL)	4 cups (1 L)	5 cups (1.25 L)
Colby cheese	2 cups (500 mL)	4 cups (1 L)	6 cups (1.5 L)	8 cups (2 L)	10 cups (2.5 L)
Cheddar cheese	2 cups (500 mL)	4 cups (1 L)	6 cups (1.5 L)	8 cups (2 L)	10 cups (2.5 L)
onion powder	1 tsp (5 mL)	2 tsp (10 mL)	1 tbsp (15 mL)	4 tsp (20 mL)	5 tsp (25 mL)
hash browns	1 lb (500 g)	2 lbs (1 kg)	3 lbs (1.5 kg)	4 lbs (2 kg)	5 lbs (2.5 kg)
13x9 pans	1	2	3	4	5

Roasted Candied Sweet Potatoes

Warning: eating too much of this dish may result in extreme feelings of taste-bud joy. Side effects also include cravings for yummy sweet potatoes for many days after eating them. My family has a tradition of making this marshmallow-covered, buttery, brown-sugared sweet potato bake for every holiday we celebrate. *Makes 8 servings.*

5 large sweet potatoes (about 2½ lbs/1.25 kg)

½ cup (125 mL) butter

1¼ cups (310 mL) packed brown sugar

1 tsp (5 mL) vanilla extract

2 cups (500 mL) mini marshmallows (optional)

1. Preheat oven to 400°F (200°C).

2. Using a sharp knife, poke holes all over the sweet potatoes. Place potatoes on a baking sheet lined with foil. Bake in preheated oven for 1½ hours or until tender.

3. Remove sweet potatoes from oven and let cool for 5 minutes. Peel and cut crosswise into 1-inch (2.5 cm) slices. Layer potatoes, overlapping slightly, in a 13- by 9-inch (33 by 23 cm) baking dish.

4. In a small, microwave-safe bowl, combine butter and brown sugar. Melt in the microwave on High for 1 minute, until bubbling. Add vanilla and stir. Pour evenly over sweet potatoes.

MAKE IT NOW Preheat oven to 350°F (180°C). Cover baking dish with foil. Bake in preheated oven for 1 hour, until sauce is bubbling all over. Remove foil and sprinkle mini marshmallows, if using, evenly overtop. Preheat broiler. Broil for about 1 minute, checking every 20 seconds, until marshmallows are golden brown. Let cool for 10 minutes; serve.

MAKE IT A FREEZER MEAL Let cool completely. Wrap baking dish tightly with plastic wrap, pressing down gently to remove air. Cover with foil, label and freeze.

THAW AND COOK Place in the refrigerator for at least 12 hours or up to 24 hours to thaw. Preheat oven to 350°F (180°C). Remove plastic wrap and foil. Cover with new foil. Bake in preheated oven for 1 hour and 10 minutes. Remove foil and sprinkle mini marshmallows, if using, evenly overtop. Preheat broiler. Broil for about 1 minute, checking every 20 seconds, until marshmallows are golden brown. Let cool for 10 minutes; serve.

BULK BATCH	Servings	8 (1 batch)	16 (2 batches)	24 (3 batches)	32 (4 batches)	40 (5 batches)
	sweet potatoes	5	10	15	20	25
	butter	½ cup (125 mL)	1 cup (250 mL)	1½ cups (375 mL)	2 cups (500 mL)	2½ cups (625 mL)
	brown sugar	1¼ cups (310 mL)	2½ cups (625 mL)	3¾ cups (925 mL)	5 cups (1.25 L)	6¼ cups (1.56 L)
	vanilla	1 tsp (5 mL)	2 tsp (10 mL)	1 tbsp (15 mL)	4 tsp (20 mL)	5 tsp (25 mL)
	marshmallows	2 cups (500 mL)	4 cups (1 L)	6 cups (1.5 L)	8 cups (2 L)	10 cups (2.5 L)
	13x9 dishes	1	2	3	4	5

Garlic Herb Smashed Potatoes

Not only are these potatoes a popping new way to serve your usual starchy staple, but after a long day it can be so much fun to get in the kitchen and smash those little potatoes! This side goes really well with my Steak with Gorgonzola Butter (page 209), and it makes a great party appetizer too!

Makes 6 servings.

1½ lbs (750 g) yellow-fleshed or red baby potatoes

¼ cup (60 mL) olive oil

¼ tsp (1 mL) garlic salt

¼ cup (60 mL) butter

½ tsp (2 mL) dried parsley

¼ tsp (1 mL) ground sage

Salt and freshly ground black pepper

Garnish

Chopped fresh sage (optional)

1. Preheat oven to 450°F (230°C).

2. In a large bowl, combine potatoes, olive oil and garlic salt. Spread on a rimmed baking sheet lined with foil.

3. Bake in preheated oven for 20 minutes or until tender.

4. In a small saucepan, melt butter over low heat. Add parsley and sage; stir. Remove from heat and let cool slightly.

5. Remove potatoes from oven and immediately smash them gently with a potato masher or the bottom of a glass until about half their original height.

6. Spoon a little of the butter mixture over each smashed potato. Season to taste with salt and pepper.

MAKE IT NOW Place sauced smashed potatoes back in the oven and bake for 15 to 20 minutes, until golden and crispy. Serve sprinkled with chopped sage, if desired.

MAKE IT A FREEZER MEAL Freeze potatoes on baking sheet for about 1 hour, until solid. Remove from freezer and transfer to a labeled gallon-size (4 L) freezer bag. Seal, removing as much air as possible, and freeze.

REHEAT Preheat oven to 450°F (230°C). Place frozen smashed potatoes on a rimmed baking sheet lined with lightly greased foil, spacing them apart. Bake in preheated oven for 18 to 22 minutes, until crispy and golden. Serve sprinkled with chopped sage, if desired.

BULK BATCH GUIDE	Servings	6 (1 batch)	12 (2 batches)	18 (3 batches)	24 (4 batches)	30 (5 batches)
	baby potatoes	1½ lbs (750 g)	3 lbs (1.5 kg)	4½ lbs (2.25 kg)	6 lbs (3 kg)	7½ lbs (3.75 kg)
	olive oil	¼ cup (60 mL)	½ cup (125 mL)	¾ cup (175 mL)	1 cup (250 mL)	1¼ cups (310 mL)
	garlic salt	¼ tsp (1 mL)	½ tsp (2 mL)	¾ tsp (3 mL)	1 tsp (5 mL)	1¼ tsp (6 mL)
	butter	¼ cup (60 mL)	½ cup (125 mL)	¾ cup (175 mL)	1 cup (250 mL)	1¼ cups (310 mL)
	dried parsley	½ tsp (2 mL)	1 tsp (5 mL)	1½ tsp (7 mL)	2 tsp (10 mL)	2½ tsp (12 mL)
	ground sage	¼ tsp (1 mL)	½ tsp (2 mL)	¾ tsp (3 mL)	1 tsp (5 mL)	1¼ tsp (6 mL)
	gallon bags	1	2	3	4	5

Mashed Potatoes

Bet you didn't know you could freeze mashed potatoes! Well, you can, and the good news is they can be quickly reheated and taste just as good as the day you made them. I like pairing these with Bacon Love Pork Tenderloin (page 174) or Cranberry Pork Roast (page 177). Makes 6 servings.

2 lbs (1 kg) yellow-fleshed or russet potatoes, peeled and cut into 1- to 2-inch (2.5 to 5 cm) chunks

1 cup (250 mL) butter, diced

½ cup (125 mL) milk

Salt and freshly ground black pepper

1. Place potatoes in a large stockpot and add just enough cold water to cover. Bring to a boil over high heat. Reduce heat to medium-high and boil gently for about 15 minutes, until the largest pieces are very tender when pricked with a fork, about 15 minutes.

2. Drain potatoes over a large bowl, reserving about 1/4 cup (60 mL) liquid. Off the heat, return potatoes and reserved liquid to pot.

3. Sprinkle diced butter over potatoes, cover and let stand for 2 minutes. Remove lid and, using a hand masher, thoroughly mash potatoes, until most of the big lumps are gone. Add milk and continue to mash until smooth. Season to taste with salt and pepper.

MAKE IT NOW Serve immediately.

MAKE IT A FREEZER MEAL Let mashed potatoes cool for about 25 minutes, to room temperature. Place in a labeled gallon-size (4 L) freezer bag. Seal, removing as much air as possible, and freeze.

REHEAT Place bag in refrigerator for at least 12 hours or up to 24 hours to thaw. Preheat oven to 375°F (190°C). Transfer mashed potatoes to a 13- by 9-inch (33 by 23 cm) baking dish. Cover with foil and bake in preheated oven for 20 to 25 minutes, stirring occasionally, or until heated through. (You can also do this in the microwave. Transfer potatoes to a large, microwave-safe bowl and heat on High for 2-minute periods, stirring after each, for 4 to 5 minutes, until heated through.)

BULK BATCH	Servings	6 (1 batch)	12 (2 batches)	18 (3 batches)	24 (4 batches)	30 (5 batches)
	potatoes	2 lbs (1 kg)	4 lbs (2 kg)	6 lbs (3 kg)	8 lbs (4 kg)	10 lbs (5 kg)
	butter	1 cup (250 mL)	2 cups (500 mL)	3 cups (750 mL)	4 cups (1 L)	5 cups (1.25 L)
	milk	½ cup (125 mL)	1 cup (250 mL)	1½ cups (375 mL)	2 cups (500 mL)	2½ cups (625 mL)
	gallon bags	1	2	3	4	5

Dirty Rice

Don't let the name of this recipe fool you. This rice may be called "dirty" but it's actually quite wholesome and delicious. It's wonderful when paired with any soul food, from Flower's Seafood Gumbo (page 246) to a good old-fashioned crayfish bake or down-home barbecue, but it also works well as a stand-alone meal. Makes 6 servings.

½ medium onion, quartered

1 tsp (5 mL) minced garlic

2 medium green bell peppers, divided

1 lb (500 g) ground beef

1 tbsp (15 mL) olive oil

¼ tsp (1 mL) hot pepper flakes

1 tbsp (15 mL) Creole seasoning

1½ tsp (7 mL) dried parsley

2 cups (500 mL) long-grain white rice

1 cup (250 mL) beef broth or Homemade Beef Stock (page 350)

2 cups (500 mL) water

1. In a food processor or high-powered blender, process onion, garlic and 1 bell pepper, until smooth. Set aside.

2. Chop the second bell pepper, by hand, into small dice.

3. In a large saucepan or stockpot with a tight-fitting lid, cook ground beef over medium-high heat, stirring and breaking up clumps with a spoon, for 4 to 5 minutes, until browned and no longer pink inside. Remove from heat and drain off fat through a fine-mesh sieve. Return beef to saucepan over medium-high heat.

4. Add olive oil, onion mixture, diced bell pepper, hot pepper flakes, Creole seasoning and parsley; cook, stirring, for 2 minutes, until bell pepper is tender. Add rice to saucepan and stir for 1 minute, until rice is hot and sizzling.

5. Add beef broth and water; stir. Turn up heat to high and bring to a boil. Cover with lid and immediately reduce heat to low. Cook for 20 minutes, until rice is tender and liquid is absorbed. Remove from heat. Let stand with the lid on for 10 minutes, then fluff with a fork.

MAKE IT NOW Serve immediately.

MAKE IT A FREEZER MEAL Run water over a large rimmed baking sheet, then pour off excess but do not dry. Evenly spread cooked rice on baking sheet (do not press down). Place in the refrigerator until completely cooled. Transfer rice to a labeled gallon-size (4 L) freezer bag. Seal, removing as much air as possible, and freeze.

REHEAT Place bag in refrigerator for at least 12 hours or up to 24 hours to thaw. Empty contents into a large, microwave-safe bowl. Cover loosely with a wet cloth or paper towel. Microwave in 1-minute increments on Medium, stirring after each, until rice is hot. (You can also reheat it on the stove. Transfer rice to a large saucepan, sprinkle with 1 tsp/5 mL water, cover and heat over medium heat, occasionally stirring gently, until hot.)

BULK BATCH GUIDE	Servings	6 (1 batch)	12 (2 batches)	18 (3 batches)	24 (4 batches)	30 (5 batches)
	onions	½	1	1½	2	2½
	garlic	1 tsp (5 mL)	2 tsp (10 mL)	1 tbsp (15 mL)	4 tsp (20 mL)	5 tsp (25 mL)
	bell peppers	2	4	6	8	10
	ground beef	1 lb (500 g)	2 lbs (1 kg)	3 lbs (1.5 kg)	4 lbs (2 kg)	5 lbs (2.5 kg)
	olive oil	1 tbsp (15 mL)	2 tbsp (30 mL)	3 tbsp (45 mL)	¼ cup (60 mL)	⅓ cup (75 mL)
	hot pepper flakes	¼ tsp (1 mL)	½ tsp (2 mL)	¾ tsp (3 mL)	1 tsp (5 mL)	1¼ tsp (6 mL)
	Creole seasoning	1 tbsp (15 mL)	2 tbsp (30 mL)	3 tbsp (45 mL)	¼ cup (60 mL)	⅓ cup (75 mL)
	dried parsley	1½ tsp (7 mL)	1 tbsp (15 mL)	1½ tbsp (22 mL)	2 tbsp (30 mL)	2½ tbsp (37 mL)
	white rice	2 cups (500 mL)	4 cups (1 L)	6 cups (1.5 L)	8 cups (2 L)	10 cups (2.5 L)
	beef broth	1 cup (250 mL)	2 cups (500 mL)	3 cups (750 mL)	4 cups (1 L)	5 cups (1.25 L)
	water	2 cups (500 mL)	4 cups (1 L)	6 cups (1.5 L)	8 cups (2 L)	10 cups (2.5 L)
	gallon bags	1	2	3	4	5

Spanish Rice

After many years of taste-testing Spanish rice from various restaurants, friends and online recipes, I finally did it! I made the fluffiest, yummiest Spanish rice that is a perfect copy of the one I enjoy at my favorite Mexican restaurant. I love to eat it all on its own, but I also serve it alongside my Cilantro Lime Chicken Tacos (page 156) and my Killer Chicken Enchiladas (page 159). Makes 6 servings (about 6 cups/1.5 L).

½ medium onion, quartered

1 carrot, quartered

½ medium tomato

1¾ cups (425 mL) hot water

3 tbsp (45 mL) caldo de tomate seasoning (see Tip, below)

2 tbsp (30 mL) olive oil

1 cup (250 mL) long-grain white rice

1 can (8 oz/227 mL) tomato sauce

Tip

Caldo de tomate is my secret weapon in this recipe. It's a Mexican-seasoned bouillon powder available in jars (Knorr is a common brand). Look for it in the Latin foods section in grocery stores, specialty stores or online.

1. In a high-powered blender, combine onion, carrot and tomato; purée on High until smooth. Set aside.

2. In a small bowl, combine hot water and caldo de tomate seasoning; stir and set aside.

3. In a fine-mesh sieve, rinse rice under cold water for about 5 minutes, until rinse water runs clear.

4. Heat a medium skillet over medium-high heat. Add olive oil and rice; cook, stirring constantly, for 3 to 4 minutes, until rice is barely starting to turn golden brown.

5. Add vegetable purée mixture to skillet and cook, stirring, for 1 minute, until heated through. Add tomato sauce and cook, stirring, for 1 minute, until heated through.

6. Carefully pour caldo de tomate solution over rice. Bring to a boil, then immediately reduce heat to low. Cover and simmer for 20 minutes, until rice is tender and liquid is absorbed. Remove from heat. Let stand with the lid on for 10 minutes, then fluff with a fork.

MAKE IT NOW Serve immediately.

MAKE IT A FREEZER MEAL Run water over a large rimmed baking sheet, then pour off excess but do not dry. Evenly spread cooked rice on baking sheet (do not press down). Place in the refrigerator until completely cooled. Transfer rice to a labeled gallon-size (4 L) freezer bag. Seal, removing as much air as possible, and freeze.

REHEAT Place bag in refrigerator for at least 12 hours or up to 24 hours to thaw. Empty contents into a large, microwave-safe bowl. Cover loosely with a wet cloth or paper towel. Microwave in 1-minute increments on Medium, stirring after each, until rice is hot. (You can also reheat it on the stove. Transfer rice to a large saucepan, sprinkle with 1 tsp/5 mL water, cover and heat over medium heat, occasionally stirring gently, until hot.)

BULK BATCH GUIDE	Servings	6 (1 batch)	12 (2 batches)	18 (3 batches)	24 (4 batches)	30 (5 batches)
	onions	½	1	1½	2	2½
	carrots	1	2	3	4	5
	tomatoes	½	1	1½	2	2½
	water	1¾ cups (425 mL)	3½ cups (875 mL)	5¼ cups (1.31 L)	7 cups (1.75 L)	8¾ cups (2.175 L)
	caldo de tomate seasoning	3 tbsp (45 mL)	6 tbsp (90 mL)	9 tbsp (135 mL)	¾ cup (175 mL)	¾ cup + 3 tbsp (220 mL)
	olive oil	2 tbsp (30 mL)	¼ cup (60 mL)	6 tbsp (90 mL)	½ cup (125 mL)	⅔ cup (150 mL)
	white rice	1 cup (250 mL)	2 cups (500 mL)	3 cups (750 mL)	4 cups (1 L)	5 cups (1.25 L)
	tomato sauce	8 oz (227 mL)	16 oz (454 mL)	24 oz (681 mL)	32 oz (908 mL)	40 oz (1.135 L)
	gallon bags	1	2	3	4	5

Wild Rice Pilaf

Sing out loud with me: "Wild rice, I think I love you!" I love changing up from boring white rice to my wonderful wild rice pilaf. Maybe it's the variety of colors or the pleasing nutty, earthy taste, but either way, just break with the boring and add this lively side dish to your meal. I especially like it with Rosemary Pot Roast (page 205) or Balsamic Short Ribs (page 213). Makes 6 servings.

2 tbsp (30 mL) butter

2 tbsp (30 mL) diced or puréed onion

½ tsp (2 mL) minced garlic

1½ cups (375 mL) unseasoned wild rice blend (about 9½ oz/270 g)

2¼ cups (560 mL) vegetable broth or Homemade Vegetable Stock (page 351)

Pinch garlic salt

Garnish

Chopped fresh Italian (flat-leaf) parsley (optional)

1. In a large saucepan with a tight-fitting lid, melt butter over medium-high heat. Add onion and garlic and cook, stirring, for 1 to 2 minutes, until fragrant.

2. Add rice and cook, stirring, for about 3 minutes, until rice is fragrant and edges begin to brown.

3. Add vegetable broth and garlic salt. Stir, turn up heat to high and bring to a boil. Immediately cover with lid and reduce heat to low. Cook for about 20 minutes, until rice is tender and liquid is absorbed. Remove from heat. Let stand for 10 minutes, then fluff with a fork.

MAKE IT NOW Sprinkle parsley overtop, if using, then stir gently and serve.

MAKE IT A FREEZER MEAL Run water over a large rimmed baking sheet, then pour off excess but do not dry. Evenly spread cooked rice on baking sheet (do not press down). Place in the refrigerator until completely cooled. Transfer rice to a labeled gallon-size (4 L) freezer bag. Seal, removing as much air as possible, and freeze.

REHEAT Empty contents of bag into a large, microwave-safe bowl. Cover loosely with a wet cloth or paper towel. Microwave in 1-minute increments on Medium, stirring after each, until rice is hot. (You can also reheat it on the stove. Transfer rice to large saucepan, sprinkle with 1 tsp/5 mL of water, cover and heat over medium heat, occasionally stirring gently, until rice is hot.) Sprinkle parsley overtop, if using, then stir gently and serve.

	Servings	6 (1 batch)	12 (2 batches)	18 (3 batches)	24 (4 batches)	30 (5 batches)
BULK BATCH	butter	2 tbsp (30 mL)	¼ cup (60 mL)	6 tbsp (90 mL)	½ cup (125 mL)	⅔ cup (150 mL)
	onion	2 tbsp (30 mL)	¼ cup (60 mL)	6 tbsp (90 mL)	½ cup (125 mL)	⅔ cup (150 mL)
	garlic	½ tsp (2 mL)	1 tsp (5 mL)	1½ tsp (7 mL)	2 tsp (10 mL)	2½ tsp (12 mL)
	wild rice blend	1½ cups (375 mL)	3 cups (750 mL)	4½ cups (1.125 L)	6 cups (1.5 L)	7½ cups (1.875 L)
	vegetable broth	2¼ cups (560 mL)	4½ cups (1.125 L)	6¾ cups (1.675 L)	9 cups (2.25 L)	11¼ cups (2.81 L)
	gallon bags	1	2	3	4	5

Cilantro Lime Corn

Love side dishes with attitude? Then freeze a batch of this corn. I serve this as a side with (or even on top of) Perfect Pork Carnitas Tacos (page 203) or Great Northern Enchiladas (page 274).

Makes 6 servings.

1 lb (500 g) frozen sweet corn

½ cup (125 mL) minced red onion (optional)

¼ cup (60 mL) chopped fresh cilantro

1 tsp (5 mL) grated lime zest

Juice of 2 limes (about ¼ cup/60 mL)

½ tsp (2 mL) honey

1 tsp (5 mL) salt

¼ tsp (1 mL) freshly ground black pepper

1. In a medium bowl, combine corn, red onion, if using, cilantro, lime zest, lime juice, honey, salt and pepper.

MAKE IT NOW Let ingredients stand at room temperature for 30 minutes or until corn has thawed and flavors meld together. Transfer to the refrigerator until ready to serve, for up to 12 hours. Serve cold.

MAKE IT A FREEZER MEAL Pour corn mixture into a labeled gallon-size (4 L) freezer bag. Seal, removing as much air as possible, and freeze.

THAW AND SERVE Remove from freezer and place bag on the counter at room temperature. Let stand for 30 minutes or until corn is thawed and flavors meld together. Place in refrigerator until ready to serve, for up to 12 hours. Serve cold.

BULK BATCH GUIDE	Servings	6 (1 batch)	12 (2 batches)	18 (3 batches)	24 (4 batches)	30 (5 batches)
	corn	1 lb (500 g)	2 lbs (1 kg)	3 lbs (1.5 kg)	4 lbs (2 kg)	5 lbs (2.5 kg)
	red onion	½ cup (125 mL)	1 cup (250 mL)	1½ cups (375 mL)	2 cups (500 mL)	2½ cups (625 mL)
	cilantro	¼ cup (60 mL)	½ cup (125 mL)	¾ cup (175 mL)	1 cup (250 mL)	1¼ cups (310 mL)
	lime zest	1 tsp (5 mL)	2 tsp (10 mL)	1 tbsp (15 mL)	4 tsp (20 mL)	5 tsp (25 mL)
	limes	2	4	6	8	10
	honey	½ tsp (2 mL)	1 tsp (5 mL)	1½ tsp (7 mL)	2 tsp (10 mL)	2½ tsp (12 mL)
	salt	1 tsp (5 mL)	2 tsp (10 mL)	1 tbsp (15 mL)	4 tsp (20 mL)	5 tsp (25 mL)
	pepper	¼ tsp (1 mL)	½ tsp (2 mL)	¾ tsp (3 mL)	1 tsp (5 mL)	1¼ tsp (6 mL)
	gallon bags	1	2	3	4	5

DESSERTS

Blackberry Almond Crumble   304

Brown Butter Pecan Pie   307

Mascarpone Key Lime Mini Pies   308

Island Coconut Angel Cake   311

Salted Caramel Pumpkin Cheesecake   312

Molten Hot Fudge Lava Cakes   315

Layered Chocolate Mousse Cake   318

Chocolate Chip Cookies   321

Churros   324

Minty Melts   327

Blackberry Almond Crumble

I will never tire of eating this satisfying dessert, which perfectly combines warm blackberry filling with a crunchy oat and almond crumb topping. It's total dessert bliss, especially when served warm with a heaping scoop of vanilla ice cream or fresh whipped cream. Makes 6 servings.

Filling

3½ cups (875 mL) fresh blackberries or 1 lb (500 g) frozen blackberries, thawed

3 tbsp (45 mL) cornstarch

¾ cup (175 mL) granulated sugar

¼ cup (60 mL) freshly squeezed orange juice

½ tsp (2 mL) almond extract

Topping

1 cup (250 mL) packed brown sugar

1 cup (250 mL) all-purpose flour

¾ cup (175 mL) large-flake (old-fashioned) rolled oats

½ tsp (2 mL) ground cinnamon

½ tsp (2 mL) ground nutmeg

¼ cup (60 mL) finely chopped almonds

½ cup (125 mL) butter, melted

1. *Filling:* In a medium bowl, combine blackberries and cornstarch. Add sugar, orange juice and almond extract; stir gently to combine. Pour into a greased 8-inch (20 cm) metal or foil square pan.

2. *Topping:* In another medium bowl, combine sugar, flour, oats, cinnamon, nutmeg and almonds. Pour in melted butter and stir until crumbly. Spread topping evenly over fruit mixture.

MAKE IT NOW Preheat oven to 375°F (190°C). Place pan on a rimmed baking sheet to catch any drips. Bake crumble in preheated oven for 35 to 40 minutes, until fruit is bubbling and topping is a deep golden brown. Let cool for at least 15 minutes before serving.

MAKE IT A FREEZER MEAL Wrap pan tightly with plastic wrap, pressing down gently to remove air. Cover with foil. Label and freeze.

COOK FROM FROZEN Preheat oven to 375°F (190°C). Remove foil and plastic wrap. Place pan on a rimmed baking sheet to catch any drips. Bake crumble in preheated oven for 50 to 55 minutes, until fruit is bubbling and topping is a deep golden brown. If the topping starts to brown too quickly during baking, cover with foil. Let cool for at least 15 minutes before serving.

Servings	6 (1 batch)	12 (2 batches)	18 (3 batches)	24 (4 batches)	30 (5 batches)
blackberries	3½ cups (875 mL)	7 cups (1.75 L)	10½ cups (2.625 L)	14 cups (3.5 L)	17½ cups (4.375 L)
cornstarch	3 tbsp (45 mL)	6 tbsp (90 mL)	½ cup (125 mL)	¾ cup (175 mL)	¾ cup + 3 tbsp (220 mL)
granulated sugar	¾ cup (175 mL)	1½ cups (375 mL)	2¼ cups (560 mL)	3 cups (750 mL)	3½ cups (875 mL)
orange juice	¼ cup (60 mL)	½ cup (125 mL)	¾ cup (175 mL)	1 cup (250 mL)	1¼ cups (310 mL)
almond extract	½ tsp (2 mL)	1 tsp (5 mL)	1½ tsp (7 mL)	2 tsp (10 mL)	2½ tsp (12 mL)
brown sugar	1 cup (250 mL)	2 cups (500 mL)	3 cups (750 mL)	4 cups (1 L)	5 cups (1.25 L)
all-purpose flour	1 cup (250 mL)	2 cups (500 mL)	3 cups (750 mL)	4 cups (1 L)	5 cups (1.25 L)
rolled oats	¾ cup (175 mL)	1½ cups (375 mL)	2¼ cups (560 mL)	3 cups (750 mL)	3½ cups (875 mL)
cinnamon	½ tsp (2 mL)	1 tsp (5 mL)	1½ tsp (7 mL)	2 tsp (10 mL)	2½ tsp (12 mL)
nutmeg	½ tsp (2 mL)	1 tsp (5 mL)	1½ tsp (7 mL)	2 tsp (10 mL)	2½ tsp (12 mL)
almonds	¼ cup (60 mL)	½ cup (125 mL)	¾ cup (175 mL)	1 cup (250 mL)	1¼ cups (310 mL)
butter	½ cup (125 mL)	1 cup (250 mL)	1½ cups (375 mL)	2 cups (500 mL)	2½ cups (625 mL)
8x8 pans	1	2	3	4	5

BULK BATCH GUIDE

Brown Butter Pecan Pie

If you've only ever had traditional pecan pie, be prepared to have your socks knocked off. Browning the butter gives it such a deep, nutty flavor. This is one dessert I thoroughly enjoyed testing, eating, testing and eating again for this cookbook. It was all done for my readers' benefit of course (wink, wink). Makes 6 to 8 servings.

½ cup (125 mL) butter

1¼ cups (310 mL) pecan halves or pieces

½ batch Pie Crust (page 331), pre-baked and cooled

1 cup (250 mL) corn syrup

½ cup (125 mL) granulated sugar

½ cup (125 mL) packed brown sugar

4 large eggs, lightly beaten

1 tsp (5 mL) vanilla extract

Pinch salt

1. In a small saucepan, melt butter over medium-low heat, stirring occasionally. Cook for 5 to 8 minutes, until golden brown and foamy. Set aside to cool completely.

2. Place pecans in cooled baked pie crust.

3. In a large bowl, whisk together corn syrup, granulated sugar, brown sugar, eggs and vanilla, until smooth. Add cooled browned butter and whisk until creamy and smooth. Pour over pecans in crust.

MAKE IT NOW Preheat oven to 350°F (180°C). Place pie dish on a rimmed baking sheet to catch any drips. Bake pie for 45 to 55 minutes, until filling puffs up above edges of pie shell. If crust begins to brown too early, cover loosely with foil. Remove from oven and let cool completely before serving.

MAKE IT A FREEZER MEAL Place unbaked pie in freezer and freeze until firm, about 2 to 3 hours. Wrap tightly with several layers of plastic wrap, pressing down gently to remove air. Cover with foil, label and freeze.

COOK FROM FROZEN Preheat oven to 350°F (180°C). Remove foil and plastic wrap from pie. Place pie dish on a rimmed baking sheet to catch any drips. Bake frozen pie for 60 to 70 minutes, until filling puffs up above edges of pie shell. If crust begins to brown too early, cover loosely with foil. Remove from oven and let cool completely before serving.

BULK BATCH GUIDE	Servings	6 to 8 (1 batch)	12 to 16 (2 batches)	18 to 24 (3 batches)	24 to 32 (4 batches)	30 to 40 (5 batches)
	butter	½ cup (125 mL)	1 cup (250 mL)	1½ cups (375 mL)	2 cups (500 mL)	2½ cups (625 mL)
	pecans	1¼ cups (310 mL)	2½ cups (625 mL)	3¾ cups (925 mL)	5 cups (1.25 L)	6¼ cups (1.56 L)
	Pie Crust	½ batch	1 batch	1½ batches	2 batches	2½ batches
	corn syrup	1 cup (250 mL)	2 cups (500 mL)	3 cups (750 mL)	4 cups (1 L)	5 cups (1.25 L)
	granulated sugar	½ cup (125 mL)	1 cup (250 mL)	1½ cups (375 mL)	2 cups (500 mL)	2½ cups (625 mL)
	brown sugar	½ cup (125 mL)	1 cup (250 mL)	1½ cups (375 mL)	2 cups (500 mL)	2½ cups (625 mL)
	eggs	4	8	12	16	20
	vanilla	1 tsp (5 mL)	2 tsp (10 mL)	1 tbsp (15 mL)	4 tsp (20 mL)	5 tsp (25 mL)
	9-inch pie plates	1	2	3	4	5

Mascarpone Key Lime Mini Pies

These mini pies are truly my biggest addiction. The refreshing light, sweet flavor of Key limes and the creamy, airy mascarpone are the obvious stars, but the real surprise lies in the unique taste of cardamom in the graham cracker crust. It's a magical combination! Makes about 12 mini pies.

Filling

8 oz (250 g) mascarpone cheese, softened

1 can (14 oz or 300 mL) sweetened condensed milk

¾ cup (175 mL) freshly squeezed or bottled Key lime juice

2 cups (500 mL) frozen whipped topping (Cool Whip), about 6 oz/175 g

Crust

1¼ cups (310 mL) graham cracker crumbs (about 4½ oz/130 g)

¼ cup (60 mL) butter, melted

½ tsp (2 mL) ground cardamom or ground cinnamon

Garnishes

Additional frozen whipped topping (Cool Whip), optional

Sliced Key limes (optional)

1. *Filling:* In the bowl of a stand mixer (or in a medium bowl, using an electric hand mixer), beat mascarpone cheese on High for about 1 minute, until creamy. Add condensed milk and lime juice; beat on Medium for about 1 minute, until smooth. Gently fold in whipped topping, until blended.

2. Place 12 silicone muffin liners in a 12-cup muffin tin. Scoop mixture into cups until three-quarters full.

3. *Crust:* In a medium bowl, combine graham cracker crumbs, melted butter and cardamom, stirring well.

4. Sprinkle crust mixture evenly over each mini pie. Press gently with the back of a spoon to flatten. Freeze for about 2 hours, until firm.

MAKE IT NOW Remove from freezer. Gently remove silicone liners and invert mini pies onto a serving plate, crust side down. Top with additional whipped topping and a slice of Key lime, if using. Serve frozen.

MAKE IT A FREEZER MEAL Remove from freezer. Transfer mini pies, in their silicone liners, to 2 labeled gallon-size (4 L) freezer bags. Seal, removing as much air as possible, and freeze.

SERVE Remove from freezer. Gently remove silicone liners and invert mini pies onto a serving plate, crust side down. Top with additional whipped topping and a slice of Key lime, if using. Serve frozen.

BULK BATCH GUIDE	Mini pies	12 (1 batch)	24 (2 batches)	36 (3 batches)	48 (4 batches)	60 (5 batches)
	mascarpone cheese	8 oz (250 g)	1 lb (500 g)	1½ lbs (750 g)	2 lbs (1 kg)	2½ lbs (1.25 kg)
	sweetened condensed milk	14 oz (300 mL)	28 oz (600 mL)	42 oz (900 mL)	56 oz (1.2 L)	70 oz (1.5 L)
	Key lime juice	¾ cup (175 mL)	1½ cups (375 mL)	2¼ cups (560 mL)	3 cups (750 mL)	3¾ cups (925 mL)
	frozen whipped topping	2 cups (500 mL)	4 cups (1 L)	6 cups (1.5 L)	8 cups (2 L)	10 cups (2.5 L)
	graham cracker crumbs	1¼ cups (310 mL)	2½ cups (625 mL)	3¾ cups (925 mL)	5 cups (1.25 L)	6¼ cups (1.56 L)
	butter	¼ cup (60 mL)	½ cup (125 mL)	¾ cup (175 mL)	1 cup (250 mL)	1¼ cups (310 mL)
	cardamom	½ tsp (2 mL)	1 tsp (5 mL)	1½ tsp (7 mL)	2 tsp (10 mL)	2½ tsp (12 mL)
	gallon bags	2	4	6	8	10

Island Coconut Angel Cake

No, you're not dreaming . . . you're just lost in a sweet tropical trance as you eat this coconut angel cake. This dessert is super easy to make and looks beautiful at any luau party or barbecue.

Makes 8 servings.

1 large (about 10 oz/300 g or 9-inch/23 cm diameter) baked angel food cake

4 cups (1 L) frozen pineapple chunks (about 20 oz/560 g)

2 tsp (10 mL) pure maple syrup

16 oz (500 g) frozen whipped topping (Cool Whip)

2 cups (500 mL) sweetened shredded coconut

1. Place three 20-inch (50 cm) pieces of plastic wrap on your counter, overlapping slightly. Using a serrated knife, slice angel food cake in half horizontally, like a big bagel. Place bottom half in center of plastic wrap, cut side up.

2. In a high-powered blender or food processor, combine frozen pineapple and maple syrup; blend on High until smooth. Spread pineapple mixture over bottom half of cake. Place other half of cake on top of filling, cut side down.

3. Using a spatula, spread whipped topping over outside of whole cake and a thin layer inside the hole. Sprinkle coconut all over top and sides of cake; press to adhere.

4. Lift up edges of plastic wrap to cover cake; wrap tightly with additional plastic wrap if necessary. Then wrap in foil. Place cake in freezer for at least 4 hours.

MAKE IT NOW Remove cake from freezer and gently remove foil and plastic wrap. Place on a serving platter or cutting board. Let thaw at room temperature for 20 to 30 minutes. Serve.

MAKE IT A FREEZER MEAL Keep in the freezer for up to 4 months.

THAW AND SERVE Remove from freezer and gently remove foil and plastic wrap. Place on a serving platter or cutting board. Let thaw at room temperature for 20 to 30 minutes. Serve.

BULK BATCH	Servings	8 (1 batch)	16 (2 batches)	24 (3 batches)	32 (4 batches)	40 (5 batches)
	angel food cakes	1	2	3	4	5
	frozen pineapple	4 cups (1 L)	8 cups (2 L)	12 cups (3 L)	16 cups (4 L)	20 cups (5 L)
	maple syrup	2 tsp (10 mL)	4 tsp (20 mL)	2 tbsp (30 mL)	8 tsp (40 mL)	10 tsp (50 mL)
	frozen whipped topping	16 oz (500 g)	32 oz (1 kg)	48 oz (1.5 kg)	64 oz (2 kg)	80 oz (2.5 kg)
	shredded coconut	2 cups (500 mL)	4 cups (1 L)	6 cups (1.5 L)	8 cups (2 L)	10 cups (2.5 L)

Salted Caramel Pumpkin Cheesecake

Confession time here: I have eaten an entire cheesecake by myself on more than one occasion. Oh, the humanity — but totally worth it! This cheesecake has just a hint of pumpkin and perfectly blended spices to give it that special fall flavor. Add the oozy, gooey salted caramel on top and you've reached heaven, for reals. Makes 12 servings.

Crust

1¼ cups (310 mL) graham cracker crumbs (about 4½ oz/130 g)

¼ cup (60 mL) unsalted butter, melted

½ tsp (2 mL) ground cardamom

¼ tsp (1 mL) ground ginger

Filling

1 lb (500 g) cream cheese

1 cup (250 mL) granulated sugar

¾ cup (175 mL) unsweetened pumpkin purée (not pie filling)

1½ tsp (7 mL) ground cinnamon

½ tsp (2 mL) ground nutmeg

¼ tsp (1 mL) ground cloves

1 lb (500 g) frozen whipped topping (Cool Whip)

Caramel Topping

1 cup (250 mL) granulated sugar

1 tbsp (15 mL) water

6 tbsp (90 mL) unsalted butter, cubed and softened

¾ cup (175 mL) heavy or whipping (35%) cream, at room temperature

½ tsp (2 mL) salt

1. *Crust:* In a medium bowl, combine graham cracker crumbs, melted butter, cardamom and ginger; stir to combine. Press mixture into bottom of a 10-inch (25 cm) springform pan. Place in freezer until you've finished preparing the filling.

2. *Filling:* In a large bowl, using an electric hand mixer or stand mixer, beat cream cheese and sugar on High for 1 minute, until creamy. Add pumpkin, cinnamon, nutmeg and cloves; beat for 30 seconds or until evenly blended and smooth. Gently fold in whipped topping until well combined.

3. Pour filling over crust and, using the back of a spoon, smooth out evenly. Place in refrigerator for 2 to 3 hours, until set and firm.

4. *Caramel Topping:* In a medium saucepan over medium heat, heat sugar and water, stirring constantly, until sugar is dissolved. Boil without stirring, but gently swirling the pot occasionally, until sugar turns amber, being careful not to burn. Immediately add butter and whisk like crazy until melted (it will bubble up on you, which is normal). Remove from heat. Slowly, whisking vigorously, add cream (sauce will bubble up again). Add salt and whisk to combine. Set aside for 35 to 45 minutes to cool.

MAKE IT NOW Serve cheesecake immediately with caramel topping spread overtop. You can also transfer the topping to an airtight container and cover the cheesecake, then store in the refrigerator for up to 3 days. Slice and serve.

MAKE IT A FREEZER MEAL Transfer cheesecake from fridge to freezer and freeze for 2 to 3 hours, until firm. Pour cooled caramel sauce into a quart-size (1 L) freezer bag. Seal, removing as much air as possible, and freeze. Once cheesecake is firm, remove from pan and wrap in several layers of plastic wrap. Place bag of caramel sauce on top of plastic wrap and wrap foil around both. Label and freeze.

THAW AND SERVE Place cake and sauce in refrigerator for at least 12 hours or up to 24 hours to thaw. Gently remove foil, caramel bag and plastic wrap. Place cake on a serving platter. If caramel sauce is not soft enough to pour, transfer to a small, microwave-safe bowl and microwave on High for 20 seconds, until warm. Let cool slightly, then spread evenly over top of cheesecake. Slice and serve.

(continued on page 314)

Servings	12 (1 batch)	24 (2 batches)	36 (3 batches)	48 (4 batches)	60 (5 batches)
graham cracker crumbs	1¼ cups (310 mL)	2½ cups (625 mL)	3¾ cups (925 mL)	5 cups (1.25 L)	6¼ cups (1.56 L)
unsalted butter	¼ cup (60 mL)	½ cup (125 mL)	¾ cup (175 mL)	1 cup (250 mL)	1¼ cups (310 mL)
ground cardamom	½ tsp (2 mL)	1 tsp (5 mL)	1½ tsp (7 mL)	2 tsp (10 mL)	2½ tsp (12 mL)
ground ginger	¼ tsp (1 mL)	½ tsp (2 mL)	¾ tsp (3 mL)	1 tsp (5 mL)	1¼ tsp (6 mL)
cream cheese	1 lb (500 g)	2 lbs (1 kg)	3 lbs (1.5 kg)	4 lbs (2 kg)	5 lbs (2.5 kg)
sugar for filling	1 cup (250 mL)	2 cups (500 mL)	3 cups (750 mL)	4 cups (1 L)	5 cups (1.25 L)
pumpkin purée	¾ cup (175 mL)	1½ cups (375 mL)	2¼ cups (560 mL)	3 cups (750 mL)	3¾ cups (925 mL)
cinnamon	1½ tsp (7 mL)	1 tbsp (15 mL)	1½ tbsp (22 mL)	2 tbsp (30 mL)	2½ tbsp (37 mL)
nutmeg	½ tsp (2 mL)	1 tsp (5 mL)	1½ tsp (7 mL)	2 tsp (10 mL)	2½ tsp (12 mL)
cloves	¼ tsp (1 mL)	½ tsp (2 mL)	¾ tsp (3 mL)	1 tsp (5 mL)	1¼ tsp (6 mL)
frozen whipped topping	1 lb (500 g)	2 lbs (1 kg)	3 lbs (1.5 kg)	4 lbs (2 kg)	5 lbs (2.5 kg)
sugar for topping	1 cup (250 mL)	2 cups (500 mL)	3 cups (750 mL)	4 cups (1 L)	5 cups (1.25 L)
water	1 tbsp (15 mL)	2 tbsp (30 mL)	3 tbsp (45 mL)	¼ cup (60 mL)	⅓ cup (75 mL)
unsalted butter for topping	6 tbsp (90 mL)	¾ cup (175 mL)	1 cup + 2 tbsp (280 mL)	1½ cups (375 mL)	1¾ cups + 2 tbsp (455 mL)
cream	¾ cup (175 mL)	1½ cups (375 mL)	2¼ cups (560 mL)	3 cups (750 mL)	3¾ cups (925 mL)
salt	½ tsp (2 mL)	1 tsp (5 mL)	1½ tsp (7 mL)	2 tsp (10 mL)	2½ tsp (12 mL)
quart bags	1	2	3	4	5

This cheesecake has
just a hint of pumpkin
and perfectly blended spices
to give it
that special fall flavor.

Molten Hot Fudge Lava Cakes

I'm ashamed to say this, but these gooey, decadent molten hot fudge cakes are usually hoarded by me. I love to keep a couple stashed in the very back of the freezer, deceptively hidden from my family behind a bag of frozen vegetables, for when those chocolate cravings kick in — which may or may not be frequently. Makes 6 individual cakes.

Cakes

½ cup (125 mL) water

¼ cup (60 mL) butter

1 cup (250 mL) all-purpose flour

1 cup (250 mL) granulated sugar

¼ cup (60 mL) unsweetened cocoa powder

¾ tsp (3 mL) baking powder

¾ tsp (3 mL) baking soda

½ tsp (2 mL) salt

1 large egg, beaten

½ cup (125 mL) milk

1½ tsp (7 mL) vanilla extract

Additional unsweetened cocoa powder for dusting

Ganache Filling

¼ cup (60 mL) heavy or whipping (35%) cream

½ cup (125 mL) milk chocolate chips

½ cup (125 mL) bittersweet (dark) chocolate chips

1. *Cakes:* Preheat oven to 350°F (180°C).

2. In a small saucepan over high heat, bring water to a boil. Remove from heat. Add butter and stir until melted. Set aside to cool slightly.

3. In bowl of a stand mixer fitted with the wire whisk attachment (or in a large bowl, using an electric hand mixer), combine flour, sugar, cocoa powder, baking powder, baking soda and salt; beat together on Low for about 30 seconds, just until combined. With the motor running, add eggs, milk and vanilla, then slowly add butter mixture. Increase speed to Medium and beat for about 1 minute, until combined (batter will be thin).

4. Grease 6 cavities of 2 silicone 4-cavity fluted mini cake pans (1 cup/250 mL capacity per cavity) and lightly dust with cocoa powder. Place prepared pans on a baking sheet. Pour batter into prepared cavities until half full (leave the other two empty).

5. Bake in preheated oven for 22 to 30 minutes, or until a tester inserted in the center comes out clean. Let cool in pan for 10 minutes, then transfer cakes to a wire rack to cool.

6. *Ganache Filling:* In a small saucepan over medium heat, bring cream almost to a boil. Remove from heat. Add milk chocolate chips and bittersweet chocolate chips; stir until melted. Let cool for 5 minutes.

7. Using a spoon, drizzle half the chocolate mixture over cakes. Set aside remaining mixture to cool until thick and smooth, about 30 minutes.

8. Using a piping bag, pipe chocolate mixture into insides of cakes, leaving a dollop of chocolate on top. (You can also do this with a spoon.)

MAKE IT NOW Place each cake on a microwave-safe plate. Microwave, one at a time, on High for 20 to 30 seconds, until chocolate is bubbling out the top. Serve hot.

MAKE IT A FREEZER MEAL Place filled cakes on a baking sheet lined with parchment paper and freeze for 1 to 2 hours, until solid. Remove from freezer. Wrap each cake in plastic wrap, then place cakes in 2 labeled gallon-size (4 L) freezer bags. Seal, removing as much air as possible, and freeze.

REHEAT Remove cakes from freezer and remove plastic wrap. Place each cake on a microwave-safe plate and, one at a time, microwave on High for 45 seconds, until chocolate is bubbling out the top. Serve hot.

(continued on page 317)

Cakes	6 (1 batch)	12 (2 batches)	18 (3 batches)	24 (4 batches)	30 (5 batches)
water	½ cup (125 mL)	1 cup (250 mL)	1½ cups (375 mL)	2 cups (500 mL)	2½ cups (625 mL)
butter	¼ cup (60 mL)	½ cup (125 mL)	¾ cup (175 mL)	1 cup (250 mL)	1¼ cups (310 mL)
all-purpose flour	1 cup (250 mL)	2 cups (500 mL)	3 cups (750 mL)	4 cups (1 L)	5 cups (1.25 L)
sugar	1 cup (250 mL)	2 cups (500 mL)	3 cups (750 mL)	4 cups (1 L)	5 cups (1.25 L)
cocoa powder	¼ cup (60 mL)	½ cup (125 mL)	¾ cup (175 mL)	1 cup (250 mL)	1¼ cups (310 mL)
baking powder	¾ tsp (3 mL)	1½ tsp (7 mL)	2¼ tsp (11 mL)	1 tbsp (15 mL)	4 tsp (20 mL)
baking soda	¾ tsp (3 mL)	1½ tsp (7 mL)	2¼ tsp (11 mL)	1 tbsp (15 mL)	4 tsp (20 mL)
salt	½ tsp (2 mL)	1 tsp (5 mL)	1½ tsp (7 mL)	2 tsp (10 mL)	2½ tsp (12 mL)
eggs	1	2	3	4	5
milk	½ cup (125 mL)	1 cup (250 mL)	1½ cups (375 mL)	2 cups (500 mL)	2½ cups (625 mL)
vanilla	1½ tsp (7 mL)	1 tbsp (15 mL)	1½ tbsp (22 mL)	2 tbsp (30 mL)	2½ tbsp (37 mL)
cream	¼ cup (60 mL)	½ cup (125 mL)	¾ cup (175 mL)	1 cup (250 mL)	1¼ cups (310 mL)
milk chocolate chips	½ cup (125 mL)	1 cup (250 mL)	1½ cups (375 mL)	2 cups (500 mL)	2½ cups (625 mL)
bittersweet chocolate chips	½ cup (125 mL)	1 cup (250 mL)	1½ cups (375 mL)	2 cups (500 mL)	2½ cups (625 mL)
gallon bags	2	4	6	8	10

I'm ashamed to say this, but these gooey, decadent molten hot fudge cakes are usually hoarded by me.

Layered Chocolate Mousse Cake

I would walk through fire, or at least an un-air-conditioned room in the middle of summer, to have a slice of this gorgeous frozen dessert. Made in a loaf pan and frozen till firm, then sliced to show off the beautiful chocolate and fudge layers, it's perfect for a hot summer's day. Makes 12 servings.

1½ cups (375 mL) chocolate wafer crumbs

¼ cup (60 mL) unsalted butter, melted

1 cup (250 mL) hot fudge sauce

8 oz (250 g) mascarpone cheese, softened

1 can (14 oz or 300 mL) sweetened condensed milk

1 tsp (5 mL) vanilla extract

2 cups (500 mL) frozen whipped topping (Cool Whip), about 6 oz/175 g

Chocolate curls (optional)

Tip

To make chocolate curls: Place a 3- to 4-inch (7.5 to 10 cm) chunk of milk chocolate in a small, microwave-safe bowl. Heat in the microwave on Medium for 30 to 40 seconds, until slightly softened (do not let it melt). Using a vegetable peeler, scrape along top of chocolate to make curls. Keep curls refrigerated until ready to use.

1. Line a 9- by 5-inch (23 by 12.5 cm) loaf pan with a large piece of foil, making sure it's smooth and flat against the sides, leaving a 3-inch (7.5 cm) overhang outside the pan.

2. In a medium bowl, combine wafer crumbs and butter, stirring well. Pour into prepared loaf pan and, using the back of a spoon, press evenly into the bottom. Transfer to freezer for 5 to 10 minutes, until firm.

3. Place fudge sauce in a microwave-safe bowl and heat on High for about 20 seconds, until warm and spreadable but not boiling. Set aside 1/4 cup (60 mL) hot sauce.

4. Remove loaf pan from freezer and spread remaining ¾ cup (175 mL) hot fudge sauce evenly over crumb layer. Place back in freezer until you finish preparing the filling.

5. In a medium bowl, using an electric hand mixer, beat mascarpone cheese for about 1 minute, until creamy. Add condensed milk and vanilla; beat for 30 seconds, until smooth. Gently fold in whipped topping until smooth and blended. Transfer half of the mixture to another medium bowl; add reserved hot fudge sauce. Stir gently to combine until it's a nice, even brown color.

6. Spread half the white mascarpone mixture evenly over hot fudge layer in prepared pan. Then spread half the chocolate mascarpone mixture overtop. Repeat with remaining white mascarpone and then chocolate mascarpone mixtures.

7. Using a butter knife, swirl gently 5 or 6 times through all the mascarpone layers. Sprinkle with chocolate curls, if using. Place in the freezer for about 3 to 4 hours, until firm.

MAKE IT NOW Remove loaf pan from freezer. Holding on to foil, gently remove cake from pan. Peel foil from underneath cake as you place it on a serving platter or cutting board; discard foil. Cut cake crosswise into 1-inch (2.5 cm) slices; serve frozen.

MAKE IT A FREEZER MEAL Remove loaf pan from freezer. Holding on to foil, gently remove cake from pan. Cover completely with foil, adding more if necessary, then place in a labeled gallon-size (4 L) freezer bag. Seal, removing as much air as possible, and freeze. (If you added the chocolate curls, make sure not to place anything on top of cake in the freezer, to keep them from being crushed.)

SERVE Remove cake from freezer. Gently remove foil. Place on a serving platter or cutting board. Cut crosswise into 1-inch (2.5 cm) slices; serve frozen.

(continued on page 320)

Servings	12 (1 batch)	24 (2 batches)	36 (3 batches)	48 (4 batches)	60 (5 batches)
chocolate wafer crumbs	1½ cups (375 mL)	3 cups (750 mL)	4½ cups (1.125 L)	6 cups (1.5 L)	7½ cups (1.875 L)
unsalted butter	¼ cup (60 mL)	½ cup (125 mL)	¾ cup (175 mL)	1 cup (250 mL)	1¼ cups (310 mL)
hot fudge sauce	1 cup (250 mL)	2 cups (500 mL)	3 cups (750 mL)	4 cups (1 L)	5 cups (1.25 L)
mascarpone cheese	8 oz (250 g)	1 lb (500 g)	1½ lbs (750 g)	2 lbs (1 kg)	2½ lbs (1.25 kg)
sweetened condensed milk	14 oz (300 mL)	28 oz (600 mL)	42 oz (900 mL)	56 oz (1.2 L)	70 oz (1.5 L)
vanilla	1 tsp (5 mL)	2 tsp (10 mL)	1 tbsp (15 mL)	4 tsp (20 mL)	5 tsp (25 mL)
frozen whipped topping	2 cups (500 mL)	4 cups (1 L)	6 cups (1.5 L)	8 cups (2 L)	10 cups (2.5 L)
gallon bags	1	2	3	4	5
9x5 loaf pans	1	2	3	4	5

I would walk through fire,
or at least an
un-air-conditioned room
in the middle of summer,
to have a slice of
this gorgeous frozen dessert.

Chocolate Chip Cookies

This is the last chocolate chip cookie recipe you'll ever need. It has just the right amount of crispiness on the outside and a super-soft, chewy inside. With good reason it's one of the most popular and well-loved recipes on my blog! The best part is that you can freeze the dough in balls to enjoy a single freshly baked cookie or a small batch anytime. Makes 24 large cookies.

3½ cups (875 mL) all-purpose flour

1¼ tsp (6 mL) baking soda

1½ tsp (7 mL) baking powder

¾ tsp (3 mL) salt

1¼ cups (310 mL) unsalted butter, softened

1¼ cups (310 mL) packed dark brown sugar

1 cup + 2 tbsp (280 mL) granulated sugar

2 large eggs

2 tsp (10 mL) vanilla extract

2 cups (500 mL) good-quality milk chocolate chips (about 12 oz/375 g)

1. In a medium bowl, whisk together flour, baking soda, baking powder and salt. Set aside.

2. In bowl of a stand mixer fitted with the paddle attachment (or in a large bowl, using an electric hand mixer), cream butter, brown sugar and granulated sugar on Medium for about 15 seconds, just until blended.

3. Add eggs, one at a time, mixing well after each addition. Add vanilla and beat until well incorporated.

4. Turn off the mixer, add flour mixture, then turn mixer to Low and mix for about 30 seconds, just until combined (do not overmix). Remove bowl from mixer stand, if necessary. Add chocolate chips and, using a large spoon, stir gently until evenly distributed.

MAKE IT NOW Preheat oven to 350°F (180°C). Using a ¼-cup (60 mL) cookie scoop or measuring cup, drop batter onto a baking sheet lined with parchment paper, spacing 2 to 3 inches (5 to 7.5 cm) apart. Bake, one sheet at a time, in preheated oven for 15 to 17 minutes, until edges of cookies are just starting to turn golden brown. Remove from oven and let cool on baking sheet for 2 minutes, then transfer to a wire rack for at least 5 minutes. Repeat with additional batches. Serve.

MAKE IT A FREEZER MEAL Line a baking sheet with parchment paper. Using a ¼-cup (60 mL) cookie scoop or measuring cup, drop batter onto baking sheet, next to each other but not touching. Freeze for about 45 minutes, until cookie dough is solid. Remove baking sheet from freezer and place frozen dough balls in 2 labeled gallon-size (4 L) freezer bags. Seal, removing as much air as possible, and freeze.

COOK FROM FROZEN Place frozen cookie dough balls on a baking sheet lined with parchment paper, spacing 2 to 3 inches (5 to 7.5 cm) apart. Let thaw for about 5 minutes while oven heats. Preheat oven to 350°F (180°C). Bake in preheated oven, one sheet at a time, for 15 to 17 minutes, until edges of cookies are just starting to turn golden brown (add a few extra minutes of baking time if needed). Remove from oven and let cool on baking sheet for 2 minutes, then transfer to a wire rack for 5 minutes. Repeat with additional batches.

(continued on page 323)

Cookies	24 (1 batch)	48 (2 batches)	72 (3 batches)	96 (4 batches)	120 (5 batches)
all-purpose flour	3½ cups (875 mL)	7 cups (1.75 L)	10½ cups (2.625 L)	14 cups (3.5 L)	17½ cups (4.375 L)
baking soda	1¼ tsp (6 mL)	2½ tsp (12 mL)	3¾ tsp (18 mL)	5 tsp (25 mL)	6¼ tsp (31 mL)
baking powder	1½ tsp (7 mL)	1 tbsp (15 mL)	1½ tbsp (22 mL)	2 tbsp (30 mL)	2½ tbsp (37 mL)
salt	¾ tsp (3 mL)	1½ tsp (7 mL)	2¼ tsp (11 mL)	1 tbsp (15 mL)	3¾ tsp (18 mL)
unsalted butter	1¼ cups (310 mL)	2½ cups (625 mL)	3¾ cups (925 mL)	5 cups (1.25 L)	6¼ cups (1.56 L)
dark brown sugar	1¼ cups (310 mL)	2½ cups (625 mL)	3¾ cups (925 mL)	5 cups (1.25 L)	6¼ cups (1.56 L)
sugar	1 cup + 2 tbsp (280 mL)	2¼ cups (560 mL)	3 cups + 6 tbsp (840 mL)	4½ cups (1.125 L)	5¾ cups (1.4 L)
eggs	2	4	6	8	10
vanilla	2 tsp (10 mL)	4 tsp (20 mL)	2 tbsp (30 mL)	8 tsp (40 mL)	10 tsp (50 mL)
chocolate chips	2 cups (500 mL)	4 cups (1 L)	6 cups (1.5 L)	8 cups (2 L)	10 cups (2.5 L)
gallon bags	2	4	6	8	10

This is the last
chocolate chip
cookie recipe
you'll ever need.

Churros

My kids may not work for food but they will work for desserts. I've been able to get a lot of chores done around the house by baking up a batch of these sweet cinnamon-coated churros. Makes 12 churros.

1 cup (250 mL) water

½ cup (125 mL) butter

1 cup (250 mL) all-purpose flour

3 large eggs, beaten

2 cups (500 mL) vegetable oil (approx.)

To Serve

½ cup (125 mL) granulated sugar

2 tsp (10 mL) ground cinnamon

1. In a medium saucepan over high heat, bring water and butter to a boil. Once butter has completely melted, add flour; cook, stirring constantly with a wooden spoon, for about 10 seconds, until smooth. Reduce heat to low and cook, stirring vigorously, for about 1 minute, until a ball forms. Remove from heat.

2. Add beaten eggs one at a time, mixing until each addition is fully incorporated and dough is smooth.

3. Transfer dough to an 18-inch (45 cm) piping bag fitted with a #8B (1 inch/2.5 cm) open star tip.

4. Line a large baking sheet with parchment paper. Pipe churros onto parchment paper, working horizontally from left to right. Make them 3½ to 5 inches (7.5 to 12.5 cm) long, no longer than the width of the saucepan or fryer you will be frying them in, spacing apart. Cover loosely with plastic wrap and freeze for at least 1 hour, until solid.

5. In a medium, heavy-bottomed saucepan, heat at least 2 inches (5 cm) vegetable oil until a candy/deep-fry thermometer registers 360°F (182°C). (If you are using an electric deep-fryer, use according to the manufacturer's directions.)

6. Fry one churro at a time for 2 minutes on each side, keeping remaining churros frozen until they go into the oil. Remove from heat and place on a plate lined with paper towels to drain. Let oil return to 360°F (182°C) between churros.

MAKE IT NOW Combine sugar and cinnamon on a plate. Immediately roll hot churros in mixture until coated on all sides. Serve warm.

MAKE IT A FREEZER MEAL Let fried churros cool completely. Place in a labeled gallon-size (4 L) freezer bag. Seal, removing as much air as possible, and freeze.

REHEAT Preheat oven to 425°F (220°C). Place frozen fried churros on a baking sheet lined with parchment paper. Bake in preheated oven for 3 to 5 minutes, until crispy and heated through. Combine sugar and cinnamon on a plate. Immediately roll hot churros in mixture until coated on all sides. Serve warm.

BULK BATCH	Churros	12 (1 batch)	24 (2 batches)	36 (3 batches)	48 (4 batches)	60 (5 batches)
	water	1 cup (250 mL)	2 cups (500 mL)	3 cups (750 mL)	4 cups (1 L)	5 cups (1.25 L)
	butter	½ cup (125 mL)	1 cup (250 mL)	1½ cups (375 mL)	2 cups (500 mL)	2½ cups (625 mL)
	all-purpose flour	1 cup (250 mL)	2 cups (500 mL)	3 cups (750 mL)	4 cups (1 L)	5 cups (1.25 L)
	eggs	3	6	9	12	15
	vegetable oil	2 cup (500 mL)	2 cup (500 mL)	2 cup (500 mL)	2 cup (500 mL)	2 cup (500 mL)
	gallon bags	1	2	3	4	5

Minty Melts

Whip up a batch of these delightfully easy-to-make treats in less than 5 minutes and keep them in a safe hiding place in your freezer. When you get a little craving for something sweet, just take out one or two frozen bites at a time, pop 'em in your mouth and enjoy the cool, creamy, minty chocolate taste. Makes about 30 mini melts.

1 cup (250 mL) unsalted butter, softened

3 tbsp (45 mL) unsweetened cocoa powder

½ cup + 1 tbsp (140 mL) honey

1 tsp (5 mL) peppermint extract

⅛ tsp (0.5 mL) salt

1. In a medium bowl, whisk together butter, cocoa powder, honey, peppermint and salt, until smooth.

2. Scoop mixture into an 18-inch (45 cm) piping bag with a #8B (1 inch/2.5 cm) open star tip (or you can use a resealable plastic bag with the corner cut off to make smooth melts).

3. Squeeze bite-sized stars or mounds onto a baking sheet lined with parchment paper, spacing them apart. Place in freezer for about 20 to 30 minutes, until firm.

MAKE IT NOW Remove individual mini melts from freezer and eat while frozen (do not thaw).

MAKE IT FREEZER MEAL Transfer frozen melts to a labeled gallon-sized (4 L) freezer bag. Seal, removing as much air as possible, and freeze.

SERVE Remove individual mini melts from freezer and eat immediately (do not thaw).

BULK BATCH GUIDE Mini melts	30 (1 batch)	60 (2 batches)	90 (3 batches)	120 (4 batches)	150 (5 batches)
unsalted butter	1 cup (250 mL)	2 cups (500 mL)	3 cups (750 mL)	4 cups (1 L)	5 cups (1.25 L)
cocoa powder	3 tbsp (45 mL)	6 tbsp (90 mL)	9 tbsp (135 mL)	¾ cup (175 mL)	¾ cup + 3 tbsp (220 mL)
honey	½ cup + 1 tbsp (140 mL)	1 cup + 2 tbsp (280 mL)	1⅔ cups + 4 tsp (420 mL)	2¼ cups (560 mL)	2¾ cups + 1 tbsp (690 mL)
peppermint extract	1 tsp (5 mL)	2 tsp (10 mL)	1 tbsp (15 mL)	4 tsp (20 mL)	5 tsp (25 mL)
salt	⅛ tsp (0.5 mL)	¼ tsp (1 mL)	⅓ tsp (1.5 mL)	½ tsp (2 mL)	¾ tsp (3 mL)
gallon bags	1	2	3	4	5

BASES & SAUCES

Gnocchi 330

Pie Crust 331

Pizza Dough 332

Alfredo Sauce 333

Red Sauce 334

Vegetarian Red Sauce 335

White Sauce 336

Vegetarian White Sauce 337

Marinara Sauce 338

Easy Pesto 339

Thirty-Minute Pizza Sauce 340

Smoky BBQ Sauce 341

Basic Grilled Chicken Marinade 342

Basic Grilled Steak Marinade 343

Lip-Smackin' Chutney 344

Peanut Sauce 345

Enchilada Sauce 346

Totally Tasty Salsa 347

Avocado Crema 348

Homemade Chicken Stock 349

Homemade Beef Stock 350

Homemade Vegetable Stock 351

Blistered Roasted Peppers 353

Slow Cooker Caramelized Onions 354

Time-Saving Roasted Garlic and Onion Purée 355

Gnocchi

I can't say enough about gnocchi! These adorably cute little potato-based pasta balls are so tender and fluffy, even when you them make ahead and freeze 'em. They are delectable in my creamy Alfredo Sauce (page 333), in soups such as my Sausage and Gnocchi Soup (page 112), in Marinara Sauce (page 338), rolled in crumbs and fried, or even just tossed with some butter and garlic. You honestly can't go wrong! *Makes 3 servings, or about 12 oz (375 g) gnocchi.*

2 medium russet potatoes (about 8 oz/250 g), peeled and quartered

1 large egg, beaten

1 cup (250 mL) all-purpose flour (approx.)

1. Place potatoes in a large stockpot and add enough cold water to cover, plus 2 to 3 inches (5 to 7.5 cm). Bring to a boil over high heat. Reduce heat to medium-high and boil gently for 10 to 15 minutes, until potatoes are tender.

2. Drain potatoes and return to pot. Using a hand masher, thoroughly mash potatoes (you do want any lumps!). Let cool completely.

3. In a medium bowl, thoroughly combine 1 cup (250 mL) mashed potatoes and the egg (reserve extra potatoes for another use).

4. Begin adding flour, ½ cup (125 mL) at a time, gently mixing with your hands, just until dough is a little sticky but also very light, adding additional flour as needed.

5. Turn out dough onto a floured cutting board and knead 5 times.

6. Pat out dough into a 4-inch (25 cm) square that is about 2 inches (5 cm) thick. Cut into 8 even strips, each about ½ inch (1 cm) wide. Roll each strip into a "snake" and cut crosswise into 1-inch (2.5 cm) pieces. Roll each piece under the tines of a fork, pressing against the cutting board, to create ridges in the gnocchi.

MAKE IT NOW Fill a large stockpot with water and bring to a boil over high heat. Add gnocchi and cook, stirring gently, for 2 to 3 minutes, or until they start to float to the top. Drain and serve.

FREEZE IT Place uncooked gnocchi on a baking sheet lined with parchment paper, spacing them apart. Freeze until solid. Transfer to a labeled gallon-size (4 L) freezer bag. Seal, removing as much air as possible, and freeze.

COOK FROM FROZEN Fill a large stockpot with water and bring to a boil over high heat. Add frozen gnocchi and cook, stirring gently, for 3 to 4 minutes, or until they start to float to the top. Drain and serve.

BULK BATCH	Servings	3 (1 batch)	6 (2 batches)	9 (3 batches)	12 (4 batches)	15 (5 batches)
	russet potatoes	2	4	6	8	10
	eggs	1	2	3	4	5
	all-purpose flour	1 cup (250 mL)	2 cups (500 mL)	3 cups (750 mL)	4 cups (1 L)	5 cups (1.25 mL)
	gallon bags	1	2	3	4	5

Pie Crust

Flaky, buttery and ready for you any time, this make-ahead-and-freeze pie crust recipe will not disappoint. I usually make a massive batch all at once, so I only have one big mess to clean up.

Makes two 9-inch (23 cm) pie crusts.

2½ cups (625 mL) all-purpose flour

1 tsp (5 mL) salt

¼ cup (60 mL) shortening

½ cup (125 mL) cold butter, cubed

¼ cup (60 mL) ice water (approx.)

1. In a medium bowl, whisk together flour and salt. Add shortening. Using a pastry blender or two knives, cut shortening into flour until pea-size pieces form.

2. Add butter and cut in until pea-size pieces form.

3. Add ¼ cup (60 mL) ice water and, using a wooden spoon, combine gently, just until dough holds together. Add more water, a little at a time, if necessary. Using your hands, form dough into a ball.

4. Divide dough in half and shape each half into a disk. Wrap each disk in plastic wrap and place in the refrigerator for at least 30 minutes or up to 12 hours.

MAKE IT NOW Preheat oven to 425°F (220°C). Unwrap one disk of dough and place on a floured surface. Sprinkle a little flour on dough and rolling pin. Pressing down gently with rolling pin, roll out dough until it forms a 12-inch (30 cm) circle about ¼ inch (0.5 cm) thick, flouring underneath and on top of the dough as necessary to prevent sticking. Transfer to a 9-inch (23 cm) metal or foil pie plate and trim overhang to ¾ inch (2 cm). Fold dough edge under itself and crimp decoratively. Prick with a fork all over crust.

To prebake pie crust: Chill pastry until ready to bake. Bake in preheated oven for 15 to 17 minutes, until slightly golden. Let cool completely before filling.

For unbaked pie crusts: Follow instructions in individual recipes.

FREEZE IT Wrap each plastic-wrapped disk completely with foil. Place both disks in a labeled gallon-size (4 L) freezer bag. Seal, removing as much air as possible, and freeze.

THAW AND COOK Place dough in refrigerator for 8 to 12 hours or until thawed. Follow baking instructions in Make It Now.

BULK BATCH	Pie crusts	2 (1 batch)	4 (2 batches)	6 (3 batches)	8 (4 batches)	10 (5 batches)
	all-purpose flour	2½ cups (625 mL)	5 cups (1.25 L)	7½ cups (1.875 L)	10 cups (2.5 L)	12½ cups (3.125 L)
	salt	1 tsp (5 mL)	2 tsp (10 mL)	1 tbsp (15 mL)	4 tsp (20 mL)	5 tsp (25 mL)
	shortening	¼ cup (60 mL)	½ cup (125 mL)	¾ cup (175 mL)	1 cup (250 mL)	1¼ cups (310 mL)
	butter	½ cup (125 mL)	1 cup (250 mL)	1½ cups (375 mL)	2 cups (500 mL)	2½ cups (625 mL)
	ice water	¼ cup (60 mL)	½ cup (125 mL)	¾ cup (175 mL)	1 cup (250 mL)	1¼ cups (310 mL)
	gallon bags	1	2	3	4	5

Pizza Dough

Hand-kneading and rolling out pizza dough is one of my least favorite things to do. So here's an amazingly easy pizza dough recipe where all you have to do is press out the dough and voilà — thin- or thick-crust pizza — it's totally up to you! Makes enough dough for two 12-inch (30 cm) pizzas.

2 cups (500 mL) warm water

¼ cup (60 mL) honey

1 tbsp (15 mL) quick-rising (instant) yeast

5 cups (1.25 L) all-purpose flour (approx.)

1 tbsp (15 mL) salt

¼ tsp (1 mL) onion powder

¼ tsp (1 mL) garlic powder

¼ cup (60 mL) olive oil, divided

1. In bowl of a stand mixer fitted with the dough hook attachment, combine water, honey and yeast. Mix on Low for about 30 seconds, until just combined. Turn off mixer and let stand for 10 minutes; the mixture should bubble to show that the yeast is working.

2. Add flour, salt, onion powder and garlic powder to mixer bowl. Mix on Low until well combined. Increase speed to High and knead for 7 minutes. Gradually add up to ½ cup (125 mL) more flour, as needed, until dough just comes away from sides of bowl but still sticks to bottom.

MAKE IT NOW Pour 2 tbsp (30 mL) olive oil into 2 separate large bowls. Divide dough in half and place in bowls. Cover bowls with greased plastic wrap and let rise in a warm, draft-free place for about 45 minutes, until doubled in size. Preheat oven to 500°F (260°C) with a pizza stone on middle rack. Dump dough out of bowls onto 2 separate pieces of parchment paper, each about 12 inches (30 cm) square (or about the size you want for your pizza). Using your fingers, very gently spread out dough to about 12 inches (30 cm) in diameter for a thick crust or 14 to 16 inches (35 to 40 cm) for a thin crust (both thicknesses will taste great). Top with Thirty-Minute Pizza Sauce (page 340), cheese and desired toppings. Slide pizza, on parchment paper, onto preheated stone. Bake pizzas, one at a time, in preheated oven for 8 to 10 minutes, until crust starts to get golden, toppings are hot and cheese is melted. Remove from oven and let cool for 5 minutes before serving.

FREEZE IT Add 2 tbsp (30 ml) olive oil each to 2 labeled gallon-size (4 L) freezer bags and turn to coat all sides. Divide dough in half, then place each half in a bag, turning to coat all sides with oil. Seal bags, removing as much air as possible, and freeze.

THAW AND COOK Place bag on counter for 2 to 3 hours to thaw and rise until doubled in size. Follow shaping and baking directions in Make It Now.

BULK BATCH GUIDE	Pizza crusts	2 (1 batch)	4 (2 batches)	6 (3 batches)	8 (4 batches)	10 (5 batches)
	warm water	2 cups (500 mL)	4 cups (1 L)	6 cups (1.5 L)	8 cups (2 L)	10 cups (2.5 L)
	honey	¼ cup (60 mL)	½ cup (125 mL)	¾ cup (175 mL)	1 cup (250 mL)	1¼ cups (310 mL)
	yeast	1 tbsp (15 mL)	2 tbsp (30 mL)	3 tbsp (45 mL)	¼ cup (60 mL)	⅓ cup (75 mL)
	all-purpose flour	5 cups (1.25 L)	10 cups (2.5 L)	15 cups (3.75 L)	20 cups (5 L)	25 cups (6.25 L)
	salt	1 tbsp (15 mL)	2 tbsp (30 mL)	3 tbsp (45 mL)	¼ cup (60 mL)	⅓ cup (75 mL)
	onion powder	¼ tsp (1 mL)	½ tsp (2 mL)	¾ tsp (3 mL)	1 tsp (5 mL)	1¼ tsp (6 mL)
	garlic powder	¼ tsp (1 mL)	½ tsp (2 mL)	¾ tsp (3 mL)	1 tsp (5 mL)	1¼ tsp (6 mL)
	olive oil	¼ cup (60 mL)	½ cup (125 mL)	¾ cup (175 mL)	1 cup (250 mL)	1¼ cups (310 mL)
	gallon bags	2	4	6	8	10

Alfredo Sauce

Creating an Alfredo sauce that wouldn't separate much after freezing was no easy task. The first secret I discovered was to freshly grate the Parmesan cheese — don't buy the pre-grated stuff, because it often contains cellulose or other fillers. The second secret is the xanthan gum: this unflavored powder really helps keep the sauce together. Make sure to blend your sauce so it is super smooth, too! Makes about 3 cups (750 mL).

½ cup (125 mL) butter

2½ tbsp (37 mL) cornstarch

¼ tsp (1 mL) xanthan gum

2 cups (500 mL) half-and-half (10%) cream

1½ cups (375 mL) freshly grated Parmesan cheese (about 5 oz/150 g)

To Serve

Salt and freshly ground black pepper

1. In a medium saucepan, melt butter over medium heat. Sprinkle cornstarch and xanthan gum over melted butter; cook, whisking constantly, for 2 to 3 minutes, until foamy and simmering (do not let it brown).

2. Add cream; cook, whisking constantly, for about 3 to 4 minutes, until sauce thickens and starts to simmer. Remove from heat. Add Parmesan cheese, ½ cup (125 mL) at a time, whisking constantly until melted and smooth.

3. Pour sauce into a blender and blend on High until super smooth (you can also use an immersion blender in the pan). This step helps to keep the sauce from separating later.

MAKE IT NOW Season to taste with salt and pepper. Serve as desired. Store in an airtight container in the refrigerator for up to 3 to 4 days; reheat as directed below.

FREEZE IT Let sauce cool completely at room temperature, uncovered, stirring occasionally. Pour cooled sauce into a labeled quart-size (1 L) freezer bag. Seal, removing as much air as possible (this recipe stores best with the least possible amount of air — use a straw to remove all the air from the freezer bag), and seal. Freeze.

REHEAT Place bag in the refrigerator for at least 12 hours or up to 24 hours to thaw. (If you are in a hurry you can place the bag in a sink full of lukewarm water until thawed enough to pour. Do not use hot water — heating the sauce too quickly will cause it to separate. Ideally you want to thaw the sauce slowly and heat it slowly.) To reheat on the stovetop, pour sauce into a small saucepan and heat over medium-low heat, stirring often, for 4 to 5 minutes or until warmed through. To reheat using the microwave, pour sauce into a small, microwave-safe bowl, cover and microwave on Low for 5 to 6 minutes, stirring every 2 minutes. Season to taste with salt and pepper. Serve as desired.

Sauce	3 cups/750 mL (1 batch)	6 cups/1.5 L (2 batches)	9 cups/2.25 L (3 batches)	12 cups/3 L (4 batches)	15 cups/3.75 L (5 batches)
butter	½ cup (125 mL)	1 cup (250 mL)	1½ cups (375 mL)	2 cups (500 mL)	2½ cups (625 mL)
cornstarch	2½ tbsp (37 mL)	⅓ cup (75 mL)	⅓ cup + 2 tbsp (105 mL)	⅔ cup (150 mL)	¾ cup + 1½ tsp (182 mL)
xanthan gum	¼ tsp (1 mL)	½ tsp (2 mL)	¾ tsp (3 mL)	1 tsp (5 mL)	1¼ tsp (6 mL)
half-and-half	2 cups (500 mL)	4 cups (1 L)	6 cups (1.5 L)	8 cups (2 L)	10 cups (2.5 L)
Parmesan cheese	1½ cups (375 mL)	3 cups (750 mL)	4½ cups (1.125 L)	6 cups (1.5 L)	7½ cups (1.875 L)
quart bags	1	2	3	4	5

BULK BATCH GUIDE

Red Sauce

This recipe should also be known as "the best spaghetti sauce in the world." After slow cooking all day long, the notes of the tomatoes, garlic and beef meld together into something truly heavenly.
Makes about 9 cups (2.25 L).

1 lb (500 g) ground beef

2 onions, puréed or diced

2 garlic cloves, minced

3 cans (each 14 oz/398 mL) tomato sauce

1 can (6 oz/156 mL) tomato paste

2 celery stalks, chopped

2 tsp (10 mL) salt

¼ tsp (1 mL) freshly ground black pepper

2 tsp (10 mL) dried oregano

½ tsp (2 mL) dried thyme

1 bay leaf

1 cup (250 mL) water

1. In a large skillet over medium-high heat, cook ground beef and onions, stirring and breaking up beef with a spoon, for 4 to 5 minutes or until beef is no longer pink. Drain, then transfer to a large (approx. 5 quart) slow cooker. Add garlic, tomato sauce, tomato paste, celery, salt, pepper, oregano, thyme, bay leaf and water. Stir to combine. Cover and cook on Low for 10 to 12 hours or on High for 4 to 5 hours, until color deepens and flavors intensify. Remove bay leaf.

MAKE IT NOW Serve as desired or store in an airtight container in the refrigerator for up to 4 days. Reheat as directed below.

FREEZE IT Transfer to a shallow container and let cooked sauce cool completely. Place in a labeled gallon-size (4 L) freezer bag or divide among smaller containers, as desired. Seal, removing as much air as possible, and freeze.

REHEAT Place bag in the refrigerator for at least 12 hours or up to 24 hours to thaw. In a large saucepan over medium heat, heat sauce, stirring often, for about 15 minutes, until hot and bubbly. Serve as desired.

Sauce	9 cups/2.25 L (1 batch)	18 cups/4.5 L (2 batches)	27 cups/6.75 L (3 batches)	36 cups/9 L (4 batches)	45 cups/11.25 L (5 batches)
ground beef	1 lb (500 g)	2 lbs (1 kg)	3 lbs (1.5 kg)	4 lbs (2 kg)	5 lbs (2.5 kg)
onions	2	4	6	8	10
garlic cloves	2	4	6	8	10
tomato sauce	42 oz (1.194 L)	84 oz (2.388 L)	126 oz (3.582 L)	168 oz (4.776 L)	210 oz (5.97 L)
tomato paste	6 oz (156 mL)	12 oz (312 mL)	18 oz (468 mL)	24 oz (624 mL)	30 oz (780 mL)
celery stalks	2	4	6	8	10
salt	2 tsp (10 mL)	4 tsp (20 mL)	2 tbsp (30 mL)	8 tsp (40 mL)	10 tsp (50 mL)
pepper	¼ tsp (1 mL)	½ tsp (2 mL)	¾ tsp (3 mL)	1 tsp (5 mL)	1¼ tsp (6 mL)
dried oregano	2 tsp (10 mL)	4 tsp (20 mL)	2 tbsp (30 mL)	8 tsp (40 mL)	10 tsp (50 mL)
dried thyme	½ tsp (2 mL)	1 tsp (5 mL)	1½ tsp (7 mL)	2 tsp (10 mL)	2½ tsp (12 mL)
bay leaves	1	2	3	4	5
water	1 cup (250 mL)	2 cups (500 mL)	3 cups (750 mL)	4 cups (1 L)	5 cups (1.25 L)
gallon bags	1	2	3	4	5

BULK BATCH GUIDE

Vegetarian Red Sauce

Here is a delicious and deeply flavored red sauce lovingly created for all my vegetarian friends. The mushrooms add a lot of flavor, along with the herbs. This recipe makes enough for a hungry crowd or to freeze leftovers for later. Makes about 8 cups (2 L) sauce.

2 onions, chopped

2 celery stalks, chopped

2 carrots, cut into chunks

8 oz (250 g) cremini or white mushrooms, stems removed

1 tsp (5 mL) minced garlic

3 cans (each 14 oz/398 mL) tomato sauce

1 cup (250 mL) water

1 can (6 oz/156 mL) tomato paste

2 tsp (10 mL) salt

¼ tsp (1 mL) freshly ground black pepper

2 tsp (10 mL) dried oregano

½ tsp (2 mL) dried thyme

1 bay leaf

1. In a food processor, combine onions, celery, carrots, mushrooms and garlic. Pulse or shred until pieces are very fine.

2. Transfer vegetable mixture to a large (approx. 5 quart) slow cooker. Add tomato sauce, water, tomato paste, salt, pepper, oregano, thyme and bay leaf. Stir to combine. Cover and cook on Low for 10 to 12 hours or on High for 4 to 5 hours, until color deepens and flavors intensify. Remove bay leaf.

MAKE IT NOW Serve as desired or store in an airtight container in the refrigerator for up to 5 days. Reheat as directed below.

FREEZE IT Let cooked sauce cool completely. Place in a labeled gallon-size (4 L) freezer bag or divide among smaller containers, as desired. Seal, removing as much air as possible, and freeze.

REHEAT Place bag in the refrigerator for at least 12 hours or up to 24 hours to thaw. In a large saucepan over medium heat, heat sauce, stirring occasionally, for about 15 minutes, until hot and bubbly. Serve as desired.

BULK BATCH GUIDE

Sauce	8 cups/2 L (1 batch)	16 cups/4 L (2 batches)	24 cups/6 L (3 batches)	32 cups/8 L (4 batches)	40 cups/10 L (5 batches)
onions	2	4	6	8	10
celery stalks	2	4	6	8	10
carrots	2	4	6	8	10
cremini mushrooms	8 oz (250 g)	1 lb (500 g)	1½ lbs (750 g)	2 lbs (1 kg)	2½ lbs (1.25 kg)
garlic	1 tsp (5 mL)	2 tsp (10 mL)	1 tbsp (15 mL)	4 tsp (20 mL)	5 tsp (25 mL)
tomato sauce	42 oz (1.194 L)	84 oz (2.388 L)	126 oz (3.582 L)	168 oz (4.776 L)	210 oz (5.97 L)
water	1 cup (250 mL)	2 cups (500 mL)	3 cups (750 mL)	4 cups (1 L)	5 cups (1.25 L)
tomato paste	6 oz (156 mL)	12 oz (312 mL)	18 oz (468 mL)	24 oz (624 mL)	30 oz (780 mL)
salt	2 tsp (10 mL)	4 tsp (20 mL)	2 tbsp (30 mL)	8 tsp (40 mL)	10 tsp (50 mL)
pepper	¼ tsp (1 mL)	½ tsp (2 mL)	¾ tsp (3 mL)	1 tsp (5 mL)	1¼ tsp (6 mL)
dried oregano	2 tsp (10 mL)	4 tsp (20 mL)	2 tbsp (30 mL)	8 tsp (40 mL)	10 tsp (50 mL)
dried thyme	½ tsp (2 mL)	1 tsp (5 mL)	1½ tsp (7 mL)	2 tsp (10 mL)	2½ tsp (12 mL)
bay leaves	1	2	3	4	5
gallon bags	1	2	3	4	5

White Sauce

When I first started making freezer meals, a lot of the casseroles and creamy baked items used canned cream soup as a base. I wanted to create a recipe that had fewer calories and was less processed but still had a smooth, wonderful flavor. I discovered just how easy it is to make a creamy base from scratch, and now I always make it for my recipes such as Old-Fashioned Chicken Pot Pie (page 155), Hazelnut Chicken Wild Rice Soup (page 104) and Easy Tuna Casserole (page 242). Use one batch any time a recipe calls for one 10 oz (284 mL) can of condensed cream-based soup (diluted with equal parts milk or water). Makes 2¼ cups (560 mL) sauce.

¼ cup (60 mL) butter

¼ cup (60 mL) cornstarch

2 cups (500 mL) chicken broth or Homemade Chicken Stock (page 349)

¼ tsp (1 mL) celery salt

Salt and freshly ground black pepper

Tip
This recipe does not freeze well on its own but works very well when frozen with other ingredients, such as in casseroles, pastas and soups.

1. In a medium saucepan over medium heat, melt butter. Sprinkle cornstarch overtop and cook, whisking constantly, for 2 to 3 minutes, until foamy and simmering (do not let it brown).

2. Add chicken broth; cook, whisking constantly, for 3 to 4 minutes, until sauce thickens and starts to simmer. Remove from heat. Whisk in celery salt and season to taste with salt and pepper.

MAKE IT NOW Add to desired recipe or store in an airtight container in the refrigerator for up to 3 to 4 days. Reheat as directed below.

FREEZE IT Let cool to room temperature and add sauce to your freezer meal recipe as directed.

REHEAT Follow the reheating instructions for each recipe.

BULK BATCH	Sauce	2¼ cups/560 mL (1 batch)	4½ cups/1.125 L (2 batches)	6¾ cups/1.675 L (3 batches)	9 cups/2.25 L (4 batches)	11¼ cups/2.81 L (5 batches)
	butter	¼ cup (60 mL)	½ cup (125 mL)	¾ cup (175 mL)	1 cup (250 mL)	1¼ cups (310 mL)
	cornstarch	¼ cup (60 mL)	½ cup (125 mL)	¾ cup (175 mL)	1 cup (250 mL)	1¼ cups (310 mL)
	chicken broth	2 cups (500 mL)	4 cups (1 L)	6 cups (1.5 L)	8 cups (2 L)	10 cups (2.5 L)
	celery salt	¼ tsp (1 mL)	½ tsp (2 mL)	¾ tsp (3 mL)	1 tsp (5 mL)	1¼ tsp (6 mL)

Vegetarian White Sauce

This recipe will give you the same flavor as my traditional white sauce but is vegetarian friendly. If you'd like to make it vegan friendly, just substitute coconut oil or vegan butter for the butter. Use one batch any time a recipe calls for one 10 oz (284 mL) can of condensed cream-based soup (diluted with equal parts milk or water). Make 2¼ cups (560 mL) sauce.

¼ cup (60 mL) butter

¼ cup (60 mL) cornstarch

2 cups (500 mL) vegetable broth or Homemade Vegetable Stock (page 351)

¼ tsp (1 mL) celery salt

Salt and freshly ground black pepper

Tip
This recipe does not freeze well on its own but works very well when frozen with other ingredients, such as in casseroles, pastas and soups.

1. In a medium saucepan over medium heat, melt butter. Sprinkle cornstarch overtop and cook, whisking constantly, for 2 to 3 minutes, until foamy and simmering (do not let it brown).

2. Add vegetable broth; cook, whisking constantly, for 3 to 4 minutes, until sauce thickens and starts to simmer. Remove from heat. Whisk in celery salt and season to taste with salt and pepper.

MAKE IT NOW Add to recipes as desired or store in the refrigerator for up to 4 to 5 days.

FREEZE IT Allow sauce to cool to room temperature and add to freezer meal recipes as directed.

REHEAT Follow the reheating instructions for each recipe.

BULK BATCH	Sauce	2¼ cups/560 mL (1 batch)	4½ cups/1.125 L (2 batches)	6¾ cups/1.675 L (3 batches)	9 cups/2.25 L (4 batches)	11¼ cups/2.81 L (5 batches)
	butter	¼ cup (60 mL)	½ cup (125 mL)	¾ cup (175 mL)	1 cup (250 mL)	1¼ cups (310 mL)
	cornstarch	¼ cup (60 mL)	½ cup (125 mL)	¾ cup (175 mL)	1 cup (250 mL)	1¼ cups (310 mL)
	vegetable broth	2 cups (500 mL)	4 cups (1 L)	6 cups (1.5 L)	8 cups (2 L)	10 cups (2.5 L)
	celery salt	¼ tsp (1 mL)	½ tsp (2 mL)	¾ tsp (3 mL)	1 tsp (5 mL)	1¼ tsp (6 mL)

Marinara Sauce

Hearty, robust and fresh, this classic marinara sauce is so good it'll have you mopping up every last drop. Makes 2 cups (500 mL).

2 tbsp (30 mL) olive oil

¼ cup (60 mL) minced onion

½ tsp (2 mL) salt

⅛ tsp (0.5 mL) freshly ground black pepper

2 tbsp (30 mL) grated carrot

1 can (28 oz/796 mL) whole tomatoes, with juice

1 tsp (5 mL) dried oregano

1 tsp (5 mL) dried thyme

¼ tsp (1 mL) dried basil

1. In a medium saucepan over low heat, heat olive oil. Add onion, salt and pepper; cook, stirring occasionally, for about 10 minutes, until onion is soft. Add carrot and cook, stirring, for 5 minutes, until tender.

2. Using your hands, crush tomatoes while adding to the pot; pour in juice. Add oregano, thyme and basil; stir to combine. Increase heat to medium and bring to a boil, stirring often. Immediately reduce heat to low and simmer, stirring occasionally, for 30 minutes, until thickened.

3. Pour mixture into a blender (or use an immersion blender in the pot) and purée sauce until smooth.

MAKE IT NOW Serve as desired or store in an airtight container in refrigerator for up to 4 days. Reheat as directed below.

FREEZE IT Let sauce cool completely. Pour into a labeled quart-size (1 L) freezer bag. Seal, removing as much air as possible, and freeze.

REHEAT Place bag in the refrigerator for at least 12 hours or up to 24 hours to thaw, or run lukewarm water over bag until you can break sauce apart. To reheat on the stovetop, pour sauce into a medium saucepan and heat over medium-low heat, stirring often, for about 10 minutes, until warmed through. To reheat in the microwave, pour sauce into a small, microwave-safe bowl, cover and microwave on Low for 1 to 2 minutes. Stir, then microwave on High for 30 seconds. Serve as desired.

Sauce	2 cups/500 mL (1 batch)	4 cups/1 L (2 batches)	6 cups/1.5 L (3 batches)	8 cups/2 L (4 batches)	10 cups/2.5 L (5 batches)
olive oil	2 tbsp (30 mL)	¼ cup (60 mL)	6 tbsp (90 mL)	½ cup (125 mL)	⅔ cup (150 mL)
onions	¼ cup (60 mL)	½ cup (125 mL)	¾ cup (175 mL)	1 cup (250 mL)	1¼ cups (310 mL)
salt	½ tsp (2 mL)	1 tsp (5 mL)	1½ tsp (7 mL)	2 tsp (10 mL)	2½ tsp (12 mL)
pepper	⅛ tsp (0.5 mL)	¼ tsp (1 mL)	⅓ tsp (1.5 mL)	½ tsp (2 mL)	¾ tsp (3 mL)
carrot	2 tbsp (30 mL)	¼ cup (60 mL)	6 tbsp (90 mL)	½ cup (125 mL)	⅔ cup (150 mL)
tomatoes	28 oz (796 mL)	56 oz (1.592 L)	84 oz (2.388 L)	112 oz (3.184 L)	140 oz (3.98 L)
dried oregano	1 tsp (5 mL)	2 tsp (10 mL)	1 tbsp (15 mL)	4 tsp (20 mL)	5 tsp (25 mL)
dried thyme	1 tsp (5 mL)	2 tsp (10 mL)	1 tbsp (15 mL)	4 tsp (20 mL)	5 tsp (25 mL)
dried basil	¼ tsp (1 mL)	½ tsp (2 mL)	¾ tsp (3 mL)	1 tsp (5 mL)	1¼ tsp (6 mL)
quart bags	1	2	3	4	5

BULK BATCH GUIDE

Easy Pesto

You can use almost any nut to make a pesto that is delicious and packed full of flavor. Freeze it in ice-cube trays, transfer to a freezer bag and you'll have delicious, easy pesto whenever you like!

Makes about 2 cups (500 mL).

2 tsp (10 mL) minced garlic

3 cups (750 mL) fresh basil leaves

1 cup (250 mL) grated Parmesan cheese (about 3½ oz/100 g)

⅔ cup (150 mL) pine nuts (see Tip, below)

1 tsp (5 mL) salt

¼ tsp (1 mL) freshly ground black pepper

1 cup (250 mL) extra-virgin olive oil

Tip

If you prefer, you can use pistachios, sunflower seeds, almonds or walnuts in place of the pine nuts.

1. In a food processor, combine garlic and basil leaves; process until finely chopped. Add Parmesan cheese, pine nuts, salt and pepper; pulse until a coarse paste forms. With the motor running, slowly pour in olive oil through the feed tube and process until a smooth paste forms.

MAKE IT NOW Serve as desired or store in an airtight container in the refrigerator for up to 1 week.

FREEZE IT Measure out 1 tbsp (15 mL) portions into cups of 3 ice-cube trays. Place in freezer until solid. Transfer frozen pesto cubes to a labeled gallon-size (4 L) freezer bag. Seal, removing as much air as possible, and freeze.

THAW AND SERVE Thaw pesto in the refrigerator for at least 4 hours or up to 6 hours. Or remove desired number of pesto cubes, place in a separate quart-size (1 L) bag, seal, and run cool water over bag until thawed. Serve as desired.

Pesto	2 cups/500 mL (1 batch)	4 cups/1 L (2 batches)	6 cups/1.5 L (3 batches)	8 cups/2 L (4 batches)	10 cups/2.5 L (5 batches)
garlic	2 tsp (10 mL)	4 tsp (20 mL)	2 tbsp (30 mL)	8 tsp (40 mL)	10 tsp (50 mL)
basil	3 cups (750 mL)	6 cups (1.5 L)	9 cups (2.25 L)	12 cups (3 L)	15 cups (3.75 L)
Parmesan cheese	1 cup (250 mL)	2 cups (500 mL)	3 cups (750 mL)	4 cups (1 L)	5 cups (1.25 mL)
pine nuts	⅔ cup (150 mL)	1⅓ cups (325 mL)	2 cups (500 mL)	2⅔ cups (650 mL)	3⅓ cups (825 mL)
salt	1 tsp (5 mL)	2 tsp (10 mL)	1 tbsp (15 mL)	4 tsp (20 mL)	5 tsp (25 mL)
pepper	¼ tsp (1 mL)	½ tsp (2 mL)	¾ tbsp (3 mL)	1 tsp (5 mL)	1¼ tsp (6 mL)
extra-virgin olive oil	1 cup (250 mL)	2 cups (500 mL)	3 cups (750 mL)	4 cups (1 L)	5 cups (1.25 L)
gallon bags	1	2	3	4	5

BULK BATCH GUIDE

Thirty-Minute Pizza Sauce

Yes, you could just buy jarred pizza sauce at the store, but if you are looking for a tried-and-true, perfectly delicious and fresh-flavored homemade version, this one's a winner. Makes about 4 cups (1 L).

1 tbsp (15 mL) butter

2 tbsp (30 mL) olive oil

½ cup (125 mL) diced onion

¼ cup (60 mL) diced celery

½ tsp (2 mL) minced garlic

1 can (28 oz/796 mL) whole tomatoes, with juice

1 can (6 oz/156 mL) tomato paste

2 tbsp (30 mL) grated Parmesan cheese

1 tsp (5 mL) dried basil

1 tsp (5 mL) dried oregano

½ tsp (2 mL) granulated sugar

¼ tsp (1 mL) freshly ground black pepper

1 bay leaf

1. In a medium saucepan over medium heat, melt butter and olive oil. Add onion and celery; cook, stirring, for 3 to 4 minutes, until onion is starting to brown. Add garlic and cook, stirring, for 1 to 2 minutes, until golden and fragrant. Remove from heat.

2. In a blender, combine onion mixture, tomatoes (with juice), tomato paste, Parmesan cheese, basil, oregano, sugar and pepper; blend on High until smooth.

3. Return purée to saucepan, add bay leaf and bring to a boil over medium-high heat, stirring often. Immediately reduce heat to low and simmer, stirring occasionally, for 30 minutes, until thickened slightly. Discard bay leaf. Let sauce cool.

MAKE IT NOW Spread over pizza dough — I use about ¼ cup (60 mL) sauce for a 12-inch (30 cm) pizza — and bake as directed, or store in an airtight container in the refrigerator for up to 5 days.

FREEZE IT Divide sauce equally between 4 labeled quart-size (1 L) freezer bags, placing 1 cup (250 mL) sauce in each bag, or divide among smaller containers, as desired. Seal bags, removing as much air as possible, and freeze.

REHEAT Place a bag in the refrigerator for at least 6 hours or up to 12 hours to thaw, or run warm water over it until sauce is thawed. Stir until smooth. Spread over pizza dough — I use about ¼ cup (60 mL) sauce for a 12-inch (30 cm) pizza — and bake as directed.

Sauce	4 cups/1 L (1 batch)	8 cups/2 L (2 batches)	12 cups/3 L (3 batches)	16 cups/4 L (4 batches)	20 cups/5 L (5 batches)
butter	1 tbsp (15 mL)	2 tbsp (30 mL)	3 tbsp (45 mL)	¼ cup (60 mL)	⅓ cup (75 mL)
olive oil	2 tbsp (30 mL)	¼ cup (60 mL)	6 tbsp (90 mL)	½ cup (125 mL)	⅔ cup (150 mL)
onion	½ cup (125 mL)	1 cup (250 mL)	1½ cups (375 mL)	2 cups (500 mL)	2½ cups (625 mL)
celery	¼ cup (60 mL)	½ cup (125 mL)	¾ cup (175 mL)	1 cup (250 mL)	1¼ cups (310 mL)
garlic	½ tsp (2 mL)	1 tsp (5 mL)	1½ tsp (7 mL)	2 tsp (10 mL)	2½ tsp (12 mL)
tomatoes	28 oz (796 mL)	56 oz (1.592 L)	84 oz (2.388 L)	112 oz (3.184 L)	140 oz (3.98 L)
tomato paste	6 oz (156 mL)	12 oz (312 mL)	18 oz (468 mL)	24 oz (624 mL)	30 oz (780 mL)
Parmesan cheese	2 tbsp (30 mL)	¼ cup (60 mL)	6 tbsp (90 mL)	½ cup (125 mL)	⅔ cup (150 mL)
dried basil	1 tsp (5 mL)	2 tsp (10 mL)	1 tbsp (15 mL)	4 tsp (20 mL)	5 tsp (25 mL)
dried oregano	1 tsp (5 mL)	2 tsp (10 mL)	1 tbsp (15 mL)	4 tsp (20 mL)	5 tsp (25 mL)
sugar	½ tsp (2 mL)	1 tsp (5 mL)	1½ tsp (7 mL)	2 tsp (10 mL)	2½ tsp (12 mL)
pepper	¼ tsp (1 mL)	½ tsp (2 mL)	¾ tsp (3 mL)	1 tsp (5 mL)	1¼ tsp (6 mL)
bay leaves	1	2	3	4	5
quart bags	4	8	12	16	20

BULK BATCH GUIDE

Smoky BBQ Sauce

Trust me, this is worth every second of the 30 minutes it takes to make and cook this fantastic sauce. One batch has the equivalent yield of a large bottle of store-bought barbecue sauce. Makes about 5 cups (1.25 L).

3 tbsp (45 mL) olive oil

1 medium onion, finely chopped

2 tsp (10 mL) minced garlic

2 tbsp (30 mL) chili powder

1 tsp (5 mL) salt

1 tsp (5 mL) freshly ground black pepper

2 cups (500 mL) ketchup

1 cup (250 mL) packed brown sugar

½ cup (125 mL) yellow mustard

⅓ cup (75 mL) cider vinegar

⅓ cup (75 mL) Worcestershire sauce

¼ cup (60 mL) freshly squeezed lemon juice

¼ cup (60 mL) steak sauce

½ cup (125 mL) dark (cooking) molasses

1. In a medium saucepan, heat olive oil over medium-high heat. Add onion and garlic; cook, stirring, for 1 to 2 minutes or until soft and fragrant. Reduce heat to medium. Add chili powder, salt and pepper; cook, stirring, for 30 seconds to release flavor. Add ketchup, brown sugar, mustard, cider vinegar, Worcestershire sauce, lemon juice, steak sauce and molasses; stir to combine. Bring to a boil, then immediately reduce heat to low and simmer, stirring often, for 15 minutes or until sauce has thickened. Remove from heat.

MAKE IT NOW Let cool for 10 minutes, then serve. You can store the sauce in an airtight container in the refrigerator for up to 2 weeks.

FREEZE IT Let cool completely. Pour sauce into 2 labeled quart-size (1 L) freezer bags, or divide among smaller containers, as desired. Seal, removing as much air as possible, and freeze.

THAW AND SERVE Place bag in the refrigerator for at least 12 hours or up to 24 hours to thaw, or run hot water over bag in the sink until sauce is thawed.

Sauce	5 cups/1.25 L (1 batch)	10 cups/2.5 L (2 batches)	15 cups/3.75 L (3 batches)	20 cups/5 L (4 batches)	25 cups/6.25 L (5 batches)
olive oil	3 tbsp (45 mL)	6 tbsp (90 mL)	½ cup (125 mL)	¾ cup (175 mL)	¾ cup + 3 tbsp (220 mL)
onions	1	2	3	4	5
garlic	2 tsp (10 mL)	4 tsp (20 mL)	2 tbsp (30 mL)	8 tsp (40 mL)	10 tsp (50 mL)
chili powder	2 tbsp (30 mL)	¼ cup (60 mL)	6 tbsp (90 mL)	½ cup (125 mL)	⅔ cup (150 mL)
salt	1 tsp (5 mL)	2 tsp (10 mL)	1 tbsp (15 mL)	4 tsp (20 mL)	5 tsp (25 mL)
pepper	1 tsp (5 mL)	2 tsp (10 mL)	1 tbsp (15 mL)	4 tsp (20 mL)	5 tsp (25 mL)
ketchup	2 cups (500 mL)	4 cups (1 L)	6 cups (1.5 L)	8 cups (2 L)	10 cups (2.5 L)
brown sugar	1 cup (250 mL)	2 cups (500 mL)	3 cups (750 mL)	4 cups (1 L)	5 cups (1.25 L)
yellow mustard	½ cup (125 mL)	1 cup (250 mL)	1½ cups (375 mL)	2 cups (500 mL)	2½ cups (625 mL)
cider vinegar	⅓ cup (75 mL)	⅔ cup (150 mL)	1 cup (250 mL)	1⅓ cups (325 mL)	1⅔ cups (400 mL)
Worcestershire	⅓ cup (75 mL)	⅔ cup (150 mL)	1 cup (250 mL)	1⅓ cups (325 mL)	1⅔ cups (400 mL)
lemon juice	¼ cup (60 mL)	½ cup (125 mL)	¾ cup (175 mL)	1 cup (250 mL)	1¼ cups (310 mL)
steak sauce	¼ cup (60 mL)	½ cup (125 mL)	¾ cup (175 mL)	1 cup (250 mL)	1¼ cups (310 mL)
molasses	½ cup (125 mL)	1 cup (250 mL)	1½ cups (375 mL)	2 cups (500 mL)	2½ cups (625 mL)
quart bags	2	4	6	8	10

BULK BATCH GUIDE

Basic Grilled Chicken Marinade

This easy marinade, with its hint of lime and bursts of cilantro and garlic, is my go-to recipe for perfectly seasoned grilled chicken. You can use the chicken to top salads or add to soups, or simply grill and serve. I love having it at the ready! *Makes 6 servings.*

½ cup (125 mL) olive oil

1 tsp (5 mL) salt

½ tsp (2 mL) freshly ground black pepper

½ tsp (2 mL) paprika

½ tsp (2 mL) ground cumin

1 tsp (5 mL) minced garlic

3 tbsp (45 mL) chopped onion

¼ cup (60 mL) chopped fresh cilantro

2 tbsp (30 mL) freshly squeezed lime juice

1 cup (250 mL) warm water

2 lbs (1 kg) boneless, skinless chicken breasts

1. Place olive oil, salt, pepper, paprika, cumin, garlic, onion, cilantro and lime juice in a gallon-size (4 L) freezer bag (label the bag if freezing for later). Add water, then swish marinade around in bag. Add chicken and seal bag, removing as much air as possible. Turn and swish bag contents to coat all sides of the meat.

MAKE IT NOW Place bag in refrigerator for at least 2 hours or up to 24 hours. Remove chicken from bag, discarding marinade. Preheat barbecue grill to Medium-High. Place chicken on a well-greased rack and cook for 10 to 12 minutes, turning halfway, until no longer pink inside and internal temperature reaches 165°F (73°C). Transfer to a serving platter and let rest for 3 to 5 minutes before serving.

FREEZE IT Place bag of chicken and marinade in the freezer and freeze.

THAW AND COOK Place bag in refrigerator for at least 12 hours or up to 24 hours to thaw. Remove chicken from bag, discarding marinade. Preheat barbecue grill to Medium-High. Place chicken on a well-greased rack and cook for 10 to 12 minutes, turning halfway, until no longer pink inside and internal temperature reaches 165°F (73°C). Transfer to a serving platter and let rest for 3 to 5 minutes before serving.

BULK BATCH GUIDE — Servings	6 (1 batch)	12 (2 batches)	18 (3 batches)	24 (4 batches)	30 (5 batches)
olive oil	½ cup (125 mL)	1 cup (250 mL)	1½ cups (375 mL)	2 cups (500 mL)	2½ cups (625 mL)
salt	1 tsp (5 mL)	2 tsp (10 mL)	1 tbsp (15 mL)	4 tsp (20 mL)	5 tsp (25 mL)
pepper	½ tsp (2 mL)	1 tsp (5 mL)	1½ tsp (7 mL)	2 tsp (10 mL)	2½ tsp (12 mL)
paprika	½ tsp (2 mL)	1 tsp (5 mL)	1½ tsp (7 mL)	2 tsp (10 mL)	2½ tsp (12 mL)
cumin	½ tsp (2 mL)	1 tsp (5 mL)	1½ tsp (7 mL)	2 tsp (10 mL)	2½ tsp (12 mL)
garlic	1 tsp (5 mL)	2 tsp (10 mL)	1 tbsp (15 mL)	4 tsp (20 mL)	5 tsp (25 mL)
onion	3 tbsp (45 mL)	6 tbsp (90 mL)	½ cup (125 mL)	¾ cup (175 mL)	¾ cup + 3 tbsp (220 mL)
cilantro	¼ cup (60 mL)	½ cup (125 mL)	¾ cup (175 mL)	1 cup (250 mL)	1¼ cups (310 mL)
lime juice	2 tbsp (30 mL)	¼ cup (60 mL)	6 tbsp (90 mL)	½ cup (125 mL)	⅔ cup (150 mL)
water	1 cup (250 mL)	2 cups (500 mL)	3 cups (750 mL)	4 cups (1 L)	5 cups (1.25 L)
chicken	2 lbs (1 kg)	4 lbs (2 kg)	6 lbs (3 kg)	8 lbs (4 kg)	10 lbs (5 kg)
gallon bags	1	2	3	4	5

Basic Grilled Steak Marinade

Fast, easy and super delicious, this dark, almost teriyaki-style marinade was developed for beef, but it can also be used for chicken, pork and fatty fish such as salmon and tuna. Everyone begs me for the recipe! *Makes 6 servings.*

1 cup (250 mL) tamari sauce

1 cup (250 mL) granulated sugar

1 cup (250 mL) balsamic vinegar

2 tsp (10 mL) minced garlic

2 tsp (10 mL) seasoned salt

2 lbs (1 kg) beef flank steak

1. Place tamari sauce, sugar, vinegar, garlic and salt in a gallon-size (4 L) freezer bag (label the bag if freezing for later). Add flank steak and seal bag, removing as much air as possible. Turn and swish contents to coat all sides of the meat.

MAKE IT NOW Place bag in refrigerator for at least 2 hours or up to 2 days. Remove meat from bag, discarding marinade. Preheat barbecue grill to High. Place flank steak on a well-greased rack and close lid. Grill for about 5 to 6 minutes on one side, until well seared. Turn over meat, close lid and grill for about 3 to 4 minutes (for medium-rare). Transfer to a cutting board and let rest for 3 to 5 minutes, then slice thinly across the grain.

FREEZE IT Place bag of beef and marinade in the freezer and freeze.

THAW AND COOK Place bag in refrigerator for at least 12 hours or up to 24 hours to thaw. Remove meat from bag, discarding marinade. Preheat a barbecue grill to High. Place flank steak on a well-greased rack and close lid. Grill for about 5 to 6 minutes on one side, until well seared. Turn over meat, close lid and grill for about 3 to 4 minutes (for medium-rare). Transfer to a cutting board and let rest for 3 to 5 minutes, then slice thinly across the grain.

BULK BATCH	Servings	6 (1 batch)	12 (2 batches)	18 (3 batches)	24 (4 batches)	30 (5 batches)
	tamari sauce	1 cup (250 mL)	2 cups (500 mL)	3 cups (750 mL)	4 cups (1 L)	5 cups (1.25 L)
	sugar	1 cup (250 mL)	2 cups (500 mL)	3 cups (750 mL)	4 cups (1 L)	5 cups (1.25 L)
	balsamic vinegar	1 cup (250 mL)	2 cups (500 mL)	3 cups (750 mL)	4 cups (1 L)	5 cups (1.25 L)
	garlic	2 tsp (10 mL)	4 tsp (20 mL)	2 tbsp (30 mL)	8 tsp (40 mL)	10 tsp (50 mL)
	seasoned salt	2 tsp (10 mL)	4 tsp (20 mL)	2 tbsp (30 mL)	8 tsp (40 mL)	10 tsp (50 mL)
	flank steak	2 lbs (1 kg)	4 lbs (2 kg)	6 lbs (3 kg)	8 lbs (4 kg)	10 lbs (5 kg)
	gallon bags	1	2	3	4	5

Lip-Smackin' Chutney

Whenever I make Indian food, I always pull out some of this amazing chutney. The cilantro, spicy jalapeño and fresh mint come together to create a flavor that is out of this world. It's also great for dipping naan bread into, or even tortilla chips. I guarantee those lips are gonna smack! Makes about 1 cup (250 mL).

1½ cups (375 mL) cilantro (about 2 bunches)

8 green onions, green parts only

1 jalapeño pepper

½ cup (125 mL) fresh mint leaves

1 tsp (5 mL) minced garlic

2 tbsp (30 mL) freshly squeezed lemon juice

2 tbsp (30 mL) olive oil

1 tsp (5 mL) ground cumin

½ tsp (2 mL) ground coriander

½ tsp (2 mL) salt

¼ tsp (1 mL) freshly ground black pepper

1. In a food processor or blender, combine cilantro, green onions, jalapeño, mint, garlic, lemon juice, olive oil, cumin, coriander, salt and pepper. Process until very smooth, stopping the motor to scrape down sides of bowl as necessary.

MAKE IT NOW Serve immediately or store in an airtight container in the refrigerator for up to 2 days.

FREEZE IT Transfer chutney to a labeled quart-size (1 L) freezer bag. Seal bag, removing as much air as possible, and freeze.

THAW AND SERVE Place bag in refrigerator for at least 4 hours or up to 6 hours to thaw, or run cool water over bag until chutney is thawed. Serve cold.

Chutney	1 cup/250 mL (1 batch)	2 cups/500 mL (2 batches)	3 cups/750 mL (3 batches)	4 cups/1 L (4 batches)	5 cups/1.25 L (5 batches)
cilantro	1½ cups (375 mL)	3 cups (750 mL)	4½ cups (1.125 L)	6 cups (1.5 L)	7½ cups (1.875 L)
green onions	8	16	24	32	40
jalapeño peppers	1	2	3	4	5
mint leaves	½ cup (125 mL)	1 cup (250 mL)	1½ cup (375 mL)	2 cup (500 mL)	2½ cup (625 mL)
garlic	1 tsp (5 mL)	2 tsp (10 mL)	1 tbsp (15 mL)	4 tsp (20 mL)	5 tsp (25 mL)
lemon juice	2 tbsp (30 mL)	¼ cup (60 mL)	6 tbsp (90 mL)	½ cup (125 mL)	⅔ cup (150 mL)
olive oil	2 tbsp (30 mL)	¼ cup (60 mL)	6 tbsp (90 mL)	½ cup (125 mL)	⅔ cup (150 mL)
cumin	1 tsp (5 mL)	2 tsp (10 mL)	1 tbsp (15 mL)	4 tsp (20 mL)	5 tsp (25 mL)
coriander	½ tsp (2 mL)	1 tsp (5 mL)	1½ tsp (7 mL)	2 tsp (10 mL)	2½ tsp (12 mL)
salt	½ tsp (2 mL)	1 tsp (5 mL)	1½ tsp (7 mL)	2 tsp (10 mL)	2½ tsp (12 mL)
pepper	¼ tsp (1 mL)	½ tsp (2 mL)	¾ tsp (3 mL)	1 tsp (5 mL)	1¼ tsp (6 mL)
quart bags	1	2	3	4	5

Peanut Sauce

I love using this sauce as a dip for my Amazing Chicken Satay (page 163). It's creamy and smooth, with just the right deep, peanutty flavor and a perfect bite of gentle heat. Makes about 1 cup (250 mL).

¼ cup (60 mL) canned coconut milk

⅓ cup (75 mL) creamy peanut butter

2 tsp (10 mL) freshly squeezed lime juice

1½ tsp (7 mL) grated ginger

1 tsp (5 mL) tamari sauce

1 tsp (5 mL) packed brown sugar

⅛ tsp (0.5 mL) Sriracha sauce or hot pepper flakes

1. In a blender, combine coconut milk, peanut butter, lime juice, ginger, tamari sauce, brown sugar and Sriracha sauce. Blend on High for 30 seconds to 1 minute, until creamy and smooth.

MAKE IT NOW Serve warm or at room temperature as a dipping sauce, or use as desired. Store sauce in an airtight container in the refrigerator for up to 2 days.

FREEZE IT Place sauce in a labeled quart-size (1 L) freezer bag. Seal, removing as much air as possible, and freeze.

THAW AND SERVE Place bag in refrigerator for at least 8 hours or up to 12 hours to thaw, or run warm water over bag until sauce is thawed; stir. To serve warm, transfer to a small, microwave-safe bowl and microwave for 30 seconds on High, or serve at room temperature. Use as desired.

BULK BATCH GUIDE

Sauce	1 cup/250 mL (1 batch)	2 cups/500 mL (2 batches)	3 cups/750 mL (3 batches)	4 cups/1 L (4 batches)	5 cups/1.25 L (5 batches)
coconut milk	¼ cup (60 mL)	½ cup (125 mL)	¾ cup (175 mL)	1 cup (250 mL)	1¼ cups (310 mL)
peanut butter	⅓ cup (75 mL)	⅔ cup (150 mL)	1 cup (250 mL)	1⅓ cups (325 mL)	1⅔ cups (400 mL)
lime juice	2 tsp (10 mL)	4 tsp (20 mL)	1 tbsp (30 mL)	8 tsp (40 mL)	10 tsp (50 mL)
ginger	1½ tsp (7 mL)	1 tbsp (15 mL)	1½ tbsp (22 mL)	2 tbsp (30 mL)	2½ tbsp (37 mL)
tamari sauce	1 tsp (5 mL)	2 tsp (10 mL)	1 tbsp (15 mL)	4 tsp (20 mL)	5 tsp (25 mL)
brown sugar	1 tsp (5 mL)	2 tsp (10 mL)	1 tbsp (15 mL)	4 tsp (20 mL)	5 tsp (25 mL)
Sriracha sauce	⅛ tsp (0.5 mL)	¼ tsp (1 mL)	⅓ tsp (1.5 mL)	½ tsp (2 mL)	¾ tsp (3 mL)
quart bags	1	2	3	4	5

Enchilada Sauce

This is one amazingly smooth and creamy enchilada sauce, created by my brother Jordan, an aspiring chef. The secret is the combination of peanut butter, which adds depth of flavor, and the peppery spices. Trust me, this is the best enchilada sauce ever! Makes 2½ cups (625 mL).

2 cups (500 mL) warm water

6 tbsp (90 mL) tomato paste

1 tsp (5 mL) ground cumin

½ tsp (2 mL) garlic powder

1 tsp (5 mL) salt

2 tbsp (30 mL) all-purpose flour

2 tbsp (30 mL) chili powder

2 tbsp (30 mL) vegetable oil

¼ medium onion, diced

2 cans (4½ oz/127 mL) mild green chiles, with juices

2 tbsp (30 mL) creamy peanut butter

1. In a medium bowl, combine water, tomato paste, cumin, garlic powder and salt. Set aside.

2. In a small bowl, combine flour and chili powder. Set aside.

3. In a large saucepan, heat vegetable oil over medium-high heat. Once it is hot and shimmering, add onion. Cook, stirring, for 2 to 3 minutes, until softened and golden brown. Sprinkle in flour mixture; cook, whisking constantly, for 1 minute, until simmering.

4. Add tomato paste mixture, whisking constantly; bring to a simmer, whisking. Immediately reduce heat to medium-low. Add green chiles with juices and simmer, stirring often, for 10 minutes, until sauce is slightly thickened. Remove from heat. Add peanut butter and stir to combine. (If you love your sauce super smooth, use an immersion blender.)

MAKE IT NOW Use immediately or store in an airtight container in the refrigerator for 4 to 5 days.

FREEZE IT Let sauce cool to room temperature. Pour into a labeled quart-size (1 L) freezer bag. Seal, removing as much air as possible, and freeze.

REHEAT Place bag in refrigerator for at least 8 hours or up to 12 hours to thaw, or run lukewarm water over bag until you can break sauce apart. Pour contents into a large saucepan over medium heat; heat, stirring often, for about 10 minutes, until warmed through. Serve as desired.

BULK BATCH GUIDE Sauce	2½ cups/625 mL (1 batch)	5 cups/1.25 L (2 batches)	7½ cups/1.75 L (3 batches)	10 cups/2.5 L (4 batches)	12½ cups/3.125 L (5 batches)
water	2 cups (500 mL)	4 cups (1 L)	6 cups (1.5 L)	8 cups (2 L)	10 cups (2.5 L)
tomato paste	6 tbsp (90 mL)	¾ cup (175 mL)	1 cup + 2 tbsp (280 mL)	1½ cups (375 mL)	1¾ cups + 2 tbsp (455 mL)
cumin	1 tsp (5 mL)	2 tsp (10 mL)	1 tbsp (15 mL)	4 tsp (20 mL)	5 tsp (25 mL)
garlic powder	½ tsp (2 mL)	1 tsp (5 mL)	1½ tsp (7 mL)	2 tsp (10 mL)	2½ tsp (12 mL)
salt	1 tsp (5 mL)	2 tsp (10 mL)	1 tbsp (15 mL)	4 tsp (20 mL)	5 tsp (25 mL)
all-purpose flour	2 tbsp (30 mL)	¼ cup (60 mL)	6 tbsp (90 mL)	½ cup (125 mL)	⅔ cup (150 mL)
chili powder	2 tbsp (30 mL)	¼ cup (60 mL)	6 tbsp (90 mL)	½ cup (125 mL)	⅔ cup (150 mL)
vegetable oil	2 tbsp (30 mL)	¼ cup (60 mL)	6 tbsp (90 mL)	½ cup (125 mL)	⅔ cup (150 mL)
onions	¼	½	¾	1	1¼
green chiles	9 oz (254 mL)	18 oz (508 mL)	27 oz (762 mL)	36 oz (1.016 L)	45 oz (1.27 L)
peanut butter	2 tbsp (30 mL)	¼ cup (60 mL)	6 tbsp (90 mL)	½ cup (125 mL)	⅔ cup (150 mL)
quart bags	1	2	3	4	5

Totally Tasty Salsa

Have an overabundance of fresh garden tomatoes? Turn them into delicious freezer salsa to enjoy over enchiladas or tacos, or mix it with some sour cream for a vibrant dip or salad dressing. Makes about 6 cups (1.5 L).

2 lbs (1 kg) tomatoes (about 5 large)

1 large onion, chopped

1 to 2 jalapeño peppers

½ cup (125 mL) tomato paste

2 tbsp (30 mL) freshly squeezed lime juice

1 tbsp (15 mL) granulated sugar

1 tsp (5 mL) salt

2 tsp (10 mL) garlic powder

¼ cup (60 mL) chopped fresh cilantro

1. Fill a large stockpot with water and bring to a boil over high heat. Add tomatoes, in batches, and blanch for 2 minutes. Using a slotted spoon, remove and transfer tomatoes to a large bowl of ice water; let stand for 1 minute. Once cool enough to handle, use a knife to cut out the cores, then use the knife or your fingers to peel off the skins. Halve tomatoes and spoon out the seeds, then chop.

2. In a large saucepan, combine chopped tomatoes, onion, jalapeño to taste, tomato paste, lime juice, sugar, salt and garlic powder. Bring to a boil over medium-high heat, stirring often. Cover and immediately reduce heat to low. Simmer, stirring frequently, for 25 minutes, until flavors intensify. Remove lid and continue to simmer, stirring often, for 20 minutes, until color deepens. Remove from heat and let cool to room temperature. Stir in chopped cilantro.

MAKE IT NOW Refrigerate salsa until cold, about 2 hours. Serve as desired or store in an airtight container in the refrigerator for up to 1 week.

FREEZE IT Let salsa cool completely. Scoop into 2 labeled quart-size (1 L) glass jars, leaving 1/2 inch (1 cm) headspace, seal with lids and freeze. You can also divide salsa among smaller or larger containers as desired.

THAW AND SERVE Place jar in the refrigerator for at least 12 hours or up to 24 hours to thaw. Serve as desired.

	Salsa	6 cups/1.5 L (1 batch)	12 cups/3 L (2 batches)	18 cups/4.5 L (3 batches)	24 cups/6 L (4 batches)	30 cups/7.5 L (5 batches)
BULK BATCH GUIDE	tomatoes	2 lbs (1 kg)	4 lbs (2 kg)	6 lbs (3 kg)	8 lbs (4 kg)	10 lbs (5 kg)
	onions	1	2	3	4	5
	jalapeño peppers	1 to 2	2 to 4	3 to 6	4 to 8	5 to 10
	tomato paste	½ cup (125 mL)	1 cup (250 mL)	1½ cups (375 mL)	2 cups (500 mL)	2½ cups (625 mL)
	lime juice	2 tbsp (30 mL)	¼ cup (60 mL)	6 tbsp (90 mL)	½ cup (125 mL)	⅔ cup (150 mL)
	sugar	1 tbsp (15 mL)	2 tbsp (30 mL)	3 tbsp (45 mL)	¼ cup (60 mL)	⅓ cup (75 mL)
	salt	1 tsp (5 mL)	2 tsp (10 mL)	1 tbsp (15 mL)	4 tsp (20 mL)	5 tsp (25 mL)
	garlic powder	2 tsp (10 mL)	4 tsp (20 mL)	2 tbsp (30 mL)	8 tsp (40 mL)	10 tsp (50 mL)
	cilantro	¼ cup (60 mL)	½ cup (125 mL)	¾ cup (175 mL)	1 cup (250 mL)	1¼ cups (310 mL)
	quart jars	2	4	6	8	10

Avocado Crema

I like to add this delicious, creamy sauce to tacos, nachos and salads, especially my Rio-Style Sweet Pork Salad (page 185). Makes about 1½ cups (375 mL).

1 cup (250 mL) chopped avocado, fresh or frozen (about 1 large)

½ cup (125 mL) sour cream or plain Greek yogurt

½ tsp (2 mL) salt

1 tsp (5 mL) freshly squeezed lime juice

1. In a food processor or blender, combine avocado, sour cream, salt and lime juice. Process until smooth.

MAKE IT NOW Spoon over tacos or use as a dipping sauce. Store in an airtight container in the refrigerator for up to 2 days.

FREEZE IT Pour sauce into a labeled quart-size (1 L) freezer bag. Seal, removing as much air as possible. (This recipe is best stored with the least amount of air possible. If you have a vacuum sealer, use it here. Or use a straw to remove all the air from the freezer bag before sealing.) Freeze.

THAW AND SERVE Place bag in the refrigerator for at least 6 hours or up to 8 hours to thaw. Pour into a medium bowl and whisk until smooth. Spoon over tacos or use as a dipping sauce.

BULK BATCH — Sauce	1½ cups/375 mL (1 batch)	3 cups/750 mL (2 batches)	4½ cups/1.125 L (3 batches)	6 cups/1.5 L (4 batches)	7.5 cups/1.875 L (5 batches)
avocado	1 cup (250 mL)	2 cups (500 mL)	3 cups (750 mL)	4 cups (1 L)	5 cups (1.25 L)
sour cream	½ cup (125 mL)	1 cup (250 mL)	1½ cups (375 mL)	2 cups (500 mL)	2½ cups (625 mL)
salt	½ tsp (2 mL)	1 tsp (5 mL)	1½ tsp (7 mL)	2 tsp (10 mL)	2½ tsp (12 mL)
lime juice	1 tsp (5 mL)	2 tsp (10 mL)	1 tbsp (15 mL)	4 tsp (20 mL)	5 tsp (25 mL)
quart bags	1	2	3	4	5

Homemade Chicken Stock

If I have the time before a big freezer-cooking marathon, I love to make a big ol' pot of homemade chicken stock to help me save money. It also makes the recipes I'm adding it to more complex and flavorful than store-bought chicken broth. Makes about 24 cups (6 L).

1 raw whole chicken (5 to 6 lbs/2.25 to 3 kg)

2 onions, halved

3 celery stalks with leaves, cut into chunks

3 carrots, cut into chunks

2 bay leaves

5 whole black peppercorns (or 1/4 tsp/ 1 mL freshly ground black pepper)

2 tbsp (30 mL) white vinegar

1 bunch fresh parsley

24 cups (6 L) water

2 tbsp (30 mL) salt

Freshly ground black pepper

1. In a large (approx. 20 quart) stockpot, combine chicken, onions, celery, carrots, bay leaves, peppercorns, vinegar, parsley and water. Let stand for 30 minutes, allowing the vinegar to draw all those glorious minerals out of the bones.

2. Bring stockpot to a gentle simmer over medium heat, then immediately reduce heat to low. Skim off any foam. Cover and simmer gently on low heat for 12 hours. (You don't want it to come to a full rolling boil at any time. There should be only a few bubbles breaking the surface.)

3. Remove from heat, uncover and place stockpot in an ice-water bath. Let stock cool, refreshing ice water as necessary to keep it cold.

4. Place a colander over a large bowl or container. Line colander with a flour-sack towel or cheesecloth and pour stock through. Press down on solids with the back of a large spoon to get out as much liquid as possible. Remove meat from bones (you can use it in recipes that require cooked chicken, such as Old-Fashioned Chicken Pot Pie, page 155). Discard bones, skin and remaining solids. Season stock to taste with salt and pepper.

MAKE IT NOW Use immediately or transfer to an airtight container and store in the refrigerator for up to 2 days, spooning off and discarding any hardened fat on the top.

FREEZE IT Refrigerate stock until completely cooled and fat rises to the top. Spoon off and discard any hardened fat. Transfer stock to 12 labeled quart-size (1 L) freezer bags, allotting 2 cups (500 mL) stock per bag. (You can also divide it among smaller or larger containers as desired.) Seal bags, removing as much air as possible, and freeze.

THAW AND USE Place a bag in refrigerator for at least 12 hours or up to 24 hours to thaw, or run lukewarm water over bag until you can break apart stock. Use in recipes as desired. To heat, pour bag contents into a large saucepan and warm over medium heat for about 10 minutes, stirring often, until heated through.

Stock	24 cups/6 L (1 batch)	48 cups/12 L (2 batches)	72 cups/18 L (3 batches)	96 cups/24 L (4 batches)	120 cups/30 L (5 batches)
whole chickens	1	2	3	4	5
onions	2	4	6	8	10
celery stalks	3	6	9	12	15
carrots	3	6	9	12	15
bay leaves	2	4	6	8	10
peppercorns	5	10	15	20	25
white vinegar	2 tbsp (30 mL)	1/4 cup (60 mL)	6 tbsp (90 mL)	½ cup (125 mL)	⅔ cup (150 mL)
parsley bunches	1	2	3	4	5
water	24 cups (6 L)	48 cups (12 L)	72 cups (18 L)	96 cups (24 L)	120 cups (30 L)
salt	2 tbsp (30 mL)	1/4 cup (60 mL)	6 tbsp (90 mL)	½ cup (125 mL)	⅔ cup (150 mL)
quart bags	12	24	36	48	60

BULK BATCH GUIDE

Homemade Beef Stock

Homemade stocks are one of my favorite ways to give my food a little extra kick. Not only is its flavor rich, delicious and rustic, this beef stock is also very healthy, filled with beneficial minerals, collagen, calcium and more. Makes about 16 cups (4 L).

4 lbs (2 kg) meaty beef shin or neck bones

2 onions, cut into 1-inch (2.5 cm) chunks

3 celery stalks, cut into 1-inch (2.5 cm) chunks

3 large carrots, cut into 1-inch (2.5 cm) chunks

⅓ cup (75 mL) olive oil

2 tsp (10 mL) salt

16 cups (4 L) water

2 bay leaves

5 whole black peppercorns (or 1/4 tsp/ 1 mL freshly ground black pepper)

Additional salt and freshly ground black pepper

1. Preheat oven to 400°F (200°C).

2. In a large roasting pan, combine beef bones, onions, celery and carrots. Drizzle olive oil evenly overtop and toss to coat; sprinkle with salt. Roast in preheated oven for about 1 hour, turning every 15 minutes, until vegetables are golden brown and tender.

3. In a large (approx. 20 quart) stockpot, combine water, bay leaves and peppercorns. Add roasted vegetables and bones, scraping in brown bits from the pan. Bring to a gentle simmer over medium-high heat. Immediately reduce heat to low and skim off any foam. Cover and simmer gently on low heat for 8 hours. (You don't want it to come to a full rolling boil at any time. There should be only a few bubbles breaking the surface.)

4. Remove from heat, uncover and place stockpot in an ice-water bath. Let stock cool, refreshing ice water as necessary to keep it cold.

5. Place a colander over a large bowl or container. Line colander with a flour-sack towel or cheesecloth and pour stock through. Press down on solids with the back of a large spoon to get out as much liquid as possible. Discard solids. Season stock to taste with salt and pepper.

MAKE IT NOW Use immediately or transfer to an airtight container and store in the refrigerator for up to 2 days. Spoon off and discard any hardened fat on the top.

FREEZE IT Refrigerate stock until completely cooled and fat rises to the top. Spoon off and discard any hardened fat. Transfer stock to 8 labeled quart-size (1 L) freezer bags, allotting 2 cups (500 mL) stock per bag. (You can also divide it among smaller or larger containers as desired.) Seal bags, removing as much air as possible, and freeze.

THAW AND USE Place a bag in refrigerator for at least 12 hours or up to 24 hours to thaw, or run lukewarm water over bag until you can break apart stock. Use in recipes as desired. To heat, pour bag contents into a large saucepan and warm over medium heat, stirring often, for about 10 minutes, until heated through.

Stock	16 cups/4 L (1 batch)	32 cups/8 L (2 batches)	48 cups/12 L (3 batches)	64 cups/16 L (4 batches)	80 cups/20 L (5 batches)
beef bones	4 lbs (2 kg)	8 lbs (4 kg)	12 lbs (6 kg)	16 lbs (8 kg)	20 lbs (10 kg)
onions	2	4	6	8	10
celery stalks	3	6	9	12	15
carrots	3	6	9	12	15
olive oil	⅓ cup (75 mL)	⅔ cup (150 mL)	1 cup (250 mL)	1⅓ cups (325 mL)	1⅔ cups (400 mL)
salt	2 tsp (10 mL)	4 tsp (20 mL)	2 tbsp (30 mL)	8 tsp (40 mL)	10 tsp (50 mL)
water	16 cups (4 L)	32 cups (8 L)	48 cups (12 L)	64 cups (16 L)	80 cups (20 L)
bay leaves	2	4	6	8	10
peppercorns	5	10	15	20	25
quart bags	8	16	24	32	40

BULK BATCH GUIDE

Homemade Vegetable Stock

This roasted vegetable stock is so easy, flavorful, healthy and nourishing — and it only takes a few hours to make. To save money you can stockpile leftover vegetable scraps (about 6 to 7 cups/1.5 to 1.75 L) in a bag in your fridge or freezer to use in this recipe. Makes about 8 cups (2 L).

2 onions, cut into 1-inch (2.5 cm) chunks

2 celery stalks, cut into 1-inch (2.5 cm) chunks

3 large unpeeled carrots, cut into 1-inch (2.5 cm) chunks

⅓ cup (75 mL) olive oil

2 tsp (10 mL) salt

Freshly ground black pepper

8 cups (2 L) water

10 sprigs fresh parsley

2 bay leaves

Additional salt and freshly ground black pepper

1. Preheat oven to 400°F (200°C).

2. Place onions, celery and carrots on a rimmed baking sheet lined with parchment paper. Drizzle olive oil evenly over vegetables; sprinkle with salt and pepper.

3. Roast in preheated oven for about 1 hour, turning every 15 minutes, until golden brown and tender.

4. In a large stockpot, combine water, parsley and bay leaves. Add roasted vegetables and bring to a boil over high heat. Immediately reduce heat to low, cover and simmer gently for 1 hour.

5. Remove from heat and let cool for 30 minutes.

6. Place a colander over a large bowl or container. Line colander with a flour-sack towel or cheesecloth and pour stock through. Press down on solids with the back of a large spoon to get out as much liquid as possible. Discard solids. Season stock to taste with salt and pepper.

MAKE IT NOW Use immediately or transfer to an airtight container and store in the refrigerator for up to 2 days.

FREEZE IT Let stock cool completely. Place in 4 labeled quart-size (1 L) freezer bags, allotting 2 cups (500 mL) stock per bag. (You can also divide it among smaller or larger containers as desired.) Seal bags, removing as much air as possible, and freeze.

THAW AND USE Place a bag in refrigerator for at least 12 hours or up to 24 hours to thaw, or run lukewarm water over bag until you can break apart stock. Use in recipes as desired. To heat, pour bag contents into a large saucepan and warm over medium heat for about 10 minutes, stirring often, until heated through.

BULK BATCH GUIDE Stock	8 cups/2 L (1 batch)	16 cups/4 L (2 batches)	24 cups/6 L (3 batches)	32 cups/8 L (4 batches)	40 cups/10 L (5 batches)
onions	2	4	6	8	10
celery stalks	2	4	6	8	10
carrots	3	6	9	12	15
olive oil	⅓ cup (75 mL)	⅔ cup (150 mL)	1 cup (250 mL)	1⅓ cups (325 mL)	1⅔ cups (400 mL)
salt	2 tsp (10 mL)	4 tsp (20 mL)	2 tbsp (30 mL)	8 tsp (40 mL)	10 tsp (50 mL)
water	8 cups (2 L)	16 cups (4 L)	24 cups (6 L)	32 cups (8 L)	40 cups (10 L)
parsley sprigs	10	20	30	40	50
bay leaves	2	4	6	8	10
quart bags	4	8	12	16	20

Blistered Roasted Peppers

I love freezing blistered peppers in ice-cube trays and using them in soups, sauces and (my favorite) quesadillas. Just wait till you try my version with Smashed Bean and Red Pepper Quesadillas (page 270). Charred bell peppers really add a unique depth of smoky, earthy flavor to any dish.

Makes about 3 cups (750 mL).

6 red bell peppers, halved

½ cup (125 mL) olive oil

Salt and freshly ground black pepper

1. Preheat broiler.

2. Arrange peppers, skin side up, on a large rimmed baking sheet. Drizzle with olive oil and sprinkle with salt and pepper.

3. Broil peppers for 5 minutes or until you see charred spots. Flip peppers and broil for an additional 5 minutes, until charred on the second side. Remove from oven, place in a bowl and cover until cool enough to handle (this steams the skins, making them easier to remove). Peel off and discard skins.

MAKE IT NOW Slice or purée roasted peppers and serve as desired. You can store them in an airtight container in the refrigerator for up to 2 days.

FREEZE IT Let roasted peppers cool completely. Using a blender, process until smooth. Divide equally among the cups of 2 ice-cube trays; freeze until solid. Transfer frozen cubes to a labeled gallon-sized (4 L) freezer bag. Seal bag, removing as much air as possible, and freeze. (You can also divide the cubes among smaller or larger containers as desired.)

THAW AND USE Remove frozen cubes from bag as needed. Add frozen to soups or stews on the stovetop, or thaw in an airtight container in the refrigerator for 4 to 5 hours. Use in any recipe that calls for blistered or roasted red peppers.

BULK Roasted peppers	3 cups/750 mL (1 batch)	6 cups/1.5 L (2 batches)	9 cups/2.25 L (3 batches)	12 cups/3 L (4 batches)	15 cups/3.75 L (5 batches)
red bell peppers	6	12	18	24	30
olive oil	½ cup (125 mL)	1 cup (250 mL)	1½ cups (375 mL)	2 cups (500 mL)	2½ cups (625 mL)
gallon bags	1	2	3	4	5

Slow Cooker Caramelized Onions

I am telling you, this is the easiest method for caramelizing onions, hands down. Make ahead to use in sandwiches, homemade pizza, hamburgers or soups. Makes about 3 cups (750 mL).

3 tbsp (45 mL) olive oil

6 large onions (about 4½ lbs/2.25 kg), thinly sliced

1. Pour olive oil into a medium to large (approx. 3½ to 6 quart) slow cooker. Rub all over bottom and sides until stoneware is well coated. Add onions; stir until well coated with oil.

2. Cover slow cooker and cook onions on Low for 6 to 8 hours, or until deep golden brown and caramelized.

MAKE IT NOW Use immediately or store in an airtight container in the refrigerator for up to 5 days.

FREEZE IT Let onions cool completely. Divide into 1-cup (250 mL) portions and place in 3 labeled quart-size (1 L) freezer bags. Seal, removing as much air as possible, and freeze.

THAW AND USE Place a bag in refrigerator for at least 8 hours or up to 12 hours to thaw, or run hot water over bag until onions are thawed.

BULK BATCH	Onions	3 cups/750 mL (1 batch)	6 cups/1.5 L (2 batches)	9 cups/2.25 L (3 batches)	12 cups/3 L (4 batches)	15 cups/3.75 L (5 batches)
	olive oil	3 tbsp (45 mL)	6 tbsp (90 mL)	½ cup (125 mL)	¾ cup (175 mL)	¾ cup + 3 tbsp (220 mL)
	onions	6	12	18	24	30
	quart bags	3	6	9	12	15

Time-Saving Roasted Garlic and Onion Purée

This is my time-saving way of packing in a lot of flavor with the least amount of chopping possible. I make a big batch of this stuff, freeze it in ice-cube trays and use it whenever a recipe tells me to cook onions and garlic. When a recipe calls for ¼ cup (60 mL) diced onions and ½ tsp (2 mL) minced garlic, I add ¼ cup (60 mL) of this roasted purée. Makes about 3 cups (750 mL).

6 large onions (about 4½ lbs/2.25 kg), unpeeled

½ cup (125 mL) olive oil, divided

6 heads garlic, unpeeled

1. Preheat oven to 400°F (200°C).

2. Line a 13- by 9-inch (33 by 23 cm) baking dish with foil. Place onions in baking dish. Drizzle 2 tbsp (30 mL) olive oil overtop.

3. Slice tops off garlic heads to just expose cloves underneath. Place garlic heads, cut side down, on a piece of foil. Drizzle 2 tbsp (30 mL) olive oil overtop. Fold up foil around garlic, sealing bulbs inside. Place package in baking dish alongside onions.

4. Roast vegetables in preheated oven for 1 hour, until tender.

5. Squeeze garlic cloves out of their skins into a food processor or blender. Add onions and remaining 1/4 cup (60 mL) olive oil. Process until smooth.

MAKE IT NOW Use as desired or store in an airtight container in the refrigerator for 4 to 5 days.

FREEZE IT Measure out 1 tbsp (15 mL) portions and place in cups of 4 ice-cube trays. Freeze for about 2 hours, until solid. Remove from ice-cube tray and place in 2 labeled gallon-sized (4 L) freezer bags. Seal, removing as much air as possible, and freeze. (You can also divide them among smaller or larger containers as desired.)

THAW AND USE Remove frozen cubes from bags as needed. Add frozen to soups or stews on the stovetop, or thaw in an airtight container in the refrigerator for 4 to 5 hours. Use in recipes that call for roasted or sautéed garlic and onions.

BULK BATCH	Purée	3 cups/750 mL (1 batch)	6 cups/1.5 L (2 batches)	9 cups/2.25 L (3 batches)	12 cups/3 L (4 batches)	15 cups/3.75 L (5 batches)
	onions	6	12	18	24	30
	olive oil	½ cup (125 mL)	1 cup (250 mL)	1½ cups (375 mL)	2 cups (500 mL)	2½ cups (625 mL)
	garlic heads	6	12	18	24	30
	gallon bags	2	4	6	8	10

ACKNOWLEDGMENTS

When I think about all the incredible people who have helped make this cookbook a reality, my heart gets all tender and my eyes a little misty. Writing this cookbook has been no easy task. Many, many people worked tirelessly alongside me with a dream and vision to match my own. I will be forever grateful to my family, friends, blog readers, talented experts and freezer-meal enthusiasts. So, thank you, from the wee little bottom of my heart for letting me follow my dreams of sharing my love of freezer meals with the world.

To my husband, Matt: thank you for always believing that I could write this cookbook, even on the days when I didn't believe it myself. Your love pushed me to work hard and to put my heart and soul into this project. Thank you for being Mr. Mom and handling pretty much everything our family needed during this process, even when you were tired after working in an office all day. Thank you for your humorous inspiration and for taste-testing every single recipe. You are my hero, babe, and I love you to pieces.

To my fun and amazing kids, Monica, Micah, Grace and Liam: thank you for taste-testing countless recipes, even when the food didn't always look perfect — and for doing many loads of dishes. That is real love, guys, real love.

To Mom: thank you for teaching me to love cooking. You have been my cheerleader and ray of positive sunshine throughout this process. To Dad-Dee, thank you for teaching me to follow my dreams and for showing me the absolute best facial expressions of pure delight and joy whenever I cook you something delicious. It totally makes me want to keep making more yummy food. I love you, my papaaaa.

To my sister Ashleigh: thank you for your love, keeping me laughing, making countless freezer meals with me and busting out the best car-dance moves I've ever seen. You have a way of brightening my spirits and encouraging me to keep pushing through like no one else. Thanks for your hilarious, creative ideas for headnotes and reviewing them all with me for hours. And last, thanks for being the best sister and friend in the whole wide world. I love you, sis.

To Angela Truman, who spent exhausting weeks with me during the photo shoot for this book, cooking, washing dishes and prepping food. Even when we were so tired each night, you not only kept me going but you made the work fun. You are so wonderful I will never, EVER forget your friendship and kindness. You are a true rock star.

To my forever friend Flower: thank you for constantly dropping everything to support me while I was writing this cookbook. Without you there would have been no way I would have finished. Thank you for your endless hours helping me to develop recipes and headnotes, slaving away during the photo shoot, and laughing while gulping down way too many Red Bulls. You've shown me what true friendship means. I love you. I promise to be the first in line to buy your cookbook someday.

To my amazing, generous and supportive blog readers: seriously, thank you for following me on my blog, HappyMoneySaver. Your excitement and passion for freezer meals is the true reason I created this cookbook. Thank you for all your love, support and comments. It means the world to me.

To my talented food photographer, Charity Burggraaf: thank you for capturing such beauty, warmth and love in every photo. I am so grateful for the countless hours you spent photographing, traveling, planning, editing and being open to my ideas during the entire process. To my genius food stylist, Nathan Carrabba: thank you for showing the world how beautiful freezer meals can be — you are a true talent. Thank you also to the many people and companies who helped me out during the intense 3½ weeks of cookbook shooting, including Emily Bleazard, Megan Tegen, Jaclyn Redman, Cheryl Hassell and Le Creuset.

Thank you to Barrie MacLauchlin, Melissa Gregoire, Susan Longo, Stephanie Skaggs, Kristi Summit, Jennifer Dobbie, Patrona Dyck, Cathy Messner, Emily Rife, Tammi Vik, Karen Hughes, Allison Vaupel, Lisa Philips, Kandy Tobin, Trish Mears, Tera Campbell, Gia Jacobson, Shari L. Jensen, Julie Mattox, Janet Morrison, Jamie Starr, Annemarie Seymour, Marci Wendt, Tiffany Meyer, Becky Redeker, Kristen Stone, Louise Monico, Bethany Vaughn, Jordan Lloyd, Dayana Lloyd and Lara Floyd, who helped test recipes in their kitchens, even when the recipes were sometimes (ahem) less than perfect. Your thoughtful feedback and ideas were so very helpful and necessary. I hope this book is something you can be proud to say you were a part of.

To my publisher, Robert Rose, and editor, Meredith Dees. I knew from our very first conversation that working together was going to be an incredible experience. Thank you for believing in me and helping me to create this wonderful cookbook.

To my literary agent, Sally Ekus, and Kelly Glover, Martine Quibell and Nina McCreath and the rest of the hard-working team at Robert Rose: thank you for sharing all your expertise and guiding me through writing my first cookbook. You all worked so very hard to make this dream a reality. You are the true heroes behind this whole journey.

And last, I need to thank my Heavenly Father, whom I prayed to for help countless times when I felt at my wits' end. Thank you for inspiring my mind and giving me the strength and energy to push forward and keep writing. I am so grateful for all you have blessed me with.

INDEX

A

Alfredo Sauce, 333
    Artichoke Dip, 68
    Bacon Carbonara Pasta Pie, 190
    Broccoli Chicken Alfredo Bake, 151
    Chicken Pesto Parmesan Shells, 152
    Spinach Gnocchi Alfredo, 258
Almond Lemon Poppyseed Muffins, 64
almonds and almond flour
    Blackberry Almond Crumble, 304
    Frosted Cinnamon Roll Granola, 59
    Morning Energy Bars, 60
Amazing Chicken Satay with Peanut Sauce, 163
Amazing Macaroni and Cheese, 254
appetizers and snacks, 67–93
Artichoke Dip, 68
Asian Chicken Lettuce Wraps, 160
Avocado Crema, 348

B

bacon
    Bacon Carbonara Pasta Pie, 190
    Bacon Love Pork Tenderloin, 174
    Bacon-Wrapped Chicken Bites, 83
    California Breakfast Casserole, 48
    Cashew Basil Chicken, 131
    Sun-Dried Tomato and Bacon Chicken, 132
    Twice-Baked Potatoes, 93
baked goods, 19, 63–64, 284
Balsamic Short Ribs, 213

Basic Grilled Chicken Marinade, 342
Basic Grilled Steak Marinade, 343
basil
    Cashew Basil Chicken, 131
    Coconut Cashew Basil Curry Soup, 99
    Easy Pesto, 339
    Sun-Dried Tomato Basil Pesto Quiche, 273
batch cooking, 24–39
    beginner (7 meals), 30–31
    intermediate (30 meals), 32–34
    advanced (50 meals), 35–39
    planning and pre-prep, 24–25
BBQ Beef Brisket, 214
beans, 17
    Chili, Seriously Good, 119
    Cilantro Black Bean Taco Salad, 269
    Great Northern Enchiladas, 274
    Mini Meatball Soup, 116
    Mole Tamale Pie, 229
    Mongolian Beef and Green Beans, 217
    Rio-Style Sweet Pork Salad, 185
    Smashed Bean and Red Pepper Quesadillas, 270
    Smoky Ham and White Bean Soup, 103
    Sweet & Spicy Pork Carnita Soup, 115
    White Bean Chicken Chili, 122
beef
    freezing, 19
    Balsamic Short Ribs, 213
    Basic Grilled Steak Marinade, 343
    BBQ Beef Brisket, 214
    Beef Barley Stew, 125
    Brown Sugar Meatloaf, 210
    Chili, Seriously Good, 119

    Dirty Rice, 295
    French Dip Sandwiches, 235
    Homemade Beef Stock, 350
    Mole Tamale Pie, 229
    Mongolian Beef and Green Beans, 217
    Red Sauce, 334
    Rosemary Pot Roast, 205
    Sizzlin' Steak Fajitas, 232
    Steak with Gorgonzola Butter, 209
    Sweet-and-Sour Meatballs, 79
    Tempting Taco Pasta Shell Casserole, 226
    Thai Beef Stir-Fry, 218
    Venezuelan Steak, 221
berries
    Blackberry Almond Crumble, 304
    Blueberry Orange Smoothie Kits, 43
    Cranberry Pork Roast, 177
blanching, 18
Blistered Roasted Peppers, 353
    Asian Chicken Lettuce Wraps, 160
    Smashed Bean and Red Pepper Quesadillas, 270
Boneless BBQ Pork Ribs, 189
Breakfast Burritos, 44
breakfasts, 41–64
broccoli
    Broccoli Chicken Alfredo Bake, 151
    Buffalo Ranch Roasted Cauliflower and Broccoli, 280
    Creamy, Cheesy Broccoli Soup, 100
    Deep-Dish Cheesy Broccoli Brown Rice, 261
Brown Butter Pecan Pie, 307
Brown 'n' Serve Rolls, 284
Brown Sugar Meatloaf, 210
Buffalo Ranch Roasted Cauliflower and Broccoli, 280

butter, 18
buttermilk
　　Buttermilk Dill Chicken
　　　Sandwiches, 128
　　Homemade Chicken Strips,
　　　89
Buttery Cinnamon French Toast
　　Bake, 56

C

California Breakfast Casserole,
　　48
Candied Sweet Potatoes,
　　Roasted, 288
Caramelized Onions, Slow
　　Cooker, 354
carrots. *See also* vegetables
　　Chicken Pot Pie,
　　　Old-Fashioned, 155
　　Chicken Tortellini Soup, 107
　　Hazelnut Chicken Wild Rice
　　　Soup, 104
　　Herbed Chicken and
　　　Dumpling Soup, 111
　　Mini Meatball Soup, 116
　　Peanut Perfection Pad Thai,
　　　167
　　Rosemary Pot Roast, 205
　　Stuffed Mini Sweet Peppers,
　　　80
cashews
　　Cashew Basil Chicken, 131
　　Cashew Mushroom Fried
　　　Rice, 265
　　Coconut Cashew Basil Curry
　　　Soup, 99
cauliflower
　　Buffalo Ranch Roasted
　　　Cauliflower and Broccoli,
　　　280
　　Cauliflower Chickpea Curry
　　　Bake, 257
　　Cauliflower Crave Soup,
　　　96
celery. *See also* vegetables
　　Herbed Chicken and
　　　Dumpling Soup, 111
　　Smoky Ham and White Bean
　　　Soup, 103
cheese, 18. *See also specific*
　　　types (below)
　　Artichoke Dip, 68
　　Baked Ziti, 222

California Breakfast
　　Casserole, 48
Cauliflower Crave Soup, 96
Cheesy Eggplant Parmigiana,
　　266
Cheesy Potatoes, 287
Chicken Enchiladas, Killer, 159
Chicken Parmigiana, 139
Chicken Pesto Parmesan
　　Shells, 152
Creamy, Cheesy Broccoli
　　Soup, 100
Creamy Cilantro Chicken
　　Taquitos, 86
Deep-Dish Cheesy Broccoli
　　Brown Rice, 261
Great Northern Enchiladas,
　　274
Hazelnut Mushroom Potatoes
　　au Gratin, 277
Hazelnut Pear Chicken, 136
Lasagna, Momma's, 225
Macaroni and Cheese,
　　Amazing, 254
Mole Tamale Pie, 229
Spicy Buffalo Chicken Hot
　　Dip, 71
Steak with Gorgonzola Butter,
　　209
Stuffed Mini Sweet Peppers,
　　80
Sun-Dried Tomato Basil Pesto
　　Quiche, 273
Sweet & Spicy Pork Carnita
　　Soup, 115
Taco Pasta Shell Casserole,
　　Tempting, 226
Twice-Baked Potatoes, 93
cheese, Cheddar
　　Breakfast Burritos, 44
　　Cauliflower Chickpea Curry
　　　Bake, 257
　　Crescent Chicken Divine, 135
　　Easy Tuna Casserole, 242
　　Empanada Hand Pies, 90
　　Hash-Brown Casserole, 199
　　Hearty Breakfast Bowls, 47
　　Smashed Bean and Red
　　　Pepper Quesadillas, 270
cheese, cream and mascarpone
　　Layered Chocolate Mousse
　　　Cake, 318
　　Mascarpone Key Lime Mini
　　　Pies, 308

Salted Caramel Pumpkin
　　Cheesecake, 312
Sun-Dried Tomato and Bacon
　　Chicken, 132
cheese, mozzarella
　　Pepperoni Blossoms, 76
　　Perfect Pizza Any Way You
　　　Top It, 194
　　Stromboli, 193
cheese, Parmesan
　　Alfredo Sauce, 333
　　Bacon Carbonara Pasta Pie,
　　　190
　　Broccoli Chicken Alfredo
　　　Bake, 151
　　Cashew Basil Chicken, 131
　　Cilantro Lime Chicken Tacos,
　　　156
　　Easy Pesto, 339
　　Homemade Chicken Strips,
　　　89
　　Spinach Gnocchi Alfredo,
　　　258
　　Thirty-Minute Pizza Sauce,
　　　340
chicken and turkey. *See also*
　　　chicken breasts; chicken,
　　　cooked
　　bulk cooking, 29
　　freezing, 19
　　Asian Chicken Lettuce Wraps,
　　　160
　　Chicken Tikka Masala, 164
　　Herbes de Provence
　　　Chicken, 140
　　Homemade Chicken Stock,
　　　349
　　Maple Dijon Chicken, 147
　　Smoky Grilled Louisiana
　　　Turkey Legs, 148
chicken breasts
　　Amazing Chicken Satay with
　　　Peanut Sauce, 163
　　Bacon-Wrapped Chicken
　　　Bites, 83
　　Basic Grilled Chicken
　　　Marinade, 342
　　Buttermilk Dill Chicken
　　　Sandwiches, 128
　　Cashew Basil Chicken, 131
　　Chicken Parmigiana, 139
　　Coconut Cashew Basil Curry
　　　Soup, 99
　　Hazelnut Pear Chicken, 136

chicken breasts (continued)
    Homemade Chicken Strips,
        89
    Honey Lime Chicken, 143
    Lemon Tarragon Chicken, 144
    Peanut Perfection Pad Thai,
        167
    Shrimp Jambalaya, 251
    Spicy Buffalo Chicken Hot
        Dip, 71
    Sun-Dried Tomato and Bacon
        Chicken, 132
    White Bean Chicken Chili,
        122
chicken, cooked
    Broccoli Chicken Alfredo
        Bake, 151
    Chicken Pesto Parmesan
        Shells, 152
    Chicken Tortellini Soup, 107
    Cilantro Lime Chicken Tacos,
        156
    Creamy Cilantro Chicken
        Taquitos, 86
    Crescent Chicken Divine, 135
    Hazelnut Chicken Wild Rice
        Soup, 104
    Herbed Chicken and
        Dumpling Soup, 111
    Killer Chicken Enchiladas, 159
    Old-Fashioned Chicken Pot
        Pie, 155
    Teriyaki Chicken, 170
    Zesty Tortilla Soup, 108
chickpeas
    Cauliflower Chickpea Curry
        Bake, 257
    Sausage and Gnocchi Soup,
        112
chilis, 119–22
chocolate and cocoa powder
    Chocolate Chip Cookies, 321
    Layered Chocolate Mousse
        Cake, 318
    Minty Melts, 327
    Molten Hot Fudge Lava
        Cakes, 315
    Morning Energy Bars, 60
Churros, 324
cilantro
    Chicken Satay with Peanut
        Sauce, Amazing, 163
    Cilantro Black Bean Taco
        Salad, 269

Cilantro Lime Chicken Tacos,
    156
Cilantro Lime Corn, 300
Creamy Cilantro Chicken
    Taquitos, 86
Lip-Smackin' Chutney, 344
Mole Tamale Pie, 229
Peanut Perfection Pad Thai,
    167
Sizzlin' Steak Fajitas, 232
Cinnamon Mini Donut Muffins,
    63
coconut
    Island Coconut Angel Cake,
        311
    Morning Energy Bars, 60
coconut milk
    Cauliflower Chickpea Curry
        Bake, 257
    Chicken Satay with Peanut
        Sauce, Amazing, 163
    Coconut Cashew Basil Curry
        Soup, 99
    Peanut Perfection Pad Thai,
        167
    Peanut Sauce, 345
corn
    Cilantro Black Bean Taco
        Salad, 269
    Cilantro Lime Corn, 300
    Great Northern Enchiladas,
        274
    Mole Tamale Pie, 229
    Sweet & Spicy Pork Carnita
        Soup, 115
    Zesty Tortilla Soup, 108
Cranberry Pork Roast, 177
cream, 18. See also milk
    Alfredo Sauce, 333
    Cauliflower Crave Soup,
        96
    Chicken Pot Pie, Old-
        Fashioned, 155
    Chicken Tikka Masala, 164
    Creamy, Cheesy Broccoli
        Soup, 100
    Hazelnut Chicken Wild Rice
        Soup, 104
    Molten Hot Fudge Lava
        Cakes, 315
    Salted Caramel Pumpkin
        Cheesecake, 312
    Sun-Dried Tomato Basil Pesto
        Quiche, 273

Creamy Cilantro Chicken
    Taquitos, 86
Crescent Chicken Divine, 135

D
dairy products, 18, 19. See also
    specific items
Deep-Dish Cheesy Broccoli
    Brown Rice, 261
desserts, 303–27
Dill Pickles, Fried, 72
Dirty Rice, 295

E
Easy Pesto, 339
Easy Tuna Casserole, 242
Eggplant Parmigiana, Cheesy,
    266
eggs
    Breakfast Burritos, 44
    Buttery Cinnamon French
        Toast Bake, 56
    Hearty Breakfast Bowls, 47
    Sun-Dried Tomato Basil Pesto
        Quiche, 273
Empanada Hand Pies, 90
Enchilada Sauce, 346
    Chicken Enchiladas, Killer, 159
    Great Northern Enchiladas,
        274
    Rio-Style Sweet Pork Salad,
        185
    Taco Pasta Shell Casserole,
        Tempting, 226

F
fat separator, 27
fish and seafood
    freezing, 19
    Baked Shrimp Scampi, 241
    Easy Tuna Casserole, 242
    Flower's Seafood Gumbo,
        246
    Lemon Dill Tilapia Tacos, 245
    Savory Salmon in Foil, 238
    Shrimp Jambalaya, 251
flash freezing, 17–19
Flower's Seafood Gumbo, 246
freezer bags, 15
    labeling, 22
    removing air from, 21

freezer burn, 21
freezer meals, 12–14
  batch cooking, 24–39
  pre-prep for, 24
  swapping, 25
  thawing, 23
  tools and supplies for, 15, 27
freezers, 16, 22
freezing
  containers for, 13, 15
  duration, 19
  foods to avoid, 17
  quickly, 21–22
French Dip Sandwiches, 235
French Toast Bake, Buttery
  Cinnamon, 56
Fried Dill Pickles, 72
Frosted Cinnamon Roll Granola,
  59
fruit. See also berries; specific
  fruits
  freezing, 17, 19
  Blueberry Orange Smoothie
    Kits, 43
  Hazelnut Pear Chicken, 136

G

garlic. See also vegetables
  Easy Pesto, 339
  Garlic Herb Smashed
    Potatoes, 291
  Time-Saving Roasted Garlic
    and Onion Purée, 355
Gnocchi, 330
  Sausage and Gnocchi Soup,
    112
  Spinach Gnocchi Alfredo,
    258
graham cracker/wafer crumbs
  Layered Chocolate Mousse
    Cake, 318
  Mascarpone Key Lime Mini
    Pies, 308
  Salted Caramel Pumpkin
    Cheesecake, 312
Great Northern Enchiladas,
  274
greens. See also lettuce
  Blueberry Orange Smoothie
    Kits (variation), 43
  Mini Meatball Soup, 116
  Sausage and Gnocchi Soup,
    112

  Spinach Gnocchi Alfredo,
    258
group swaps, 25

H

ham
  Hash-Brown Casserole, 199
  Smoky Ham and White Bean
    Soup, 103
  Stromboli, 193
hazelnuts
  Hazelnut Chicken Wild Rice
    Soup, 104
  Hazelnut Mushroom Potatoes
    au Gratin, 277
  Hazelnut Pear Chicken, 136
Hearty Breakfast Bowls, 47
Herbed Chicken and Dumpling
  Soup, 111
Herbes de Provence Chicken,
  140
Homemade Beef Stock, 350
Homemade Chicken Stock, 349
Homemade Chicken Strips, 89
Homemade Vegetable Stock,
  351
honey
  Honey Lime Chicken, 143
  Honey Pork Chops, 178
  Minty Melts, 327

I

Island Coconut Angel Cake, 311
Island Pork, 181

K

kale. See greens
ketchup. See tomato sauces
Killer Chicken Enchiladas, 159

L

Lasagna, Momma's, 225
Layered Chocolate Mousse
  Cake, 318
lemon
  Almond Lemon Poppyseed
    Muffins, 64
  Baked Shrimp Scampi, 241
  Lemon Dill Tilapia Tacos, 245
  Lemon Tarragon Chicken, 144

  Mascarpone Key Lime Mini
    Pies, 308
  Rosemary Pot Roast, 205
  Savory Salmon in Foil, 238
Lentil Supreme Shepherd's Pie,
  262
lettuce
  Asian Chicken Lettuce Wraps,
    160
  Cilantro Black Bean Taco
    Salad, 269
  Lemon Dill Tilapia Tacos, 245
  Rio-Style Sweet Pork Salad,
    185
lime
  Cilantro Lime Corn, 300
  Honey Lime Chicken, 143
  Mascarpone Key Lime Mini
    Pies, 308
  Smoky Grilled Louisiana
    Turkey Legs, 148
Lip-Smackin' Chutney, 344
  Smashed Bean and Red
    Pepper Quesadillas, 270

M

Macaroni and Cheese, Amazing,
  254
maple syrup
  Island Coconut Angel Cake,
    311
  Maple Breakfast Sausage
    Patties, 51
  Maple Dijon Chicken, 147
marinades, 342–43
Marinara Sauce, 338
  Cheesy Eggplant Parmigiana,
    266
Mascarpone Key Lime Mini Pies,
  308
Mascarpone Lemon Wontons,
  75
Mashed Potatoes, 292
meat, 17. See also specific
  meats
milk (dairy and non-dairy),
  18. See also buttermilk;
  coconut milk; cream
  Broccoli Chicken Alfredo
    Bake, 151
  Buttery Cinnamon French
    Toast Bake, 56
  Cheesy Potatoes, 287

milk (continued)
    Chicken Pesto Parmesan
      Shells, 152
    Hazelnut Mushroom Potatoes
      au Gratin, 277
    Macaroni and Cheese,
      Amazing, 254
    Morning Energy Bars, 60
    Perfect Freezer Pancakes,
      55
milk, condensed
    Layered Chocolate Mousse
      Cake, 318
    Mascarpone Key Lime Mini
      Pies, 308
Mini Meatball Soup, 116
Minty Melts, 327
Mole Tamale Pie, 229
Molten Hot Fudge Lava Cakes,
    315
Momma's Lasagna, 225
Mongolian Beef and Green
    Beans, 217
Morning Energy Bars, 60
muffins, 63–64
mushrooms
    Cashew Mushroom Fried
      Rice, 265
    Hazelnut Mushroom Potatoes
      au Gratin, 277
    Vegetarian Red Sauce, 335
mustard
    Maple Dijon Chicken, 147
    Smoky BBQ Sauce, 341

N

noodles. *See* pasta and
    noodles
nuts, 19. *See also specific types
    of nuts*
    Brown Butter Pecan Pie, 307
    Easy Pesto, 339

O

oats (rolled)
    Blackberry Almond Crumble,
      304
    Frosted Cinnamon Roll
      Granola, 59
Old-Fashioned Chicken Pot Pie,
    155
onions. *See also* vegetables

    Slow Cooker Caramelized
      Onions, 354
    Time-Saving Roasted Garlic
      and Onion Purée, 355
orange juice
    Blueberry Orange Smoothie
      Kits, 43
    Cranberry Pork Roast, 177
    Pork Carnitas Tacos, Perfect,
      203

P

Pancakes, Perfect Freezer, 55
pasta and noodles
    freezing, 17, 19
    Bacon Carbonara Pasta Pie,
      190
    Baked Shrimp Scampi, 241
    Baked Ziti, 222
    Broccoli Chicken Alfredo
      Bake, 151
    Cauliflower Chickpea Curry
      Bake, 257
    Chicken Pesto Parmesan
      Shells, 152
    Chicken Tortellini Soup, 107
    Easy Tuna Casserole, 242
    Lasagna, Momma's, 225
    Macaroni and Cheese,
      Amazing, 254
    Mini Meatball Soup, 116
    Peanut Perfection Pad Thai,
      167
    Taco Pasta Shell Casserole,
      Tempting, 226
peanut butter
    Enchilada Sauce, 346
    Morning Energy Bars, 60
    Peanut Sauce, 345
Peanut Sauce, 345
    Chicken Satay with Peanut
      Sauce, Amazing, 163
    Peanut Perfection Pad Thai,
      167
peas
    Chicken Pot Pie, Old-
      Fashioned, 155
    Crescent Chicken Divine, 135
    Lentil Supreme Shepherd's
      Pie, 262
pepperoni. *See* sausage
peppers, chile
    Chutney, Lip-Smackin', 344

    Coconut Cashew Basil Curry
      Soup, 99
    Enchilada Sauce, 346
    Great Northern Enchiladas,
      274
    Mole Tamale Pie, 229
    Salsa, Totally Tasty, 347
    Sizzlin' Steak Fajitas, 232
    Sweet & Spicy Pork Carnita
      Soup, 115
peppers, sweet. *See also*
      Blistered Roasted Peppers
    Chili, Seriously Good, 119
    Dirty Rice, 295
    Pork 'n' Pepper Stir-Fry, 186
    Sizzlin' Steak Fajitas, 232
    Stuffed Mini Sweet Peppers,
      80
    Sweet-and-Sour Meatballs,
      79
    Thai Beef Stir-Fry, 218
    Venezuelan Steak, 221
Perfect Freezer Pancakes, 55
Perfect Pizza Any Way You Top
    It, 194
Perfect Pork Carnitas Tacos,
    203
pesto, 339
    Chicken Pesto Parmesan
      Shells, 152
    Mini Meatball Soup, 116
    Sun-Dried Tomato Basil Pesto
      Quiche, 273
Pie Crust, 331
    Brown Butter Pecan Pie, 307
    Chicken Pot Pie, Old-
      Fashioned, 155
    Empanada Hand Pies, 90
pineapple
    Blueberry Orange Smoothie
      Kits (variation), 43
    Honey Lime Chicken, 143
    Island Coconut Angel Cake,
      311
    Island Pork, 181
    Pork 'n' Pepper Stir-Fry, 186
    Sweet-and-Sour Meatballs,
      79
Pizza Dough, 332
    Perfect Pizza Any Way You
      Top It, 194
    Stromboli, 193
pizza sauce. *See* Thirty-Minute
    Pizza Sauce

pork
    freezing, 19
    Bacon Love Pork Tenderloin, 174
    Boneless BBQ Pork Ribs, 189
    Cranberry Pork Roast, 177
    Honey Pork Chops, 178
    Island Pork, 181
    Maple Breakfast Sausage Patties, 51
    Perfect Pork Carnitas Tacos, 203
    Pork 'n' Pepper Stir-Fry, 186
    Rio-Style Sweet Pork Salad, 185
    Rosemary Brown Sugar Pork Chops, 182
    Smoky Pulled Pork Sandwiches, 200
    Sweet & Spicy Pork Carnita Soup, 115
potatoes, 17. See also potatoes, hash brown
    Breakfast Burritos, 44
    Garlic Herb Smashed Potatoes, 291
    Gnocchi, 330
    Hazelnut Mushroom Potatoes au Gratin, 277
    Lentil Supreme Shepherd's Pie, 262
    Mashed Potatoes, 292
    Rosemary Pot Roast, 205
    Twice-Baked Potatoes, 93
potatoes, hash brown
    California Breakfast Casserole, 48
    Cheesy Potatoes, 287
    Chicken Pot Pie, Old-Fashioned, 155
    Hash-Brown Casserole, 199
    Hearty Breakfast Bowls, 47
    Savory Sausage Hash, 52
    Sun-Dried Tomato Basil Pesto Quiche, 273
Pumpkin Cheesecake, Salted Caramel, 312

Q

quick freezing, 21–22

R

Red Sauce, 334
    Baked Ziti, 222
    Chicken Parmigiana, 139
    Momma's Lasagna, 225
refreezing, 17
rice. See also rice, wild
    freezing, 17, 19
    Cashew Mushroom Fried Rice, 265
    Deep-Dish Cheesy Broccoli Brown Rice, 261
    Dirty Rice, 295
    Shrimp Jambalaya, 251
    Spanish Rice, 296
rice, wild
    Hazelnut Chicken Wild Rice Soup, 104
    Wild Rice Pilaf, 299
Rio-Style Sweet Pork Salad, 185
Rolls, Brown 'n' Serve, 284
Rosemary Brown Sugar Pork Chops, 182
Rosemary Pot Roast, 205

S

Salmon in Foil, Savory, 238
salsa, 347
    California Breakfast Casserole, 48
    Cilantro Black Bean Taco Salad, 269
    White Bean Chicken Chili, 122
Salted Caramel Pumpkin Cheesecake, 312
sandwiches, 128, 200, 235
sauces, 333–38, 340–41, 345–46
sausage
    Breakfast Burritos, 44
    Hearty Breakfast Bowls, 47
    Mini Meatball Soup, 116
    Pepperoni Blossoms, 76
    Perfect Pizza Any Way You Top It, 194
    Sausage and Gnocchi Soup, 112
    Savory Sausage Hash, 52
    Seafood Gumbo, Flower's, 246
    Shrimp Jambalaya, 251

Sweet-and-Sour Meatballs, 79
Savory Salmon in Foil, 238
Savory Sausage Hash, 52
seafood. See fish and seafood
seasonings, 19
seeds
    Almond Lemon Poppyseed Muffins, 64
    Morning Energy Bars, 60
    Teriyaki Chicken, 170
Seriously Good Chili, 119
Shrimp Jambalaya, 251
Shrimp Scampi, Baked, 241
Sizzlin' Steak Fajitas, 232
Slow Cooker Caramelized Onions, 354
slow cookers, 27
Smashed Bean and Red Pepper Quesadillas, 270
Smoky BBQ Sauce, 341
    Bacon Love Pork Tenderloin, 174
    BBQ Beef Brisket, 214
    Boneless BBQ Pork Ribs, 189
    Brown Sugar Meatloaf, 210
    Smoky Pulled Pork Sandwiches, 200
Smoky Grilled Louisiana Turkey Legs, 148
Smoky Ham and White Bean Soup, 103
soups, 96–118
sour cream
    Avocado Crema, 348
    California Breakfast Casserole, 48
    Cheesy Potatoes, 287
    Hash-Brown Casserole, 199
    Twice-Baked Potatoes, 93
    White Bean Chicken Chili, 122
Spanish Rice, 296
    Empanada Hand Pies, 90
Spicy Buffalo Chicken Hot Dip, 71
spinach. See greens
Steak with Gorgonzola Butter, 209
stocks, 19, 349–51
Stromboli, 193
Stuffed Mini Sweet Peppers, 80
Sun-Dried Tomato and Bacon Chicken, 132
Sun-Dried Tomato Basil Pesto Quiche, 273

Sweet-and-Sour Meatballs, 79
Sweet Potatoes, Roasted
    Candied, 288
Sweet & Spicy Pork Carnita
    Soup, 115

T

Tempting Taco Pasta Shell
    Casserole, 226
Teriyaki Chicken, 170
Thai Beef Stir-Fry, 218
Thirty-Minute Pizza Sauce,
    340
    Pepperoni Blossoms, 76
    Perfect Pizza Any Way You
        Top It, 194
    Stromboli, 193
Time-Saving Roasted Garlic and
    Onion Purée, 355
tomatoes. See also tomato
    sauces
    Chili, Seriously Good, 119
    Cilantro Black Bean Taco
        Salad, 269
    Marinara Sauce, 338
    Mole Tamale Pie, 229
    Salsa, Totally Tasty, 347
    Seafood Gumbo, Flower's,
        246
    Shrimp Jambalaya, 251
    Sun-Dried Tomato and Bacon
        Chicken, 132
    Sun-Dried Tomato Basil Pesto
        Quiche, 273
    Sweet & Spicy Pork Carnita
        Soup, 115
    Thirty-Minute Pizza Sauce,
        340
    Zesty Tortilla Soup, 108
tomato sauces (as ingredient)
    Balsamic Short Ribs, 213
    Beef Barley Stew, 125
    Brown Sugar Meatloaf, 210
    Chicken Tikka Masala, 164
    Enchilada Sauce, 346
    Mole Tamale Pie, 229
    Red Sauce, 334
    Smoky BBQ Sauce, 341
    Spanish Rice, 296
    Vegetarian Red Sauce, 335
    Venezuelan Steak, 221

tortillas, 19
    Breakfast Burritos, 44
    Chicken Enchiladas, Killer, 159
    Cilantro Lime Chicken Tacos,
        156
    Creamy Cilantro Chicken
        Taquitos, 86
    Great Northern Enchiladas,
        274
    Lemon Dill Tilapia Tacos, 245
    Pork Carnitas Tacos, Perfect,
        203
    Sizzlin' Steak Fajitas, 232
    Smashed Bean and Red
        Pepper Quesadillas, 270
Totally Tasty Salsa, 347
Turkey Legs, Smoky Grilled
    Louisiana, 148
Twice-Baked Potatoes, 93

V

vacuum sealers, 15, 21
vegetables. See also greens;
    specific vegetables
    blanching, 18
    freezing, 17, 19
    prechopped/frozen, 27
    Beef Barley Stew, 125
    Cashew Mushroom Fried
        Rice, 265
    Homemade Beef Stock, 350
    Homemade Chicken Stock,
        349
    Homemade Vegetable Stock,
        351
    Lentil Supreme Shepherd's
        Pie, 262
    Red Sauce, 334
    Seafood Gumbo, Flower's,
        246
    Spanish Rice, 296
    Thirty-Minute Pizza Sauce,
        340
    Vegetarian Red Sauce, 335
Vegetarian White Sauce, 337
Venezuelan Steak, 221

W

water chestnuts
    Artichoke Dip, 68

    Asian Chicken Lettuce Wraps,
        160
whipped topping, frozen
    Island Coconut Angel Cake,
        311
    Layered Chocolate Mousse
        Cake, 318
    Mascarpone Key Lime Mini
        Pies, 308
    Salted Caramel Pumpkin
        Cheesecake, 312
White Bean Chicken Chili, 122
White Sauce, 336
    Cauliflower Chickpea Curry
        Bake, 257
    Cauliflower Crave Soup, 96
    Cheesy Potatoes, 287
    Chicken Pot Pie, Old-
        Fashioned, 155
    Creamy, Cheesy Broccoli
        Soup, 100
    Crescent Chicken Divine,
        135
    Deep-Dish Cheesy Broccoli
        Brown Rice, 261
    Easy Tuna Casserole, 242
    Hazelnut Mushroom Potatoes
        au Gratin, 277
    Macaroni and Cheese,
        Amazing, 254
    Sun-Dried Tomato and Bacon
        Chicken, 132
wild rice
    Hazelnut Chicken Wild Rice
        Soup, 104
    Wild Rice Pilaf, 299

Y

yogurt, 18
    Almond Lemon Poppyseed
        Muffins, 64
    Avocado Crema, 348
    Blueberry Orange Smoothie
        Kits, 43
    Freezer Pancakes, Perfect,
        55

Z

Zesty Tortilla Soup, 108
Ziti, Baked, 222